Praise for *Poker & Pop Cult*

CW00801284

"This book had to be written, and only
er's place in our culture has been Martin's
I've known him. Poker is a story of a thous... ...., ...

Tommy Angelo, author of *Elements of Poker* and *Painless Poker*

"A thorough, well-informed and highly entertaining exploration of the
cultural riches bred by poker, explaining why the game remains so quintessentially American while growing ever more universal."

Anthony Holden, author of *Big Deal* and *Bigger Deal*

"Martin Harris's *Poker & Pop Culture* is a lively, well researched, highly
readable account of the game's hold on the popular imagination, revealing
its history - from Shakespeare to ESPN, Flash Kate to James Bond, Tony
Soprano to Daniel Negreanu - with 1,001 telling details. A+ Americana,
and then some."

James McManus, author of *Positively Fifth Street* and *Cowboys Full*

"Heralded or condemned, in good times, bad times, dead or alive, poker has been through it all, and proven itself to be the ultimate survivor.
Kudos to Martin Harris for his staggeringly in depth look at its intriguing
history. *Poker & Pop Culture* holds all the cards and knows where the
bodies are buried. So I highly suggest you pull up a comfy chair and deal
yourself in for a terrific read!"

Joseph Walsh, actor, screenwriter and co-producer of *California Split*

"*Poker & Pop Culture* is more than the most detailed history of America's favorite card game I've read yet. Martin Harris has written a mon-
umentally readable, always engaging look at how poker has appeared in
literature, television, movies, and other places. Filled with fascinating anecdotes about real-life and fictional poker games, this book is worth reading
and re-reading. From John Wayne to William Shatner, Mississippi riverboats to online sites and countless places in between, Harris covers it all."

David G. Schwartz, author of *Roll the Bones: The History of Gambling*

"Martin has always been one of my favorite poker writers - and I'm
looking forward to seeing what he's created in *Poker & Pop Culture*. It's
sure to be interesting and lively!"

Maria Konnikova, author of *Mastermind* and *The Confidence Game*

"Do not believe the absent-minded professor shtick. Martin Harris is the smartest person in poker. Like all great professors, he has the uncanny ability to boil down complex subjects and unravel tangled history to present a succinct timeline and understandable narrative of events."

Paul "Dr. Pauly" McGuire, author of *Lost Vegas*

"I always wondered what 'exhaustively researched' really meant. Now I know. Harris has unearthed a staggering array of juicy poker facts and lore from literature, movies, television, music and history, but his accomplishment goes far beyond its remarkable thoroughness, giving context, stature and meaning to America's game, conveying it all in a delightfully elegant prose that is as heady and surprising as hitting a one-outer on the river. *Poker & Pop Culture* is a fist-pumping winner of a book."

Peter Alson, author of *Take Me to the River* and co-author of *One of a Kind*

"That the beautiful game of poker has spawned the tales of cheats and cardsharps and the most unsavory of muckrakers for me only adds to the allure. Poker is a game about character, after all, and what would character entail if not the basest things about us? Martin Harris swims in the details, glowingly, unflinchingly, and boldly peeling back the layers on the narrative of our game. I salute him for compiling these stories, for we who love the beautiful game of poker, we are the sons and daughters of riverboat gamblers, the descendants of presidents, and the sixth cousins of the baddest Stetson to ever pull a six-shooter from their waistband when laying down a paltry two pair. This tome is the definitive fabric of poker."

Jesse May, author of *Shut Up and Deal*

"I'm insanely jealous of Martin Harris. At major poker events where we worked together side-by-side, Martin always seemed to arrive first, and leave last -- long after the workday was done. His tenacity usually paid off with outstanding content. Martin got the stories the rest of us missed. Now, Martin has penned a new book about poker and culture packed with brilliant insights. Damn you, Martin Harris!"

Nolan Dalla, poker writer and co-author of *One of a Kind*

MARTIN HARRIS

POKER & Pop Culture

TELLING THE STORY OF AMERICA'S FAVORITE CARD GAME

D+B

POKER

First published in 2019 by D&B Publishing

British Library Cataloguing-in-Publication Data
A catalogue record for this book is available from the British Library.
ISBN: 978 1 909457 98 0

Cover and book design by Horacio Monteverde.
Printed and bound by Versa Press in the US.

All sales enquiries should be directed to D&B Publishing:
info@dandbpoker.com

POKER
www.dandbpoker.com

Martin Harris

Martin Harris is a writer, teacher, and poker reporter who has covered the game for the last dozen years. He earned a Ph.D. in English from Indiana University at Bloomington and has taught full- and part-time at the university level for two decades. He currently teaches in the American Studies program at the University of North Carolina Charlotte, where his courses include "Poker in American Film and Culture" and "Tricky Dick: Richard Nixon, Poker, and Politics."

Contents

Acknowledgments

Poker is not a team game, but you need others to play. The same goes for writing a book, a task necessarily performed alone, but in most cases impossible to achieve without the support of others. In my case, the list of those who have helped is a long one.

Special thanks to Haley Hintze for recruiting me to write and report on poker long ago and also for suggesting to me the idea of writing articles about "poker & pop culture." Thanks to David G. Schwartz who played an important role early on that set me on the path to writing this book, then helped provide support again during the project's latter stages. Thanks to Dan Addelman and Byron Jacobs for making the idea of the book a reality. Thanks as well to James McManus for his encouragement to me along the way, and to Howard Swains for his important guidance and advice at the end.

Thanks to Paula Eckard and the American Studies program at the University of North Carolina at Charlotte, and to the many students in my Poker in American Film and Culture course whose responses to some of the material presented here helped shape my own thinking about poker's significance. Also thanks to the University of Nevada Las Vegas and the Center for Gaming Research for their support which added greatly to the final product.

Thanks to John Caldwell, Garry Gates, Brad Willis, Simon Young, Dave Allan, Paudie O'Reilly, Michael Craig, Matt Showell, Eric Ramsey, Ging Masinda, Maryann Morrison, Donnie Peters, Matthew Parvis, and Frank Op de Woerd for having provided me opportunities to write and report on poker. Being part of numerous poker reporting teams over the years has not only been a rewarding professional experience (and useful to opening my eyes further to poker's impact not just in America but in the 20 or so countries to which I've had the chance to travel while following the game), but also introduced me to many other great colleagues and friends. Besides those already mentioned, I want especially to acknowledge Stephen Bartley, Dave

Behr, Marc Convey, Joe Giron, Jason Kirk, Paul McGuire, Carlos Monti, Sergio Prado, Rich Ryan, Jack Stanton, Reinaldo Venegas, Alexander Villegas, and Nick Wright for having helped make those "work" experiences so much fun. Thanks as well to Lane Anderson, Kristy Arnett, Kristen Bihr, Gene Bromberg, Josh Cahlik, Anthony Charter, Heath Chick, Matt Clark, Brett Collson, Sam Cosby, Valerie Cross, Rick Dacey, Marty Derbyshire, Benjamin Gallen, Mickey Doft, Tim Duckworth, Yori Eskamp, Lynn Gilmartin, Adam Goulding, Chris Hall, Mad Harper, Sarah Herring, Chad Holloway, Steve Horton, Dana Immanuel, Aleeyah Jadavji, Thomas Koo, Jan Kores, Pamela Maldonado, Kevin Mathers, Danny Maxwell, Mickey May, Maria Paula Montero, B.J. Nemeth, Jennifer Newell, Mo Nuwwarah, Will O'Connor, Paul Oresteen, Brittany Paige, Mateusz Pater, Matthew Pitt, Remko Rinkema, Matt Savage, Will Shillibier, Tomas Stacha, Neil Stoddart, Kevin Taylor, René Velli, Matt Wehner, Jessica Welman, and Christian Zetzsche for their friendship and support as we together followed poker being played all over the globe.

Among the many other "poker people" from whom I've received encouragement and/or inspiration are Andre Akkari, Peter Alson, Tommy Angelo, Karridy Askenasy, David Aydt, Lance Bradley, Rick Bennet, Andrew Brokos, Amy Calistri, Tricia Cardner, David Carrion, Gareth Chantler, Barbara Connors, Chris Cosenza, Tom Cummins, Nolan Dalla, Zachary Elwood, Mike Fasso, Alan Fowler, Shari Geller, Barry Greenstein, John Hartness, Anthony Holden, Scott Huff, Phil Ivey, Ross Jarvis, Ryan Kallberg, Maria Konnikova, Eugene Katchalov, Carol Kline, Paul Kobel, Curtis Krumel, Michele Lewis, Jonathan Little, Jesse May, James McManus, Nate Meyvis, Dan Michalski, Lara Miller, Mike Mock, Chris Moneymaker, Andrew Moxon, Tri Nguyen, Seth Palansky, Tim Peters, Al Rash, Ben Saxton, Tom Schneider, Alan Schoonmaker, Adam Schwartz, Howard Schwartz, Kara Scott, Paul Seldon, Jennifer Shahade, Dave Smith, Joe Stapleton, Eileen Sutton, Chris Tessaro, Jennifer Tilly, Carlos Welch, Nathan Williams, Matt Waldron, Joey Walsh, Michael Wein, and Robert Woolley. Thanks also to Chad Brown, Robbie Davies, Rachel Kranz, Lou Krieger, and Barry Tanenbaum who before leaving us helped me in important ways as well.

Thanks to my brother Joe and my parents Laura and Frank, and to my other family, Hope, Tim, and Henry Benziger for all their love and support. Thanks to Tess and John McCullough who were special, loving parents to me as well.

And thanks most of all to my wife, Heather McCullough, whom I love more than the 2,598,960 ways of constructing a five-card poker hand. "Vera" first motivated me to keep writing about poker long ago, and she continued to provide love and encouragement to me throughout the writing of this book, which is dedicated to her.

Martin Harris, May 2019

Introduction

It's a Saturday afternoon in 1944. You've wandered into the local theater for a few hours of entertainment, hoping perhaps to avoid the newsreels covering recent battles in Europe or attacks in the Pacific in favor of some lighter fare. Or say it's last week and after a spin through the dial you've paused on one of the classic film networks, again seeking something less dispiriting than what's streaming from the news channels.

You've happened upon the western *Tall in the Saddle* with John Wayne and Gabby Hayes. The Duke enters an older gentleman's office. "Mr. Rocklin," begins the older fellow, an actor named Donald Douglas who squints uncertainly through a pair of round bifocals. "What happened between you and my stepson last night?" It cuts to Wayne – that is, Mr. Rocklin – who hesitates just a moment as if considering the best way to answer. Then, with an earnest look, he says, "Poker."

"Oh," comes the nodding response, and the pair and plot move on.

Nothing more needs to be said. The audience nods as well, then and now. We all know poker, after all, whether we play America's favorite card game or not.

We know it as a game played by cowboys and card sharps, by soldiers and scouts, by presidents, peasants, and painted dogs. We know that unlike many other card games, poker requires players to match not only wits, but egos and nerve as well. It's a game in which the competition can be intellectual, emotional, mental, psychological, analytical, verbal, and – as might have been the case with Rocklin and the elderly gentleman's stepson – even physical. It's a game that suits the familiar image of Wayne's Old West cowboy, a figure of rugged independence who commands respect, who instinctively understands the relationship between risk and reward, and who never shies from conflict. It's also a game befitting the image of America itself, the country in which poker was first introduced and for which the mythic cowboy – part real, part imagined – also stands as an emblem.

In other words, when Wayne says "poker," you don't *have* to be a player yourself to have an idea what he means. You don't even need to know the rules in order to understand the game's logical place in a story such as this. A game of cards would provide a ready context for characters to clash, given how poker occupied such a prominent place in the culture during the time of the Old West. Or during the 1940s, for that matter. Or today.

In fact, the history of poker runs parallel with that of the United States, starting with its origins as a game whose features are largely borrowed from other cultures' card games before being assimilated into something distinctly "American." Playing cards date from ninth century imperial China, evolving constantly over the next millennium as they were employed in a variety of games throughout Asia and Europe. By the late 18th century, most characteristics of the modern deck had been established, including the size and thickness of the cards, the rankings, and the four suits. Card games like *Poch* (from Germany), *primiera* (from Italy), *brag* (from Britain), and *mus* (from Spain) had all been carried to America by its early settlers and eventual founders, with another French game – *poque* – brought to the Louisiana Territory during the first decades of the 19th century. Poker emerged from all of those games, and as the new country's border marched westward over the coming decades, the game likewise swiftly spread via steamboats, wagon trains, stagecoaches, and locomotives.

From the beginning, three essential elements defined poker: cards, money, and bluffing. With the cards players build hands, not unlike the construction of a homestead with available materials. On such five-card combinations bets are placed, with the introduction of a draw adding an additional chance to set one's price. These financial commitments, like those routinely made on tracts of land or other futures, help make poker much more than an idle amusement, adding an urgent connection between the value of the cards and the lives of those holding them. Each hand be-comes a complicated negotiation, with each player's personal idea of mon-ey's significance directly affecting the amounts set when selling, or costs agreed to when buying.

Of course such negotiations, like others that carried the country's in-habitants across the continent, don't *have* to be entered into in good faith. Perhaps more than any other element, the possibility of misrepresenting the value of one's hand with a bluff makes poker fundamentally different from other card games, and more readily representative of the nation of bold risk-takers playing it. The possibility of the bluff likewise adds layers of psychological complexity that help make poker – as the saying goes –

not just a game of cards played by people, but a game of people played with cards.

But connections between poker and America go much deeper than the coincidence of chronology or the way the game can be said to reflect the "pioneer spirit" of the nation's early history. That's because many values and ideals compiled and endorsed by the country's founders and championed by generations thereafter find ready expression at the poker table.

Ideas of individual liberty start with the freedom to make those daring bluffs or to play one's hand however one sees fit. They extend to the potential of actually earning a living from playing cards and chart a career path measured by pots won rather than hours clocked or goods sold. There are numerous examples from the game's earliest days of individuals discovering that poker could provide for them more readily than other forms of employment – that what others viewed as "play" could for them count as "work." Thus a well-timed raise while holding a winning hand might amount to a kind of personal declaration of independence. Similarly a correct fold could become a demonstration of self-reliance, smartly trusting one's instinct regarding the strength an opponent's hand as signaled by the bet amount or the faint but perceptible tremor in his voice when he announced it.

For a country shaped by capitalist ideology, there's no more appropriate game to reflect both its individual-promoting benefits and antagonism-stirring drawbacks. A player's chips become a kind of property, necessary to defend with every deal. The rules of the game are necessarily agreed upon like citizens assenting to laws governing their conduct. And by buying into the game each player assumes certain unalienable rights to continued life at the table, to the liberty to bet or fold or call or raise, and to the pursuit of happiness that comes from scooping a pot after winning a hand.

Some argue that poker uncannily exemplifies the "American dream" insofar as it provides all who wish to play an equal opportunity to succeed. Of course, those making the argument for the egalitarian nature of poker generally tend not to emphasize how much class distinctions matter. Players' financial wherewithal not only affects their ability to take a seat, but also how they will play once they do. Bluffing is central, no doubt, but nothing can dissuade a player from boldly raising with inferior cards quite as much as the knowledge that he cannot afford to get called and lose.

Even so, it's true to say that poker doesn't "discriminate," at least when the game is square and rules are respected. As in America, where laws dictate guidelines within which citizens can pursue their livelihood, poker suggests a similar ideal, even if that ideal is not always realized. Indeed, if you were to stick with *Tall in the Saddle* a little longer you'd find it was a dispute over rules that caused the conflict between Rocklin and the stepson. You'd also discover that his need during the poker game to make a show of force in order to enforce those rules prefigures the rest of the plot when he is later called upon to restore order to a lawless Old West town.

There's one other factor poker's champions always need to acknowledge: the importance of luck. A sound grasp of odds and probabilities certainly provides a meaningful edge to some, as does being able to suss out the significance of opponents' actions, words, and other non-verbal "tells" while masking the meaning of one's own. Yet as anyone who has played poker knows only too well, a hand perfectly played does *not* guarantee a positive result. "Bad beats," "suckouts," and "coolers" happen all the time, the variety of terms players use to describe such misfortunes reflecting the frequency of their occurrence. Speaking of laws, the relative weight of luck and skill in poker has been the subject of many legal arguments in the U.S. dating almost from the time of the game's first introduction. Proponents wishing to distinguish poker from other gambling games have emphasized the significance of skill, while those wanting to prohibit the game have pointed to luck's undeniable role. Both are right, and it isn't that surprising to find judges over the years ruling in favor of either side many times over.

But that, too, is "American." Writing in the 1830s when both poker and the nation were amid early stages of growth and development, Alexis de Tocqueville remarked with astonishment on Americans' unwillingness to shy away from risk. "For them, the desire for well-being has become an anxious, burning passion that grows even as it is satisfied," wrote the Frenchman in *Democracy in America*, adding that while the need to emigrate began as matter of survival, "it has become a game of chance, which they love as much for the emotions it stirs as for the profit it brings."[1] To be sure, Americans particularly value honest work being duly compensated. Over the course of the nation's history, the idea of lifting oneself up by one's bootstraps has evolved into a persuasive ethic by which many swear. But Americans also love the adrenaline spike of a good gamble, with the promise of great rewards easily obtained providing equal encouragement to many.

Again, though, many of us know these things about poker – or a lot of them, anyway. When Tocqueville speaks of the nation's early entrepreneurs in terms that sound like he could be referring to poker players, there's something familiar about that to most of us as well. Whether we're playing or not we're "talking poker" to each other all the time, and there's no other game – not even baseball – that has established itself so prominently within the American vernacular. We know what it means when someone laments that "the chips are down." We watch out for the fellow with "an ace up his sleeve," knowing he could use such an advantage to "up the ante." We're always "passing the buck" when dodging an obligation (an archaic reference to the dealer's button), or insisting "the buck stops here" when taking responsibility ourselves. We keep our "hand in the game" when wanting to stay involved, but try to remain mindful always to "have an out" when we do. When it's time to make our meaning clear we'll put our "cards on the table." But when it becomes necessary to hide what we're thinking from others, we'll put on a "poker face."

Mark Twain, himself a poker player, is said to have complained that not enough Americans were acquainted with the game. "There are few things that are so unpardonably neglected in our country as poker," goes the quote. "The upper class knows very little about it. Now and then you find ambassadors who have sort of a general knowledge of the game, but the ignorance of the people is fearful. Why, I have known clergymen, good men, kind-hearted, liberal, sincere, and all that, who did not know the meaning of a 'flush.' It is enough to make one ashamed of one's species."[2]

It's a favorite reference among poker players, although more often than not those who share it do not acknowledge that the writer of some of the greatest works of American satire was most assuredly bluffing. Usually the observation is repeated as a straightforward lament over poker's lack of cultural standing. Yet poker was hardly neglected at the time, and Twain's admonishment of the nation's wealthy, the politically powerful, and its spiritual leaders was undoubtedly delivered with tongue firmly in cheek. In fact, evidence abounds from Twain's era that poker was far from being neglected in America, with all three of the groups referenced by Twain well represented at the tables.

Stephen Crane's short story "A Poker Game" presents a hotel-room game between a moneyed real estate maven and young heir to millions as entirely customary, with poker described as having by then become "one of the most exciting and absorbing occupations known to intelligent American manhood."[3] Such a scene is reflected further by Cassius M. Coolidge's contemporaneous "Dogs Playing Poker" series of paintings which likewise suggest in a less sober way that poker was a favorite pastime of the middle and upper classes. Ample evidence shows the nation's elected officials were also avid players in Twain's day. In *Jack Pots: Stories of the Great American Game*, Eugene Edwards declares that by the end of the 19th century "Washington is popularly regarded as the great poker center of the United States" in large part because "when Congress is in session, the whole town is in a fever of excitement, and the easiest way to work off the surplus steam is with a pack of cards."[4] At the time Twain made his declaration, the president who had just left office, Ulysses S. Grant, was an especially dedicated poker player. In fact a former Congressman who had been Grant's Minister to Great Britain, Robert C. Schenck, had earned widespread notoriety for compiling a book of rules for draw poker regarded as among the first of its kind. (In other words, Schenck was an ambassador with more than just a "general knowledge of the game.") The clergy, too, are sometimes described taking seats in poker tales of the period. There's Rev. Thankful Smith of the Thompson Street Poker Club stories written by Twain's contemporary Henry Guy Carleton. Smith is the poker-playing preacher who well knows what a flush is, and how sometimes a flush can be beaten because "Dat's de way wif cyards" since "Gamblin' 's onsartin."[5] In fact, a decade before, Twain himself had written a humorous short story, "Science vs. Luck," in which a group of clergymen play cards for money versus expert players as a test of card games' skill component. Such historical and literary evidence belies Twain's claim about poker's general lack of notice. But it also suggests there's more to poker's story – a *lot* more – than many of us might realize.

The game is so deeply embedded in American culture, its profound significance and even influence on the country's history has perhaps been taken for granted. For example, even the game's most ardent enthusiasts are likely unaware that Grant was a poker player. But he's part of a long, storied tradition of poker-playing presidents for whom acquaintance with the game was much more than incidental. Such a point can be argued with reference to domestic programs like the "Square Deal" and "New Deal" (both of which borrow from poker's egalitarian features), Cold War decisions influenced directly by game theory (a discipline borne from the study of "parlor games" including poker), and the game having provided at least one future president enough income to launch his first congressional campaign (the one nicknamed "Tricky Dick").

Stories like these often surprise students in the American Studies course I've taught for several years at UNC Charlotte, "Poker in American Film and Culture." So do others we cover that shed light on the many cultural contexts in which poker has appeared over the two centuries the game has been played. Each semester we travel through the game's colorful and varied history, often marveling at the sheer quantity of references to poker that appear initially in letters, memoirs, news accounts, and early strategy primers, then eventually extend into paintings, fiction, drama, music, film, and television.

We study poker's significance during the Civil War and reconstruction periods, then move into the 20th century to discover the game's popularity spreading to practically all social groups, traveling from steamboats and saloons to kitchen tables and living room parlors. We explore the game's significance to soldiers during both World Wars and other conflicts, the advent of casino culture and legalized poker, the birth of the World Series of Poker and later boom in popularity of tournaments spurred in part by televised poker, as well as the comparatively recent growth of the online version of the game. While we move through poker's past, we're simultaneously reminded again and again of poker's prominence in the present when yet another politician accuses an opponent of "stacking the deck," another legal commentator describes a defendant's "ace in the hole," or another coach declares his team's readiness to go "all in" behind its star player. Often there will arise as well one more sitcom or drama using a poker game to further relationships between characters, not unlike *Tall in the Saddle* with its poker scene midway through the film.

Poker? Sure, we know poker. But how well do we know poker, really? After all, every hand of poker ever played has featured a combination of the known and unknown, with the distinction between the two deliberately complicated by the efforts of everyone involved. As historian John Lukacs once said of poker: "The important thing is not what happens but what people think happens."[6] Similarly, poker's portrayal in popular culture has always been rife with embellishments and intentional distortions that have collectively helped assign or reinforce certain ideas of what the game means. Thus the story of poker and its significance to American history and culture includes much that seems readily apparent, but also much that needs further explanation.

You really want to know "what happened"? Let's go back to the beginning and take a closer look at the story of America's favorite card game. Let's look as well at the many stories that have been told *about* poker – some true, some pure bluffs, and many somewhere in between – that have both increased the game's importance to American history and culture and shaped the way we think about poker and its significance.

Everyone seated? Good.

Here's the deal.

1   Poker in the Past

Before we get into the game and some early hands, a few questions.

What do you think of when someone mentions poker? What connotations, positive or negative, do you associate with the card game played for two hundred-plus years on steamboats and in saloons, in kitchens and casinos, for matchsticks and for millions? What is your response to "America's favorite card game" being declared uniquely emblematic of the country's values and history, as being not only "more than the national game," as poker historian Al Alvarez once proclaimed, but "part of the American way of life"?[1]

Such questions likely produce a wide variety of responses. So, too, would questions asking what springs to mind when someone speaks of "America" or "the American way of life." How you respond likely depends a lot on your personal experience.

If you've played poker yourself and gained some enjoyment and/or profit while doing so, you probably have good things to say about the game. If your experience has been less positive, you might be less quick to speak well of it. But if you haven't played poker at all, and have only heard or read stories of others playing or watched it played on television or in the movies, your opinion has necessarily been shaped by these many cultural representations. Even dedicated players have likely had their opinions influenced by the game's frequent portrayal in popular culture.

Poker rarely exists as an entirely neutral activity about which those who play or watch are indifferent. It's a game about which people are constantly delivering *judgments* – moral, ethical, evaluative, analytical, and even legal. And more often than not, when it comes to cultural representations of poker or instances when the game has earned "mainstream" attention, those judgments are *not* positive. As poker's popularity has increased and more people have been introduced to the game, so, too, have objections to it become louder and more prevalent. Poker is not only America's favorite card game to play, but also to condemn.

Among the first to write extensively about the game, Jonathan Harrington Green introduced poker to his readers in 1843 as "a game that is immensely destructive – perhaps more so than any other short game at cards now in use."[2] During the Civil War, confederate soldiers gambling on cards distressed Robert E. Lee so greatly in 1862 he wrote a "General Order" forbidding the activity, describing "the vice" as "wholly inconsistent with the character of a Southern soldier and subversive of good order and discipline in the army."[3] It's the same game at which the gambler John Oakhurst excels in Bret Harte's 1869 short story "The Outcasts of Poker Flat" – too well, actually, as his winning ways are enough to inspire "a spasm of virtuous reaction" among the town's leaders who decide to include him among a group of "improper persons" sent into exile. An unfortunate sequence of events thereafter results in the death of Oakhurst, who writes his own epitaph to say he "struck a streak of bad luck" begun on the day of his banishment, "and handed in his checks."[4]

Debts accrued from a poker game were also said partly to have ignited the real-life dispute between James Butler "Wild Bill" Hickok and David Tutt, a conflict ending in the latter's demise after their games of draw poker led to one of the first and most famous "quick-draw" duels. After achieving national fame, Hickok himself also died by gunfire in 1876 while playing five-card draw in a saloon in the Dakota Territory, the aces and eights in his hand (as the story was later told) having perhaps proved distracting enough for the celebrity gunslinger to have lowered his guard. Poker, so it went, was a dangerous recreation. Indeed, as Hickok's tale was later styled, poker was a card game in which you could even be dealt something called "the dead man's hand."

Such a possibility was illustrated vividly by Frederic Remington in his 1897 painting *A Misdeal* depicting a saloon filled with gunsmoke, chairs overturned and four poker players on the floor either dead or dying while a fifth scoops what appears to be the game's last pot. N.C. Wyeth's 1916 painting *Wild Bill Hickok at Cards* furthered the connection by showing the famed lawman at the table drawing a pistol and not cards. In his satirical dictionary *The Cynic's Word Book*, later revised and republished in 1911 as *The Devil's Dictionary*, Ambrose Bierce dismissively defined "poker" as "a game said to be played with cards for some purpose to this lexicographer unknown."[5]

Early motion pictures picked up the theme as well. The 1899 short *Poker at Dawson City* produced by the Edison Manufacturing Company consists of players fighting, spilling beer, and waving guns for 20 seconds, while the one-reeler *A Cure for Pokeritis* from 1912 invented a word in order to present poker as a kind of disease in need of remedy. Warren

An old postcard humorously depicting "A Sunday School Class in the West." The description on the back finds it necessary to explain this "jolly group of old time Cowboy friends" playing poker, smoking, and drinking (one of whom is conspicuously armed) "are not disturbers of the peace as might be inferred from the photograph."

G. Harding's abbreviated tenure in the White House (1921-23) didn't do much for the reputation of the office of the presidency, marked as it was by unprecedented corruption, widespread scandal including criminal behavior among members of his administration, and extra-marital affairs. Nor did Harding help poker's reputation very much, hosting twice-a-week games in the White House during which alcohol flowed despite Prohibition. Though he was still popular at the time of his sudden death by heart attack, later revelations severely damaged Harding's legacy, with his predilection for poker – and alleged loss of a set of White House china while gambling on cards – further diminishing poker's status amid an era of temperance.

Poker is likewise the cause of strife (and, often, violence) in numerous westerns appearing throughout the genre's extended golden age, causing trouble in films like *Destry Rides Again* (1936), *Tall in the Saddle* (1944), *Winchester '73* (1950), *The Lawless Breed* (1953) and *Rio Bravo* (1959). Even non-westerns presented poker in a less than flattering light, such as in *A Streetcar Named Desire* (1951), the adaptation of Tennessee Williams' stage play in which a poker game evolves into a scene of shocking domestic violence. The loss of a hand of Spit in the Ocean is the final straw triggering Stanley Kowalski to physically abuse his pregnant wife.

The 1965 film *The Cincinnati Kid* explored a poker player's travails, despite the commonly held view that poker wasn't just a dangerous or even deadly game to play, it was deadly to watch. Director Norman Jewison explained: "There were many people who felt that a card game was death – that there was no way you could make a film about a card game, because it was just so totally uncinematic."[6] While the film ultimately succeeds in creating a compelling story punctuated by a suspenseful, climactic high-stakes game, reviewers held poker against it. *The New York Times* found the subject matter less than inclusive, making the movie "strictly for those who relish, or at least play, stud poker."[7] *Time* judged "nearly everything about *Cincinnati Kid* is reminiscent of *The Hustler*," the 1961 gambling film in which pool was the featured game. "Director Jewison can put his cards on the table [and] let his camera cut suspensefully to the players' intent faces," the *Time* reviewer explains, "but a pool shark sinking a tricky shot into a side pocket undoubtedly offers more range."[8] More than three decades later the 1998 poker drama *Rounders* also endured similar dismissals by some critics calling it "a tiresome rip-off of *The Hustler*"[9] plagued by "slow-moving card game sequences" that only "avid poker players" might enjoy.[10]

Negative judgment about poker's commercial appeal had to be overcome in order for a short documentary about the 1973 World Series of Poker to air on CBS, an experiment not attempted again for several years. By 1980 card games expert John Scarne estimated 65 million Americans were playing poker in one form or another,[11] but not many were exerting much effort to defend the game. In a tongue-in-cheek opener to a 1983 column for *The New York Times Magazine*, TV critic and reporter Walter Goodman begins a discussion of home-game poker by wryly noting "the first thing to be said in poker's behalf is that it is absolutely unedifying; it is not intellectually stimulating or morally uplifting." His monthly game, much like others "across this poker-infatuated land," provides a refuge from "obligations and responsibilities," an admittedly selfish escape "from family and job" to a more child-like sphere "when play was the most serious thing in the world."[12]

Meanwhile if recreational poker players were being drawn as adults abdicating responsibilities, the more serious "professionals" examined by anthropologist David Hayano for his 1982 study *Poker Faces: The Life and Work of Professional Card Players* found themselves mired in existential crises borne from the day-to-day uncertainty about their livelihood and inescapable doubts about the significance of their lives. "Living, playing, and surviving in the chancy world of the cardroom repeatedly assaults the sensibilities," writes Hayano after having spent an extended period among full-time players in the California clubs of the era, "and several pros have openly commented on the difficulties of 'lasting' and explaining 'what this all means.'"[13]

A remarkable confluence of events in the late 1990s and early 2000s dramatically increased poker's profile, helping carry the game from the cultural fringe and into the public eye. *Rounders* not only successfully attracted "avid poker players," but soon began to create new ones as well, with the concurrent advent of online poker providing many of those newly interested a fast and convenient way to play. Meanwhile the rise of reality TV exerted an important influence on televised poker, with producers incorporating commercially-successful elements from shows such as *Survivor* and *American Idol,* as well as from sports programming and game shows, to build big audiences eager to watch poker.

Not everyone found such shows so compelling. "TV Poker's a Joker," judged sports writer Rick Reilly in 2004, summarily dismissing "the televised poker craze" as "the biggest waste of time" and potentially harmful to younger viewers. "Poker isn't a sport, it isn't for kids, and it sure as hell shouldn't be on my damn sports channels," Reilly complains.[14] Comedian and talk show host Bill Maher continued the theme in a 2006 compilation of jokes titled *New Rules: Polite Musings from a Timid Observer.* "No more TV gambling," Maher declares. "First, there was *Celebrity Poker*, then there was *Celebrity Blackjack.* I saw one show that was just Camryn Manheim scratching lottery tickets. What gets on TV has to be at least as interesting as what's on the average security monitor at a convenience store."[15] The poker boom continued, nonetheless, bringing enough fame to players to land some of them on non-poker reality shows. In 2009 Annie Duke found herself on the receiving end of a memorable anti-poker rant by comedian and television personality Joan Rivers on an episode of *Celebrity Apprentice*. "You're a *poker* player. A *poker* player!" bellows Rivers, the pronouncing of the very word causing her to cringe. "Poker players! Poker players are trash, darling. Trash!"[16]

As more and more Americans took seats at both real and virtual tables and online poker grew into a multibillion-dollar industry worldwide, the nearly decade-long efforts of a few of the nation's lawmakers suddenly came to fruition with the surprise passage of the Unlawful Internet Gambling Enforcement Act (UIGEA) of 2006. While not targeting online poker in particular, the law significantly affected Americans' access to online games by prohibiting "financial service providers" from facilitating transactions to and from sites located outside the U.S. Several chose to stop allowing American players entirely, while those who continued to accept U.S.-based players were faced with regulations that made it increasingly arduous to move money to facilitate games.

Cheating scandals on a couple of those sites – Absolute Poker and UltimateBet - were reported on by *The Washington Post* and CBS' *60 Minutes* in late 2008, with an above-the-fold *Post* headline "Players Gamble on Honesty, Security of Internet Betting" hardly helping to make playing poker online seem like an innocuous pastime.[17] Eventually those two sites along with PokerStars and Full Tilt Poker were targeted by the Department of Justice and dramatically driven from the U.S. with the 2011 unsealing of an indictment and civil complaint charging them not only with violating the UIGEA, but a host of other crimes including money laundering and bank fraud. Poker players immediately dubbed the day "Black Friday." Charged with returning player funds to Americans no longer allowed to play, only PokerStars actually had the money available to be withdrawn. It prompted the DOJ to amend the civil complaint to add new charges that Full Tilt Poker's owners had defrauded players by funneling nearly $440 million from player accounts to themselves. The accompanying press release declared: "Full Tilt was not a legitimate poker company, but a global Ponzi scheme."[18] It was a characterization loudly (and often uncritically) repeated over every media outlet, creating a dubious pocket pair between a couple of five-letter words starting with "p" – one referring to a fraudulent investment operation, the other to a card game.

At the time, *Rounders* co-writer Brian Koppelman echoed the sentiment of many poker players, finding the virtual annihilation of online poker in America by the federal government "wrong on every level" and hoping "the absurdity" of the situation would be resolved soon so amateurs and pros alike could "get back to playing the game we love in the comfort and privacy of our homes." That said, the situation recalled for Koppelman an earlier, more romantic version of the game, the one promoted by popular culture in which poker was largely the province of outlaws "plying their trade at the edges of society, not its center." After several years of the game conspicuously enjoying the bright-hot spotlight, poker had been abruptly forced to retreat to the periphery. "Poker is... finally back in the shadows, where, mythically at least, it belongs," said Koppelman.

Such a survey omits poker's positives, of course, both in the game's history and in the various cultural representations of poker which will be our primary focus going forward. It nonetheless raises the question: from where did all this animosity toward poker and poker players come?

Well, in truth, it was there even before the first hand was dealt.

2 Before Poker

"In the beginning, everything was even money."[1]

So quipped Mike Caro, the self-proclaimed "mad genius of poker" and author of numerous strategy books and articles. Though Caro deliberately alludes to another famous opening line, he does *not* in fact mean to refer to a certain gamble once taken in the Garden of Eden. Rather, he's describing the point of view of an uninformed gambler, who before gathering and analyzing relevant data might well erroneously view *any* bet as a 50-50 proposition.

Back in Eden, as John Milton imagined the scene in *Paradise Lost*, Eve listens with keen interest to the arguments of a surprisingly loquacious serpent – Earth's first tout, we might call him – all of which concern a certain "tree we may not taste or touch." Having weighed risk and reward and concluded there to be no hindrance "to reach, and feed at once both body and mind," Eve takes a chance. "She plucked, she ate," and in an instant the

Poker & Pop Culture

Earth responds with "signs of woe, that all was lost."[2] Not only does the Puritan poet make the case for free will in his dramatization, with Eve (and then Adam) ultimately shown culpable for the fateful choices they make, but he also suggests that even before the fall there existed within human agency a willingness – perhaps even an innate desire – to gamble.

The other message delivered here, of course, is that gambling is *bad*. As Caro implies, and Eve and Adam demonstrate, gambling is especially bad when done without sufficient understanding of the risks involved. But even after having sampled from the Tree of Knowledge of Good and Evil, those who gamble willingly frequently open themselves up to censure and even punishment. Well before a card game called poker first appeared in the south and west United States during the early 19th century, and before all of the many stories helped build interest in it, cultural prejudice against gambling games was already firmly established. We hardly need to go back to Genesis to support the argument that as a species, humans have pretty much *always* been ready and willing to gamble, and other humans have always been there to raise objections.

Many have observed how the risk-taking urge may have been bred in us as a necessary corollary of survival-of-the-fittest selection, a genetic legacy handed down by our hunter-gatherer ancestors. Among archeological records there exist many concrete signs of gambling, including precursors to favored modern games. The title of David G. Schwartz's comprehensive history of gambling, *Roll the Bones*, points all of the way back to the tossing of *astragali* or the huckle-bones of sheep and goats by early humans. Such *astragali* have been recovered in numerous archeological sites throughout Europe, the Mediterranean, and the Near East, in some cases associated with the activities of fortune-tellers who regarded the results as indicators of future events. From there, Schwartz suggests, our ancestors needed little encouragement to start placing bets upon which of the four unsymmetrical sides the bones would settle.[3] Later in Mesopotamia (now northern Iraq) more examples of *astragali* from various periods have been discovered, including filed down, six-sided versions marked with insignia said to date as far back as 3,000 B.C.

Another divinatory practice involved the throwing of arrows as found among several ancient cultures, among them the Babylonians, Scythians, and Greeks. Practitioners of "belomancy" marked feathered arrows with symbols or written phrases then cast them aloft, watching to see where they landed (or where higher powers were thought to have carried them) with the results taken as indications of the best course of action. Writing in the late-19th century, Stewart Culin outlined possible connections between belomancy and a few gambling games, including the theory that early playing cards directly descended from these arrows. In multiple works Culin describes Korean arrows of the sixth century A.D. evolving a few centuries later into *htou-tjyen* or "fighting tablets" – that is, long (eight inches) and narrow (a quarter-inch) strips of paper with uniform designs on one side and numerals and early suits on the other.[4] A pack consisted of anywhere from 40 to 60 cards, some with pictures of arrow feathers on their backs. Culin's contemporary Sir William Wilkinson similarly described these early Korean "cards," and both of them are among historians who propose that the earliest card games emerged during the T'ang dynasty in ninth century Imperial China. Some of the games overlap closely with tile-based games often considered the first versions of dominoes and mahjong.[5]

From Asia playing cards wound their way west to Europe, with appearances along the way in India, Persia (Iran), and Egypt. By the end of the medieval period and start of the modern era, most countries had their own decks as well as burgeoning traditions of games played with them. Catherine Perry Hargrave's 1930 compilation *A History of Playing Cards* provides hundreds of examples, showing how card designs frequently chronicled various cultural values and traditions. Early Chinese cards sometimes resembled paper notes used as currency, with some featuring portraits of characters from folk tales. Some of the circular-shaped cards from India depicted various incarnations of Vishnu. Meanwhile the cards in Europe showed kings and other nobles, eventually becoming the "court cards" of the modern deck. Some early "vying" games played with these cards featured the wagering of money or other items of value and in some cases bluffing. Games like *Poch* from Germany, *primiera* from Italy, *brag* from England, *mus* from Spain, and especially *poque* from France all arguably contributed elements to poker, with poque perhaps being the game's most direct precursor thanks to French settlers bringing it to the Louisiana Territory both before and after its acquisition by the United States.[6] Indeed, many have speculated that incorrect pronunciation of the word "poque" (emphasizing the second syllable) provided a basis for the name "poker."

In other words, like much of America's population, poker was "parented" elsewhere, having descended from other, earlier card games originating in other countries. Not only that, the often dubious cultural standing of poker – as a game for outlaws, cheats, and ne'er-do-wells – was largely inherited, too.

"Poker is Not Responsible for All the Charges Brought Against It"

"As in any game of chance or speculation there are in poker opportunities to cheat," William J. Florence wrote in his 1892 book *The Gentleman's Handbook on Poker*. "Long before poker, however, was even invented, cheating at chance games was practiced by the unprincipled. I have seen loaded dice taken from the ruins of Pompeii and Herculaneum and now preserved in the Government Museum in Naples; so poker is not responsible for all the charges brought against it."[7]

It is a given that cheating at gambling games predated poker. So, too, did other objections to gambling as a both a means to squander away this life while ensuring damnation in the next. Such was the message repeatedly delivered via poetry, fiction, drama, in philosophical writings and paintings, and elsewhere during the centuries preceding the first hands of poker.

As we have seen, Milton's Satan encouraged the first couple to indulge their predilection for risk-taking in the Garden of Eden. It's fitting, then, that Dante reserved a place in the seventh circle of hell for gamblers. In the *Inferno*, the first part of his early 14th-century epic *The Divine Comedy*, Dante condemned "wanton spendthrifts" to a region designated for those guilty of "violence against oneself." There's no card playing in Chaucer's *Canterbury Tales*, although the Pardoner in his tale does rail against gambling, describing "hasardrye" (the dice game Hazard, or gambling generally speaking) as the "mooder of lesynges" (the mother of lies).[8] In fact, during the late 1300s authorities in Italy, France, Switzerland, Spain, Germany, and the Netherlands issued a number of ordinances and prohibitions outlawing several different card games. Hargrave refers to a "Paris decree" in 1397 that "forbade working people to play at 'tennis, bowls, dice, cards or ninepins, on working days.'"[9] More legal proscriptions against cards appeared in the following century, further attesting to the continued popularity of the games as well as how much they bothered some. Reservations about gambling on cards additionally surface in a story of uncertain veracity regarding the initial voyage of Christopher Columbus across the Atlantic in 1492 and sailors playing primero on board. After encountering rough weather, the story goes, the cards were tossed overboard, declared to be the "devil's picture-books."[10]

By the time Francois Rabelais wrote his great satire *Gargantua and Pantagruel* during the mid-16th century, the manufacture of cards and development of still more games had expanded significantly. Early in the book Rabelais describes the giant Gargantua finishing a large meal, then having a green cloth laid out over a table and cards, dice, and game-boards set upon it. Then in suitably hyperbolic fashion he's said to play some 200-plus different games, many of which appear to be card games. Later translators expanded the list even further. If you pick up the book today you'll find an even longer list including primero, glic (a precursor of poque), and post and pair (a relative of brag). Rabelais doesn't really offer an opinion on whether gambling games are good or bad, making him different from most other cultural commentators who bring up the subject. His contemporary Thomas More, for instance, described the inhabitants of his *Utopia* shunning gambling as a bad pleasure and the source of social ill. Erasmus in *The Praise of Folly* also censures gamblers as foolish, addicted, given to cheating, and their games often leading players into senseless conflict.

During the 1560s an Italian mathematician and physician named Gerolamo Cardano wrote a short treatise titled *Liber de Lude Aleae* or a *Book on Games of Chance* that neatly summarizes cultural attitudes toward gambling, including gambling on cards. Cardano was himself a gambler, and spent time in a debtors' prison due to his gambling losses. Amid explorations of the math behind various games of chance, Cardano maintains that gambling produces destructive and unhealthy effects, and should only be pursued in moderation. He acknowledges how gambling on cards and dice can make some irrational to the point of madness. Gambling, he surmises, "would seem a natural evil" and "for that reason it ought to be discussed by a medical doctor like one of the incurable diseases."[11] Cardano defends certain forms of gambling, and maintains card games like primero might be even better than dice, rewarding those with good memories and offering more opportunities for the skillful to gain an edge. "In play with dice... everything depends entirely on pure chance, if the die is honest" he writes. "But in cards, apart from the recognition of cards from the back [i.e., marked cards] there are a thousand other natural and worthy ways of recognizing them which are at the disposal of the prudent man." Thus, Cardano concludes, "it is more fitting for the wise man to play at cards than at dice."[12] Some have speculated that Cardano was motivated to write the book not so much by curiosity about odds and probabilities, but by a desire to rationalize his own predilections. In any case, the book went unpublished until nearly a century after Cardano's death.

Gambling of various forms continued to flourish throughout Europe while raising the ire of countries' moral stewards. Betting on the outcomes of papal elections had become prevalent enough for Pope Gregory XIV to ban the practice in 1591, with anyone found doing so subject to the penalty of excommunication. In Italy the emergence of the wildly popular "ridotti" gambling dens featured card games like basset and faro. Legislation to prohibit them proved ineffective, and in 1638 Venice authorities gave in and opened Il Ridotto, a government-sanctioned gambling house, essentially history's first casino.

In common with most Elizabethan playwrights, William Shakespeare mentions card-playing frequently. The plot of *The Merry Wives of Windsor* hinges on Falstaff's attempt to make money, having stopped gambling at cards, by trying to court two wealthy (and married) women at once. "I never prospered since I forswore myself at primero," Falstaff explains.[13] Miguel de Cervantes, Shakespeare's contemporary and author of *Don Quixote*, was himself a gambler. In his short story "Rinconete y Cortadillo" published early in the 17th century, characters cheat at *veintiuna* or "twenty-one," thought to be the earliest reference in literature to the game now known as blackjack. And near the end of Part Two of *Don Quixote*, a maid angrily bids the knight-errant goodbye wishing him bad luck at cards in the future, stating if he ever plays "los cientos" (or piquet) or "primera," she hopes he only gets dealt bad cards.

Alexander Pope particularly targets the game of ombre (a bridge-like trick-taking game) in his early 18th-century mock-heroic *The Rape of the Lock*, describing a game played among the upper-class as like an epic battle (with added sexual connotations). Pope's friend Jonathan Swift often played and gambled on cards, although he apparently regretted the time wasted upon such games. Other of their contemporaries also associated card games with idle foolishness and even evidence of a certain moral decay among the wealthy. As Samuel Johnson once wrote in a *Rambler* essay, he greatly valued visiting and meeting new people, but when those meetings occurred "at card tables, however brilliant, I have always thought my visit lost." Johnson said the games were "too trifling for me when I was grave, and too dull when I was cheerful."[14]

Georges de la Tour, *Cheat with the Ace of Diamonds* (ca. 1635)

Much as writers began focusing more intently on everyday life in their works, so, too, did certain European painters turn their attention toward scenes of people engaged in commonplace activities and recreations. Card playing was a favorite subject for such "genre painting," with cheating often present to emphasize anti-gambling messages. Caravaggio's *The Cardsharps* (ca. 1594) depicts a young primero player being doubly duped by an older man peering over his shoulder at his hand while his younger opponent hides a card behind his back. Around 1620 Flemish painter Nicolas Régnier associated card playing with palm reading, pickpockets, and prostitution amid a crowded evening scene in *Cardsharps and Fortune Teller*, with cheating again in evidence as a soldier slyly removes a card from play. Valentin de Boulogne likewise chooses a dark, sinister setting for his *Soldiers Playing Cards and Dice (The Cheats)* (ca. 1618-20), with the integrity of the game played by two figures in the foreground compromised by another in the back signaling to an accomplice.

Like Régnier and Boulogne, the French painter Georges de La Tour was influenced by Caravaggio to paint two companion works, *Cheat with the Ace of Clubs* (ca. 1626-29) and *Cheat with the Ace of Diamonds* (1635). Both show nearly identical scenes of a young wealthy man in a card game being set up to fall by a trio of accomplices: a courtesan, an older card player, and a wine-serving maid. Sex, alcohol, and gambling are intertwined, with the older man surreptitiously pulling an ace from his belt further underscoring the painting's moral warning. Adding to the painting's drama are the sidelong glances of the conniving trio, including the cheater in the foreground looking over his shoulder at the viewer as though to make us somehow complicit. (More than two and a half centuries later, Cassius M. Coolidge's poker-playing dogs, especially the cheating bulldog passing an ace in *A Friend in Need* offered a wagging tongue-in-cheek nod to the European sharps.)

Poker Stirs the Melting Pot
Such was the context into which poker was introduced in early-19th century America. Not only did the game acquire elements from precursor card games played elsewhere, but poker likewise inherited centuries' worth of censure and vitriol.

It wasn't long after the colonies were established that authorities did what they could to prevent the gambling madness from spreading. In 1638 Puritans in Massachusetts revised a previously passed "Idleness Statute" outlawing the possession of cards, dice, or other gambling-related paraphernalia to make more specific the prohibition against gambling. Quakers in Pennsylvania enacted a similar law in 1682. Both New Hampshire (in 1721) and New Jersey (in 1748) passed laws prohibiting gambling.

In 1752, Reverend William Stith encouraged lawmakers to continue to curb the vice when he delivered a sermon to Virginia's General Assembly at Williamsburg titled "The Sinfulness and Pernicious Nature of Gaming." A historian and one of the first presidents at the College of William & Mary, Stith sensibly allows that "even Gaming for Money, in some Instances and Degrees, may be a lawful and innocent Diversion." The problem, however, is that "the Spirit of Gaming is of a very growing and encroaching Nature," utterly consuming those who engage to such a degree that it "totally engrosses and enslaves" its victims.[15] Thus do those who gamble sin against their neighbors, their country, their families, themselves, and ultimately God. Stith concludes by advising lawmakers "there is no reigning Evil among us at present, so virulent and outrageous, and which seems so greatly to demand their Regard and healing Hand, as this of Gaming; nor any Thing, wherein they can do their Country a more real and substantial Service, than by putting an effectual Stop to it."[16]

In 1790 the newly acquired Northwest Territory passed an "act for suppressing and prohibiting every species of gaming for money or other property," including rendering "null and void" any exchange of money or goods "won or obtained... by playing at cards" or other games of chance. In 1806 Louisiana made gambling illegal everywhere in the state except New Orleans (helping ensure the city would become an early gambling capital in the southern U.S.), while in 1814 the legislature in Missouri passed an anti-gambling law including specific provisions prohibiting the operation of any gaming tables.[17]

While entrepreneurship and "speculation" was the order of the day, especially after the new country declared its independence, the kind of risk-taking represented by gambling and card-playing was condemned from all sides. Stories of gamblers meeting tragic ends occasionally provided plots in early American fiction and drama. In a study connecting American fiction of the era to burgeoning economic anxieties, Karen A. Weyler discusses a number of anti-gambling novels such as *St. Hubert* (1800) which connects card playing and adultery as together causing ruin to its married protagonist; *The Gambler, or the Memoirs of a British Officer* (1802) in which the main character gambles away his family's fortune and ends the story in prison; and Caroline Matilda Warren Thayer's *The Gamesters* (1805) in which a character gets seduced into the vice by an acquaintance, gambles away his inheritance, then takes his own life. Novels such as these, Weyler argues, illustrate the effort to distinguish honest trade from "gambling, which is universally damned in early American fiction and belles lettres."[18] Plenty of similar warnings were being delivered from the pulpit, of course.

In the beginning, then, everything *wasn't* "even money" as far as poker's place in the culture was concerned. It was a game destined to cause trouble right from the start.

You could say the deck was stacked against it.

t chance slip by of partaking of a little *rational*
·ment. What do you agree to?"

" Let's go to Rodger's," said Corporal Stephe
nd talk about old times, over a venison steak an
ɔp of whiskey."

" Not so," said Benson. " The M—— lost so
ɔl hundreds last night at poker,* in camp, and i
:et some brother officers at Rodger's to night.
ɪt won't do."

    * A favorite game of cards at the south and west.

3

Poker in Print

    The search for the earliest references to the new game of poker leads us directly to the American frontier. The game and nation grew and developed together, with both experiencing significant territorial expansion throughout the 19th century. Just as the ever-shifting concept of what "America" was and stood for swelled to include a multitude of different ideals and values, so, too, did poker evolve into a uniquely adaptable game allowing for a remarkable variety of rules, variants, and methods of play.

    The first mentions of poker in print help provide an estimate of when the early games played with 20 or 25 cards took place, then also when variants requiring 52 cards, such as draw poker and stud poker, emerged. They also confirm right from the start poker's curious "outlaw" status, with even the very first stories including many details that later became commonplace or even clichéd.

The First Hand History

In the spring of 1833, Congress created a new military organization called the United States Regiment of Dragoons. Its duties included exploring the Mississippi Valley to seek treaties with Native American tribes while also defending the newly established frontier. Over that summer officers were recruited to serve from every state in the Union, all 24 of them. By year's end five companies' worth of men belonging to what would subsequently be called the "First Regiment of Dragoons" were sent to Fort Gibson in the Arkansas Territory, with five more companies joining them the next spring.

Accounts of the First Regiment's campaigns began appearing shortly after they were conducted, including in an official journal kept by Lieutenant T.B. Wheelock. In 1836 a lively telling of the First Regiment of Dragoons' story was published titled *Dragoon Campaigns to the Rocky Mountains; Being a History of the Enlistment, Organization, and First Campaigns of the Regiment of United States Dragoons; Together With Incidents of a Soldier's Life, and Sketches of Scenery and Indian Character.* The book presents a series of letters written by "A Dragoon" from August 1833 to the fall of 1834 and contains a full and occasionally critical picture of the regiment's organization and operation. It also contains a important moment in the history of poker: the very first reference in a book to the game.[1]

The particular story was written from Fort Gibson during the spring of 1834. It begins with a small group of officers discussing plans to enjoy a final evening before decamping. One of them suggests having dinner at the dwelling of an affluent Cherokee named "old Rodger" located a short walk across the prairie. However, another member of the group quickly objects, noting how "The M–– lost some cool hundreds at poker last night, in camp, and is to meet some brother officers at Rodger's to night." Aware that his audience may not be familiar with the game, the author supplies a footnote defining "poker" as "A favorite game of cards at the south and west." They decide instead to have one of the group sneak away from camp to old Rodger's in order to secure a quart of whiskey to help enliven their evening. After losing a "toss up," the author is selected to make the trip. "The business I had in hand was one of double risk and severe penalty," he explains, noting how not only was alcohol forbidden, but also being caught away from the barracks without a pass was strictly prohibited. Upon arriving at Rodger's, he first listens through a window and hears the Major and Captain engaged in an animated discussion.

Soon he realizes what is going on: his superiors are once more playing that "favorite game" of the region. "I'll stake you another ten," the Major says. "Done," replies the Captain, a response that appears to indicate a responding raise. The Major continues to up the stakes to "twenty," "fifty," then "another hundred." None of these bets cause the Captain any consternation as he steadfastly remains in the hand. At last the Major stops raising, "and throwing down his cards exclaimed, 'There's four kings! What have you got?'" "Only four aces!" responds the Captain who then gathers his winnings. An incensed Major curses, "at the same time splitting the pine table with a blow of his fist." "We shall probably have an hour's extra drill in the morning," the author reflects grimly.

Thus the first reference to poker in print includes several details that would be repeated frequently in subsequent poker tales. The nighttime setting, with the air of illicitness thickened further by the author's surreptitious run for contraband, introduces poker as a game played in the shadows, an "outlaw" activity of dubious legality. The hand then features multiple raises concluding with a dramatic showdown, resembling a verbal battle ending in violence. That also prefigures future stories of poker hands (especially those from the Old West), with the Major's breaking of the table afterwards illustrating the short step from intellectual intrigue to physical frustration. The mathematically improbable outcome of four aces beating four kings will likewise emerge as a clichéd concluding twist in numerous subsequent poker stories.

The *Dragoon Campaigns* author – whose identity is uncertain, but is usually believed to be either a young soldier named James Hildreth or an older veteran of the campaigns, originally from Britain, named William L. Gordon-Miller – refrains from casting any judgments about the prudence of gambling at cards. His account implies he's more comfortable risking getting caught on a booze run than he would be betting hundreds on a hand of poker. The storyteller does not hint that anything untoward might have happened in the hand between the Major and the Captain. While the showdown of quad aces over quad kings might appear to provide compelling circumstantial evidence pointing to the possibility of a stacked deck, both the physical distance between the author and the game and his seemingly slight knowledge of poker might have made it hard for him to recognize if anyone had cheated.

More Hands, More Warnings

Although not specified, it's likely the variant dealt in the *Dragoon Campaigns* poker game was what would come to be called "Twenty-Deck Poker." This first form employed only the aces, kings, queens, jacks, and tens, with five cards dealt to each player, no discards or draws, and only a single round of betting. Suits were of no consequence, with only high card, one pair, two pair, "triplets" (three of a kind), "full" (full house), and four of a kind being recognized hands, and neither straights nor flushes considered. The twenty-card variant also appears in other early references to poker including in Jonathan Harrington Green's *An Exposure to the Arts and Miseries of Gam-*

bling; *Designed Especially as a Warning to the Youthful and Inexperienced Against the Evils of That Odious and Destructive Vice* (1843) and Joe Cowell's *Thirty Years Passed Among the Players in England and America* (1844).

Green and Cowell are much more direct about potential dangers associated with the new card game of poker. As a teenager and young adult, Green was among the first wave of steamboat sharps fleecing travelers on the Mississippi. In 1842, however, he abruptly gave up gambling to campaign against it, becoming a popular lecturer and author of nearly a dozen books warning readers against gambling's many ills, including professional cheats like his former self. Adopting the role of "The Reformed Gambler" (the self-referencing title of one of his later books), Green even became involved in efforts to legislate against gambling and root out illegal houses.

As suggested by the less than subtle title of his first book, Green explicitly tries to dissuade readers from engaging in gambling games of all kinds. This purpose partially prevents Green from sharing certain particulars of how poker is actually played so as not to encourage his readers to learn it. "I would that all were ignorant of it," he claims amid wide-eyed warnings against poker, a game he believes to be an early step along a fateful "road to ruin." According to Green, what starts with innocent pursuits such as dominoes, checkers, and whist, leads to faro, roulette, horse racing, cock-fighting, and worse. Even so, Green does flesh out the basic rules of twenty-card poker, including explaining "there are no limits to the bets." As he explains it, the game "frequently… begins as low as a quarter of a dollar, and runs up to thousands in one or two minutes."[2]

Green remarks how poker can involve bluffing, insofar as "the man who has the most money will frequently bet so high on a poor hand, as to run his adversary off and win," a tactic he calls "a run off." He identifies the "southern and western portions of our country" as the most likely areas in which to encounter the game, dwelling in particular upon a game he says was played in New Orleans in 1835. He also describes "a game of full deck poker, which is played with the full pack of fifty-two cards," a change allowing for more than four players to be dealt into a hand.[3]

When it comes to poker, Green's warning to readers is twofold. Not only does playing the game mean risking the general moral degradation caused by all forms of gambling, but the preponderance of cheaters in poker ensures "the uninitiated need never expect to win any thing." The twenty-card game affords more opportunities for cheaters than does "full deck poker," Green believes, since the reduced number of cards makes it "very easy to keep the eye on particular cards, and to stock them, and deal off particular hands." Reading Green explain the cheater's method of "frequently giving out hands that are seldom got in the common course of fair play, and are seldom dealt out but by design," it is easy to entertain the thought that he's given us an explanation for the Captain's good fortune versus the Major back in old Rodger's cabin.[4]

In his 1844 follow-up *Gambling Unmasked: Or The Personal Experience of the Reformed Gambler*, Green describes a game of poker he played aboard the Caspian on the Red River in 1833 in which he demonstrated that very method in a game versus a young Frenchman. Having "stocked" the deck, Green dealt himself what in twenty-card poker (with no straights or flushes) constitutes an unbeatable hand of two aces, two kings, and a queen and his opponent a near-miss with two aces, two kings, and a jack. Having cleaned out the Frenchman for $2,500, the latter leaves the game cursing "all America, and the day his father came to America."[5]

In common with similar examples of heavy-handed moral instruction, there's something disingenuous about Green's sensational handling of his subject, which tends to be more exploitative than educational. He often seems equally keen to champion his own cleverness while censuring the professional gamblers' deceitful craft. That said, Green's account is valuable for helping us pinpoint when and where poker began to be played. He establishes poker to have already become a popular pastime by the 1830s, even suggesting that by then the game had gone through a generation's worth of change to produce a kind of nostalgia for its earlier form. "There was a time when this game was not so dangerous as it has come to be of late years," he writes in *An Exposure to the Arts and Miseries of Gambling*. "It was then common to see men of almost all classes amuse themselves at this game; and landlords would join their guests for social amusement. Captains and other officers of packets and steamboats, generally, would engage freely in a game with their passengers for recreation. And little if anything was wagered or lost at the game, and all got up pleased, and seldom had any cause of dissatisfaction."[6]

It's a dubious sketch, positing the existence of a kind of "before-the-fall" version of poker in which players somehow competed without self-interest. Against that portrait Green contrasts the later corrupt player of "a game that it is immensely destructive – perhaps more so than any another short game at cards now in use."[7] In any case, it's clear that by the time poker began to be written about during the 1830s and 1840s, the game had existed long enough to have developed a brief history with a subculture having already grown up around it.

A year after Green's book, British stage actor Joe Cowell released a memoir titled *Thirty Years Passed Among the Players in England and America*. In it Cowell further attests to poker's spread up the Mississippi and through the American south thanks to a story of a poker game in December 1829.[8] An inexperienced card player himself ("my skill only extending to a homely game at *whist*"), Cowell is introduced to several card games while on a tour of American theaters. (The book also includes an early mention of "uker" or euchre.) His poker story develops aboard a ship called the *Helen M'Gregor* during a "foggy, wretched night" of low visibility, with hostility already brewing. Near the beginning of the episode – before the game switches to poker – a suspicion of cheating results in a player suddenly chopping another's finger off with a Bowie knife. Such wariness continues into the poker game during which opponents' cards are "carefully concealed from one another" while "old players pack them in their hands, and peep at them as if they were afraid to trust even themselves to look."

The game once more is the twenty-card version of poker, and in his introduction Cowell presents it as "exclusively a high-gambling Western game, founded on [the British game] *brag*." Cowell actually describes the game in which he participated to have been played "with twenty-five cards only, and by four persons," though confusingly adds that only aces, kings, queens, jacks, and tens are used (totaling 20). Cowell comes away from the game a loser, and when the boat accidentally hits an island, "the hubbub formed a good excuse to end our game, which my stupidity had made desirable long before." Before stopping, though, one final hand is played involving four others, with bets starting at $10, then $20, then suddenly $500 and $1,500. Three players remain at showdown, with one player's four kings and an ace proving an unbeatable hand, remarkably besting the four queens with an ace held by one opponent and four jacks with an ace of the other.

It appears to be yet another incredible hand of poker, although in this case Cowell is able to confirm that "the truth was, the cards had been *put up*, or *stocked*, as it is called." Even so, the discovery of cheating does not cause Cowell to follow Green's lead and censure the game or those who play it. "After the actors, there is no class of persons so misrepresented and abused behind their backs as the professional gamblers," Cowell writes, lamenting how "as in my trade, the depraved and dishonourable are selected as the sample of all." Cowell rather wishes to promote the gambler, a character he encountered repeatedly during his travels while on steamboats and in hotels, and to insist "they cannot be excelled by any other set of men who make making money their only mental occupation."

Was poker an opportunity for socializing and satisfying intellectual curiosity, or a breeding ground for vice and financial ruin? The debates began almost from the very beginning.

Poker According to *Hoyle*

A year after Cowell's book, poker received its first mention in an edition of *Hoyle's Games*, the popular series of rule books whose publication continued well after the death in 1769 of its original author Edmond Hoyle.

The 1845 American edition of *Hoyle's* compiled by Henry F. Anners added games described in the prefatory advertisement as "*entirely new* in this country," among them "Poker, or 'Bluff'" or the "full deck" version of the game played with 52 cards.[9] The entry covers how the dealer is chosen, procedures for handling exposed cards and misdeals, the employment of "counters" or "chips" to indicate stakes being wagered, and, significantly, the addition of flushes (better than three of a kind, not as high-ranking as a "full hand" or full house), though not yet straights. Straight and royal flushes are also yet to be included, leaving four of a kind atop the list of hand rankings.

Other variations to game play are also outlined, including the option to "double head" or "treble head," that is, to double or triple the stakes should all players decide not to "enter for the pool." Players can additionally agree to have the one sitting left of the dealer post a "blind" bet to induce action, with the minimum raise thereafter being twice the blind. A postscript referring to "Twenty-Deck Poker" appears to show that the twenty-card variant was still sometimes played, though such references soon became less frequent and faded entirely by the time of the Civil War.

An even more meaningful innovation soon arrived, the first indication of which can be found in *Bohn's New Hand-Book of Games* from 1850.[10] Here the poker discussion from the 1845 *Hoyle's* is repeated verbatim, with the addition of another short, important addendum describing "Draw Poker."[11] The entry tells of a game similar in all respects except that "the player can draw from the pack as many cards as he may wish, – not exceeding five, – which must be given him by the dealer; but previous to drawing he must take from his original hand the same number as he may wish to draw."

Such an invitation to invest further and try to improve one's hand echoes the "frontier spirit" often ascribed to those who were carrying the game westward. Rather than accept a poor hand as fate-determining, players could seek to improve their standing via the

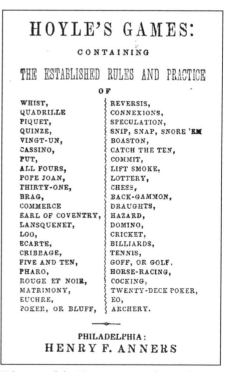

Title page of the 1845 American edition of Hoyle's Games (including references to "Poker, or Bluff" and "Twenty-Deck Poker")

discard and draw, thus demonstrating "that practical, inventive turn of mind, quick to find expedients" Frederick Jackson Turner later famously listed among the "traits of the frontier."[12]

The initial reference to draw poker in Bohn's book describes a betting round before the draw, though does not mention a second round afterwards. The first edition of the 1864 *American Hoyle* compiled by William Brisbane Dick (under the pseudonym "Trumps") similarly describes a betting round before the draw but not one after. However, follow-up editions include a longer section on "Draw Poker" that describes among its "laws" a second betting round post-draw. Other particulars also resemble the variation most latter day players would encounter when introduced to poker over the next century, often as "five-card draw."[13]

A lot of familiar terminology was already in place, though a few terms have now been rendered obsolete. The word "brag" is used as a synonym for betting and "age" refers to the player with the "eldest hand" sitting to the left of the dealer, who is charged with acting first before the draw (akin to today's "under the gun"). Hand rankings are gradually coming to resemble the modern-day chart, although a "straight, sequence, or rotation" is here ranked below "triplets"; later straights will be permanently placed higher than trips. (Hinting at their relatively new acceptance, a note cautions: "It should always be determined whether [straights] are to be admitted at the commencement of the game.") Meanwhile flushes ("five cards of all the same suit") are less equivocally included as part of the newly-accepted rankings.

The straight flush is also mentioned in the revised 1864 *American Hoyle* as a current topic of debate among the game's rule-makers. "It is strongly urged by some experts that the strongest hand at Draw Poker should be a *Straight Flush*," a footnote explains, "for the reason that it is more difficult to get than four of a kind, and removes from the game the objectionable feature of a known invincible hand."

Two other variations added as postscripts appear further designed to satisfy the desire to alter and change one's destiny. One, "Whiskey Poker," failed to capture much interest, despite being enthusiastically presented as "a neat variation of Draw Poker" and "a most amazing game." This version involved the dealing of an additional five-card hand with which players could swap their original cards. Players could also then exchange their cards with opponents' discards prior to the actual drawing round.

The other variation, however, did catch on: "Stud Poker."

Dick offers only one short paragraph of explanation of this game with a "not very euphonious name," almost reluctantly sharing how the five cards are dealt with the first face down followed by four face up. No explanation of betting is described, although the game soon adopted the procedure of including betting rounds after the first two cards are dealt (one down, one up), then after each of the next three to offer four chances to bet.

The spread of stud poker westward was also documented by the California legislature's decision in 1885 to amend a statute prohibiting gambling games to include faro, twenty-one, roulette, a card game called lansquenet, and "stud-horse poker." The proscription against stud remained on the books for a full century afterwards. Shedding the original "horse" designator that further connected poker with the frontier, five-card stud came to rival draw poker's popularity in certain areas of the country by the end of the 19th century. A seven-card variation of stud began to be played not long after the five-card game was introduced, although five-card stud remained the more popular format well into the 20th century. In seven-card stud, after anteing players are dealt three cards initially, two down and one up, followed by the first round of bets. The next three "streets" are dealt face up then a seventh card face down, with further betting after each making for five betting rounds total.

The additional betting rounds made seven-card stud much less suitable for the no-limit betting that characterized most games of five-card draw and five-card stud, and so often fixed limits were followed with "small" bets on the first two rounds and "big" bets (twice the small) on the final three. That last down card came to be called "the river" with "Down-the-River" sometimes used as an alternate name for the game. It is one of a few details that survived into the game's later evolution into Texas hold'em.

The draw and stud variations incorporated strategy components that had been lacking from original "Straight Poker," enabling players who understood odds and probabilities to use that knowledge to their advantage. Even so, despite devoting additional space to poker in the revised 1864 *American Hoyle*, Dick (or "Trumps") is less than enthusiastic about the game's rise. Elaborating on a brief note in the 1845 *Hoyle* saying poker "depends more on hazard than any other game played with cards," Dick insists that "Success in playing the game of Poker (or Bluff, as it is sometimes called) depends rather on luck and energy than skill. It is emphatically a game of chance, and there are easier ways of cheating, or playing with marked cards, than in any other game."

"Poker Literature is Assuming Formidable Proportions"

As poker and its new variants continued to spread so, too, did references to the game in print. In fact, it wasn't that long after poker earned notice in editions of *Hoyle's* that conversation about the game turned to address its sudden rise in prominence and popularity, with some observers even suggesting – either jokingly, with dismay, or in earnest – that poker be considered America's new "national game."

On May 4, 1872 in a syndicated column appearing in *The Atlanta Con-*

stitution, Washington, D.C. correspondent Tommy Hauck reports how gambling games like faro and roulette had fallen out of favor in the nation's capital, replaced instead by "short cards" or poker. With tongue somewhat in cheek, Hauck opines that "Draw poker is more of a national game at present than base ball, backgammon or President making."[14]

That possibility was considered once more in an unsigned article titled "The National Game" in the February 12, 1875 issue of *The New York Times*.[15] In this case, the author doesn't seem to find the development quite as amusing. "It has been claimed for base-ball that it is the national game," the article begins, acknowledging how the relatively new sport had captured America's imagination so thoroughly that attending a "match" had become a great way for "foreign visitors" to learn something pertinent about American culture. However, "if we are to judge anything from a new variety of literature that is spreading through the newspapers, we are forced to the conclusion that the national game is not base-ball, but poker." The writer takes solace in the fact that when it comes to poker "its diffusion is by no means national" but adds that we cannot "shut our eyes to the fact that poker literature is assuming formidable proportions." Supporting the assertion is a compilation of recent articles and books about poker. These include a reference to Bret Harte's short story "The Outcasts of Poker Flat," a review of Henry T. Winterblossom's just published *The Game of Draw-Poker, Mathematically Illustrated*, and a short discussion of Robert C. Schenck's short pamphlet *Draw. Rules for Playing Poker* that had been originally circulated privately in Britain in 1872 and had been reprinted by *The New York Tribune* the previous week.

Regarding the latter, the author alludes to the *Tribune*'s self-described motto when facetiously explaining how "One newspaper, which delights to call itself a 'great moral organ,' has published an elaborate treatise on the game, and daily uses the technical terms of poker to illustrate the manner in which political questions strike the Thoughtful Patriot." In other words, not only does poker's increasing popularity bother the writer, but the fact that the game's vocabulary has begun to appear in political discourse is even more distressing.

The reprinting of Schenck's rules in the *Tribune* inspired a letter that appeared on February 13, 1875 in which a reader from Arkansas wrongly challenges Schenck's order of hand rankings, citing incorrect probabilities to argue that three of kind (or "threes") should beat a straight (or "sequence"). The letter writer twice refers to "our great National game of draw-poker" while making his case. Given the urgency with which the Arkansan wishes to argue the rules, he seems to mean it.[16] In any event, such references help confirm poker's rapid spread during the middle decades of the 19th century, having already gone from requiring a footnote of explanation in the 1830s to becoming a contender for America's "national game" by the 1870s.

4

Poker on the Mississippi

The evening setting, the improbable showdown, the suspicions of cheating, the uncertain historical veracity, and, of course, the violence in Joe Cowell's report of the 1829 poker game aboard the *Helen M'Gregor* will all feature time and again in subsequent accounts of the newly popular "short card" game of poker.

So, too, will the setting aboard a steamboat, whether it be traveling up and down the Mississippi River from New Orleans to Minnesota and back, or along the numerous tributaries extending well into the northeast, or westward throughout the massive territory gained via the Louisiana Purchase in 1803. In fact, so many of the earliest accounts of poker take place in card parlors aboard these new "floating palaces," practically every later attempt to reconstruct a scene aboard such vessels in popular culture

Poker & Pop Culture

made sure to include a poker game. It was usually a crooked one involving marked cards, cold decks, hair triggers, ruthless card sharps and their hapless targets.

It follows that any survey of poker's history in America – in particular the many cultural representations of the game – must discuss how poker appeared in three frequently evoked contexts during the 19th century: steamboats, saloons, and the Civil War.

Relative Freedoms Out on the Water

Following some initial late 18th-century trials by others, engineer Robert Fulton helped realize the first successful steamboat run when his *Clermont* navigated its way through a two-day voyage on the Hudson River in 1807. A few years later Fulton and others designed the much larger *New Orleans* that managed a three-month trip from Pittsburgh all the way to New Orleans via the Ohio and Mississippi Rivers, landing in early 1812.

Though the original *New Orleans* sank within a couple of years, several large steamboats regularly traversed the Mississippi by the mid-1810s and more than 1,200 were in operation by the 1830s. Accidents were frequent, many causing fatalities. Boiler explosions destroyed more than 250 steamboats during the 1830s alone, including the *Helen M'Gregor* only a couple of months after Cowell's ride. Estimates of the number killed ranged from 30 to 60 of its 400-plus passengers. In 1865, nearly 1,200 people died aboard the *Sultana* in the worst recorded steamboat disaster.

Despite these accidents, steamboats proved a popular means of travel, greatly facilitating various types of commerce and enabling farmers to ship crops to markets far and wide in the still primarily agrarian society of the first half of the 1800s. Poker spread up and down the Mississippi from the gaming dens of New Orleans, which was one of several important ports. During the early days trips between Ohio and the Gulf Coast took more than three weeks and even though journey times quickly reduced thanks to advances in boat construction and navigation techniques, there remained plenty of leisure time during the trips for hundreds of passengers to indulge in various recreations, including gambling.

Also relevant to poker's progress on these vessels was the more general difficulty of regulating the steamboats' commerce, traffic, manufacture, and operation. Particularly before mid-century, the nascent federal government exerted only limited purview over the states, with the country's waterways even more difficult to manage. It wasn't until 1838 that the Interstate Steamboat Commerce Commission was established to regulate traffic. It took still longer for the federal government to pass the Steamboat Act of May 30, 1852, which enforced inspections and other measures in response to the many fatal accidents. At a time when various states were attempting to prohibit certain forms of gambling – inaugurating what would become an inconsistent, patchwork pattern of gambling legislation that has continued throughout America's history – oversight of "steamboat poker" fell primarily to those in command. As Herbert Asbury explains in his gambling history *Sucker's Progress*, "the Captain was the veritable autocrat" aboard the steamboats whose "will was the law of the boat."[1] That included allowing (and in some cases encouraging) gambling games such as faro, chuck-a-luck (a dice game), and various card games including euchre, vingt et un, seven-up (a.k.a. "old sledge"), whist, brag, and poker.

A number of players soon emerged who made their living exclusively via gambling on the steamboats. Asbury estimates that by the early 1830s, not even a couple of decades into the steamboats' history, "between 1,000 and 1,500 professional gamblers more or less regularly worked the steamboats between New Orleans and Louisville." He describes their presence as initially creating tension, but eventually evolving into a more routine state of affairs in which the sharps' being on board wasn't just tolerated but even desired. "The status of the river-going sharper had changed," Asbury writes, alluding to earlier incidents of gamblers being sent off the ships. In fact, by the time Cowell took his ride in 1829 the professional gambler "had become almost as much a member of a steamboat's personnel as the pilot, and many captains considered it bad luck to leave port without at least one gambler among the passengers."[2]

Robert K. DeArment lowers the estimate to "six to eight hundred professionals" making a living gambling aboard the steamers in his historical survey *Knights of the Green Cloth*. "The golden age of riverboat gambling lasted from about 1835 until the beginning of the Civil War," DeArment writes, and indeed the majority of stories about poker on the Mississippi take place during that period.[3] Supporting that observation is Sol Smith, the theater manager and humorist who in *Theatrical Management in the West and South for Thirty Years* (1868) tells of having first encountered "the interesting game of 'poker'" while traveling aboard the *New Orleans* in 1835. "Card-playing was a very common amusement then," writes Smith, who adds "it was not unusual to see half a dozen tables occupied at the same time in the gentlemen's cabin of a Mississippi boat" (111).[4]

Eugene Edwards reflects how before the railroads came to prominence (the first transcontinental line was completed in 1869) and the "gangs of professional gamblers" and "sharpers" began to work the trains in earnest, the poker action aboard the steamboats was nonstop. "It was nothing unusual for an open game to be run in the saloon all day and night from the time the boat left the wharf on the upper river until she landed at her destination," Edwards writes. "Private coteries were made up and played twenty-four hours at a stretch, the deck hands had their games at intervals and the pilot at the wheel took a hand when he was off duty," he continues. "In short, everybody played or looked on, ready to play at the first chance, if they had the money." It was "the paradise of the professional poker player," Edwards says.[5]

Mark Twain and "Them Fellers on the Boats"

Probably the most enduring tale of poker on the Mississippi comes via one of the 19th century's greatest storytellers, the American humorist Mark Twain.

Born Samuel Langhorne Clemens in Missouri in 1835, Twain's family moved to Hannibal along the Mississippi River when he was a child. As a teenager, Twain began writing for the Hannibal newspaper run by his brother. Eventually he moved to New York and spent a few years in the north working as a printer, then made his way back to Missouri as a young man to work as a steamboat pilot. The Civil War intervened, halting traffic on the Mississippi and curtailing Twain's burgeoning career. Six months after the South's surrender, Twain's initial literary success, the short story "The Celebrated Jumping Frog of Calaveras County," was published in late 1865, and a few years later his travel narrative *The Innocents Abroad* (1869) became his first bestseller. From there Twain embarked on an illustrious literary career, producing numerous landmarks of American fiction, among them the great novels *The Adventures of Tom Sawyer* (1876) and *Adventures of Huckleberry Finn* (1884).

Twain chronicled steamboat culture extensively in many of his writings. In fact, Twain's adopted pen name memorialized his time on the steamboats, referring to a leadsman's call of "mark twain" signaling that the lead line indicated waters were at least two fathoms (12 feet) deep and safe for passage. Twain also played and observed others playing poker during his travels.

Twain shared his tongue-in-cheek observation that "there are few things that are so unpardonably neglected in our country as poker" during a speech at the Fifth Avenue Theatre in New York in 1877 prior to the curtain lifting on the comedy *Ah Sin, The Heathen Chinee*, a collaboration between Twain and Bret Harte. Previewing the play, Twain jokes how a poker scene had been included "for the instruction of the young."[6] Like everything else in the prologue, Twain is being sarcastic. He well knew poker was hardly being neglected. He also knew that when it came to America's youth, many didn't need to be introduced to the idea of gambling on cards. In his 1870 short story "Science vs. Luck" a group of young Kentucky boys playing "old sledge" or "seven-up" (the same trick-taking game the Duke and the Dauphin play in *Huckleberry Finn*) are charged with gambling, but a clever lawyer manages to establish the game on which they were betting was *not* a game of chance. The proof comes from a match between men believing in the "science" of the game and a group of clergymen who think the game is all luck. The "science" players win handily, proving the game's skill component.

Comments about poker appear occasionally in Twain's fiction. In *The Gilded Age* (1873), the main characters take a brief trip via steamer from Alton, Illinois to St. Louis when one notices a Congressman taking part in a "five cent ante" poker game in the ship's saloon. "I shouldn't think a representative in Congress would play poker any way in a public steamboat," he says. "Nonsense," replies his traveling companion. "You've got to pass the time."[7] Later on in Twain's dark satire *A Connecticut Yankee in King Arthur's Court* (1889), he employs a poker analogy when his 19th-century time-traveler Hank Morgan tricks hundreds of sixth-century knights into believing he has enough ammunition to kill them all. "It was a 'bluff' you know," Morgan explains. "At such a time it is a sound judgment to put on a bold face and play your hand for a hundred times what it worth; forty-nine times out of fifty nobody dares to 'call,' and you rake in the chips."[8] Unfortunately for Morgan, the knights do call his bluff and rush him. But they lose their nerve after he kills several more and, not knowing his ammunition is limited, they give in to the "magical" Yankee.

As far as Twain's own abilities were concerned, his comments suggest he was a skilled though circumspect poker player. During the mid-1860s he contributed articles under various names to the San Francisco weekly *The Golden Era*, and in one series from 1865 (written under a false name) he humorously described himself being put on trial for fraud (for writing under a false name). In the piece Twain has his colleague Charles Webb, a.k.a. "C. H. W. Inigo," testify to his "good character" claiming "he can play draw poker equal to any man. Consider myself some at draw poker, but he can discount me every time. He won those sleeve buttons that he has on from me at draw poker."[9] That said, Twain apparently made it a rule to avoid mixing it up with the card sharps populating those Mississippi riverboats he helped guide. An item in the September 9, 1912 issue of *The New York Times*, a couple of years after the author's death, quotes William H. Davis, a fellow pilot who worked with Twain. "Mark wouldn't gamble with them fellers on the boats," Davis insisted. "They were full of gamblers in those days. Mark liked a little game of poker as well as the rest of us, but he was mighty particular who he played with."[10]

The threat posed by those steamboat sharps is described most memorably in the poker story "The Professor's Yarn" included in *Life on the Mississippi* (1883), a memoir chronicling Twain's experiences as a pilot. Twain inserts the story as it was told to him by a fellow traveler aboard the *Gold Dust* in 1882, a tale the unnamed Professor dates from the "early days" of steamboat travel. After accepting a job in California, the Professor embarks on a several-week journey that includes a trip by sea up the continent's west coast. He describes the other passengers generally, then focuses on the "three professional gamblers on board – rough, repulsive fellows." He tries to avoid the trio, but "could not help seeing them with some frequency, for they gambled in an upper-deck stateroom every day and night," and during evening walks he often "had glimpses of them through their door, which stood a little ajar to let out the surplus tobacco smoke and profanity." "They were an evil and hateful presence," says the Professor, espousing a not uncommon view of the era. "But I had to put up with it, of course."[11]

The trip becomes more pleasant once the Professor befriends a young cattleman named John Backus. At one point Backus suggests a proposal whereby the Professor, in his capacity as a surveyor, might allot him some free land in exchange for payment, with Backus showing the Professor his stash of a thousand dollars' worth of gold as he does. The Professor declines the invitation, then is later dismayed when he finds Backus having been recruited by the gamblers to play in their poker game. From all appearances, the gamblers are taking advantage of the naïve country boy, plying him with drink as they soberly work to extricate as much money from him as they can. "It was the painfulest night I ever spent," the Professor laments.[12]

The tale's climax is a big hand of five-card draw involving Backus and one of the gamblers named Hank Wiley. After Wiley draws one card and the other players take three each, a series of bets leave only Wiley and Backus in the hand and an enormous "yellow pyramid" of coins in the middle, with one last raise and call bringing the pot to $20,000. "What have you got?" asks Backus, and his opponent confidently reveals his hand. "Four kings, you d––d fool!" he says. Backus then tables his cards. "Four *aces,* you ass!" he bellows. Backus knows, however, the declaration of his hand may not be enough to ensure his collection of the winnings. While "covering his man with a cocked revolver," he delivers an additional statement: *"I'm a professional gambler myself, and I've been laying for you duffers all this voyage!"*[13]

As it turns out, one of the other three gamblers had joined forces with Backus, thereby ensuring the four-kings-versus-four-aces scenario in the latter's favor. The accomplice acted as a double-agent of sorts, having previously misled Wiley to believe he would deal Backus four *queens* which would make Wiley's quad kings best. It's a "stocked" deck hand directly recalling the one Joe Cowell observed aboard the *Helen M'Gregor.* In fact, as the Professor later finds out, Backus had been putting *him* on as well by posing as a cattleman, establishing a persona that would help him fool the gamblers into thinking he was more rube than rogue.

The resolution echoes "The Celebrated Jumping Frog of Calaveras County" in which an apparent hustler himself gets hustled by a stranger in a bet over a frog-jumping contest. The story well presents the danger and unpredictability the gamblers introduced into the world of the steamboat. It also neatly presents the figure of the "professional gambler" as Backus very deliberately calls himself. It's an emphatic line, suggesting not only that Backus believes himself worthy of the respect due to someone in his "profession," but also that being able to cheat successfully is in fact one of the requisite tricks of his trade. So, too, is the ability to defend oneself as Backus does by holding aloft his cocked revolver.

George Devol, Gambling Superhero

The rules of civilized society often didn't apply when it came to steamboat poker. Or, rather, there were other, different rules, often changing and arbitrary, adding considerable unsteadiness to the boats' passage.

If you were to cheat in a regular saloon poker game, your tenure there would only last as long as you were able to avoid being discovered by the regulars. Then the guns could well come out and you'd likely never return – assuming you made it to the exit the first time. Getting caught cheating on a steamboat, however, merely meant a quick hunt for another of the hundreds of floating card games on offer. Wait long enough and you could even return to the very same vessel from which you were ejected, given the constant turnover of passengers.

Such realities were well understood by George Devol, who became one of the steamboats' most infamous sharpers. Born in 1829 in Ohio, Devol spent nearly his entire life in transit, mostly on steamboats, then later on trains on the country's growing railroad lines. His 1887 memoir *Forty Years a Gambler on the Mississippi* presents Devol's story, arranged in roughly chronological fashion via 177 short chapters, each presenting a brief anecdote from his colorful life.

A runaway at age 10, Devol finds work as a cabin boy on various steamboats, immediately learning a number of card games and how to cheat at them. "I learned to play 'seven-up' and to 'steal card' so that I could cheat the boys," he explains in an early chapter. "I felt as if I was fixed for life." He eventually learns other card-based gambling games like "red and black" and three-card monte while working on the steamboats for the next seven years. During that time he also discovers other means of cheating including how to "stock a deck."[14] He derives additional income running games of faro, keno, and roulette.

A short stint back home helping his brother caulk steamboats did little to convince Devol to give up the gambling life. After dramatically dumping his caulking tools in the river, Devol declares his life plan to his brother.

legendary steamboat gambler George Devol

"I told him I intended to live off fools and suckers," he writes. "I also said, 'I will make money rain;' and I did come near doing as I said."[15] Poker soon emerges as the game Devol finds most lucrative, whether playing "on the square" or, more often than not, with some ill-gotten edge. With barkeeps and deck hands working as accomplices on seemingly every boat, in addition to the more steady partners with whom Devol worked over the years, the stream of cash flowing into Devol's pockets is as reliable as the Mississippi itself.

Many of Devol's stories follow familiar plot-lines. Several feature the "narrow escape" in which our hero has to jump off moving boats and swim ashore or sneak out amid crowds to avoid being caught and punished by those he's swindled. Others show "the fighting gambler" able to win physical battles following gambling victories, usually landing solid blows after his attackers swing and miss. Often the "soft-hearted hero" returns winnings to "suckers" on whom he takes pity, including several churchmen. In "Lost His Wife's Diamonds," for example, Devol wins a few hundred from a gentleman who leaves and returns with a velvet box full of jewelry. Devol gives him $1,500 for it, then proceeds to win that off of him as well. The next day Devol spots the man with his wife and child, and notices "the lady's eyes were red, as if she had been crying."[16] He has the box full of diamonds delivered to the family's room, benevolently refusing to give the man his address to allow him the chance to pay him back.

However, the most frequently evoked story type in Devol's book is the "outcheating the cheaters" tale, resembling Twain's yarn of the bogus cattleman. In "He Knew My Hand," a poor gentleman approaches Devol for a ten-cent ante game of poker. "We played along, and I was amused to see him stocking the cards (or at least trying to do so)," Devol observes, allowing the fellow to cheat him out of a few small pots. The stakes go up, and eventually Devol is dealt three jacks. By then, however, he's already held out four fives from the deck, and after a series of raises shows his quads at showdown. "'That is not the hand you had,'" his opponent objects, giving away that he'd cheated. "How the d––l do you know what I had?" Devol responds. "You are a gambler," says the man accusingly as he pulls a knife, the word "gambler" clearly being used as a synonym for "cheater." But Devol raises him, weapon-wise, by drawing "Betsy Jane," which is "one of the best tarantula pistols in the Southern country."[17]

Cheating other cheaters satisfies an inner sense of justice for Devol. "When a sucker sees a corner turned up, or a little spot on a card in three-card monte, he does not know that it was done for the purpose of making him think he has the advantage," Devol explains. "It is a good lesson for a dishonest man to be caught by some trick, and I always did like to teach it."[18]

That Devol himself was a dishonest man doesn't seem to suggest any self-contradiction. He is content with himself from a moral standpoint and makes early reference to a familiar code of honor. "A gambler's word is as good as his bond," he says, "and that's more than I can say of many business men who stand very high in a community."[19] It's a fine sentiment, although it reads much differently when you remember the designation "gambler" *also* indicates a willingness to cheat.

The Honorable Gambler, Canada Bill

William "Canada" Bill Jones was another larger-than-life figure from the 19th-century steamers, a contemporary of Devol's who along with a couple of others occasionally teamed up with the *Forty Years* author to perpetrate hustles up and down the nation's waterways.

Originally from northern England, Jones emigrated to Canada as a young adult, then eventually found a home on the Mississippi where he pursued a lucrative career fleecing all comers until his death, at 40, around 1880.

"Canada" Bill Jones

Much of what is known about Canada Bill comes from Devol who introduces him as "a character one might travel the length and breadth of the land and never find his match." Hardly an imposing figure, Devol describes Jones as "a medium-sized, chicken-headed, tow-haired sort of a man" who dressed poorly and never weighed more than 130 pounds. He also looks slow-witted – he "resembled an idiot" – but that was all an act, a put-on that *he* was the sucker when in actuality it was whomever he could fool into making that mistake about him.[20]

Jones often gets credited with several famous poker quotes, including the line "it's immoral to let a sucker keep his money" that Matt Damon's Mike McDermott attributes to Jones in *Rounders*. (It's a line that likely also indirectly inspired the title of the 1941 W.C. Fields comedy *Never Give a Sucker an Even Break*.) Devol confirms that Jones "often said suckers had no business with money," a sentiment that might be said to form part of Canada Bill's personal ethical code.[21] The other part was his overwhelming generosity, shown by a tendency to give away money to the needy nearly as fast as he took it away from those reckless enough to lose it. "There never lived a better hearted man," Devol writes. "He was liberal to a fault. I have known him to turn back when we were on the street and give to some poor object we had passed." One time, says Devol, he saw Jones "win $200 from a man, and shortly after his little boy came running down the cabin, Bill called the boy up and handed him the $200 and told him to give it to his mother."[22]

Devol outlived Canada Bill and includes an epitaph to his former partner lamenting how he died penniless in Pennsylvania, with friends having to raise funds to pay for a funeral. Indeed, Canada Bill's charity seems partly to blame for his end-of-life destitution, although as Devol explains it, there was one other likely cause for the loss of his riches. "While he was a great man at monte, he was a fool at short cards" or poker. "I have known men who knew this to travel all over the country after Bill, trying to induce him to play cards with them. He would do it, and that is what kept him poor."[23]

Devol goes on to defend Canada Bill against an unflattering portrait of him by Mason Long in his moralistic 1878 memoir *The Life of Mason Long: The Converted Gambler*. After presenting Jones as "the most notorious and successful thief who ever operated in this country," Long suggests Jones "squandered his money very lavishly and drank himself to death." Devol vehemently rejects both charges, though he has a good idea why Long and others are so ready to condemn card players: "The public put all sporting men into one class, called gamblers; likewise they put all church members into classes and call them Christians, etc. There is as wide a difference between a true gambler and one who styles himself a sport, as there is between a true Christian and one who puts on the cloak of Christianity to serve the devil in."[24]

It's a difficult defense to make given the complicated morality espoused by Devol, Jones, and other sharps – that is, one that endorses cheating under certain terms and against certain targets but not others. Indeed, given the frequency of cheating and violence in stories of steamboat poker, it's easy to see how finer distinctions regarding the "true gambler" get washed away in all of these stories' wake.

Jim Bowie, Knight-Errant of the Steamboats

Another larger-than-life figure who stars frequently in steamboat poker stories is James "Jim" Bowie, the pioneer perhaps best known for once having literally brought a knife to a gunfight.

After attending a duel between other acquaintances, Bowie found himself in a deadly fight in which he stabbed to death a longtime rival with a large hunting knife. The story of the "Sandbar Fight" became so well known that the association between Bowie and his weapon of choice came to be reflected in the branding of the Bowie knife. Bowie was also known for fighting in the Texas Revolution, losing his life while defending the Alamo with Davy Crockett in 1836.

Bowie's heroism is also part of poker's history largely because of an incident during a trip he took a few years earlier aboard a rebuilt *New Orleans*. Asbury summarizes various accounts of the incident, said to have taken place in the fall of 1832. The story begins with a poker game involving three colluding card sharps (posing as two planters and a merchant) and an unsuspecting dupe from Natchez.[25] With Bowie watching and recognizing the game of twenty-card poker to be crooked, the gamblers eventually take $50,000 off their mark – every dollar he had – and the man becomes so distraught he nearly throws himself overboard. But Bowie and his wife prevents him. Soon afterwards Bowie finds the sharps, and after using a "bulging wallet" as enticement, he accepts their invitation to play with them. Eventually a hand arises in which Bowie is dealt four kings and a ten, his hand strength signaling to Bowie they had reached the hand "intended for the big cleanup."

A huge pot develops between Bowie and one of the "planters," with $70,000 on the table by the time betting finished. Suddenly Bowie rises from his chair, grabbing his opponent's wrist with one hand and pulling out his knife with the other. "Show your hand," Bowie declares. "If it contains more than five cards I shall kill you!" The sharp hesitates nervously, and Bowie twists his hand to cause his cards to fall – four aces, a queen, *and* a jack.

According to Asbury there are two versions of what happens next, with Bowie letting the sharp off with a warning in one and killing him in a duel in the other. The latter version sounds as though it might conflate the *New Orleans* story with another later one involving Bowie playing poker aboard the *Rob Roy* in 1835, a game that also ended with Bowie killing an opponent in a post-game duel. Both have Bowie giving the young man two-thirds of his winnings while making him swear "never to touch another card."[26]

The story fits with other anecdotes of Bowie acting as one of a few "knights-errant of the steamboats" (as Asbury calls him) looking out for the welfare of those unable to help themselves against the many card cheats on board. This figure was heralded not long after Bowie's death as "the friend of the feeble, the protector of the oppressed, and the sworn enemy of tyrants."[27]

Rules Out on the River

Stories of poker games on the nation's waterways and the colorful characters who played in them continued to be told well after the popularity of steamboat travel had waned.

In multiple books New York-based journalist David A. Curtis helped chronicle poker as it was played aboard steamboats and elsewhere. His 1899 collection *Queer Luck* is set in a New York underground club where a "gray-haired young-looking man" is telling the stories. Not old enough to have traveled aboard the steamers prior to the Civil War, the tale-teller nonetheless saw enough during the 1860s and 1870s to convince him that tales told of characters like Devol, Jones, and Bowie were well within the realm of the credible.

"There were a good many stories told about the old-time Mississippi boats that I am fully prepared to believe," the gray-haired man reflects. "That the game of poker flourished on the river as it never has elsewhere, before or since, seems entirely probable. I have seen games that made me hold my breath because of the size of the stakes, and because of the fact that I knew the players were all armed, and a shot or stab was certain to follow a hasty word or suspicious act."[28]

To prove the point, he shares an account of a game he did witness while traveling from Memphis to Natchez. Over the course of two nights he watches two seasoned "professionals" apply their trade, with the unusual participation of a woman known as "Flash Kate" making the episode even more memorable. His tale ends with a twist, a huge hand in which a cattle-dealer whom the sharps were targeting manages to pull off his own remarkable trick. While cutting the cards for one of the sharps, the cattle-dealer somehow substitutes a fresh "cold" deck right under their noses, which "sounds like an impossibility, but wonderful things are possible to a sleight-of-hand performer."[29] The subsequent hand is a howler – the cattle-dealer's four aces beats four kings, four queens, and four jacks – and even though everyone knows the deal was crooked, the cattle-dealer's drawn revolver ensures he collects the pot.

Curtis added further to the legacy of post-Civil War steamboat poker with his 1906 collection *Stand Pat, Or Poker Stories from the Mississippi*. This time he concentrates on a group of card-playing characters inhabiting a Mississippi River town in Arkansas he had visited a few decades before. The book reminds us that while poker was constantly being played on the steamboats themselves, the many ports at which the boats stopped tended to become poker hot spots as well. Over the course of 20 stories Curtis describes the card-related adventures of Long Mike, Stumpy, Gallagher, the one-eyed man, and a varied supporting cast as they match wits with each other and a series of opponents either fresh off steamboats or waiting to depart.

Some of the stories in *Stand Pat* are light-hearted, such as an early one in which players end a hand showing five aces, a full house (kings full of aces), and four red jacks, then realize they were playing with two pinochle decks. Others are less full of mirth, including one in which a visitor shoots the one-eyed man dead following the discovery of marked cards. Long Mike is nearly drowned in the nearby river during another fight, and Gallagher survives getting shot in the head in another. Visitors stopping by having come off the *Rosa Lee,* the *Creole Belle,* the *Natchez,* and other steamboats additionally accrue numerous injuries at the tables. The source of intrigue – and conflict – in most of the tales is the gradual discovery of cheating, initially only suspected, then finally proven with varying degrees of violence. Decks are stacked, cards dealt from the bottom, hidden cards accessed surreptitiously from pockets, partners look over shoulders and transmit signals, and six-card hands are dealt, among other transgressions.

"I don't know what the reason is, but poker don't 'pear to be respected now, like it used to be," observes one of Curtis' storytellers, an Arkansas City saloon owner and veteran of steamboat poker referred to as "old man Greenhut." "Call poker immoral, I've heard tell," he complains, incredulous that anyone would object to the game he regards as "the greatest educator an' highest moral training known to civilization." He makes the statement without irony, just before relating the story of a game played aboard the *River Belle* in 1876 involving colluding players, expert card "manipulators," and yet another eyebrow-raising quads-over-quads climax.[30]

While ostensibly defending the game, old man Greenhut also reveals why poker became less respected during the "golden age of riverboat gambling." On the one hand, Greenhut insists "the game of draw-poker is about as nigh perfect as anything that was ever devised by the mind o' man," but he acknowledges "there is times when even the best players is obliged to rely on outside influences to help 'em out o' some great emergency o' the game." By "outside influences" he refers both to the need to cheat when the cards aren't cooperating *and* to defend oneself (including physically) against the occasional "unscrupulous stranger." According to Greenhut's way of thinking, methods such as marking cards or bottom dealing are "all part o' draw-poker, same as it's a part o' the game not to be found out when you're obliged to change the natural order o' the cards."

"I maintain so long as they're done slick enough to not be seen, they are as legitimate as anything else in draw-poker," he says.[31]

Rolling Forward From Steamboat Poker

Connections between poker and 19th-century steamboats don't end there. The "river" itself even becomes part of the vocabulary of the game as a reference to the final card dealt in seven-card stud and (much later) the last community card in Texas hold'em.[32]

In a way, the steamboats presented a kind of paradox floating through 19th-century America. On the one hand, they were a marvel of human ingenuity, an emblem of industrial advancement that enabled civilization to grow and prosper as never before. But once they left their ports and moved out onto those rolling waters, they also became detached from the societies they were helping to advance, transforming into discrete worlds not necessarily bound by the rules observed on land.

The boats were also a lot like poker tables, self-enclosed spaces populated by individuals drawing their own particular distinctions regarding what would be allowed and what would not. Viewed from without, the ethics governing the action could often appear ambiguous or even self-contradictory, and different enough from life away from the boats or the tables to make it seem especially hazardous to the uninitiated. That's just one reason why most later cultural attempts to reproduce those scenes along the Mississippi and other rivers – be they silly or serious – tended to emphasize the potential dangers they contained.

It's no surprise, then, when Bugs Bunny finds himself accidentally aboard a steamboat in the 1949 short *Mississippi Hare*, he instantly encounters a card sharp firing his weapons and shouting out challenges. "I'm the rip-roaringest, gol-dingenest, sharp-shootinest, poker-playingest riverboat gambler on the Mississippi," cries the shooter. "Yahooo!!!! Be thar anyone man enough to sit in a poker game with Colonel Shuffle?" "Thar be," answers Bugs, who plays out the farce by cleaning out Shuffle, in the last hand topping his opponent's five aces with six aces of his own.

It is similarly unremarkable to find poker frequently played aboard the steamboats on television westerns like *Maverick* (1957-62) (see Chapter 20), *Yancy Derringer* (1958-59), and *Riverboat* (1959-61) where the games help create conflicts that animate plots such as when players are robbed or cheating occurs. In *Yancy Derringer* the title character owns a steamboat (named after the ill-fated *Sultana*), and in the first scene of the first episode he ends a high-stakes hand by showing four aces and drawing a weapon. Meanwhile *Riverboat* also begins with cheating at cards and violence aboard the titular vessel (won by the captain in a poker game), including a murder avenged by the killer being thrown into a paddlewheel.

It is also believable that when Earl Scruggs and Lester Flatt sing Tom T. Hall's ballad "I'm Gonna Ride That Steamboat" for their 1967 album *Hear the Whistle Blow* the tale of a young man from Natchez, Mississippi concerns a son's desire to avenge the death of his father killed in a poker game by a cajun gambler aboard the *Delta Queen*. The song doesn't spell out exactly how the father met his end, though it's clear he lost his money before losing his life, having learned it's impossible to win versus a stacked deck.

Such was the enduring image of 19th-century steamboats, long after people stopped riding them. They were at the very least unsafe and at worst potentially deadly. That's also how many thought of poker.

5 Poker in the Old West

As we step off of 19th-century steamboats we step back onto land to visit games happening at poker tables elsewhere in America – and again find ourselves amid scenes of colorful, larger-than-life characters and too-good-to-be-true tales. As with stories of poker on the Mississippi, stories of poker in the Old West importantly shaped the game's legacy, in particular encouraging a romanticized view of poker as primarily played by rough-hewn cowboys in darkened saloon corners, the seats around the tables often occupied by outlaws of various stripes, most armed and ready to draw their guns along with the cards. Such stories also supplement later generations' understanding of America's early history, fitting well amid periods marked by conflict, internal division, and the ongoing struggle to contain lawlessness along the westward-moving frontier.

Cowboys and Cards

The "Old West" era dates back well before the earliest references to poker in print. The United States' acquisition of the massive Louisiana Territory from France in 1803 often serves as an inaugurating event and the admission of New Mexico and Arizona to statehood in 1912 (the last of the 48 contiguous states) provides a kind of culmination. Benefiting from Napoleon Bonaparte's need to fund his military, the U.S. under President Thomas Jefferson began the century having suddenly acquired more than 820,000 square miles of land extending from the west bank of the Mississippi all the way to the Rocky Mountains. The area included all or part of 15 present-day states and more than doubled the new nation's size. A year later the Corps of Discovery Expedition began, with Captain Meriwether Lewis and Second Lieutenant William Clark leading a group of Army volunteers from Wood River, Illinois to the Pacific Ocean and back to St. Louis. Millions of settlers and their descendants followed the explorers' path westward, drawn to the land and its many resources, including mines rich with gold and silver. Collectively they helped contribute to what journalist John L. Sullivan described in 1845 as "our manifest destiny to overspread and to possess the whole of our continent which Providence has given us for the development of the great experiment of liberty."[1]

Further expansion by the U.S. also supported such a vision, highlighted by the Texas Annexation (1845); the Oregon Treaty (1846) that included present-day Oregon, Washington, Idaho, and parts of Montana and Wyoming; the Mexican Cession following the Mexican-American War (1848) that included present-day California, Nevada, and Utah; and the Gadsden Purchase (1853) that included present-day New Mexico and Arizona. Meanwhile, despite the original diplomatic intentions of Jefferson and the explorers, many of the dozens of Native American tribes encountered by Lewis and Clark were later either displaced or in some cases violently eliminated. (Belatedly this led by way of reparations to the significant involvement of the tribes' descendents in the history of gambling in the U.S.)

Conflicting views regarding slavery were also carried throughout the expanding nation. The Missouri Compromise of 1820 allowed for the admission to statehood of one slaveholding state (Missouri) along with one free state (Maine), additionally formalizing a division of the nation along the 36°30' parallel that disallowed slavery north of the line among lands obtained via the Louisiana Purchase. With the addition of new territories the issue continued to fester, and following the Mexican-American War another legal maneuver, the Compromise of 1850, admitted California as a free state while leaving other territories to decide via "popular sovereignty" whether or not to permit slavery. Challenges to the earlier Missouri Compromise followed, with the Kansas-Nebraska Act (1854) essentially repealing it and leading to the "Bloody Kansas" battles between those for and against slavery. The subsequent *Dred Scott vs. Sandford* decision by the U.S. Supreme Court in 1857 then found the earlier law unconstitutional, stripping the federal government's power to regulate slavery in newly acquired territories while also denying citizenship to African Americans (whether free or enslaved). Proponents of slavery found vindication in the ruling, abolitionists loudly dissented, and the stakes rapidly raised thereafter, ultimately precipitating the South's secession and the Civil War.

Meanwhile throughout the century these new settlements became settings in which gambling could thrive, with the rapid, uneven accumulation of wealth providing further fuel to the games. While the majority of stories of steamboat poker date from the 1820s through the 1870s, starting to fade after completion of the transatlantic railroad in 1869, most stories of poker in the Old West come after the Civil War (also true of western films and television shows in general).

While many of the earliest poker stories emanate from either the steamboats or important port cities along the Mississippi such as New Orleans, Natchez, Vicksburg, and St. Louis, a host of other locations throughout the central and western regions emerged as sites of later tales, among them Dodge City and Abeline (Kansas), Deadwood (South Dakota), Tombstone (Arizona), Denver (Colorado), San Francisco (California), Ingalls (Oklahoma), Kansas City (Missouri), and El Paso (Texas). Practically every city or town of significant size west of the Mississippi contained saloons and/or gambling houses, usually several of them. For (an extreme) example, the gold rush of the late 1840s that heralded a wave of migration into northern California gave rise to a remarkable number of gambling establishments to attract the American argonaut, by some estimates as many as a thousand of them.[2] Wherever there were sufficient resources to attract migrating settlers, income derived from those resources was put at risk in games of faro, roulette, three-card monte, chuck-a-luck, hazard (or craps), vingt et un (or blackjack), brag, and poker.

As with the image of the steamboat sharp, the common portrayal of the card-playing cowboy was based in historical reality but has been greatly informed by subsequent attempts to reimagine it in popular culture. There the two figures stand in stark contrast. The 19th-century gamblers riding the nation's waterways are often depicted dressed to the nines in black suits, decorated vests with gold or pearl buttons, and fine white dress shirts, with other conspicuous accoutrements like rings and gold pocket watches signaling their status as "professionals." By contrast, those drawing and dealing around tables in Old West saloons are usually portrayed as rugged, athletic, less refined figures, their colored long-sleeved shirts, woolen trousers and then later denim jeans (more often brown than blue), neckerchiefs, bolo ties, and boots covered with dust from ranch work or driving cattle over open ranges. They are all topped by the ever-present hats with wide brims and tall crowns such as were first manufactured by John B. Stetson in 1865.

Common to these two figures, of course, are the ubiquitous firearms, weapons that often became crucial elements in the poker tales in which they feature. In fact, to employ an idiom of the era, when it comes to stories and images of Old West poker, the transition from game-play to gunplay was often swift as thought.

Frederic Remington
Among the early shapers of Old West mythology was the artist Frederic Remington whose paintings, illustrations, and sculptures exerted direct influence not only on how the era looked to his own and future generations, but also what it meant. Among Remington's works were a couple of especially popular paintings depicting card playing in the Old West context. They came to have enormous influence over poker's later reputation and place in the culture.

Remington was born in New York in 1861 at the start of the Civil War. His father was a Union colonel, and young Remington was similarly nurtured early on for a military career. However a talent for drawing carried him down a different path that included a short stint at art school at Yale University during the late 1870s. As a young adult Remington was able to travel west and see many of the landscapes and scenes he'd spend his later life reproducing, getting involved early on with the popular *Harper's Weekly* where his first drawings were published. More schooling back in New York followed, and by the age of 25 he'd scored his first *Harper's Weekly* cover, a sketch of a scout tracking Geronimo amid the decades-long Apache Wars. Remington's burgeoning reputation also earned him the chance to illustrate future president Theodore Roosevelt's 1887 book *Ranch Life and the Hunting Trail*.

During further travels out west, Remington witnessed first-hand the aftermath of the 1890 massacre at Wounded Knee from which he produced numerous paintings and illustrations. A one-man exhibition at the American Art Galleries in New York then furthered his fame, and by the end of the century Remington was one of the country's best known artists, even having a couple of his paintings appear on postage stamps. He later reunited with Roosevelt while serving as a war correspondent and illustrator for the *New York Journal* during the Spanish-American War. He died at 48 in 1909 after complications with appendicitis, but by that point had also written novels, sculpted, and continued to paint and sketch, even if the popularity of his naturalistic style started to wane as tastes moved toward impressionistic art.

Remington's series titled *The Evolution of the Cowpuncher* (1893) – a collaboration with the fiction writer Owen Wister best known for his 1902 book *The Virginian* (see Chapter 17) – was especially influential. From these images and stories steps the mythic cowboy: manly, tough, athletic, and possessed with an understanding of the importance of work and how to survive. Such self-sufficiency mirrors the fiercely independent spirit of the nation itself, for which in many of these stories he's made to stand as an emblem. He also has a sense of justice, can be hospitable and/or serving of the cause of justice, is full of *gravitas* and takes a no-nonsense approach to most issues, capable of violence when needed. Meanwhile Indians are made to serve as the "other," with additional ideas, including the relative status of men and women and "gender roles," firmly established and re-inforced. Poker playing becomes part of the mythic cowboy's character, adding an element of intelligence and acumen to the portrait.

Remington's two most famous illustrations of Old West poker games reinforce connections between violence and poker, depicting the "before" and "after" of card-playing conflicts. The first is a woodblock print titled *A Quarrel Over Cards – A Sketch from a New Mexican Ranch* that first appeared in an 1887 issue of *Harper's Weekly*. Though darkly-lit, the scene

Frederic Remington's A Quarrel Over Cards -- A Sketch from a New Mexican Ranch (1887)

Poker & Pop Culture

is vivid, showing seven men gathered around a crowded table covered by chips and cards. One man stands, pointing aggressively at a seated opponent who is holding a deck of cards. The suggestion is clear: the accuser has detected a problem with the dealing, while the accused responds defensively, his open palm conveying innocence. Others look on with concern, while a servant at the stove holds a hand upwards as if in anticipation of the argument taking a more threatening turn. Meanwhile a player in the foreground is studying the scene carefully, one hand rubbing his cheek and the other firmly grasping the pistol in his holster. The standing man has a hand on his gun as well.

The accompanying text in *Harper's* explains how the man on the dealer's right is his confederate. "It was his deal before, and then the trick was done," that is, the stacking of the deck. We're also directed to notice the player on the dealer's left hastily covering his chips, having "a shrewd suspicion that in the 'muss' the table might be overturned." The description insists the scene is typical, and characterizes all poker games of the day as both crooked and prone to violence. A game of "draw-poker," we're told, is rife with cheating, either by a dealer acting in concert with another player or cards being saved from the deck and produced thereafter. The explanation continues: "A hidden card produced at the exact nick of time, makes 'four of a kind,' and the pot is raked in."

Occasionally players are wise to such deceit. "Sometimes," we're told, "there comes a player who... knows all the ways which are crooked. It even adds to his zest to play not only against the luck of the cards, but the talents of the gamblers." Gunplay is therefore to be expected, as "there would be little excitement about the game without drawing of cards and revolvers." In other words, the writer concludes, "Mr. *F. Remington* has made a typical gambling scene." Readers who have never seen such a game are assured the picture "is something that happens somewhere or other every day in the Territories."[3]

A decade later Remington produced a painting titled *A Misdeal*, capturing in oil on canvas what could be read as a kind of sequel to the earlier work. In this instance, however, the phrase "four of a kind" could be used to refer to the dead or wounded: there are three on the floor, one at his seat. As the bartender and those outside the saloon cower, the aggrieved party appears in the process of collecting the session's final pot. Though perhaps again meant to present a typical gambling scene, the painting wasn't that typical for Remington who more often focused on outdoor settings and didn't necessarily highlight frontier violence, even when illustrating some of the battles he'd witnessed. It also wasn't necessarily typical of every saloon poker game, although the painting helped establish the impression of poker being dangerous, furthering the association of such carnage with card playing.

Wyatt Earp and Doc Holliday, a Premium Pair

Our survey of Old West poker heroes, and how they have been represented in popular culture, starts with two of the most famous: Wyatt Earp and John "Doc" Holliday.

Earp was born in Illinois in 1848 and lived in several locations in the West with his family during his youth, including time in California during the Civil War. He continued moving around throughout adulthood, marrying multiple times while mining for gold and silver, hunting buffalo, owning saloons, and even running a brothel. Earp was in and out of legal trouble before ultimately serving in various capacities as a lawman, including as a U.S. Marshal, all the while enlarging his fame as a gambler and gunfighter.

Holliday was born in Georgia in 1851, the son of a Confederate soldier. At 19 he traveled to Philadelphia and in a couple of years earned a degree in dental surgery. He started his practice in Missouri before eventually moving back to Georgia, then was diagnosed with tuberculosis from which he would suffer throughout his adult life. He became an alcoholic and dependent on laudanum in part to relieve the pain of the disease. In search of a warm, drier climate, Holliday moved to Dallas, Texas in 1873 and thereafter traveled throughout the West while drinking, fighting, and gambling at faro and poker.

Earp and Holliday first met briefly in Texas while Earp was searching for outlaws, then they later reunited in Dodge City, Kansas where Holliday is said to have famously saved Earp's life during a shootout. The pair met

Wyatt Earp, ca. 1870s

up again multiple times thereafter, most famously in Tombstone, Arizona where Earp deputized Holliday, and along with Earp's brothers engaged in a famous gunfight versus a group of outlaws including Ike and Billy Clanton. Historians suggest the battle lasted no more than half a minute, though the fight and circumstances surrounding it were considerably expanded by later storytellers as the legendary "gunfight at O.K. Corral." Holliday died from his illness aged 36, while Earp would survive into the late 1920s before dying in Los Angeles at 80.

Before Earp's death, writer Stuart Lake visited him multiple times to gather stories that would appear in Lake's 1931 bestselling biography *Wyatt Earp: Frontier Marshal.* Accepted initially by many as a true account, Lake's book was later found to be rife with historical inaccuracies, embellishments, invented quotes, and outright fictions, though that didn't affect its popularity. Nor did it discourage others from using Lake's book as a starting point for their own versions of Earp and Holliday's story, starting with two film adaptations titled *Frontier Marshal* (from 1934 and 1939). Writers also recast Earp and Holliday's stories more overtly as fiction, including W.R. Burnett whose 1930 novel *Saint Johnson* alters names and details though includes a note beforehand alerting the reader the story is based on the famous feud and gunfight. (Yet another early film, 1932's *Law and Order*, adapted Burnett's book for the silver screen.)

One of director John Ford's great triumphs *My Darling Clementine* (1946) was also based on Lake's book, although Ford himself was well aware of the many discrepancies between the story told on screen and historical fact. Ford tried to persuade studio head Darryl F. Zanuck to let him change the character names altogether, making them fictions rather than suggest they were based on actual Old West figures. Latterly, Ford came to argue for the film's historical accuracy, telling Peter Bogdanovich about having met Earp who would visit film sets during the silent era. "He told me about the fight at the O.K. Corral," Ford said. "So in *My Darling Clementine*, we did it exactly as it had been. They didn't just walk in the street and start banging away at each other; it was a clever military maneuver."[4]

The divergence from history in the film begins with Earp (portrayed by Henry Fonda) arriving in Tombstone in 1882 (a year after the shootout took place). He immediately discovers it to be an unruly place when the cattle he and his brothers are driving to California get rustled and one of his brothers is killed. (This is another inaccuracy: the Earps were not cattle-drivers.) Soon after Earp has to take matters into his own hands when a drunk starts shooting up the town, and he accepts a position as marshal in part to try to exact revenge on his brother's killers. It isn't long after that Earp finds himself in a game of five-card draw, where once again the lawlessness of Tombstone reveals itself.

"I love poker... yes sir, I really love poker," Earp says as he contemplates a post-draw bet from his opponent. "Every hand a different problem. I've gotta do a little figuring here. What would I do if I was in your boots, Mr. Gambler? You drew three cards and I stood pat, and yet you raised

Doc Holliday, March 1872 graduation photo from the Pennsylvania School of Dentistry me. Now the question is, what should I do?" Meanwhile a woman standing behind Earp has signaled to "Mr. Gambler" that Earp is holding three of a kind. "Yeah, mighty interesting game poker... game of chance," Earp adds, then suddenly he rushes the woman out of the saloon, and after she slaps him Earp unceremoniously dumps her in a horse trough. Holliday (Victor Mature) arrives soon after and breaks up the game. "Sure is a hard town for a fellow to have a quiet game of poker in," Earp complains.

Much as Earp has to exert authority over the poker game in order to keep it on the square, so, too, does he have to take responsibility for justice to be served more generally in Tombstone, including upon the Clantons who were responsible for the theft of his cattle and his brother's murder. He also has to negotiate with Holliday over the course of the story, with the pair eventually agreeing to share in the authority needed to establish order.

Gunfight at the O.K. Corral (1957), directed by John Sturges, expands the story even further, starting in Dodge City and culminating in the big showdown at Tombstone. The film positions Holliday as the primary poker player of the pair. Early on Holliday, portrayed by Kirk Douglas, is said to have killed one person for cheating at cards, then is shown killing that player's brother in self-defense, supporting another character's judgment that "trouble just naturally seems to find him." As happens in *My Darling Clementine*, Holliday's terminal illness again gives his character a philosophical edge. At one point he explains to Earp, played by Burt Lancaster, how knowing he hasn't long to live gives him an edge at the tables,. "I never lose," he boasts. "See, poker's played by desperate men who cherish money. I don't lose because I have nothing to lose, including my life."

Before they leave Dodge for Tombstone and the climactic gun battle, there's one last hilarious sequence in which Holliday is in a heads-up poker match and won't quit despite shots being fired all around him by a group of hell-raisers who have ridden into town. "Sure are noisy," Holliday says, ignoring the pleas of his opponent who wants to run for cover. Though here presented light-heartedly, Holliday's seeming death-wish suggests he possesses not only the nerve to be a strong poker player, but a better gunfighter, too. The idea is supported again later in the film when at Tombstone Earp says, "All gunfighters are lonely. They live in fear. They die without a dime or a woman or a friend." Holliday may be lonely, and destined to die alone. But as for the rule about gunfighters living in fear, he seems an exception.

Among other films featuring Earp and Holliday, the pair returned once more in 1964's *Cheyenne Autumn*, a later work by John Ford that attempted to give more play to the Native Americans' side of the Old West story. In truth, Earp and Holliday appear as a mere digression within the film's larger plot, part of the "Dodge City interlude" Ford said was intended to function like an "intermission – a comedy sequence in the middle of an otherwise tragic story."[5] In fact, as played by Jimmy Stewart (Earp) and Arthur Kennedy (Holliday), they almost seem a comic duo, especially when sitting in a three-handed poker game against an opponent whom they suspect might be cheating.

Later the pair return to form in the sprawling, violent *Tombstone* (1993) directed by George P. Cosmatos. They are shown engaging in numerous conflicts and gunfights both before and after the central battle at the O.K. Corral in which Holliday, memorably portrayed by Val Kilmer, is again the primary poker player. Doc's struggle with tuberculosis and alcoholism is accentuated here, with his poker-playing often presented as another kind of disease he cannot shake.

Several poker scenes occur during the film, most featuring Holliday winning hands frequently enough to encourage suspicions of cheating, with his slow rolling and trash talking further heightening opponents' frustration. For example, an early scene shows Holliday turn over four queens to win a big five-card draw pot, chirping "isn't that a daisy?" to his opponent before violence ensues, ending with Holliday stabbing the player to death. Another poker game gets interrupted by a fight involving Earp (Kurt Russell). Then another finds a sickly, drunk Holliday at the end of a 36-hour session, coughing his way through a 12th-straight winning hand and inviting still more suspicion from eventual-O.K. Corral combatant Ike Clanton. "Son of a bitch, nobody's that lucky," snarls Clanton. "Maybe poker's just not your game," says a slurring Holliday. "I know... let's have a spelling contest!" Needless to say, Clanton isn't amused. But Earp intervenes, thwarting more violence – temporarily, anyway.

The film ends with Holliday at death's door in a Colorado sanitarium. Earp comes to visit, producing a deck of cards to deal a final game with his friend, a pathos-filled scene with Holliday expressing regrets about his life and encouraging Earp to try to live a better one. Meanwhile, the fact that Earp has to hold and play Holliday's cards for him offers an unsubtle reminder that Holliday has become a faint echo of his former self.

The pair's story was likewise echoed throughout popular culture in dime novels, comic books, dozens of other films, television shows, and even a 1957 doo-wop song by the Marquees featuring a young Marvin Gaye called "Wyatt Earp." As in the films, many of these iterations employed poker not only to add intrigue to plots but to add wit and intellect to the heroic image of the Old West cowboy both Earp and Holliday exemplified.

The Many Versions of Bat Masterson
Intersecting with Earp and Holliday, and with many other notorious figures from the Old West, was the famous hunter, gambler, gunfighter, occasional lawman, and later journalist Bat Masterson.

Born in Quebec in 1851, Masterson's family moved about until settling in Kansas, before he and his brothers left the farm to hunt buffalo. Some time after in Texas, Masterson apparently participated in a battle defending a small town from the siege of a Comanche tribe, though details of his involvement are sketchy. A couple of years after that came the most discussed event of Masterson's young life when he found himself in a deadly shootout in a Sweetwater, Texas saloon in early 1876 amid card playing and carousing.

Few details exist from the gunfight at the Lady Gay Saloon, and even those that do are disputed. Some say Masterson found himself in a draw poker game involving an ill-tempered and drunk Army corporal named Melvin A. King who stormed out after losing. Masterson began chatting with Mollie Brennan, a former prostitute and current dance hall girl, and some time later an angry King returned with his pistol drawn. It isn't clear whether King was mad about the game or upset with the attention Brennan was giving Masterson, but it's more certain that King's first shot hit Masterson in the pelvis and his second felled Brennan, killing her. Masterson then returned fire, killing King.

Masterson was wounded severely enough to require a cane to walk thereafter and some even suggest Masterson earned his nickname "Bat" from his use of the cane as a weapon to help keep the peace as a lawman. But there's more invention than truth in that idea. Masterson was born Bartholomew and later took the name William Barclay Masterson; "Bat" was a name he had used before.

The Sweetwater gunfight story essentially ends there, though many repetitions thereafter helped vault Masterson to the status of one of the West's most legendary gunfighters. His reputation as a poker player and gambler continued to grow as well, thanks to his travels through several states and many instances of winning large sums at the tables. Along the way he befriended Earp and his brothers as well as Holliday, becoming part of the famous "Dodge City Gang" (a.k.a. the "Dodge City Peace Commission") that for a time took on the task of policing the Kansas town. Masterson likewise served as a sheriff in Kansas and a marshal in Colorado as he further built an eclectic résumé.

Besides his charge to uphold the law

Bat Masterson in a three-piece suit and bowler hat (ca. 1879)

and keep order, Masterson frequently also managed the gambling wherever he went, overseeing poker and faro games along with roulette and other fare.

He was involved in other gunfights as well, although historians argue over whether he actually ever killed anyone else. One story involves Masterson avenging the shooting of his brother, Ed, although it isn't clear if he actually was the one pulling the trigger to administer frontier justice. Masterson was certainly involved in one other gunfight alongside Earp in Dodge. He also found himself with Earp in Tombstone not long before the O.K. Corral clash, dealing faro in the Oriental Saloon when another twist of fate arrived to further the legend-making of Bat Masterson, gunfighting gambler.

An enterprising writer for the *New York Sun* named William Young was in Gunnison, Colorado in late summer 1881 in search of "a sensational shoot-'em-up western story to titillate his eastern readers," explains Robert K. DeArment.[6] Young met a certain Dr. W. S. Cockrell who pointed out the famous Bat Masterson, describing a man who by age 27 had already killed 26 others. Cockrell went on to provide further details of Masterson's exploits, which included one story of Masterson having shot and killed seven men in one vicious swoop in response to his brother's murder. Young went back to New York and published the stories, which were soon reprinted and shared throughout the country, making Masterson into a larger-than-life emblem of the "Wild West." Truth be told, Masterson was nowhere near Gunnison at the time of the reporter's visit. The man Cockrell pointed out to the reporter was someone else, and the stories he told about Masterson were all spun from his own imagination, nothing more than a cheeky bluff.

For the next several decades Masterson consistently denied the popular stories that portrayed him as a cold-blooded killer, though the legend continued to follow him wherever he went. Theodore Roosevelt (himself a poker player) even later sought to meet Masterson thanks to those stories, as did many others. As DeArment reports, a Fourth of July celebration in 1885 in Dodge City included a vote among residents to name the town's most popular man. Masterson won in a landslide and was awarded a gold watch and gold-tipped cane.[7]

The last act of Masterson's life involved him moving to New York City and pursuing a career as a columnist for *The Morning Telegraph*. A boxing enthusiast, Masterson attended and reported on the biggest bouts while also writing on other subjects for his thrice-weekly column, "Masterson's Views on Timely Topics." In other words, it was the erroneous reporting of another New York writer that partly positioned Masterson to become a journalist himself, as the fame created by those stories opened doors for Masterson to pursue his writing career.

While in New York Masterson became friends with fellow scribe (and fellow gambler) Damon Runyon, who after spending his early career writing in Colorado moved to New York City shortly after the turn of the century and began writing about baseball for the Hearst newspapers. Runyon also wrote numerous memorable short stories about gambling, including one called "The Idyll of Miss Sarah Brown" featuring a character named "Obadiah Masterson," nicknamed "The Sky." That story, along with an account of a craps game borrowed from another, formed the basis for the later Broadway production of *Guys and Dolls*. (Marlon Brando played Sky Masterson in the 1955 film adaptation.) The Masterson of Runyon's story and the musical, closely identified with the big city and willing to bet on *anything*, is also somewhat removed from the original, primarily sharing only the gambling theme and status as a ladies man. Indeed other famous gamblers like Titanic Thompson provided as much or more direct inspiration for the character, though the name was unmistakably an homage to Bat.

Masterson died in 1923 but his legend grew still further, with characters often based on the exaggerated version of him that appeared in Old West histories and early western films. In the late 1950s came a couple of television series featuring the character, one of them a *Gunsmoke*-style drama *The Life and Legend of Wyatt Earp* (1955-61). It was the competing series *Bat Masterson* (1958-61), however, that had the most influence on the historical figure's reputation. Based in part on a 1957 biography by Richard O'Connor, the light-hearted series featured Gene Barry as a forty-ish Masterson whose fashion sense – a derby hat, vest and jacket, and always-present cane – made him something of a dandy. This version of Masterson often didn't even carry a gun, instead seeing off trouble with his cane.

Gene Barry as Bat Masterson
(from the 1958-61 TV series)

A comic book was simultaneously produced as a tie-in with the TV series, and countless other iterations of the character followed, including an episode of Hanna-Barbara's early 1960s cartoon *Punkin' Puss & Mushmouse* (a cat-versus-mouse Tom and Jerry ripoff) relating the story of "The Legend of Bat Mouseterson" (Mushmouse's cousin who comes for a visit). The character is a cane-wielding fop, hardly related to the Old West context in which the historical Masterson existed.

Lady Gamblers and Poker Alice

The Old West saloon was a male-dominated arena, primarily occupied by single men seeking respite from labor by drinking, gambling, and fighting. "Saloon culture" (as some scholars of the era have called it) was therefore predictably masculine, with the swinging doors shutting out domestic obligations and – for the most part – women.

Especially in the westernmost states, temperance movements didn't gain much traction until later in the century, well after areas became settled, men got older, and more families were begun. That further sustained the trend of saloons being almost solely the province of men, with poker's early history likewise reflecting the predominance of men at the tables. The mere entrance of a woman into a saloon as a patron was itself often noteworthy. Her taking a seat at a table and buying into a game of poker would be even more of a story. But there *were* women who played – and some earned as much notoriety as the most famous Old West gunslingers.

At the end of the 18th century, a few decades prior to poker's introduction in America's south and west, stories of women at the gambling tables in Europe evoked a cultural response that prefigured what came later in the United States. In Britain, legal restrictions were placed upon various gambling games, including the popular faro games that had captured the fancy of the upper classes. The games persisted, however, in some cases hosted privately in an attempt to avoid the notice of the authorities. "Well-off women with no other income sometimes allowed their houses to be turned into gambling houses," explains David G. Schwartz. He identifies Lady Archer and Lady Buckinghamshire as "the most prominent of a circle of 'Faro Ladies' who owned banks in private homes."[8]

The games caused legal trouble for the "Faro Ladies," who had to pay fines when they were broken up. They also exposed the women to criticism from the culture at large. Schwartz tells of *The Morning Post* mocking Lady Archer's penchant for applying lots of makeup in a report on the games, an extraneous, unwarranted censure. Another *Post* article reporting a bust added how the women hosting such games were to be regarded as "the disgrace of human nature."[9] As the latter comment suggests, "lady gamblers" were perceived as doubly threatening. Not only did they run afoul of both moral and legal prohibitions against gambling, exposing themselves to the negative consequences (both real and imagined) of such risk-taking, but they also challenged social norms by participating in what were thought to be activities only fit for men, believed by some to be an even worse transgression.

Back across the Atlantic, several women appear in Old West gambling narratives. These women likewise encountered frequent criticism and significant hardship in life, then often were elevated afterwards to storybook status as their tales were told and retold, each iteration adorned with added details to heighten their drama.

Belle Ryan and partner Charles Cora were two of many gold-seekers arriving in California in 1849. They earned their share of those new riches not through mining, but by running games of poker and faro in saloons and eventually their own gambling den in Marysville. Later they opened a second place in Sonora that doubled as a brothel, and after a few skirmishes with the law Charles was eventually hanged for killing a marshal. A few years later Ryan was dead aged 30.

Then there was Kitty Leroy who gambled her way into her twenties at faro and other games while also working as a dealer, a dancer, a prostitute, and even owning her own saloon. She was said to have been involved in gunfights as well, with various stories of her having either shot or stabbed more than a few people she had caught cheating at cards. Her story eventually carried her to Deadwood, intersecting briefly with that of Wild Bill Hickok. Like Hickok, Leroy's life was abruptly cut short when she was killed at the Lone Star Saloon in late 1877 by her fifth husband in a murder-suicide.

Reportedly born in France, Eleanora Dumont dealt all over the west from Deadwood to Tombstone, eventually opening a gambling parlor called Vingt-et-un (i.e., "21") and later a brothel. Maria Gertrudis "Tules" Barceló – either Mexican or French, depending on which historian you read – ran a popular saloon in Santa Fe. Belle Siddons, a.k.a. Madam Vestal, was a dancer turned "faro queen" in several Midwest saloons. And Kate O'Leary was another dealer who eventually owned a gambling den in Dodge City, Kansas.

Although usually associated with faro, many of these women also played poker. When not involved with rustlers, bootleggers, and other notorious Old West types, Belle Starr regularly played and won in saloon poker games before her mysterious shooting death in 1889. Minnie Smith was another dealer and poker player in Colorado. Lottie Deno played poker throughout Texas before moving to New Mexico with her husband Frank where the pair ran a gambling den. Mary Hamlin, a.k.a. "Mary the Owl," was a poker player and con artist said to have been involved in some celebrated heists. One lucrative scheme involved selling false shipping rights on the Mississippi to investors, while in another Hamlin and some accomplices swindled a San Francisco bank via a diamond hoax.

Most accounts of these women gamblers (both contemporary and otherwise) make sure to draw attention to their beauty, with their attractiveness to men said to serve them well at the tables while also occasionally being cited as a factor in stories of violent conflicts. Chris Enss, author of more than a dozen books about women of the Wild West, described Belle

"Poker Alice" Ivers, ca. 1860s

Ryan (for example) as "a voluptuous creature with dark hair, hazel eyes, and a fair complexion."[10] In some cases the prominence of these women in the male-centric world of saloons and cards also shaped contemporary responses to them. Much was made, for instance, of Kitty Leroy's penchant to dress in men's clothing. A late 19th-century novelist styled Belle Starr a "female Jesse James." And in later life, Eleanora Dumont earned the unfortunate nickname of "Madame Moustache" thanks to a shadowy upper lip.

Of all the women courageous enough to compete in the saloon poker games, however, Alice Ivers has easily earned the most notice. Born in the early 1850s in the southern English county of Devon, Ivers grew up in Virginia before moving to Colorado as a teenager. Her first husband, a miner named Frank Duffield, was a poker player, and after his death in a mining accident Ivers began dealing poker, faro, and twenty-one as a means to provide for herself. She played poker, too, and her early success netted her still more income while quickly earning her wide renown – and a nickname, "Poker Alice."

Alice was soon recruited to deal and play at various western saloons, where her celebrity became a marketable draw for the proprietors. While in Deadwood, South Dakota she met her second husband, a fellow dealer named Warren G. Tubbs, with one early story describing Alice defending his life against a drunkard by drawing a pistol. Their marriage lasted two decades and produced seven children before Tubbs died of tuberculosis in 1910. Having set poker aside during her marriage to Tubbs, Alice took up the game again in her fifties, and once more earned

"Poker Alice" Ivers, ca. 1920s

a steady income. By some accounts (including her own) she earned somewhere around $250,000 at the tables.

Eventually Alice opened her own saloon-slash-brothel in South Dakota, called "Poker's Palace." There was a third short marriage (again ending with the premature death of her husband), as well as numerous run-ins with the law. Those resulted in occasional fines and prison time for Alice due to various transgressions related to her hosting the games, managing the brothel, and becoming involved in bootlegging during the Prohibition-era 1920s. Alice enjoyed drinking herself (her drunkenness occasionally led to arrests) and smoking cigars, and references to these "masculine" behaviors are often conspicuous in accounts of her. One of the most well known photos of Alice, taken in her seventies, depicts a masculine-seeming Old West gambler, but the photo belies other accounts of Alice's beauty and love of "feminine" fashion. She apparently enjoyed traveling to New York to spend her poker winnings on dresses during her younger years.

Unlike some of the more tragic Old West stories of lady gamblers' lives shortened by violence, Alice lived to a ripe age of 79, establishing her legacy well enough to elevate her to the forefront of 19th-century women poker players. Her celebrity also inspired the makers of a TV film from the late 1980s to borrow her name and vaguely reference her story in an otherwise fictional Western starring Elizabeth Taylor.

The Long, Strange Life of the Dead Man's Hand

Looming large over all of the poker played in the Old West is the figure of James Butler "Wild Bill" Hickok, whose final hand of five-card draw is undoubtedly the most famous hand of poker played in the 19th century, perhaps even in all of poker.

Hickok was a well known figure for several years prior to that fateful August afternoon in Deadwood. Born in Illinois in 1837, by his late twenties Hickok had already collected a number of adventures, including enduring a bear attack, working with the Pony Express, and serving the Union Army in various capacities during the Civil War. He had also been involved in a couple of shootings, most notably the first widely reported "quick draw" duel in which he killed a man named David Tutt following a dispute about poker debts (and, likely, a woman). In the fall of 1865 – not long after the Tutt duel – Hickok's notoriety had grown enough to earn him a visit from journalist George Ward Nichols. Later, in the February 1867 issue of *Harper's New Monthly Magazine*, Nichols told Hickok's story to a national audience, going to great lengths to present Hickok as a gun-slinging god among men.

Nichols sketches Hickok as the epitome of rugged, Old West manhood, possessed with the "handsomest physique I had ever seen" and "a singular grace and dignity of carriage." Nichols seems spellbound by Hickok's ap-

James Butler "Wild Bill" Hickok

pearance, describing his eyes as "gentle as a woman's." Continuing his impression of Hickok, he even suggests "the woman nature seems prominent throughout" – until, that is, Nichols remembers that "you were looking into eyes that had pointed the way to death to hundreds of men." In case you missed that, Nichols repeats it. "Yes, Wild Bill with his own hands has killed hundreds of men. Of that I have not a doubt."[11] It's an exaggeration, of course, not unlike the fabricated Bat Masterson stories and other tall tales of the Old West.

Nichols briefly relates the shootout with Tutt, then asks Hickok if he ever felt fear. Hickok admits he has. "They may shoot bullets at me by the dozen, and it's rather exciting if I can shoot back," Hickok says. "But I am always sort of nervous when the big guns go off." A demonstration of Hickok's skill with a pistol follows, then Nichols wraps up his report noting "it would be easy to fill a volume with the adventures of that remarkable man." Before departing, Nichols asks Hickok if he might be permitted to share his story with the world. "Certainly you may," Hickok replied. "I'm sort of public property."[12]

The *Harper's* story catapulted Hickok to nationwide fame, accompanying him as he proceeded to work in various locales as a lawman. Stories of his poker playing continued as well, and it was in both contexts – as an upholder of the law and at the card tables – that Hickok became involved in more shootouts. One such scene was imagined later in N.C. Wyeth's 1916 oil painting of "Wild Bill Hickok at Cards." Another oft-repeated (and perhaps invented) story attributes a classic Old West poker line to Hickok. While playing an opponent he suspected was cheating, Hickok called a bet and saw his opponent turn over jacks full. Hickok responded by showing his hand and declaring a winner, aces full of sixes. When his opponent saw only three aces and a single six, he objected. "There's only one six," he said. Hickok then pulled out his pistol. "Here is the other six," he said, and his opponent conceded the pot.

Hickok's career as a lawman ended with him losing a position as a marshal in Abilene, Kansas after accidentally shooting and killing a deputy. (Poor eyesight, perhaps caused by glaucoma, may have contributed to the mistake.) He married an older woman in Wyoming, and soon after a

39-year-old Hickok traveled to the Black Hills of South Dakota in search of gold while his new wife stayed behind in Cheyenne. He reached Deadwood in July, not long after another notorious Old West figure, Martha Jane Cannary, a.k.a. "Calamity Jane," had arrived. Rumors of a romance between the two (later furthered by Jane herself) were likely unfounded. Hickok had only been in Deadwood about three weeks when on August 2, 1876 he found himself in a poker game at Nuttal & Mann's Saloon No. 10. Some accounts say the variant being played was five-card stud, others five-card draw. At around three o'clock a man named Jack McCall stepped into the saloon and said "damn you, take that," firing a pistol into the back of Hickok's head, killing him instantly.

McCall's motives are unclear, though various explanations include his having lost to Hickok in an earlier game then McCall having taken offense at Hickok's subsequent loan offer. Others speculate that McCall was under the impression that Hickok had killed his brother (a claim made by McCall at his first trial), or his having been encouraged and/or paid by others who desired Hickok's death. Hickok's fame likely bore some significance, too, as it surely made him a target previously both of gunslingers and card players. After a couple of trials, McCall was eventually hanged for the crime.

One oft-repeated facet of the story is Hickok sitting with his back to the saloon entrance, against his usual custom. The seat was the only one available when Hickok joined the game, with a player named Charlie Rich (who later became marshal of Deadwood) reportedly having refused a request from Hickok to switch chairs. The other detail that is always included is the hand Hickok held at the time of his death: two black aces and two black eights. Or, as it would later come to be called, the "dead man's hand."

In 1926, Frank J. Wilstach wrote a biography of Hickok that purports to provide initial evidence both of the hand and its nickname. Wilstach had corresponded with Ellis T. "Doc" Pierce who had been the barber in Deadwood and was given the duty of preparing Hickok's body for burial. Pierce shared with Wilstach details of the scene, including how Hickok's "fingers were still crimped from holding his poker hand... which read 'aces and eights.'" Wilstach underscores how "since that day" aces and eights was thereafter known as the "dead's man hand."[13]

Wilstach's account via Pierce is in fact the only one from a witness that identifies the actual hand. Meanwhile there has been a great deal of conjecture about what Hickok's fifth card was, though no consensus. In *Ghosts at the Table,* Des Wilson makes an entertaining and somewhat heroic effort to pin down the fifth card, but is forced to conclude it remains a mystery. Less well known is the fact that during the half-century between Hickok's killing and Wilstach's book, several *other* poker hands were known as the "dead man's hand." In 1978, Cecil Adams shared some research performed for his "The Straight Dope" column uncovering a number of references to other dead man's hands in articles and books, including

- jacks full of tens – *Grand Forks Daily Herald,* 1886
- jacks and eights – *Eau Claire Leader,* 1898
- tens and treys – *Trenton Times,* 1900
- jacks and sevens – *Encyclopaedia of Superstitions, Folklore, and the Occult Sciences,* 1903
- jacks and eights – *Hoyle's Games,* 1907

From these intervening decades, Adams also shares other references to aces and eights, the earliest from 1900. He concludes that by the time Wilstach wrote his book in 1926, even with the barber/undertaker's testimony there is still doubt over (1) whether Hickok actually held aces and eights, and (2) whether aces and eights were thereafter exclusively known as the "dead man's hand."[14] In any case, thanks to the hundreds of cultural references to the hand that have followed Wilstach's account, aces and eights have easily become the last "dead man's hand" standing. Or lying on the ground, as it were.

Numerous films have highlighted the hand, including John Ford's 1939 western *Stagecoach* in which a character holding aces and eights is killed by the hero portrayed by John Wayne. It earns a cameo early in the Coen brothers' 2018 anthology film *The Ballad of Buster Scruggs* as a hand the title character superstitiously refuses to play. Several television shows have incorporated references as well, as have works of fiction including multiple novels in a variety of genres carrying the title *Dead Man's Hand*. In Ken Kesey's 1962 novel *One Flew Over the Cuckoo's Nest,* the protagonist R.P. McMurphy is described as having a couple of tattoos, one being "a poker hand fanned out across his muscle – aces and eights."[15] (Later McMurphy runs poker games among the patients in the psychiatric hospital to which he's been assigned after faking insanity to get out of a prison sentence.) The "dead man's hand" is a frequent reference in song lyrics as well, with Bob Seger's "Fire Lake," Motörhead's "Ace of Spades," and Bob Dylan's "Rambling, Gambling Willie" among the better known examples. There's a "Dead Man's Hand" video game set in the Old West (a first-person shooter, of course). It's the name of both a Belgian-brewed stout and a Las Vegas bar. And the Las Vegas Metropolitan Police Department Homicide Section has even adopted aces and eights as its logo, a grim allusion to history's best known poker-related murder.

Just as Hickok himself recognized he'd become "sort of public property" thanks to his fame as a gunslinger, the dead man's hand has been appropriated by the public at large, whether ironically or in earnest, as an all-purpose method to convey ominous foreshadowing. Meanwhile, the hand stands as an ultimate symbol of poker in the Old West, instantly evoking both the image of the cowboy and the game's frequent association with danger and violence, a legacy that extended well into the 20th century and still exists today. The story behind the hand perhaps adds more nuance to the symbol, in particular Hickok being caught completely unaware, never having had an opportunity to defend himself against his murderer. If we were to extend the mythologizing of Hickok begun in *Harper's Magazine* a century-and-a-half ago, poker becomes a fatal flaw for our "hero," the concentration required by the game – or the exhilarating thrills it sometimes offers – proving for him a deadly distraction.

In other words, as storytellers and others continue to wax lyrical about the dead man's hand, its endless reiterations haven't necessarily helped poker's image in the culture at large, suggesting a sinister deadliness potentially revealing itself with every deal.

6 Poker in the Civil War

As we've already seen, the story of poker in America begins early in the 19th century in the south and west, but by April 12, 1861 – the day Confederate forces fired on a Union garrison at Fort Sumter in South Carolina to launch the first battle of the Civil War – the game had already found its way both north and east via steamboats, trains, and by other means. The war hastened the spread of the game even more, both during the four years of fighting and afterwards. In fact, many thousands of young men on both sides were first introduced to poker (and other gambling games) during those years.

An excellent source of information about the daily lives of both Union and Confederate soldiers is the Civil War historian Bell I. Wiley whose books *The Life of Johnny Reb: The Common Soldier of the Confederacy* (1943) and *The Life of Billy Yank: The Common Soldier of the Union* (1952) draw heavily from soldiers' diaries and letters to present a thorough, detailed understanding of the day-to-day thoughts and activities of the rank-and-file. Wiley describes various recreations pursued by those on both sides during the sometimes lengthy down times of the war. They read newspapers, novels, and, of course, the Bible. They engaged in various sports including wrestling and boxing, as well as cricket and an early version of baseball. Some sang and a few even created small theater groups to perform plays.

But gambling and card playing proved the most favored between-battle activity, providing a much desired escape from the pressures of more injurious forms of combat. Additionally, like the war itself, the betting of money on cards significantly challenged some soldiers' moral sensibilities, prompting them to reconsider their judgments of what was permissible and what was not.

Betting by the Blue

In a chapter titled "Evil and Goodness" in *The Life of Billy Yank*, Wiley writes persuasively about the war having introduced many Union soldiers to activities and behaviors in which they wouldn't otherwise have participated. These include swearing, smoking, drinking, and, of course, card playing. "The degeneration came from the removal of accustomed restraints and associations, the urge to experiment with the forbidden, the desire to escape boredom and the utter inadequacy of religious and recreational facilities for soldiers of the sixties," Wiley explains.[1]

But not everyone was as enthusiastic about the prevalence of gambling in the ranks. Some described in their diaries and in letters feelings of unease over the seeming moral laxity among their fellow soldiers. Wiley quotes one Union soldier writing home in October 1864 and reflecting with a kind of awe at just how widespread gambling on card games had become among his colleagues. "So far as my observation goes, nine out of ten play cards for money," the soldier writes.[2]

Predictably gambling picked up shortly after paydays, with many of the lower officers risking more than they should from their $16 a month allowance. Those who brought prior experience to the games enjoyed an advantage over less tutored players. "Gambling sharks trained in metropolitan dens frequented some of the camps and on payday made heavy inroads on the meager resources of unsuspecting soldiers," Wiley notes.[3]

There were dice games, including craps and the popular "chuck-a-luck." Soldiers also conducted raffles, engaged in cockfighting, and even horse racing. However "the principal gambling medium was cards and the favorite game was poker, commonly called 'bluff,' which was played in several variations," Wiley writes. "Other card games included twenty-one, euchre, faro and seven-up or 'old sledge.'"[4] Despite the small stakes, the poker games – usually five-card draw – were pursued with vigor. Wiley even shares one story of a group of Union soldiers completing a hand while being fired upon by Confederates.

The experience of a young officer named C.W. Bardeen earns particular attention. Entering the army at 16, Bardeen had no prior experience with gambling games, though in his diary reports winning hundreds at poker over the course of just a few weeks. "Played Bluff as usual. Sent $50.00 home," reads one entry. "Lost $5.00 at Sweat this morning," begins another, referring to a dice game, "but won it back again at Bluff. I seem to have uniform good success at Bluff this payday." A few days after that Bardeen reports winning $20 more at Bluff: "A full hand, two Flushes. I held the Full."[5]

However later entries find Bardeen experiencing guilty feelings about gambling, expressing the same "concern for the soul" (as Wiley puts it) as others did over poker in their diaries and letters. Bardeen ultimately gives up gambling entirely, although Wiley cynically observes that many who quit poker weren't so much worried about their souls as they were about their depleting funds, having been "constrained to reform by the quick loss of badly needed wages."[6]

Soldiers playing cards (ca. 1861-65)

Gambling of the Gray

In *The Life of Johnny Reb*, Wiley reports in a chapter titled "Besetting Sins" how a higher percentage of soldiers from the South came into the war already having prior experience with poker and other gambling games. Wiley notes in particular soldiers from Louisiana (poker's birthplace), Tennessee, Mississippi, and Texas gambling as they traveled and how they found "innumerable games of chance already in progress" upon landing in Richmond.[7]

Like the "nine out of ten" figure cited by a Union soldier regarding the prevalence of soldiers' gambling, a Confederate counterpart likewise observed of his fellow fighters that "a young man cannot guard himself too closely in camp... where to be considered an accomplished gentleman it is necessary to be a scientific and successful gambler." Dice games, horse racing, and raffles were likewise popular among the soldiers of the South. There was even betting on louse "fights" as well as on how fast lice could move off a plate. But once again, "the commonest form of gambling was card playing," with poker, twenty-one, and euchre all favorites.[8]

As the war turned in the North's favor, their advantage in numbers and resources were also realized in their access to playing cards. The American Card Company even produced a special "Union deck" supplied to soldiers that featured eagles, shields, stars, and flags for the four suits. The king was a colonel, the queen the goddess of liberty, and the jack a major, with the backs also featuring patriotic imagery. By contrast, Wiley notes the generally poor quality of the cards with which the Confederate soldiers often played, especially during the war's final months. Unlike the brand new Union decks, the "cards dealt around Confederate campfires generally were as ragged and battleworn as the uniforms of the players."[9] Cash was also scarce, meaning they would more often bet with items like pocket knives, clothes, or even rations. "A Louisiana veteran recalled a card game late in the war in which the stake was a stolen chicken," Wiley writes.[10]

One other interesting phenomenon reveals something of the general opinion regarding poker at the time. When soldiers on both sides headed to battle they often rid themselves of decks of cards as they marched, cautious to avoid "being killed with the instruments of sin on their bodies." One could find cards strewn along the paths taken to battle "tossed aside by conscience-stricken gamblers fearful of their future" like so many discards in a larger, more fateful game. "The immediate prospect of battle brought fear of death and the punishment of an angry God to the hearts of many gamblers," says Wiley.[11]

Not surprisingly, those who survived picked up the cards again on their return to camp, and the games would continue.

Ulysses S. Grant: Glad to Gamble

The two men commanding the opposing sides in the Civil War stood in stark contrast to one another in terms of both ideology and personality. On the side of the South was the blue-blooded aristocrat Robert E. Lee, who was opposed to change and fighting to preserve the past. Meanwhile the North was led by the son of a tanner and willing risk-taker Ulysses S. Grant, who embraced progress and looked to the future. Such a divergence perhaps makes it less surprising to learn the two leaders also held widely differing views on poker and gambling.

Before serving as Commanding General of the Union Army, Grant was a card player from his youth and continued to be through his final years. He played while a cadet at West Point, to which he arrived in 1839, and he graduated in the middle of his class in 1843, despite rules forbidding (among other things) alcohol, tobacco, *and* card playing. During Grant's first year at the academy, he joined a secret group called T.I.O. or "Twelve in One," described by historian Charles Bracelen Flood as "a dozen classmates who pledged eternal friendship and wore rings bearing a significance only they knew." Among the T.I.O.'s pastimes was "a card game called Brag," the oft-cited precursor to poker.[12] Later Grant entered the list of poker-playing presidents (see Chapter 10) when he served two terms in the nation's highest office during the era of reconstruction.

Despite his evident enjoyment of poker, Grant did not chronicle his card playing that much. His remarkable end-of-life autobiography, the *Personal Memoirs of Ulysses S. Grant* (published by Mark Twain shortly after Grant's death in 1885) shares no stories of his own poker playing and only casual references to that of others. In fact, there are only a few small, mostly incidental references to cards in all 32 volumes of *The Papers of Ulysses S. Grant.*

Grant once mentions in a letter sending $10 to the U.S. Senator James W. Nesmith on February 14, 1867, calling the payment a "Valentine" and adding "this is the day for distributing such things." A notation clarifies the money "was a little balance on a poker transaction."[13] Another note shares journalist John Russell Young's 1879 diary entry describing a poker game with Grant.[14]

In the *Papers* there also appears evidence of Grant's notorious feud with Captain William J. Kountz, one of a few military men with whom Grant butted heads during the war. Kountz oversaw river transportation for the Union forces, and Grant's displeasure with him escalated to the point of Grant having Kountz arrested. Kountz later filed formal charges against Grant in retaliation, accusing him of being a drunk. *The Papers* list the charges, including a reference to Grant "playing Cards for money while he was a disbursing Agent (disburseing [sic] secret service money)."[15] While the episode didn't help Grant's reputation, it did not scupper his rise to prominence. Kountz, on the other hand, faded into obscurity.

The *Papers* include one other account of Grant's poker playing made by the journalist George A. Townsend, who was best known for his reporting on both the war and Lincoln's assassination. Townsend shares how Grant's love of gambling games went against both his West Point upbringing and his father's wishes. "He was dumbfounded," wrote Townsend of Grant's father, "that Grant would play poker or occasionally faro." Townsend goes on to connect Grant's poker style to his ability as a military commander, emphasizing that his readiness to take risks proved especially beneficial on the battlefield.

"You know how a man of Grant's temperament would bet," Townsend says. "The first wager he made would be with all he had for all on the cloth. 'All the downs' was his favorite bet. He did the same in war.... He felt the spirit of the game and played for big victories and promotions."[16]

Grant Picks Off Fightin' Phil's Bluff

A more explicit discussion of Grant's poker playing finally appeared well after his death in 1909 via one Ferdinand Ward, the entrepreneur who partnered with Grant's son and infamously lost a fortune through corrupt financial deals that landed him six years in Sing Sing. Grant himself was ruined by the scheme, having invested heavily as well.

Ward shared his story in a long article published in *The New York Herald* titled "General Grant As I Knew Him" covering his friendship with the elder Grant over the last four years of the ex-president's life. Ward shoulders the blame for his failed racket, absolving Grant as essentially a "child in business matters" whose only role was to play the part of a ruined investor. Of course, Grant's willingness to sink a quarter million into the venture reflected again his desire to play for "big victories," a character trait Ward emphasizes as well. "One of the characteristics of the General which impressed me most forcibly was his courage," Ward writes. "Morally and physically he was the bravest man I ever knew. I do not think he ever knew fear." In the stories Ward tells to illustrate such courage are a couple of their poker games "of which the General was inordinately fond."[17]

"I think the game appealed to him because he had to bring to it many of the same qualities which caused him to be determined to 'fight it out along this line if it takes all summer,'" Ward writes. Here he alludes to a much-quoted line of Grant's delivered in May 1864 just a couple of months after he had taken over command of the Union forces, underscoring his readiness to continue fighting in Virginia despite having endured casualties. "The possibilities for ambuscades, masking of batteries and sudden sorties in the great American indoor game appealed to him immensely," Ward continues. "It had for him the same fascination which chess has had for other military geniuses."

One story involves a memorable hand of five-card draw. The game was five-handed, also involving Grant's friend Philip Sheridan – a.k.a. "Fightin' Phil" – who had served as a Union general and whose cavalry played an important role in the war-ending Appomattox Campaign. In the hand Grant draws three cards while Sheridan stands pat, and when the latter "bet the limit" everyone folds except Grant who raises. "Sheridan promptly came back with another boost, and General Grant saw that and raised again. Then General Sheridan with his pat hand called. General Grant showed a pair of nines and won the pot, as Sheridan had nothing."[18]

With a laugh, Grant takes out his cigar and says "I knew you were bluffing, 'Phil,' and I would have kept it up until I had staked my pile." A thoroughly impressed Ward concludes that Grant "seemed to be possessed of a sort of sixth sense which enabled him to size up situations in a flash of intuition."

Reproachful Robert E. Lee

The Confederacy's commander General Lee was much less inclined to gamble at cards. In fact, he was fairly intolerant of poker as a character-compromising vice to be avoided at all costs.

Lee also attended West Point some years before Grant in the late 1820s, finishing second in his class while adhering dutifully to the prohibition against card playing, earning zero demerits during his four years as a cadet. Later during an early tour of duty at Fort Monroe, Lee observed with distaste his fellow officers' poker playing, once writing a letter to a former classmate, Jack Mackay, describing his annoyance. "I have seen minds formed for use and ornament degenerate into sluggishness and inactivity, requiring the stimulus of brandy and cards to rouse them into action," Lee wrote.[19]

Such antipathy toward poker found expression again many years later not long after Lee took over command of the Confederate forces in 1862. In one of his "General Orders" – this one addressed to the Army of Northern Virginia – Lee was unambiguous regarding his intolerance of all forms of gambling, including poker. "The general commanding is pained to learn that the vice of gambling exists, and is becoming common in this army," the Order begins. "He regards it as wholly inconsistent with the character of a Southern soldier and subversive of good order and discipline in the army. All officers are earnestly enjoined to use every effort to suppress this vice, and the assistance of every soldier having the true interests of the army and of the country at heart is invoked to put an end to a practice which cannot fail to produce those deplorable results which have ever attended its indulgence in any society."[20]

However by then it was already probably too late to inhibit the spread of such "sin." As Wiley writes, "If Lee was just then discovering this propensity of his troops he was far behind time, for that evil had flourished in the Army of Northern Virginia, as elsewhere, long before he assumed command."[21]

Despite the order, card playing remained prevalent throughout the four years of the Civil War, even when packs – like other provisions – became harder for the Confederate soldiers to come by.

When Sherman Outplayed Hood

Some of Lee's generals were known to enjoy poker as well, and in his *Cowboys Full: The Story of Poker*, James McManus compiles the stories of a few of them.

There's the brutal and odious Nathan Bedford Forrest, later to become the first Grand Wizard of the Ku Klux Klan. McManus tells of Forrest's card playing during the war and his poker-like strategies on the battlefield, also relating how Forrest continued to play poker to earn a living after the war despite his Christian wife's objections. McManus also tells of William "Little Billy" Mahone, present with Lee at the surrender at Appomattox in early April 1865. After the war Mahone became an important figure during reconstruction, involved heavily in the building of railroads. Later during the 1880s he served as a Virginia senator, taking part in the increasingly popular poker games played by Congressmen of the era.

However, the most interesting – and probably most historically significant – story of Lee's poker-playing generals concerns John Bell Hood from Kentucky who commanded Confederate forces in a couple of decisive battles during the second half of 1864. Although the North then held the advantage, the war's outcome was still in doubt, which meant Lincoln's reelection in 1864 wasn't assured either. If Lincoln remained in office, the Union could continue forward with the battle. However, things might go differently should someone else be elected, for instance the Democrats' nominee George McClellan, who was another of Grant's antagonists. Unlike Lincoln's party, the Dems were in favor of ending the war and settling with the Confederacy. Even though McClellan disagreed with his party's platform, it's clear that if he were to have claimed the presidency from Lincoln, the country's future – including whether or not slavery was abolished – would have been altered greatly.

As it happened, decisive victories by the Union during the run-up to the election assured Lincoln's success by a wide margin. One of those victories was against forces commanded by Hood, newly appointed by the Confederacy's president Jefferson Davis to lead the Army of Tennessee into the Atlanta Campaign. Hood's adversary was William Tecumseh Sherman and his larger Military Division of the Mississippi. Not knowing much about the young Hood, Sherman asked his officers if anyone had any acquaintance with him previously, perhaps at West Point. One stepped forward, either a scout or a colonel (depending on the version of the story), to share some relevant background. As Civil War historian Shelby Foote recounts, the inside source was "a Union-loyal fellow Kentuckian" who had earlier watched Hood "play old-army poker" with an aggressive style. "I seed Hood bet $2500," the source reported to Sherman, "with nary a pair in his hand."[22]

Such information helped Sherman plot a strategy versus Hood, surmising that his boldness in a hand of poker might well translate to boldness on the battlefield. That meant Sherman could go on the offensive with his troop advantage and expect Hood not to retreat as he should. "As if on cue, Hood proceeded to shatter his Army of Tennessee with four near-suicidal attacks on Sherman's well-dug-in positions," McManus explains.[23] Both

Two unidentified Union soldiers drinking whiskey and playing cards (ca. 1861-65)

sides suffered nearly the same number of casualties (more than 30,000), but the loss represented a much higher percentage of the South's numbers than the North's. The Confederate army left Atlanta, Lincoln was reelected, and by the spring came surrender. In other words, Sherman's knowledge of Hood's big bluff in a poker game directly changed the course of United States history. As poker author Mason Malmuth notes in his reflection on the story, despite the lack of specifics regarding the hand Hood played (including whether or not his big bluff had been called), it isn't hyperbole to call it "The Most Important Hand Ever Played."[24]

Lee had warned about gambling producing "deplorable results." And for the South, Hood's gambling nature had done just that.

"It's a Pity We Couldn't Have Fought the War Out in a Poker Game"
The significance of poker during this crucial period in America's history also earns acknowledgment in the 20th century's most popular representation of a Civil War narrative: Margaret Mitchell's bestselling epic novel *Gone With the Wind* (1936). Set in Georgia during the Civil War and its aftermath, Mitchell introduces poker as an essential component of manliness for Southern whites. The game also has particular relevance to the plot, adding a chance element affecting characters' fortunes in a way that mirrors the poorly-calculated, high-stakes gamble taken by the Confederacy against the Union.

The novel opens on the eve of the Civil War in April 1861, and Mitchell immediately draws a contrast between the initial object of Scarlett O'Hara's affection, the educated and worldly Ashley Wilkes (who swiftly dashes Scarlett's hopes by marrying someone else) and her 60-year-old father, the Irish immigrant Gerald O'Hara. Whereas Ashley plays poker, the game and other activities that occupy Southern men (horseback riding, hunting, and drinking, for example) do not match his interest in the arts, literature, and ideas to which he was exposed while in Europe on his Grand Tour. The whole Wilkes family, Gerald observes, are too absorbed by "reading and dreaming the dear God knows what, when they'd better be spending their time hunting and playing poker as proper men should."[25]

The fact that Ashley beat Gerald out of two hundred dollars in a poker game, as Scarlett reminds him, doesn't move Gerald from his position. "Ashley can ride with the best and play poker with the best," Gerald acknowledges. "He can do all those things, but his heart's not in it. That's why I say he's queer." He fully intends the slight against Wilkes' masculinity.[26]

Gerald enthusiastically became "in his own opinion, a Southerner" four decades earlier, shortly after emigrating from Ireland. His acclimation to the South came primarily from having "adopted its ideas and customs, as he understood them," including "poker and horse racing, red-hot politics and the code duello, States' rights and damnation to all Yankees, slavery and King Cotton, contempt for white trash and exaggerated courtesy to women."[27]

Poker tops the list, he thinks, as "the most useful of all Southern customs," not least because Gerald won his first slave in an all-night poker game on St. Simons Island off the Georgia coast. Gerald also won the 640-

A Pass Time, a lithograph by Winslow Homer showing soldiers from the Army of the Potomac playing cards (1863)

acre plantation he named Tara in another poker game in a Savannah saloon on a hot spring night. With four deuces Gerald bested his opponent's aces full, in an instant becoming the figure he yearned to be upon arriving in Georgia: a self-sufficient, slave-owning planter able to say he earned what he had by dint of "an unbefuddled Irish head and the courage to stake everything on a hand of cards."[28]

Poker is also significant to the back-story of Rhett Butler, the wealthy rogue from Charleston who serves in the Confederate Army during the war's latter stages and who becomes Scarlett's third husband (before leaving the South and Scarlett after becoming disillusioned with both). The novel particularly highlights Rhett's gambling, describing him also beating Gerald out of $500 in a poker game, then having Rhett tell Scarlett about his own father throwing him "out into the world without a cent and no training whatsoever to be anything but a Charleston gentleman, a good pistol shot and an excellent poker player." As Rhett explains to Scarlett, he subsequently "put my poker playing to excellent advantage and supported myself royally by gambling," much to his father's chagrin.[29]

In a later scene, Rhett's gains plot-turning information during a poker game with two drunk Yankee captains who unwittingly reveal to him more than just the value of their hands. Rhett's skill at poker contributes to an image of self-assured manhood, adding further to his stature as an independent figure who doesn't shy away from risk.

While the award-winning 1939 film adaptation makes less of Rhett's poker playing (nor is there any mention of how Gerald O'Hara came to own Tara), it does include a scene not in the novel in which Rhett (Clark Gable) plays poker in an Atlanta prison with his captor, a Union army major. The major wins a hand with two pair, kings and treys – one of many, apparently, as we soon learn Rhett is down $340 for the session. Rhett takes the loss of another hand in good spirits, saying, "You know, it's a pity we couldn't have fought the war out in a poker game. You'd have done better than General Grant with far less effort."[30]

There were in fact stories of Union and Confederate soldiers playing poker against one another between battles, such as one colorful account that first appeared in the St. Louis Globe Democrat and was syndicated in several U.S. newspapers some years after the war's conclusion.[31] The tale is attributed to a Confederate officer named Andrew Danner. The scene he describes takes place shortly after the conclusion of the brutal Battle of Shiloh in April 1862, a Union victory in which both sides suffered heavy casualties, with opposing troops posted a few hundred yards apart.

"We shot at each other until we got tired of the sport, then we swapped newspapers, coffee and tobacco," Danner explains. Soon "a daredevil young yankee corporal" brazenly walks into the Confederates' post "and asked us if we knew how to play draw poker." Danner and the others confirm they do, and after the corporal produces a deck of cards they sit down to play. Soon others follow his lead, with six Union men ultimately joining the game with their adversaries to play what Danner describes as "a wide-open game, forgetting that the cruel war was not over."

Danner enjoys the upper hand in the game, cleaning out everyone save the Yankee corporal until the fun is interrupted by the sound of a Yankee sergeant cocking his musket. With four men by his side, the sergeant declares the Union men under arrest as another horse arrives, startling all as it carries General Grant. "The blue coats got up looking like a lot of whipped schoolboys, and saluted their commander, who eyed them sternly as a sphinx." The Yankee corporal and other men are ordered to leave, and after removing a cigar from his mouth, Grant lingers to ask the Rebels a question.

"Who's ahead?" Grant asks. "Oh, we are," comes the response. "Those chumps you've brought down here can't play poker a little bit." Danner steps forward quickly to qualify his colleague's immodesty. "'But they can fight, General,' I remarked. 'Have to sometimes,' said Grant, dryly, and rode away."

The card playing of Civil War combatants was pursued with the same variety of motives as other poker players before and after – for profit or for fun, as an amusing diversion or with great seriousness. Of course, as Rhett's reflection to the Yankee major grimly acknowledges, no matter how high the stakes were in such games, they always paled in comparison with the much greater ones faced by the soldiers. More than six hundred thousand perished either in combat or by starvation and disease.

In any event, the Civil War undoubtedly helped accelerate the game's spread throughout the U.S. After the South's surrender and President Andrew Johnson's declaration of the end of fighting on May 9, 1865, the survivors took poker back to their home states, increasing the game's popularity and further intensifying its cultural impact during subsequent decades.

7   Poker in Clubs

In addition to the games played on steamboats, in saloons, and in military encampments poker also grew popular in the latter decades of the 19th century in private clubs. These establishments not only furnished ready contexts for games between members, but often also provided a kind of cover for players in jurisdictions where gambling was illegal. While many states established prohibitions and/or restrictions on gambling, the clubs could promote regular poker games among known parties where the risk of being cheated, physically harmed, or subject to being raided and shut down was often reduced. The clubs were also a refuge for those who would have liked to have played poker at home but who could not, for whatever reason – say, a disapproving spouse.

Gentlemen's clubs were founded in most major American cities during the 19th and 20th centuries, organized with varying degrees of administrative formality and exclusivity as places for men of similar interests to fraternize. Precursors to some of these establishments can be found among the famous 18th-century London clubs of St. James's Street and Piccadilly. Some, like White's and Brooks's (formerly Almack's), became notorious for their wildly popular gambling rooms in which members eagerly bet on cards, dice, and other games of chance. The many gambling dens and houses that began appearing in the U.S. during the 1820s and 1830s (first in the south and east, then spreading west) also bear relation to these men's clubs. However, as nicknames including "wolf-traps" and "skinning houses" or "brace rooms" suggest, they operated more as businesses designed to extricate as much money as possible from unwitting marks than as social settings.

Where to Find an Honorable, Discreet Game
Besides exploring steamboat poker, journalist David A. Curtis' 1899 book *Queer Luck* also provides a useful introduction to the idea of a poker club, at least in this historical setting. The book presents a collection of poker stories originating from "one of those up-town club-rooms that are so quietly kept as to be entirely unknown to the police and general public" in New York City.[1]

While the stories Curtis shares are generally marked by extraordinary hands and outcomes and a few eccentric characters, they tend to emphasize camaraderie over conflict, differing sharply with the antagonistic tales involving steamboat sharps and Old West gunslingers. The opening story "Why He Quit the Game" sets the tone. It is an account of an entertaining session of five-card draw jacks-or-better involving players named only by their professions: the Editor, the Congressman, the Colonel, the Doctor, and the Lawyer. As the evening nears its end, the stakes have been raised and an enormous pot builds in which the Lawyer's straight flush beats the Colonel's four aces. The story doesn't conclude with the showdown, however, and as the Lawyer soberly rakes the huge pot the others remain tense wondering whether "some strange climax was coming, and none could even guess what it could be."[2]

If the game had taken place in the card parlor of the *River Belle* along the Mississippi or in a darkened saloon in Dodge City or Tombstone, we might well expect the revelation of marked cards or bottom dealing followed by gunplay. Instead, the Lawyer gives the money back to the Colonel, confessing that he has "stepped across the border line of dishonor" during the hand. Additionally, he says he has now resolved to quit poker.[3] What was his transgression? He mistakenly put money in the pot belonging to a client, and had he lost the hand could not have immediately replaced what he had taken. The contrast with Mark Twain's Jim Backus rising up with weapon drawn and roaring to others about his status as a "professional gambler" at the conclusion of "The Professor's Yarn" could not be more glaring.

The Lawyer's principled action exemplifies the "honor" that marks the club games and how their participants share a kind of obligation to play square. The idea returns in Curtis' final story, titled "The Club's Last Game," in which a couple of regulars in an otherwise friendly, low-stakes weekly game end up revealing themselves to be "professionals." Unsurprisingly, their lack of honesty with the others causes the game to be discontinued.

Cheating, of course, remained a risk even in such apparently friendly games. Even so, the club often tends to represent a kind of safe haven in these poker stories, a place where players could go when other alternatives weren't available. As Curtis' narrator explains in the book's final entry, clubs well serve poker players who find themselves living in areas where it is difficult to play without suffering society's censure, "where you have to keep very quiet about your card playing unless you don't give a rap for your standing in the business community, to say nothing of your social position."[4]

The Thompson Street Poker Club
by Henry Guy Carleton (1888)

The Thompson Street Poker Club

Another notable example of the poker "club report" provides an interesting contrast to *Queer Luck*. The famous Thompson Street Poker Club stories, written by humorist Henry Guy Carleton for *Life* magazine, feature a cast of mainly African American players. Carleton's stories are occasionally grouped with other late 19th-century examples of "black humor" or "slice of life" representations of urban blacks, although they arguably fit within the tradition of minstrel shows and other forms of entertainment created by whites and demeaning to blacks.

The son of a famous Union general, Carleton was a playwright and inventor credited with introducing early versions of smoke detectors and fire alarms. Prior to his first comedies making it to Broadway, Carleton served as managing editor for *Life* upon its debut in 1883, and it was in that capacity that he contributed his stories about an imaginary Manhattan

Poker & Pop Culture

poker club, presenting the tales as minutes of a committee's meetings. The stories proved popular enough that a collection of 13 of them was published in a slim volume in the spring of 1884, titled *The Thompson Street Poker Club*. Carleton produced a sequel five years later, titled *Lectures Before the Thompson Street Poker Club*, containing six longer stories featuring the same cast of characters.

The stories are illustrated with drawings by E.W. Kemble, best known for having been the illustrator for Mark Twain's *Adventures of Huckleberry Finn* (1884). In fact, it was after seeing Kemble's work in *Life* that Twain got in touch with the artist and eventually got him to agree to illustrate his landmark novel.

The Thompson Street stories include several familiar scenarios from other poker fiction. For example, one titled "The Scraped Tray" reaches a climax with a draw-poker hand being bet and raised for all the two players possess, then ends with a showdown of four kings versus four aces. (Twain's "The Professor's Yarn," published around the same time, is among countless tales with the same denouement.) A twist here is the manner of the cheating involved to produce such a showdown: one player has used a razor to scrape a three of diamonds to appear to be an ace. Indeed, the "razzer" is the favored weapon used to settle disputes in the Thompson Street games. The opening story in the collection – "Two Jacks an' a Razzer" – is essentially a variation of the old Wild Bill Hickok story in which the lawman claims to have a full house with three aces and one six, then produces his pistol and announces "Here is the other six."

In common with other stories of the era in which black characters appear, an invented dialect is used to represent characters' speech and distinguish them from the narrator's standard English. Titles include "Triflin' Wif Prov'dence," "Dar's No Suckahs in Hoboken," and "Dat's Gamblin,'" for example. Kemble's caricature-like illustrations similarly play upon stereotypes, although not as blatantly as found elsewhere. Characters are given inspired names like Professor Brick, Mr. Cyanide Whiffles, Mr. Tooter Williams, and Elder Jubilee Anderson. The Rev. Thankful Smith is also a frequent participant, and in one story has to answer for himself after making an aggressive raise. "Dat's not de speret ob de Gospil," his opponent complains, to which the reverend responds, "Dis ain't no prar meetin.'"[5]

Much of the humor in Carleton's stories stems from the running gag of mapping a sometimes unruly poker game onto the civilized proceedings of a committee meeting. That said, one cannot ignore the racial angle of fun being had at the characters' expense, with the less "civilized" black poker club functioning something like a parody of the more refined version referenced in *Queer Luck*. (Later the two Thompson Street titles were sold along with another collection from 1888 titled *The Mott Street Poker Club*

A poker game at the club gets busted (or does it?) in *A Cure for Pokeritis* (1912)

written by Alfred Trumble in which the activities of a group of Asian players in Chinatown are presented with markedly less racial sensitivity.)

Prescribing *A Cure for Pokeritis*

The 1912 short film *A Cure for Pokeritis,* directed by Laurence Trimble for Vitagraph, is among the very first examples of poker in film, and it provides another depiction of poker in clubs.

The one-reeler features John Bunny, one of the country's most famous comic celebrities at the time and star of more than 150 silent films. The rotund comedian frequently played the role of a henpecked husband, often appearing opposite Flora Finch as one of cinema's first comedy teams. *A Cure for Pokeritis* typifies that formula, pitting the two against one another and making poker the wedge that divides them.

Following an initial title card – "A game of poker. Loser again." – the story opens on a bustling poker club where multiple tables are in action, likely located in New York (the Vitagraph Studios were in Brooklyn). Bunny plays George Brown, who is shown departing the club and stopping to borrow money from another player to cover his fare home. He returns home late, endures a berating from his wife Mary, and tries to smooth things over by swearing to her he'll never play poker again.

A week passes, and George receives an invite to be initiated into the "Sons of the Morning," a men's lodge that meets every Wednesday night. According to the terms of the lodge, failure to appear incurs a fee of ten dollars, thus giving Mary no choice but to agree to her husband's participation. Of course it's all a ruse, as the "Sons of the Morning" is a cover for the same weekly poker game at the club where Brown had been playing before.

The plan works until George starts talking in his sleep, giving away his secret to his wife. Mary recruits strait-laced Cousin Freddie to help with her plight, and his investigation exposes George's subterfuge. Freddie and Mary host "an indignation meeting" for other wives angry about their husbands' poker playing, while Freddie plots a course of action. With the help of his own club – a Bible club – Freddie and his colleagues dress up as policemen and conduct a faux raid on George's poker game, with the wives in tow.[6] Fears of arrest soon dissolve into animated expressions of relief among the players, with George and Mary's film-ending embrace apparently signaling his having once and for all agreed to stop playing poker.

The club in *Pokeritis* is conspicuously presented as having been contrived as a poker retreat for the men. Another less than subtle idea put forth by the film's title is that poker represents a kind of disease or illness. The women, as organized by Cousin Freddie, directly evoke the many female-led temperance groups of the era whose influence ultimately helped create conditions for the passage of the Volstead Act and the 18th amendment heralding the era of prohibition in 1920. Such groups often also had religious affiliations, here provided by Freddie's Bible club. Though presented in a humorous vein, the association of poker and gambling with other vices in need of a "cure" is clear enough and would be recognized by audiences as representative of a common view that clubs like George's were detrimental to American society.

The Thanatopsis Pleasure and Inside Straight Club

After the First World War, a number of social and cultural changes occurred during a period of relative growth and prosperity in the United States. School children learning American history are taught to remember the "Roaring Twenties" as a booming decade, a time marked by the introduction of mass-produced automobiles, of planes that could fly from coast to coast, of motion pictures with sound, "speakeasies," "flappers," and radios providing a constant soundtrack of jazz music. Card games were among the many fancies that occupied Americans in the period preceding the stock market crash of 1929 and the Great Depression that followed.

As Ben Yagoda notes in *About Town: The New Yorker and the World It Made*, "part of the unreal frivolity of the twenties was that intelligent people should have occupied themselves with card, board, and parlor games to a degree not seen before or since." As an example, Yagoda speaks of how members of the famed Algonquin Round Table – a group of writers, actors, and wits who met daily for lunch at the Algonquin Hotel in Manhattan – would constantly battle with one another at "cribbage, backgammon, obscure word games, pachisi, casino, [and] hearts," among other forms of competition. However, "the most important game was poker."[7]

The group's daily gatherings began in 1919 and continued over the next decade-plus. Members included some of America's best known newspaper columnists, actors, poets, playwrights, and critics, which meant their ongoing poker game was perhaps one of the most famous of the era. Among the group's charter members were Franklin Pierce Adams (noted columnist for various New York newspapers), Harold Ross (founder of *The New Yorker*), Robert Benchley (editor of *Vanity Fair*), George S. Kaufman (playwright), and Dorothy Parker (writer). Actors Tallulah Bankhead and Harpo Marx also became regulars at the Algonquin, as did the composer Irving Berlin and producer and screenwriter Herman J. Mankiewicz. Membership was never constant, and in all there were probably three dozen or more individuals associated with the "Vicious Circle," an early name applied to the group for its members' wickedly savage wit. The Algonquin Round Table provided opportunities both to socialize and to share ideas, with many of those ideas eventually disseminated through the wide array of the group's cultural productions. Like the round table of Arthurian legend, this one exerted significant influence on the culture at large.

In her history of the Algonquin Round Table, Margaret Case Harriman, daughter of Algonquin Hotel owner Frank Case, says the poker club was founded by Adams in Paris during the war where he and fellow *Stars and Stripes* writers regularly played in a bistro. The games and club then continued after their return home. She reports how games took place each Saturday in the clubroom on the hotel's second floor, often lasting all night and sometimes all weekend, and that "the clubroom in the Algonquin usually looked, after a Poker session, as though carnage had taken place there" – much to her father's chagrin.[8] Club members were joined occasionally by non-Round Table players when seats needed to be filled. Adams is credited with having come up with the name for the group: "The Thanatopsis Pleasure and Inside Straight Club," which plays on the name of a woman's study group – the Thanatopsis Club – appearing in Sinclair Lewis' 1920 satirical novel *Main Street*.

It might sound like an especially grim name for a poker club, given that "thanatopsis" is the practice of thinking about or meditating on death. One can sense the dark humor in the choice, though, considering how it associates playing poker – and, perhaps, foolishly gunning for inside straights – with thoughts of one's demise. The name also in a half-joking way referred to how most members of the club approached poker as a life-or-death affair, and Harriman shares examples of arguments and the occasional fight that would enliven the games.

The critic Alexander Woollcott once wrote a two-act play lampooning the club's games, although it was never published. Adams also sometimes reported on the sessions, and it is thanks to him that some of the more memorable quotes and witticisms from the game have survived. For example, Herbert Ransom, an actor who sometimes joined in the game, apparently wasn't particularly talented when it came to concealing from his opponents the value of his hand. Thus Adams once suggested that the club institute a new rule taking into account how bad Ransom's poker face was. "Anyone who looks at Ransom's face is cheating," Adams proposed.[9]

Another source for the club's activities is a piece written by Heywood Hale Broun whose parents – the columnist Heywood Broun and the women's rights activist Ruth Hale – both played in the game. In the 1960s Broun contributed an article to *American Heritage Magazine* titled "A Full House" in which he shared several anecdotes of what he called "as colorful a group of poker players as ever sat down together outside a Bret Harte short story."[10] According to Broun, the group generally played three rounds of five-card draw, followed by a round of five-card stud, with "no wild cards or seven-card games." Women occasionally sat in on the game, with their participation sometimes providing the impetus for ongoing debates about women's equality (although Harriman reports "women were not encouraged to play").[11]

Broun's summary statement about the game's significance to its members suggests it provided something especially meaningful to those who participated – namely, a chance to stop being so damn clever all the time and enjoy the "pleasure" of competition and each other's company. "The general feeling was one of unbuttoned relaxation," Broun writes. "The Thanatopsis Club was perhaps the one place where all the erstwhile small-town boys who had to slick their hair down and talk fancy most of the time could get off the treadmill of sophistication for a few hours."[12]

According to Harriman, the typical buy-in was $500, although a few stories speak of players winning and losing thousands. One account suggests Harpo Marx won as much as $30,000 in one game, though Marx himself insisted he never won more than "a few thousand dollars" in a session.[13]

The Marx Brothers continue their poker game while the house burns down around them in this lost scene from *Horse Feathers* (1932)

Poker & Pop Culture

His autobiography *Harpo Speaks* tells more about poker's connection to the Marx Brothers, including the story of how the brothers got their nicknames during a game of five-card stud played backstage between shows in Illinois around 1914. As Harpo explains, the monologist Art Fisher was dealing a hand when he jokingly invented nicknames for the others. "A hole card for – 'Harpo.' A card for 'Chicko,'" Fisher said, landing on the names because of Harpo's harp playing and Chico's girl-chasing. Fisher added the "o" after the fashion of a popular comic strip of the day, *Knocko the Monk* (a.k.a. *Sherlocko the Monk*). Groucho's name came from the "grouch-bag" in which he carried his money, while Gummo's came from his "gumshoe way of prowling around backstage and sneaking up on people." Later when Gummo left and their younger brother joined, he followed suit by adopting the name Zeppo. "You never could tell what you might get dealt in a poker game in those days," Harpo's account concludes.[14]

According to another story, the Marx Brothers' first Broadway show, *I'll Say She Is* (1924), was kick-started by financial backing from another acquaintance from the poker table. The compilation sketch show featured a courtroom sequence in which Chico plays draw poker with a judge. At one point he asks Harpo to cut the cards, and the latter chops the deck in half with a hatchet. The gag was reprised in the 1932 film *Horse Feathers*, a film from which another scene was cut in which the four brothers play poker while Huxley College burns down around them. (Yet another possibly apocryphal story involves Zeppo losing a Beverly Hills house in a poker game.)

The Thanatopsis Club games eventually wound down and the club dissolved by the early 1930s. Harriman explains the primary reason was the same as has ruined other club poker games: the stakes got too high, and "the game degenerated into a cutthroat project rather than a friendly gathering."[15] The "unreal frivolity of the twenties" was over.

The California Clubs
Though the early poker clubs generally operated outside of the law, they were often tolerated by authorities and found themselves in a kind of liminal space of uncertain legality. The concept of the poker club found a new model, however, following the appearance of legal, licensed clubs in California in the late 1930s, which turned the small suburb of Gardena into the self-proclaimed "Poker Capital of the World."

It all started with a bold bet by businessman Ernest "Ernie" Primm, who seized on more than half a century's ambiguity among Californian lawmakers and judges regarding poker's legality. Poker had long been popular in California, well suiting the risk-taking spirit shared by gold seekers arriving in the late 1840s with games further fueled by the spoils they had mined.

Writing in 1888 about poker's progress in the state, historian Hubert Howe Bancroft shares an opinion proclaiming "California is the land where the game has been most favorably received and industriously cultivated as a science." Bancroft further connected poker's popularity "rising with the march of civilization."[16] An 1879 prohibition in the state's constitution against many different kinds of gambling did not include draw poker among the list of forbidden games. Further legislation in 1891 once more outlawed gambling without including draw. That led to a 1911 opinion by the state's Attorney General Ulysses S. Webb that once again specifically distinguished draw poker from other chance-based games, thereby keeping games going in the state over the next couple of decades.

Primm had run illegal casinos in Los Angeles during the 1930s, though eventually found it prudent to leave the city ahead of a new mayor's crackdown. Fifteen miles south in Gardena, Primm opened a gambling club in 1936 where draw poker eventually became the featured game. A raid on the room (and others) led to a courtroom showdown, with the judge ultimately following the 1911 ruling and exempting draw poker as a skill game, thereby allowing the clubs to operate as long as the community was in favor of their doing so, as was the case in Gardena.[17] Primm was able to continue operating his club, then opened a second. Before long a half-dozen were up and running in Gardena: the Embassy (later the El Dorado), the Monterey, the Rainbow, the Normandie, the Gardena, and the Horseshoe.

Max Votolato has extensively chronicled the scene in both his 2015 documentary *Freeway City* and 2017 book *Gardena Poker Clubs: A High-Stakes History*. Votolato describes how the games ran similarly to the way in which those in private clubs might, even though they were revenue creators both for the clubs' owners and for Gardena. (The clubs paid tax as well as ever increasing license and table fees.) Players dealt themselves and were responsible for self-policing the action while club staff provided additional security and other services. Despite their legal sanction, various political and business machinations were still required in order for the clubs to stay open, usually to retain the support of the community and those in power. Primm and other club owners made philanthropic donations to various projects and charities in Gardena. Frequent challenges from anti-gambling groups made the continuance of the clubs a central campaign issue with every election, and advertising on the poker tables helped inform patrons which candidates to vote for to keep the rooms open. Such elections became national news, such as in 1954 when *Life* magazine told its readers of "three pro-poker men" who had won seats on the Gardena five-person city council, thereby thwarting efforts of "local churchmen" to change the law. The headline "Poker Wins Over Prayers" sat above an article describing how the club owners "still held all the aces."[18] The clubs

Inside the Gardena Club, ca. early 1970s

also engaged in various other public relations efforts, including publishing a magazine about Gardena and giving out coupons for children to go to Disneyland, all of which helped ensure the cardrooms – very deliberately called "clubs" and not "casinos" – retained vital support.

Over subsequent decades Gardena became a true poker destination whose regular, popular games provided an alternative to those found in the glitzy casinos across the border in Nevada. "Gardena called itself the Poker Capital of the World," recounts Mike Caro, alluding to a phrase used in advertisements. "And it really was."[19] The dense collection of cardrooms – and, for a time, relative paucity of other types of businesses – transformed Gardena into a kind of "gambling town," seen from the outside by some as a mini-version of Las Vegas, although the scene was quite modest by comparison. Blaine Nicholson, a retired ad man who did public relations for Primm, explains in *Freeway City* how his former boss had envisioned the Gardena clubs as communal gathering spots for poker enthusiasts. "You could come there and play poker among friends, and every hour a chip girl

The Gardena Club boardman, ca. early 1970s

would show up and would collect money from everyone that was there," Nicholson says. Despite such an idyllic vision, Votolato documents multiple violent incidents (including murders) associated with the clubs, which helped ensure both their ongoing notoriety and constantly uneasy relationship with the community.

Meanwhile the games became increasingly competitive, especially at the higher stakes. By the 1960s and 1970s they had attracted many serious, full-time players described as "professionals" by anthropologist David Hayano in his 1982 book *Poker Faces: The Life and Work of Professional Card Players*. Hayano studies the players in the clubs as though they were a self-contained subculture, not unlike his approach when writing his dissertation on the isolated tribes of Papua New Guinea, the only difference being Hayano himself participated as a player, becoming part of the "world" he was examining. "Poker... is not a spectator sport," Hayano states. "The real action in poker is concealed.... The observable movements of chips wagered and cards dealt do very little to reveal the genuine heart of the game."[20]

Admitting he applies the term "professionals" somewhat loosely and that the players themselves would more likely use terms like "*hustler*, *player*, *rounder*, or no special title at all,"[21] Hayano meticulously divides high-volume players into categories according to their respective attitudes toward the game while also documenting details of their habits and demographic makeup. He additionally sheds light on "the relentless instability and uncertainty of day-to-day gambling" and how a significant number of players struggle with thoughts about their lives lacking meaning. "Many people, including poker players themselves, do not see card-playing as particularly productive," he writes, adding how the life of the poker pro is beset by "existential" worrying. Also, for many full-time players, "there is no finality of gain and no peak existence, except perhaps winning a major tournament." The game just goes on and on and on, a situation that "manifests itself in an existential, if not socio-psychological, kind of imbalance."[22]

Hayano characterizes the card clubs themselves as hermetic spaces, isolated from external influence much like the remote tribes he previously studied. "In contrast to the Old West and riverboat gamblers, most professional gamblers today operate in a completely distinct social and legal environment," Hayano writes.[23] In other words, while the games of old in saloons and on steamboats might have encouraged a lot of interaction between regular players and "normal" folks, the games he observed and participated in take place in closed-off "small-life worlds, with all their arcane symbols and skills."[24]

In a 1967 *Sports Illustrated* article profiling California card clubs, table tennis star and sports writer Dick Miles shares a similar impression conveyed in part by the piece's title "Lowball in a Time Capsule." Miles describes the games and players as existing in a "world of their own, isolated from outside life and its problems." It seems to him as though "in some prehistoric age they had been quick-frozen and tucked into a time capsule until, thawed by the California sun, they resumed their play heedless of the interruption."[25] Journalist David Spanier offers a less favorable assessment of the Gardena clubs in his 1977 book *Total Poker*, finding them "totally lacking in atmosphere" and "the scene... just too mechanical" when compared with his much favored Las Vegas.[26] Financial author Aaron Brown played at the El Dorado a few dozen times when a college student, and in his 2006 book *The Poker Face of Wall Street* describes how he experienced "the same timeless sense that the place existed in a different dimension from the everyday world."[27] He also found the games incredibly intense, one reason being the way the rooms' "economy" only allowed a very small percentage of Hayano's "professionals" to profit while the many "break-even" players struggled mightily. Meanwhile "tourists" and "hobbyists" were certain to lose. "Gardena is not a place to play poker for fun," judges Brown.[28]

Even so, all of these observers recognize in different ways the important social aspect of the California club games, especially for the older players. "Gambling seems only a partial motive for their play," Miles observes. "What matters as much to these veterans, apparently, is the sense of belonging... and the opportunity to shuffle through later life with their coevals, however competitive or hostile that mingling may be."[29]

The fictional California Club in the 1974 feature film *California Split* provides an uncanny recreation of this world. Directed by Robert Altman, who co-produced the film with screenwriter Joseph Walsh, the movie presents a purposely non-glorified depiction of gambling, starting with a 10-minute sequence taking place in what looks for all the world to be an actual California card room, though was in fact manufactured on a set.

As the opening credits roll, we see a staff member manning the chalkboard with player lists, as the film's central characters Charlie (Elliott Gould) and Bill (George Segal) are separately assigned seats at a $10/$20 lowball table where they first meet. Players deal each other hands while griping incessantly about the cards they are dealt and the wasting of time for which they are being charged. Things then turn violent after a player named Lew (played by Walsh's brother, Edward) wrongly suspects collusion between Charlie and Bill during a hand in which Charlie takes the last of Lew's stack. As Mike Caro confirms, the players dealing themselves often meant that while "Old Gardena was a poker garden where money grew... there was also treachery, and you had to avoid the cheating. You dealt your own cards, which was fine, but so did they, and there was always danger."[30] Lew is enraged at Charlie, though Bill is the one who ends up taking a punch, and in the ensuing chaos, everyone scrambles to scoop up his or her chips. A later scene at the California Club in which Charlie and Bill get soundly beaten by a group of elderly ladies similarly bucks the trend in American cinema by presenting poker in a fashion much more realistic than romantic.

Having played in the Gardena clubs, screenwriter Walsh found the setting and those who inhabited it both compelling and entirely apt for a film intended to counter glamorized depictions of poker and gambling. Such an intention is evident from Walsh's colorful stage directions describing "POKER PARLOR - GARDENA, CALIFORNIA" kicking off an early draft of his screenplay: "It's not pretty, but it's neat looking, very neat! The tables are all full. Possibly a few hundred people or more grouped closely around each other, yet it's morgue-like quiet. The waitresses walk around professionally, serving full-course meals at the tables where the players eat and never miss a hand, ever ready for the kill. Eyes lazily, and at times furtively, glance around for any live ones that might enter the club."[31]

"It was strange… but it was fascinating," Walsh recalls.[32] "My brain was kind of cooking. I thought this *has* to be created one day [in a film]. This is a different world, my god! It doesn't exist in Chicago. It doesn't exist in Kentucky. It only is in California. In Gardena… it was a total novelty at the time…. This collage of the strangest people I've ever seen… was nothing like what had been presented ever before. I mean this was an eclectic group, playing for life and death out there. And surly!"

The filmmakers initially planned to shoot at the Gardena Club, but the idea had to be scuttled. "They could only give us four hours, and it had to be from 4 a.m. to 8 a.m., when basically they had only a few tables going," Walsh recalls. "Altman and I said no, the poker room has got to be central to this picture. We went to Leon Ericksen who was a genius at set design. He went down to see those clubs in Gardena, then we found this big empty dance hall somewhere in Hollywood and took the bars out of it and he built that room."

The California Club is so realistic, it has even fooled veterans of the very card rooms upon which it was based. "To this day guys will tell me 'oh no, no… that *was* the Gardena Club or that was the Normandie Club – I *played* there. And I say 'really?' And I ask them how much they'd like to bet." The sequence took 10 days to shoot, with many seats around the tables filled by gamblers Walsh knew as well as extras from Synanon, a drug rehabilitation program located in Santa Monica. They were "people who had been gambling their whole life," Walsh says. "That recreation is so good it fools the gambler… you are seeing the real thing."

To borrow Miles' metaphor, the film and other recollections of the Gardena clubs function a bit like a time capsule insofar as they together preserve a particular variety of poker that no longer exists. In 1980 the nearby city of Bell voted to legalize poker, heralding the opening of more clubs. The Monterey Club closed that year, with owner Primm passing away in 1981. Then in May 1987 stud and Texas hold'em were made legal in both Los Angeles and Santa Cruz counties. "Legalized Vegas-Style Poker Offers Area Casinos New Deal" went the July 12, 1987 headline in the *Los Angeles Times* above an article describing the changed law and bright prospects for larger properties seeking to "compete for the first time on equal footing with casinos in Nevada." "'Forget Vegas!' and play 'America's favorite games' close to home" an advertisement for the Commerce Casino advised.[33]

Having lost their unique status, the era of smaller clubs' prominence swiftly faded. Most of the other original "Gardena six" clubs closed during the 1980s and 1990s, with the Normandie the last to shut down in 2016. Larry Flynt's Hustler Casino opened in 2000 on the site of the old El Dorado, with the Normandie also replaced by another Flynt property, the transition emblematic of the move from poker-only clubs to Vegas-like flash.

Back to the New York Underground

Aside from the clubs in California and casinos in Nevada, where gambling had been legal since 1931, authorities in the rest of the country continued to resist legalizing gambling in their states. It meant that card clubs populating many major American cities all remained outside the law – including a number of prosperous underground clubs in New York.

With a little effort (and knowing the right people from whom to earn an invite), the NYC clubs could be found in a variety of locations, most often basements or otherwise inconspicuous rooms tucked away in office suites, self-storage units, tenement houses, high-rise condos, bars and restaurants, social clubs, and even churches and synagogues. Of course, those who played there were often well served to guard against cheating and collusion perpetrated by the clubs' regulars routinely seeking to swindle those passing through.

The "underground" nature of these clubs meant they largely escaped wider notice, with only stories of raids or the occasional investigative feature highlighting their existence. Much as consistent winners in poker understand the benefit of winning quietly, poker clubs able to keep a low profile and spread safe, well-managed games were more likely to prosper than those that did not. One example was the Mayfair Club, which somehow remained secretive despite enjoying a storied past as a renowned bridge club, earning more attention after producing some of poker's most successful tournament players, then having the spotlight shone on it again after helping inspire a major feature film.

Founded in 1943 on the lower floor of a high-rise apartment building near Gramercy Park, the Mayfair Bridge Club (as it was initially known) attracted many top players with proprietor and multiple championship winner Harry Fishbein one of the country's best. Another great of the game Alvin Roth (also an eventual American Contract Bridge League Hall of Famer) succeeded Fishbein as "Master of the Mayfair" in 1966. Roth managed the club into the mid-1990s, overseeing its 1988 move to the basement of another apartment building on East 25th Street. Events including Roth's ascension and the club's relocation earned notice in *The New York Times* via Alan Truscott's daily bridge columns.

Truscott also noted Roth's intention "to enlarge the Mayfair's bridge activities, which in recent years have taken second place to other card games and to backgammon."[34] The *Times* occasionally reported on other goings-on at the Mayfair, too, highlighting the club as a destination for backgammon enthusiasts while warning "casual players" about the financial risks of playing. "This is an establishment where a lot of money changes hands," Peter Kerr explained in 1984. "Players here are experts and they have a predilection toward huge stakes."[35]

Despite Roth's efforts to revive bridge, backgammon continued to be the Mayfair's primary game into the 1980s, with gin rummy and eventually poker also becoming favorites. Those games were also played at a high level, with the eventual poker accomplishments of several of the club's regulars at the World Series of Poker drawing further attention.

Stu Ungar, the troubled genius who won three WSOP Main Event titles before dying at 45 of a heart condition brought on by drug abuse, was said to have demonstrated his prowess at gin rummy at the Mayfair as a 13-year-old in the mid-1960s. Ungar's connection with the club wasn't especially remarked upon when he won his first bracelets in the early 1980s, but further success in Las Vegas by other Mayfair alumni brought attention to their common background. In the 1987 WSOP Main Event no fewer than four Mayfair Club players reached the final two tables: Howard Lederer (who took fifth), Dan Harrington (sixth), Mickey Appleman (eighth), and Jay Heimowitz (11th). The following year another Mayfair player, Erik Seidel, finished runner-up in the WSOP Main Event, and Harrington later won the title in 1995. These players and others like Steve Zolotow, Paul Magriel, and Jason Lester earned enough success in tournaments to extend the Mayfair Club's reputation beyond the five boroughs.

In late 1995, band manager and music producer Brian Koppelman first received an invitation to play poker at the Mayfair Club. Like others he entered the lobby, then descended a staircase where he was examined via a security camera. He was then buzzed through a metal door. After passing through another lobby he was buzzed through a second time to enter the club, encountering a front desk where players cashed in and out. As he went on to write, Koppelman lost all he had brought with him that night playing Texas hold'em, though he returned many times as he gained experience both at the game and at enduring the emotional swings associated with winning and losing. He also found inspiration both from the setting and the characters sitting around the tables, "men with names like Joel Bagels, Freddy the Watch, Joe Angel, Johnny Handsome, Johnny Dark and Johnny Boy, who was neither a boy nor named Johnny."[36]

Koppelman excitedly told his friend David Levien: "We gotta write about this world.… The setting is amazing." The pair continued to frequent the Mayfair together, spending what Koppelman recalls as "a couple of weeks of dedicated, 'Let's go every night and write down everything we hear.'"[37] They eventually produced a screenplay with a plot centered on the world of New York poker. The film was released in 1998, titled *Rounders*.

Just as *California Split* recreated the California clubs, *Rounders* shares something of the Mayfair and other New York underground poker venues via a fictional approximation, the Chesterfield. Mike Scelza, a daytime manager at the Mayfair, worked on the film as a consultant, helping the screenwriters, set designers, and director John Dahl with the recreation. With a clean look and the patina of professionalism, the stylishly furnished club incorporates several details from the Mayfair, including the security camera and buzzing-in procedure, a hostess being wired to signal the local precinct should trouble arise, a computer database used to track players' visits and to manage the allotment of credit, and food and drink delivered by a wait staff. The plot further reveals that cheating is not tolerated at the Chesterfield nor is the failure to honor debts.

Providing a contrast in the film is the seedier club run by Russian mobster Teddy KGB (played by John Malkovich). Teddy was a general nod to the Eastern European proprietors who earned some NYC clubs the nickname of "goulash joints" or "ghoulies," as well as a more specific reference to a real-life character nicknamed Eddie KGB often found hosting a game at another New York club. Teddy's club symbolically represents a kind of proving ground for the film's young poker-playing protagonist Mike McDermott (Matt Damon), a point ably delivered via hands played between Mike and Teddy KGB in scenes that bookend the film. In some ways, the story arc reflects Koppelman's own initial experience at the Mayfair, which began with him "cleaned out" by Joey Bagels (upon whom another character, Joey Knish, was based) and other "men who knew how to fold early, bet strong and run the table like Rudy runs the city," before he returned to prove at least competitive.[38]

While *Rounders* had limited influence upon its initial release, within a few years the film had a role to play in the ignition of the poker boom in the United States, in particular introducing no-limit Texas hold'em to many new players. Meanwhile its homage to the Mayfair soon became an elegy when the club shut down in 2000. It was one of many that fell victim to then-mayor Rudy Guiliani and his "Quality of Life" campaign of initiatives.

However, the games persisted, and during the mid-2000s clubs like Playstation, the Fairview, the New York Players Club, and the Straddle continued to draw high volume despite constant raids. Along with the busts, Yankee infielder Alex Rodriguez turning up at the Broadway Club in Chelsea following a late-season game in 2005 to play alongside poker pro Phil Hellmuth earned media attention. Headlines of a different sort followed a late 2007 robbery gone wrong at another club called City Limits operating on the seventh floor of a Manhattan commercial building, resulting in the shooting death of 55-year-old math teacher, Frank Desena. A couple of years later after having run high-stakes games in Hollywood, Molly Bloom set up shop on the Upper West Side (where Rodriguez again would surface), later detailing her efforts to negotiate the uncertain landscape in a 2014 bestselling tell-all *Molly's Game*.

The idea of the private poker club continues to evolve, with the arrival of online poker and associated forums adding still more virtual "communities" of players all over the globe. Despite the fact that at its heart poker is a game played by individuals, the game's social aspect makes the formation of such clubs inevitable.

8 Poker on the Bookshelf

For much of poker's early history, the prevailing opinion among writers was that the game was not only primarily a luck-based affair in which skill was minimally important, but it was also an invitation for the unwary to be mercilessly fleeced by able and willing card sharps. As we've already seen, the position was succinctly summarized by William Brisbane Dick in *The American Hoyle: Or, Gentleman's Handbook of Games* (1864) when he described poker as "emphatically a game of chance" in which "there are easier ways of cheating, or playing with marked cards, than in any other game."[1]

Similar reservations are reflected in the earliest books on poker rules and strategy, several of which seem as interested in warning readers about the perils of five-card draw as in highlighting the path to winning play. That might seem a paradox – writing books that show readers how to play poker while encouraging them not to do so. However, as some of the authors explain, arming yourself with better knowledge of odds, probabilities and other nuances of game-play can be an important first step toward avoiding poker's pitfalls. Taken together, the books provide ready evidence of the game's growing popularity as well as its constant evolution and adaptability. Despite all, these early rule books do go some way to help counter the idea of poker being "emphatically a game of chance." Additionally, some clearly demonstrate how many players were curious about how to win *without* nefarious means.

The Congressman Who Accidentally Wrote a Poker Book
Poker players from all eras have been accustomed to legislators' unending debates over their favorite game, so it is perhaps surprising to learn that the person often credited with writing the very first book about draw poker was a former United States Congressman.

It was by accident, really, that Robert C. Schenck, once a member of the House of Representatives, came to author a short book explaining how to play five-card draw. After representing his native Ohio in Congress from 1843-51, Schenck served as an ambassador in South America, supported Lincoln in the 1860 election, fought with the Union as a general in the Civil War, and served once again in Congress as one of Ohio's representatives from 1863-70. Upon losing a close race for reelection in 1870, Schenck was appointed by President Ulysses S. Grant as Minister to the United Kingdom (i.e., an ambassador) and the following summer began a five-year deployment to Britain.

While there Schenck courted controversy by agreeing to represent the Emma Silver Mining Company of Utah as a nominal director, encouraging British investment in the mine. Schenck drew criticism for the position even before the mine stopped producing silver and investors lost their fortunes, by which time he had already stepped away from the company. Diplomatic immunity shielded him from lawsuits in the U.K., though did not protect him from increased censure both overseas and back home. He remained in the position through early 1876, but faced a U.S. House investigation of his conduct on his return. He escaped punishment despite lawmakers' severe dressing down of Schenck in their report, effectively ending his political career in ignominious fashion.

While in London, Schenck also wrote his brief primer, *Draw. Rules for Playing Poker*. Some have suggested he produced the book in order to introduce the American game to Queen Victoria, although in truth it was following a weekend of card playing with friends in Somerset that Schenck was asked by his host to write down the rules. He was later surprised to see his work reprinted and circulated by his hosts as a book. Schenck's

FOR THE PROMOTION OF PUBLIC MORALS.

THE FLOWERY PATH TO WEALTH

The Intensely Interesting and Classical
American Game

DRAW POKER

AS

TAUGHT TO THE ENGLISH ARISTOCRACY

BY

MAJ. GEN. ROBERT C. SCHENCK

(OF EMMA MINE NOTORIETY)

LATE UNITED STATES AMBASSADOR AND MINISTER
TO THE COURT OF ST. JAMES.

(COPYRIGHT SECURED)

1878.

Title page of an 1878 edition of Robert Schenck's *Draw Poker*, printed without his knowledge little "how-to" manual first surfaced in 1872, well after editions of the American *Hoyle* began to include references to poker (the first occurring in 1845). Schenck's slim volume nonetheless stands as what many regard the earliest example of a book entirely devoted to poker.

It is tempting to think an ex-Congressman and U.S. ambassador writing a poker book might indicate some sort of wider cultural acceptance of the game, but that wasn't quite the case. Schenck's rules were reprinted in full in *The New-York Tribune* in early 1875, and soon after he replied by letter to a reader curious about how he came to author such a book. Schenck's response recounts the story of his English friends' request and how "as a compliment" they had reprinted his rules and brief notes about draw poker strategy. He concludes he is "very sure that nobody can be more amazed or more annoyed" than his friends "that they have thus unwittingly brought down on me the wrath and reprehension of so many good people in America." Responding to another letter sent to the *Tribune* after it had reprinted Schenck's rules, the editor defended the author though not the game itself, dismissively referring to Schenck's subject matter as "so reprehensible a science as Draw-poker."[2] Subsequent reprintings of the original work continued to appear, some adding to their title pages a parenthetical reference to Schenck being "Of Emma Mine Notoriety." Thus poker was further associated with fraudulent financial schemes.

Eventually "Poker Bob Schenck," as he was sometimes derisively called in U.S. newspapers, came reluctantly to accept his status as the author of a poker book, and in 1880 oversaw the private printing of a new edition of the work by a Brooklyn printer. Schenck may no longer have been a U.S. ambassador, though with some trepidation he had more or less accepted his role as an ambassador of America's fastest growing card game. It was to this edition Schenck prefixed "The Author's Apology" repeating the same story he had told in the earlier letter, once more acknowledging the infamy the book had brought him. As for the content of the book, Schenck does a good job outlining the rules for five-card draw while including some strategy advice as well. The rules are essentially what we know of the game, describing the deal, an opening round of betting, the draw, a second round of betting, and (if necessary) the showdown. Meanwhile, the strategy tips also conform pretty well to later ideas of draw.

Schenck actually begins by stating "The deal is of no special value and anybody can begin."[3] However, here he seems to be referring more to the logistics of getting started rather than the significance of position; later advice suggests an understanding that position matters. Schenck also shows an awareness of the role bluffing can play in the game. "It is a great object to mystify your adversaries," he writes. "To this end it is permitted to chaff or talk nonsense, with a view of misleading your adversaries as to the value of your hand, but this must be without unreasonably delaying the game."[4] Schenck addresses the subject of tells as well, noting how "a skillful player will watch and observe what each player draws, the expression of his face, the circumstances and manner of betting, and judge, or try to judge, of the value of each hand opposed to him accordingly."[5] Toward the end Schenck offers some specific suggestions about how to play certain hands, and while these pointers hardly reach Mike Caro-levels of detail they do articulate commonly agreed-upon ideas about frequently-faced situations in five-card draw.

Schenck's concluding advice to the draw-poker player indicates the former Congressman possessed not only a solid understanding of the game, but a certain level-headedness that probably helped him at the tables. "The main elements of success in the game are: (1) *good luck;* (2) *good cards;* (3) *plenty of cheek;* and (4) *good temper*" he writes.[6] Regarding the latter element, despite his many travails Schenck seemed able enough to avoid "tilt" both at the poker tables and elsewhere. In his historical survey of games' impact upon American culture *Sportsmen and Gamesmen*, John Dizikes notes how "Schenck had come back to America in 1876 in what would have conventionally been thought of as a state of disgrace. But he seems not to have felt this or to have been the least bothered by his dismissal, keeping throughout the good temper that he had identified as one of the poker player's most necessary attributes."[7]

Schenck's book came to be referenced by practically everyone who wrote about poker strategy over the next few decades. Many stories were also circulated of Schenck's poker playing both during his time in Britain and after his return to America. In *Poker Stories* (1896), John F. B. Lillard shares an account of Schenck playing a game at the Langham Hotel in London for thousands of pounds with the Prince of Wales, a member of the Rothschild family, and "a real Duchess."[8] Lillard also includes several other stories of Schenck playing poker in later life, including a game that took place the week before his death, at 80, in the spring of 1890. One of the more notable hands involves Schenck and three politicians playing at the Blossom Club in New York City. All four players incredibly make seven-high straight flushes – apparently without any stacking of the deck. Later Herbert Asbury repeats the story of the four straight flushes, adding that Schenck "in his later years was accounted the best amateur in America."[9]

Despite his numerous achievements, Schenck's tiny book about poker became his most lasting legacy. A note by the editors of *Life* magazine a few weeks after his passing shows how the name Schenck would forever be associated with America's card game. "Many a man makes his fame out of the most unexpected materials," the editors wrote. "Who ever thought of General Schenck without thinking at once of poker? And yet General Schenck's poker was only an incident in a pretty active life."[10]

Conferring Upon Poker "the Dignity of Science"

Before Schenck's own 1880 edition of his book appeared, two other more substantial titles were published providing more thorough discussions of draw poker and how to play it. Both Henry T. Winterblossom's *The Game of Draw-Poker, Mathematically Illustrated* and John Blackbridge's *The Complete Poker-Player* offer ample evidence to promote poker's skill component and to show the game a worthy subject of study. But the books also share a number of warnings and reservations about the game, confirming how poker's increasing popularity had become unsettling to many.

Described on the title page as a "Professor of Mathematics," there was little secret at the time that "Henry T. Winterblossom" was not the author's actual name. An article in *The New York Times* soon after the book's publication in early 1875 declared the author "is understood to veil himself modestly under a pseudonym; and he is said to be a member of the Lotos Club."[11] The Lotos Club was a literary club founded in 1870 in New York City whose membership included many of the era's most famous artists and writers. One of its earliest members, Mark Twain, gave the club an informal, poker-related second name: the "Ace of Clubs." Even so, the club's constitution specifically prohibited "the games of poker, loo, and others known as round games" from the "amusements" permitted in the club house – perhaps explaining why "Winterblossom" chose to hide behind an assumed name.[12] Another possibility was the general opinion that poker's growing popularity posed a significant threat both to individuals and to American society as a whole, meaning even a relatively sober analysis of the game's mathematical truths could be construed as somehow destructive.

In a similar vein to Schenck's "Author's Apology," Winterblossom begins his book distancing himself from the idea that he might be mistaken for someone encouraging others to risk money on card games. "Draw-Poker is strictly a gambling game, and one which, if [readers] will take the author's advice, they will shun as they would a faro-table or a horse-race." It's okay *not* to play poker, Winterblossom assures his readers, reminding them "their position in society will not be imperilled in the least by the ignorance of this accomplishment" of learning the game.[13]

Winterblossom's wish to explain the odds and probabilities of draw poker is meant to encourage readers to be able to weigh more accurately the risks involved, thereby making the game better understood and less apt to be entered into recklessly. He focuses at length on starting hand selection in five-card draw ("what kind of hand one should stand on, and what kind he should throw up") and the importance of not falling victim to "the fundamental error of the 'bad player' (who is the representative of bad playing generally)... [who] wants to be in every hand." He even includes a helpful table that attempts to show how much different hands are improved by various draws, predating similar tables by a century or more.[14]

Winterblossom additionally covers bluffing, profiling opponents, sports-

Front cover of John Blackbridge's *The Complete Poker-Player* (1875)

manship and etiquette. The professor favors games with betting limits, although recognizes "the unlimited game" had started to gain favor. However one plays poker, though, Winterblossom shares the opinion of others that money is an essential element of the game. Or rather, a necessary evil. "Draw-Poker, unfortunately, is one of the few games that cannot be played so as to afford any pleasure, without the interchange of money," writes Winterblossom. "Indeed one might as well go on a gunning expedition with a blank-cartridge, as to play Poker for 'fun.'"[15]

Winterblossom signs off with a final nod toward debates about "the morality of card-playing," though wishes not to "enter the lists" and argue such matters. While not denying poker's opponents their position, he concludes: "It must be admitted, however, by its most bitter enemy that, as a source of recreation, when moderately indulged in, and stripped of its objectionable features, it presents advantages not to be obtained in any other amusement."[16] It's a modest, highly-qualified endorsement, but an endorsement nonetheless.

While Winterblossom shies away from directly addressing moral objections to poker, New York City attorney John Blackbridge tackles them head-on at the start of his book *The Complete Poker-Player: A Practical Guide Book to the American National Game*, also first published in 1875. Why should games like poker be charged with "immorality," Blackbridge asks, while other forms of "gambling" like investing or buying insurance are not? "In fact every possible transaction in life is a risk, and involves the question of loss or gain," he argues. He sets the tone for a book that not only delves into the particulars of draw poker's rules and strategy but also offers a number of more abstract, even philosophical insights regarding the human condition.[17]

Blackbridge (also a "*nom de plume*"[18]) is also much more willing to address the preponderance of cheating in poker than Winterblossom (who essentially ignores it). In a fascinating early chapter, Blackbridge presents results from his interview with an expert "card-sharper" to learn about the many methods of cheating one was likely to encounter in a game among strangers. The unnamed source teaches Blackbridge about holding out cards, dealing from the bottom, and other forms of deceit including how to invite a player to cut the deck, then replace it back as it originally was without being noticed. "Much as this man told me, I am satisfied there was much he did not tell me," Blackbridge says, adding that in his interview "enough [was] disclosed to make honest card players very wary of the society of *any man who habitually wins*."[19]

The prevalence of cheating is one reason why Blackbridge encourages his poker-playing readers to stick with small stakes games. He says that none of the George Devol-like characters "will care to practice fraud where the stakes are so small as to be played for amusement only."[20] He also suggests that lower stakes allow for the game to be played "with a contented mind." Anticipating later discussions of poker "tilt" by more than a century, Blackbridge insists: "No man can play his game well if he feels that on the turn of a card depends his solvency, or the comforts of his family, or the payment of his bills."[21] Having such anxiety causes players to be overly affected by emotion when poker should be primarily an intellectual game.

This recommendation fits with even more specific advice from Blackbridge regarding bankroll management. He estimates how much discretionary income "the average American gentleman in a large city" might have to spend on "Amusements" (about $3,000), from which he suggests about a third (or $1,000) might reasonably be devoted to poker. More calculations taking into account the frequency of play (two nights a week), the amount due the "Widow" (an archaic term for the rake), and what we today would call variance ("those 'runs' of ill-fortune that cannot be averted") together lead Blackbridge to recommend "a limit of two dollars and a half" as a reasonable maximum per bet in order to avoid risk of ruin.[22]

Blackbridge moves on to discuss the importance of position in poker, even assigning points quantifying the value of the different seats around the table. Like Winterblossom, Blackbridge reviews the mathematical chances of filling straights and other hands while also dismissing as frivolous attempts to introduce non-standard hands like "blazes" (five court cards) or "skips" (e.g., a hand like 3-5-7-9-J). Blackbridge isn't too keen about the introduction of jackpots, either, which in his opinion disturb the game's integrity by forcing players both to reveal information about their hands before the showdown and to play pots of larger size than the agreed stakes. Under that heading Blackbridge notes how jackpots had yet to gain in popularity in the south, which he commends as "the conservative portion of the country, and may be relied on as the last resort of good sense in social matters." In a similar vein, Blackbridge is no fan of "unlimited poker," about which he sides with Winterblossom when calling it a "dangerous and deadly game."[23] Filling out the text is a reproduction of Schenck's book in its entirety, a copy of the American *Hoyle*'s rules, and a series of probability calculations and charts produced by William Pole, author of several works on whist.

One reviewer associated Blackbridge with "Poker Bob Schenck" for having given so much attention to the game, joking that he might be "treading on the toes of a distinguished member of our Diplomatic Corps."[24] Another applauded *The Complete Poker-Player* as "a scientific as well as a practical work" that possessed "many features worthy of commendation."[25] The book also earned belated praise from the British author Somerset Maugham who celebrated it and Blackbridge in a 1925 short story "The

Portrait of a Gentleman." In the story, an Englishman traveling abroad discovers an old copy of *The Complete Poker-Player* while perusing a second-hand bookseller's racks in Seoul. He finds it utterly delightful, deciding that besides providing instruction on five-card draw the author had also indirectly "painted a complete portrait of himself" as a witty and wise commentator on life in general.[26] A few years later the astronomer Richard A. Proctor wrote an essay titled "Poker Principles and Chance Laws" (1883) in which he credited Blackbridge as part of the reason why "the game of poker has attained in America the dignity of a science."[27]

Not everyone was enthused by such methodical treatments of America's new favorite card game, however, including one *Chicago Tribune* reviewer of Proctor's essay who found all the calculations too tedious to bear. "Unwittingly, perhaps, he has stripped the game of all that has made it so dear to the American heart," wrote the reviewer who believed Proctor's efforts diminished the romance of poker. The review laments the reduction of poker "to a mere, dry, hard, cold mathematical computation" and continues: "No! Mr. Astronomer. Poker knows no laws and spurns all conditions. The man is its measure. Let Mr. Proctor take his heaps of calculations and come into these Western wilds, if he wants to know the legions of possibilities that lurk in this noble game."[28]

Telling How to Play, But Warning Not To
As we've already seen, authors of early poker books either omitted signing their names or went with pseudonyms, unwilling to face the barrage of criticism that came with the territory in the 19th century. A further example came in an 1882 book that shared rules of the game, a bit of strategy advice, and some "amusing incidents" in the form of poker anecdotes. Its author came to be known as British bookseller Charles Welsh, although that fact was obscured initially by the way he chose to fill out the title page: *Poker: How to Play It. A Sketch of the Great American Game, Its Laws and Rules by ONE OF ITS VICTIMS*.

Another anonymous 1883 poker volume – *Talk of Uncle George to His Nephew About Draw Poker* – included the words "with timely warnings to young players" in its long title. While again referring to draw as the "Great American game," the book's preface makes clear how "Uncle George" intends to leave to others discussions of rules and laws (naming Blackbridge, Schenck, and the "American *Hoyle*" in particular). He rather aims to "expose this game *as it is* too often played – with its 'lights and shadows,' its bright parts, and 'ways that are dark.'"[29] Thus while Uncle George's stories cover a variety of situations, communicating numerous suggestions for winning play as well as thoughts regarding etiquette, he also delivers repeated warnings against various forms of cheating, including collusion.

"Nearly every day's paper has reports of ruined characters," he observes. Uncle George essentially renders his own game-play advice superfluous by concluding: "Therefore, I say, it would be better for you to quit it entirely."[30]

William James Florence did at least identify himself as the author of his 1892 book *The Gentleman's Hand-Book of Poker*, although he distanced himself from culpability for it when stating in his preface that he wrote the book in less than four weeks in order to satisfy a bet. After discussing the historical background of rules of draw poker and then covering some other variants (stud, whiskey), Florence echoes others' warnings about sharps marking cards and using reflectors or small mirrors to see cards as they are dealt. To that he adds a summary of rules (via Schenck), covers various terms and other facets of the game, and shares some discussion of position and probabilities among other tips to players. More anecdotes and the reprinting of Proctor's aforementioned essay help round out the volume.

However it's a section titled "Advice to Players" that once again delivers the most withering observation about poker, one that would seem to contradict the purpose of a book about the game. "There are no rules for playing poker so as to win," Florence states bluntly. "Advice may be given so as to limit losses."[31]

The pattern of undermining strategy advice with bleak warnings about poker's ills continues through "Uncle" Jack Abbott's 1881 volume *A Treatise on Jack Pot Poker* and John W. Keller's 1887 *The Game of Draw Poker*. In Abbott's book, he follows a cursory history of poker and discussion of rules, with familiar warnings to avoid "unlimited" games and not to play poker on credit ("when your money gives out, quit the game"). He downplays the usefulness of even trying to improve one's game from books, advising instead that players learn from "bitter experience."[32]

Keller, meanwhile, shares rules, terminology, probabilities, and even tangible "hints to players" of what he calls an increasingly popular "means of amusement to the better classes of American people."[33] But he insists the game is best played for non-meaningful stakes and has little interest in addressing those who think "a monetary consideration or stake heightens the interest of Poker." He claims the idea that money is an essential element to poker is one of several "misuses" of the game he endeavors to correct.[34]

Why So Serious?

The first wave of poker strategy books also inspired parodies, such as Garrett Brown's 1899 volume *How to Win at Poker* made up of a teasing sequence of lectures much more entertaining than edifying. One notable chapter is titled "Lucky Players and How to Beat Them." The advice is utterly silly, though there is something delightful in the tongue-in-cheek goofiness of Brown's recommendation to try to "hoodoo" such players in order to throw them off their hot streaks. All of Brown's probabilities, dealing, terminology, rules, and etiquette points are farcical, making it clear the title of the book is meant satirically. The last chapter confirms the hint by proposing that poker be taught in colleges and the book be used as a required text.

Brown's book was popular, running through several editions, although it is highly probable the author himself exaggerated its reach. In a new preface to one of the later editions, the author jokes how "the wide distribution of the work has already brought excellent results," collectively saving his readers $300,000 according to his calculations.[35] Brown's readers clearly got it, instinctively understanding the humor produced by poking fun at those who believed poker a genuinely worthy subject of academic interest.

Even so, following the turn of the century more and more poker strategy books would appear. And those who wrote them would become increasingly earnest – and much less apologetic – about their objectives.

"A Comparatively New Field in Poker Literature"
Books devoted to poker strategy began as a novelty in the 1870s, and by the turn of the century were still viewed cynically by some. However, opinions about poker were changing and the idea that the game rewarded skill – unlike other gambling games – gradually took hold, even among casual players.

In *Jack Pots* (1900), Eugene Edwards spelled out this change of attitude, noting how "thirty or forty years ago... cards were held up to scorn as the invention of the devil, and all card players were placed but a shade above a forger or a pickpocket." However, he continues: "We do not hear so much of that wild talk nowadays," describing a game "that best fits our national character," not least because of the game's skill component. "The players must have brains, and there is where we lead the world."[36] Patriotic swagger aside, the same thesis that those who win consistently at poker "must have brains" informs practically all of the best known poker strategy books from *Jack Pots* on. The argument also helped influence the game's spread into private homes and among players of all classes and backgrounds.

By the turn of the 20th century, Scottish author Robert Frederick Foster had already established rules for whist, bridge, and numerous other games when he took over the mantle as the ultimate card game authority with the publication of *Foster's Complete Hoyle* in 1897. The book not only greatly expanded the earlier *Hoyle*s' small sections on poker to more than 50 pages – including additional discussion of rules and other games in the "poker family" like brag, commerce, bouillotte, and ambigu – it also introduced advice about five-card draw strategy ("How To Win At Poker").

For Foster, "the great secret of success in Poker, apart from natural aptitude for the game, and being a good actor, is to *avoid calling.*"[37] Foster outlines why it is often better to fold with worse hands and raise with better ones, anticipating by a century the benefits of what later strategy writers would call a "tight-aggressive" style. Still, despite publishing another stand-alone title about poker rules and strategy in 1901, Foster found it necessary to expand his explanation even further with *Practical Poker* (1904), a 250-plus page discussion of rules and strategy he says was inspired by his having "to deal with an average of eighty letters per week relating to Poker disputes alone" over the previous decade thanks to his role as card editor at the *New York Sun.*[38]

Foster begins *Practical Poker* by dismissing continued "prejudice against poker as a game of chance." In so doing, he sets an important precedent: the assumed premise is that poker has a high skill component.[39] After settling various rules disputes during the first half of the book, Foster devotes much of the rest to strategic topics like odds and probabilities when drawing, pot odds, deriving information about opponents' hands from their draws and betting, tells at the table ("mannerisms and talk"), the importance of position, bluffing, and "luck and superstition" which Foster acknowledges to be a meaningful part of the game though no argument against the importance of skill.

"The most careful players, and those who have the best intellectual endowments for the game, are not always the most successful," Foster says, adding also how better players usually tend to minimize the ill effects of luck over the long term, but that "the length of time is uncertain, and life may be over before the tide turns."[40]

Underscoring poker's new status relative to other card games, Foster's New York publisher delivered *Practical Poker* to booksellers on the same day it published two other volumes by the same author, one on bridge and another on euchre.[41] *Practical Poker* earned praise in *Life* magazine as "an extremely handy and helpful manual" that highlighted "psychological generalship" in poker.[42] The book was a commercial success as well, going through nine editions over the next couple of decades.

Following Foster's lead, subsequent strategy writers would find it less vital to offer qualifications when recommending poker to their readers or outlining paths to profitable play. Algernon Crofton's 1915 entry, *Poker. Its Laws and Principles* (with a foreword from Foster), directly maintains that "poker is less a game of chance than bridge or whist," although he indirectly argues for the importance of skill in poker by showing how results are more obviously influenced by mistakes made by bad players than by the expertise of good ones. "In one sense of the word, there is no such thing in the world as a skillful poker player, but there are plenty of bad ones," Crofton explains, comparing the winning player to a knowledgeable bookmaker who simply understands the math of the game whereas his opponent does not. Crofton goes on to present "maxims for losers" designed to help identify "principal leaks through which their money is drained from them."[43]

Crofton presents his book as contributing to what he calls "a comparatively new field in poker literature."[44] Indeed strategy texts continued to appear regularly, with the next important title heralding the rise to prominence of five-card draw's most significant challenger: George Henry Fisher's *How to Play Stud Poker* (1931), later expanded as the *Stud Poker Blue Book: The Only Standard Authority* (1934). The fact that Fisher's book initially appeared as part of the Haldeman–Julius Publishing Company's popular "Little Blue Book" series of pocket-sized titles attested to the mainstream appeal of poker strategy. It also demonstrated the extent of the game's development, which had become widespread enough to warrant a volume examining how to win at a variant other than five-card draw.

In his prefatory material and an initial chapter summarizing "the evolution of poker," Fisher acknowledges how during the game's early history "poker players were universally recognized as the special advance agents of His Satanic Majesty," and how "during the last quarter of the old century the game underwent a tremendous struggle to maintain its self-respect." But according to Fisher poker had successfully rescued itself from damnation to be transformed into "the gentleman's game" in part because of the efforts of earlier authors to codify rules.[45]

Fisher's history includes a humorous anecdote of uncertain origin describing a lively game of draw poker occurring in a saloon somewhere along the Ohio River during "that reckless period which followed the Civil War." One player – a "one-eyed fellow" – found himself dealt three kings and, after a series of raises, commits his entire stake before the draw. At that point, he suddenly runs outside the saloon, unhitches his "spirited stallion," and brings the horse inside where he ties him to the back of his chair to secure himself some extra capital. However, suspecting the others to have looked at his cards during his absence and seen his three kings, the one-eyed fellow suggests a rule change. "Now I propose that to make it fair all around, each man turns three of his cards face up – discards two – and draws two more face down." He adds: "I'll gamble this here thoroughbred stud horse on my chances."

Fisher concludes, with an appropriate degree of skepticism: "Whereupon Stud Poker was born. (At least, so they tell us.)"[46]

Though highly unlikely to be based in fact, the story dramatizes how the "closed" game of draw, in which all cards are face down, could have inspired the later "open" game of stud, in which some cards are dealt face up. But more than just its improbable details, the fact that the 1864 American

Hoyle had already described a game called "stud poker" suggests this yarn is at best embellished. The name couldn't have been invented *after* the Civil War concluded a year later.

Fisher's strategy for five-card stud is genuinely insightful, with advice about starting hand selection, "how to appraise your hand" and make decisions on each street, tables and charts providing mathematical data regarding odds and probabilities, discussions of psychology and bluffing, and a thorough discussion of the rules. Fisher well positions stud as being as much of a skill game as draw, along the way distinguishing it from chance-based gambling games like faro, roulette, and craps. "In Crap[s], no special brain quality is required – not even cool-headedness," Fisher says. "But Stud is a match of wits, and experts at the game respect the tradition by injecting common sense and sound judgment into the play."[47]

The *Stud Poker Blue Book* proved popular, earning mainstream attention from reviewers and columnists including *The Chicago Tribune*'s Westbrook Pegler who mentioned Fisher's book multiple times in his nationally-syndicated column "Fair Enough." In a review of the 1934 edition, Pegler commended the book as filling a need, arguing that along with fist-fighting, poker was one of "two sports in which the average American male thinks he is a born expert and goes blundering along with seldom, if ever, a thought that he might need instruction from a master."[48] A few months later Pegler continued to recommend the book, joking how then-vice president John Nance Garner, "one of the great American experts in stud," should use his influence to "help install Mr. Fisher's Stud Poker Blue Book as one of the official studies at West Point."[49]

Much as R.F. Foster had established himself as an authority on other card games before writing about poker, so too did bridge expert Oswald Jacoby make a transition to poker from other pursuits. He wrote multiple books on the game starting in 1940 with *Oswald Jacoby on Poker*. After playing numerous games in his youth – including a great deal of poker while serving as an under-aged soldier in World War I – Jacoby came to be regarded as the greatest tournament bridge player in the world during the 1930s as a member of the famed "Four Aces" contract bridge team. Later during World War II Jacoby worked in counterintelligence for the U.S. Navy helping crack enemy codes. He subsequently continued to write books and columns on bridge, as well as works on backgammon, rummy, canasta, and other games.

In his book Jacoby immediately addresses the "popular misconception that since poker is a gambling game it is pure luck," and explains that it is a skill-based "game of money management." He says it requires both a knowledge of the "correct technical play" and an understanding that players "must deliberately make the wrong technical play on a sufficient number of occasions so that the other players in the game will never be certain as to what he is doing."[50]

Jacoby covers rules and strategy for five-card draw and five-card stud while also giving some attention to the relatively new variant of seven-card stud and other games. He shares with readers advice about hosting poker games, including how best to manage "dealer's option" games involving multiple variants. He also explains "How to Conduct Yourself in a Poker Game," offering explicit advice about table talk and tells. He shares charts covering various poker-related probabilities, discussions of psychology and etiquette, and a number of humorous anecdotes to enliven the text. Jacoby even provides a chapter of hand-based "Problems" culled from actual games to test the reader's understanding. The book was a commercial hit, earning its author a place in the poker strategy roll of honor to match the respect he commanded in the bridge world.[51]

The Education of a Poker Player

The history of poker strategy reached another significant landmark with the 1957 publication of Herbert O. Yardley's bestseller *The Education of a Poker Player*. It became the only poker strategy book many players over the next generation had ever heard of, let alone actually read.

Yardley was another code-breaker, already known for his formative role during the early days of American intelligence. In 1931, Yardley published *The American Black Chamber* in which he shared with the world details of his role as the founder and head of MI-8, a cryptanalytic organization started by the U.S. shortly after World War I and ultimately dissolved following the stock market crash of 1929. *The American Black Chamber* was a huge seller, though caused controversy as it told many secrets the U.S. did not especially want publicized. The government even considered pursuing legal claims against Yardley over the book's publication. Though these came to nothing, laws were subsequently passed regarding the publication of governmental records that prevented Yardley from producing a second book about his time with MI-8. His services no longer wanted by his country, Yardley later worked for both Canada and China as a code-breaker before retiring in the 1950s. He began work on *The Education of a Poker Player* late in life, with the book appearing nine months before his death at age 69.

The book is both a poker strategy guide and an autobiography, starting with Yardley's life as a teenager growing up in Worthington, Indiana, then moving on to describe his adventures cracking Japanese codes in China, all the while passing along specific advice about various forms of poker. Presented in three parts, the first two are both titled "Three Poker Stories" and feature Yardley weaving various poker lessons into his entertaining autobiographical tales.

The first part concentrates on Yardley's days as a teenager learning how to play poker in Indiana saloons during the first decade of the 1900s. It primarily focuses on Monty's Place, which he prefers to other establishments "because it offered more color and action." (He also adds: "Monty's Place was the only clean one."[52]) The proprietor "Monty" or James Montgomery is described in the book teaching young Yardley how to play variations of five-card draw (jacks or better), five-card stud, and five-card draw (deuces wild with the joker). Some have suggested the Monty presented in *The Education of a Poker Player* is in fact a compilation of various people Yardley knew, although the author himself insisted he was an actual person. Along with Monty's game-specific advice comes more general pointers about hand reading, tells, and other psychological issues specific to poker.

The second part presents an older Yardley working as a code-breaker in China. Here, Yardley takes on the role of mentor, offering instruction in five-card draw (lowball), seven-card stud, and seven-card stud hi-lo. As in the first part, the chapters almost all contain summaries describing highly-detailed hand examples designed to further strategic concepts. A third and final part then offers brief treatments of other stud and draw games such as Doctor Pepper, Baseball, and Spit in the Ocean.

No matter the variant, Yardley consistently advocates a "tight is right" approach that advises readers to avoid unfavorable situations with negative expected value and instead wait for less patient, less knowledgeable players to give you their money. In this way Yardley emulates his mentor Monty, who says he simply would not sit down or stay in a game unless he knew he was getting the best of it. Monty is reported to say: "I figure the odds for every card I draw, and if the odds aren't favorable, I fold. This doesn't sound very friendly. But what's friendly about poker? It's a cut-throat game, at best."[53]

Though tight as a player, Yardley's prose style is on the loose side. His stories are peppered with frequent, indulgent digressions with those in the second part designed to make Yardley appear a cool, worldly James Bond-like figure. The end-of-chapter poker lessons are soberly spelled out in table form, but the stories preceding them are often raucous. They feature colorful characters such as Hairlip Slocum who loses a huge pot, including a pair of geldings, with aces up versus three sevens; One-Eyed Jones who Monty throws out for trying to cheat; poor Bones Alverson who draws four aces in a game of draw but dies of a heart attack before the hand is over; and Ling Fan, Yardley's interpreter in China, who adopts the role of poker student in the book's second part.

By appealing both to the public's readiness for a new, modern take on poker strategy and its taste for the exotic (and likely embellished) tales of international intrigue – not to mention Yardley's standing as a famous American codebreaker – the book was an enormous commercial triumph. In his study of Yardley *The Reader of Gentleman's Mail*, David Kahn notes how a November 9, 1957 issue of *The Saturday Evening Post* in which an excerpt was included "broke all its records by selling 5.6 million copies." Yardley's publisher, Simon & Schuster, had to order a second printing to keep up with demand.[54] (Simon & Schuster's earlier success with another poker title, *Webster's Poker Book*, is discussed in the next chapter.) In *Cowboys Full*, James McManus speculates: "The *Post*'s vast middle-class readership was apparently hungry for lessons in tough, honest poker." He adds that the book's rapid sales offered further proof that "the public was primed for a serious book about poker."[55]

Differing Approaches, an Uncertain Marketplace

Both Jacoby and Yardley's books exerted considerable influence for many years after they appeared, with both authors' recommendations about draw and stud strategy continuing to serve players over subsequent decades. Even as late as 1982, an article on poker in the finance magazine *Changing Times* suggested only three texts as further reading: *Oswald Jacoby on Poker*, *The Education of a Poker Player*, as well as a recent edition of *Hoyle*.[56]

The poker strategy books published in the two decades following Yardley's tended to serve audiences primarily comprised of the most avid players. The success of the *Maverick* television series starring James Garner resulted in a 1959 book tie-in titled *Poker According to Maverick*, written by Roy Huggins although presented as though authored by the fictional hero Bret Maverick. Written in a faux-Old West style, the book offers basic draw and stud tips along with Maverick's "Ten Commandments for Poker Players" among which the author, simultaneously evoking both the 1850s and 1950s, advises "Don't play poker with women."[57]

In a different vein, an entrepreneur named Wallace Ward started his own publishing company in the late 1960s which produced numerous titles dedicated to a Scientology-like philosophy. Ward authored some of those himself under pen names, but he also wrote and published several poker strategy books as Frank Wallace, including *Poker: A Guaranteed Income for Life* (1968). The book offers advice to home-game players describing how best to exploit unskilled opponents, delivered primarily as anecdotes starring himself as the book's main "character," John Finn. Wallace's approach is especially unsparing, causing David Mamet to characterize it "a stunningly vicious book."[58]

Thomas "Amarillo Slim" Preston also managed to add to his celebrity (and bank account) by co-authoring his own strategy title, *Play Poker to*

Win (1973). Taking advantage of fame achieved by his 1972 World Series of Poker Main Event victory and subsequent publicity tour (see Chapter 20), the book interweaves tips on different poker variants with Preston's folksy stories of his own successes at the tables, all providing him plenty of opportunities to deliver various gambling-related aphorisms ("All trappers don't wear fur caps").[59] The book includes a brief chapter on Texas hold'em, the game featured at the WSOP and one Preston reports to be a favorite among high-stakes players and "on the way to becoming the most popular poker game in America." Jon Bradshaw reports in *Fast Company* how copies of the book were sold at the 1973 World Series of Poker at Binion's Horseshoe. Preston's response to an announcement over the public address system about the book being on sale gives an indication of how seriously he took the project. "You know, I never did read that son of a bitch," he says.[60]

Math professor Norman Zadeh's *Winning Poker Systems*, also published in 1973, was well regarded by serious players for its detailed starting hand charts for draw, stud, and lowball as well as its discussion of theoretical concepts. However, the bar was raised again in 1976 with David Sklansky's *Hold'em Poker*, which provided the most thorough and useful discussion of strategy to date for the game Slim had rightly predicted was on the march to prominence. Sklansky's book covered starting hand selection, strategic considerations before and after the flop, bluffing and semi-bluffing, slow playing, reading opponents' hands, tells, and other topics. The book primarily focuses on fixed-limit hold'em, with Sklansky advising "no beginner should even consider playing" the no-limit version, as "it is not a friendly game."[61]

The audience was still relatively limited, and the book was initially published not by a major house, but by the Gambler's Book Club in Las Vegas, responding to requests for a book on hold'em. A few years later Al Alvarez visited the famed bookshop while writing *The Biggest Game in Town*, meeting its founder and proprietor John Luckman. "Players aren't readers," Luckman told Alvarez, explaining that in an already niche market only a small percentage of those who played the game were taking an interest in reading even Sklansky.[62]

Uncertainty about the market for strategy books didn't deter poker pro Doyle Brunson from joining the rush to publish following his back-to-back victories in the WSOP Main Event in 1976 and 1977. As Brunson recalls in his 2009 memoir *The Godfather of Poker*, he believed "there wasn't a credible poker book out there," aside perhaps from the latest edition of *According to Hoyle*.[63] Thus Brunson called upon other poker pros to contribute to what became a mammoth, 600-plus page compendium of strategy advice covering several draw and stud poker variants, lowball and split-

Doyle Brunson, moments before winning the 1976 World Series of Poker Main Event

pot games, and both fixed-limit and no-limit hold'em. Distrusting the less than attractive terms offered to him by various publishing houses, Brunson chose to create his own company to publish the book himself in 1978 with the attention-grabbing title *How I Made Over $1,000,000 Playing Poker*. At $100 per copy, the book included chapters by Sklansky, 1978 WSOP Main Event champion Bobby Baldwin, David "Chip" Reese, Joey Hawthorne, and Mike Caro, with Brunson adding his own lengthy discussion of no-limit hold'em strategy.

Brunson later summarized the different approach to poker strategy his book espoused, a methodology more directly articulated in the revised title Brunson chose for the book's second edition: *Super/System: A Course in Power Poker*. "At the time, most poker literature was hit and miss, consisting largely of unfounded speculation," Brunson explains, adding that few authors "had much big-league poker experience" in cardrooms or other high-stakes environments. Brunson describes himself and his collaborators as having "attacked" earlier advice to "sit and wait" and only play a small selection of strong hands. The strategy won players money, Brunson concedes, "but it didn't win much, and it wasn't worthy of writing a poker book about, because you could just blurt it out in two words: tight is right." In other words, whether poker players were readers or not, Brunson believed there wasn't all that much worth reading.

By contrast, "power poker" emphasized aggression, a more exciting and potentially much more lucrative style that still involved being selective, but "knowing when you have an edge and then aggressively maximizing it."[64] It's an approach most thoroughly emphasized in Brunson's own chapter on no-limit hold'em, the game he describes as "The Cadillac of Poker Games." Most of his advice illustrates one principle: "You become a big winner at Poker by betting... raising... and re-raising – by playing aggressively."[65] Discussing the merits of various starting hands and how to handle various postflop situations, Brunson consistently reiterates the importance of maximizing value and pressuring opponents. "That has always been the *key* to No-Limit play as far as I'm concerned," he writes. "I want to put my opponent to a decision *for all his chips*."[66]

Reaction to the book was positive, with the first edition selling out and subsequent editions priced at $50 proving popular as well. Some top pros – and even Brunson himself – lamented his decision to publicize so many secrets of winning play, reacting as though he were a magician revealing how his tricks were performed. Deciding the book would result in a wholesale makeover of the entire poker world, Frank Wallace even published his own short response, the title of which includes a judgment: *An Obituary for the Public Professional Poker Player*. Of course, *Super/System* hardly signaled any sort of demise for those earning a living playing poker, instead becoming oft-referenced as something of a "bible" for serious players.

Another title earning notice beyond the Gambler's Book Shop was *Scarne's Guide to Modern Poker* (1980) by renowned gambling author, magician, casino consultant, and expert card and dice manipulator John Scarne (pronounced to rhyme with "carny"). Ever the performer and self-promoter, Scarne's swagger begins on the first page where he boasts the phrase "According to Hoyle" has been updated to "According to Scarne."[67] Expanding upon material from a couple of his earlier titles, including the influential *Scarne's Complete Guide to Gambling* (1961), the book delivers rules and strategy advice for 117 different poker variants, including five-card draw, five- and seven-card stud, a few pages on hold'em, and a host of other obscure, colorfully-named games such as Frustration (a draw variant with just two cards, the highest hand being a pair of aces), Pass the Garbage (a.k.a. Screw Your Neighbor), and Twin Beds Roll 'Em Over (a version of Spit in the Ocean).

Scarne also includes findings from a 1978 survey that determined poker to be "the leading private and commercialized gambling game in the nation"

130

both in terms of participants and money wagered. According to Scarne's estimate, about 65 million Americans played poker with more than $100 billion being wagered each year.[68] A chapter explaining "The Science and Skill of Poker" once more argued poker's distinction from other gambling games, while another long section listing methods of "Protection Against Poker Cheats" showed how the century-old warnings of John Blackbridge and other early strategy writers were still relevant. Scarne exempts the legal, licensed games of Nevada and California card rooms (while not denying cheating still sometimes occurred in those environments), focusing instead on private games where his survey revealed that on average "cheating in one form or another took place in one out of ten games."[69]

A "Boom" for Books

In 1984, *Mike Caro's Book of Tells: The Body Language of Poker* appeared, the most famous of several strategy titles from the "mad genius of poker." An elaborate treatise concentrating on the significance of physical behaviors and table talk, the book was read by many poker players, elevating to iconic status Caro's observations that when it comes to poker-playing "actors," "weak means strong" and "strong means weak."[70] Some players also sought out titles focused on tournament strategy co-authored by 1983 WSOP Main Event champion Tom McEvoy and two-time Main Event runner-up T.J. Cloutier. The late 1980s additionally saw the birth of Two Plus Two Publishing, which produced a number of other important strategy titles, among them Sklansky's *The Theory of Poker* (1987) and Sklansky and Mason Malmuth's *Hold'em Poker for Advanced Players* (1988).

The subsequent poker boom of the mid-2000s ignited a sudden surge of interest in poker strategy books, with many new players – a lot of whom were exclusively playing online – seeking help to gain edges. At the time, anyone venturing into a large chain bookstore like Borders or Barnes & Noble would encounter an enormous selection of poker books filling an entire eight-foot-high, three-foot-wide bookshelf, the majority of which focused on strategy. Two Plus Two Publishing was well represented, most notably by a three-volume series focusing on tournament strategy: *Harrington on Hold'em* (2004-06) by 1996 WSOP Main Event champion Dan Harrington and Bill Robertie. The first volume is reported to have sold more than 300,000 copies – the most of any poker strategy book. Other poker-centric publishers like ConJelCo, Cardoza Books, Dimat Enterprises, and D&B Poker additionally helped fill the shelves with popular titles.

Major publishing houses entered the poker strategy book marketplace as well. HarperResource, an imprint of HarperCollins, published 1989 WSOP Main Event champion Phil Hellmuth's *Play Poker Like the Pros* (2003). In Hellmuth's recent autobiography *Poker Brat* he tells the story of the book reaching the *New York Times* bestseller list a year later after being referenced on an ESPN broadcast of a 2004 WSOP event.[71] Simon Spotlight Entertainment, an imprint of Simon & Schuster, published *Phil Gordon's Little Green Book* (2005), modeled after *Harvey Penick's Little Red Book*, the highest selling golf book ever. And while Anthony Holden was writing a sequel to his poker narrative *Big Deal* (see Chapter 17) for Simon & Schuster, the publisher Little, Brown called on him to produce a strategy title as well, *Holden on Hold'em* (2006).

The late Lou Krieger was positioned well when publishers began showing interest in poker, having already written multiple strategy titles including *Poker for Dummies* (2000) with Richard D. Harroch. Speaking with Krieger in 2010, he pointed out how the flooding of the marketplace with poker strategy books logically followed the sudden influx of new players.[72] "All of the books on how to improve your golf or how to play tennis, they're not aimed at the pros," Krieger said. "They are aimed at the players of limited ability, like the vast majority of us who are going to go out and buy these books." As a result, with so many new players showing an interest in improving their games, "every publisher and his brother wanted a poker book written."

Nearly all of these poker strategy books focused on no-limit Texas hold'em, the game most often featured on televised broadcasts and by far the most popular variant for new players. Krieger was called on to write several books – including four in one year – although by 2010 the market had already become saturated and the major houses were backing off once more. "The publishing industry is hunkering down, they are getting very conservative about what they release, and they are unwilling to take risks," Krieger then said. "They are only playing aces and kings, whereas in the past they would take a flyer on a nine-eight suited."

Borders closed a year later, and since then Barnes & Noble and other large U.S. chains have either downsized or diversified their offerings in response to the larger trend of all books (especially print ones) becoming gradually less central to American culture.[73] Poker strategy books nonetheless continue to appear and find audiences, even though players seeking to improve their skills now have numerous other forms of instruction readily available to them via a host of other media, including online forums, videos, coaching, and live streams.

It is clear, though, that strategy books have always played a significant role in making the case to the mainstream – both in America and globally – that poker shouldn't be regarded simply as "emphatically a game of chance" (as the 1864 *Hoyle* presents it). Whereas early strategy books came accompanied with apologies and warnings, later versions omitted such disclaimers, safely assuming the reader's acceptance that poker is a game that rewards skill.

The opening montage of *Rounders* delivers a similar point. Mike Mc-Dermott is shown in his apartment readying to go play in Teddy KGB's underground game, collecting his bankroll hidden among copies of books by Malmuth, Brunson, Holden, and others (and Mike Caro videos including ones based on his *Book of Tells*). Before the voice-over narration even begins, the books point to his seriousness as a player, prefiguring the film's larger argument in favor of poker as a skill game worthy of study.

For those who want to win, anyway.

9 Poker in the Home

By the turn of the 20th century, poker had moved well beyond the saloons and steamboats and increasingly into private homes. People who had encountered poker while journeying by boat and train introduced the game to others on their return. Similarly soldiers heading home following the Civil War continued to play, helping to ensure poker's spread.

Most of the late 19th-century strategy primers mention the popularity of private poker games, many of which were played for small stakes. Early in John Blackbridge's *The Complete Poker-Player* he tells of "the average American gentleman" living in New York City during the 1870s devoting two nights per week to such games. When introducing the game to his nephew in *Talk of Uncle George*, the author references poker during the 1880s being "found in the clubs and private card parties, all over our city and country." And in the 1890s William J. Florence recommends home games to readers of *The Gentleman's Handbook on Poker*. "It is well... to be careful about going into a game of poker on an ocean steamer, in a railway carriage, or a western hotel without some knowledge of your companions," Florence explains. "But with a party of gentlemen and for limited stakes, poker is a fascinating and harmless pastime."[1]

Just as cowboys and card sharps dominated cultural representations of poker games during the 19th century, depictions of private "home games" – often less cutthroat and more friendly – become increasingly prominent during the 20th century. The often embellished stories of Old West poker created deep impressions and a lasting legacy informing poker's outlaw status, but stories of poker in the domestic sphere more closely resembled the poker experience of contemporary audiences. Such familiarity made those depictions of the game equally if not more affecting.

"A Poker Game is a Picture of Peace"
John F. B. Lillard highlights that very contrast in his 1896 collection *Poker Stories*. Immediately after a chapter of "Stories from the Wild and Woolly West" comes "Stories from the Effete East" mostly featuring upstanding members of society including a judge, a policeman, a railroad magnate, a Yale professor, and a physician. In one, a doctor is hesitant to make a house call, but once it is made clear he's being asked to play poker and not administer to the ill, "The doctor says he'll be right over."[2]

Stephen Crane's short story "A Poker Game" visits a similarly "effete" setting. Best known for his Civil War novel *The Red Badge of Courage*, Crane was also a poet and short story writer as well as a poker player, often partaking in the game during his years at school and afterwards while a reporter and war correspondent. Sadly Crane's life and output was cut short by tuberculosis at the age of 28. Among the first posthumous works of his published in 1902 was the brief though memorable tale of a private poker game among a group of wealthy New Yorkers gathered in an uptown hotel room.

"Usually a poker game is a picture of peace," the narrator begins, emphasizing the refined, respectable setting. He adds what could be called a lengthy defense of poker as worthwhile pursuit, not at all the morally questionable, dangerous game many others had described it before. "Here is one of the most exciting and absorbing occupations known to intelligent American manhood," we are told. "Here a year's reflection is compressed into a moment of thought; here the nerves may stand on end and scream to themselves, but a tranquillity as from heaven is only interrupted by the click of chips. The higher the stakes the more quiet the scene."[3]

Crane's game is five-handed and features the real-estate tycoon Old Henry Spuytendyvil and the young, naïve Robert "Bobbie" Cinch. Cinch had inherited $22 million from his recently-deceased father who had been friends with Spuytendyvil (and presumably a player in past poker games). As Cinch's name might suggest, luck is on his side and while he isn't the most skillful player he finds himself the biggest winner. Meanwhile Old Spuytendyvil (whose name means "spinning devil"), was down "a considerable amount," with his amusement lessening right along with his dwindling chip stack.[4]

A hand of five-card draw arises in which Old Spuytendyvil bets and only Cinch calls. Thanks to an onlooker we learn Old Spuytendyvil was dealt 10♦-9♦-8♦-7♦ and draws one. We also know young Bobbie picked up 9♥-8♥-6♥-5♥ and he, too, takes only a single card. With a "sinister" look Old Spuytendyvil fires a bet, and Cinch pauses to think. "Well, Mr. Spuytendyvil," he finally says, "I can't play a sure thing against you," then tosses in a white chip, just calling his opponent. "I've got a straight flush," Cinch says, showing his completed hand of 9♥-8♥-7♥-6♥-5♥. With a mixture of "fear, horror, and rage," Old Spuytendyvil then turns over his cards – J♦-10♦-9♦-8♦-7♦. "I've got a straight flush, too!" he yells. "And mine is Jack high!"[5]

It's left to an observer to signal the story's moral to the reader. "Bob, my boy... you're no gambler, but you're a mighty good fellow, and if you hadn't been you would be losing a good many dollars this minute."[6] In other words, Cinch's decision to soft play Old Spuytendyvil and only call with his straight flush saved him from losing more. His generous nature was rewarded.

It's a poker hand uncannily matching the game's gentlemanly atmosphere, preserving the "picture of peace." It also suggests a kind of variation upon the old adage "I'd rather be lucky than good," as young Bobbie's "goodness" (morally speaking, that is) directly diminishes the consequences of his bad luck. Old Spuytendyvil is furious, having been denied an obvious opportunity to get back some of his losses. The older man also misses a chance to deliver a lesson to the young heir whom he thought had yet to earn the status to go along with his wealth.

Yet unlike the stories of violent poker hands of the "wild and woolly west," which invariably end with weapons drawn, Crane's story concludes with Spuytendvyil asking to draw another glass of whisky.

Card-Playing Canines Kings of Kitsch

The cultured setting of "A Poker Game" was parodied soon after in what has to be one of the most widely recognized examples of poker in popular culture, Cassius Marcellus Coolidge's famous series of paintings known as "Dogs Playing Poker."

Everyone knows them, those absurd gatherings of different breeds of dogs smoking cigars, drinking whisky and beer, and playing poker as though they were human. You don't even have to play poker to be familiar with the card-playing canines, regarded by some as the epitome of kitsch or lowbrow culture, by others as an effective, insightful commentary on the middle and upper classes. The images may well rank among the most iconic depictions of poker ever produced by mainstream popular culture.

Born in 1844 in upstate New York, Coolidge had already pursued multiple careers before creating the paintings for which he'd achieve his greatest fame, including taking turns as a school superintendent, a town clerk, and a small business owner. He even once helped open and run a bank, a fitting occupation for someone who during childhood picked up the nickname "Cash." Such a moniker fit well with Coolidge's entrepreneurial streak, too, as he was involved throughout his life in various money-making schemes. Probably his best-known achievement (dogs aside) was his idea for "comic foregrounds" – the life-sized portraits with the faces cut out for people to stick their heads through and create funny photos. Meanwhile Coolidge additionally worked as a journalist, writing a column for which he drew his own illustrations. He even wrote a comic opera about a mosquito infestation in New Jersey titled *King Gallinipper*, once performed in the 1880s.

Along the way Coolidge always painted and drew, successfully selling a number of his illustrations to various outlets. As early as the 1870s he had begun painting dogs, with a cigar company purchasing some to include on their boxes. A few of these early depictions of dogs featured them adopting human poses, including one in particular from 1894 showing four St. Bernards playing poker. That one – simply titled "Poker Game" – proved to be a precursor to more such paintings to come.

In 1903, when Coolidge was nearly 60, he was hired by the Brown & Bigelow advertising firm to create a series of oil paintings to be used in calendars advertising cigars. Though only a fledgling company at the time, Brown & Bigelow went on to publish many of America's most popular calendars in the 20th century, ranging from Norman Rockwell's "Boy Scout" calendars to others featuring Gil Elvgren's popular "pin-up" girls. Coolidge ultimately produced 16 paintings for Brown & Bigelow, all of which featured dogs engaged in various human activities. The calendars were a big hit, and Coolidge was able to sell the original paintings for prices ranging from $2,000 to $10,000.

Of the 16 paintings for the calendars, seven featured the dogs doing non-poker activities such as attending a baseball game, conducting a trial, playing pool, struggling over a broken down Model T, and celebrating New Year's Eve. The other nine all show them playing poker, and when considered as a sequence convey many different scenarios and settings commonly associated with the game. The best known is "A Friend in Need," which features seven dogs closely gathered around a starkly-lit table studying both their cards and each other. A closer look reveals the game isn't

A Friend in Need by Cassius M. Coolidge (1903)

exactly on the up-and-up. The cigar-chomping gray bulldog in the fore-ground is holding the ace of clubs in his extended paw under the table, apparently passing it to the tan-haired mutt on his left who looks to be holding the other three aces. As the smallest dogs at the game, perhaps these two struck up an alliance for dealing with their larger opponents.

Two other paintings, "A Bold Bluff" and "Waterloo," tell a sequential story in a manner that recalls the works of the great 18th-century satirical artist William Hogarth. In "A Bold Bluff," a St. Bernard appears in the foreground on the left, while a large tower of chips sits in the center of the table before him, apparently having just been pushed forward. The other dogs look at him intently, but he gives away nothing behind the pair of spectacles resting on his snout. Then in "Waterloo," he has revealed his hand to the others: it's a modest pair of deuces. The St. Bernard grins as his paws rest on the large pile of chips he has just claimed, the other dogs registering various forms of surprise and dismay, having fallen victim to the bold bluff.

For some of the paintings, Coolidge moves the dogs' games outside a private residence. "His Station and Four Aces" shows them playing on a train, with the dogs wearing an assortment of hats and coats suitable for travel. A

Poker & Pop Culture

conductor has interrupted the game to inform an aghast-looking player that the train has reached his stop – especially unfortunate timing, as he has four aces. Another painting, "Stranger in Camp," finds the dogs at a campsite, apparently in conflict as the chips and cards are all scattered about with two of the players locked in what looks to be a pre-fight stare-down.

Moving the games back indoors, "Poker Sympathy" shows a poor boxer falling back in his chair, his beer spilled and his four aces sliding off the table in response to seeing his opponent's straight flush. "Post Mortem" shows the cards stacked on the table with only three dogs seated around it, still drinking, smoking cigars, and ostensibly discussing the night's activities. "Pinched with Four Aces" shows a game being broken up by four dogs in police uniforms. Meanwhile "Sitting Up with a Sick Friend" is the only one of the nine Brown & Bigelow paintings to feature female dogs, so designated by their fashionable hats. Given the scene, the title appears to describe the lie told by the men to the women regarding the true nature of their gathering. One of the female dogs has an umbrella raised as if poised to strike one of the players. A card falls from the table in the foreground, confirming their guilt.

Finally in 1910 came an additional painting by Coolidge featuring yet another suspenseful scene from a private game. A table full of dogs, including one more female spectator, warily eyes a dog who has just made a huge bet. The title could refer both to the hand the bettor holds and his four similarly suspicious opponents. It's called "Looks Like Four of a Kind."

All of these paintings (collectively or singly) are commonly referred to as "Dogs Playing Poker." Among the various ideas they convey, they clearly help document how by the early 1900s poker had found its way from gaming dens, saloons, and steamboats into private homes. The dogs seem to be respectable doctors and lawyers rather than miscreants or outlaws. It's worth noting also how the world inhabited by Coolidge's dogs is decidedly male-dominated, once again reinforcing poker's "masculine" subculture. As such, the choice of dogs somehow seems appropriate. In 2002, Coolidge's daughter, Gertrude Marcella Coolidge, then 92, told *The New York Times* how she and her mother actually preferred cats. She wonders what the paintings would have been like had her father gone in a different direction. "You can't imagine a cat playing poker," she ultimately decides. "It doesn't seem to go."[7]

The paintings continue to be referenced in movies, commercials, comic strips, video games, album covers, and television shows. An episode of *Cheers* from 1987 finds bar owner Sam professing his love for a "Dogs Playing Blackjack" painting, much to the chagrin of waitress Diane who loathes anything lowbrow.[8] In 1993 an installment of *The Simpsons'* "Treehouse of Horror" Halloween anthologies includes Homer becoming hysterical at the sight of a painting of dogs playing poker.[9] In a 1998 episode of

NewsRadio parodying the blockbuster *Titanic* film from the year before, the ship's owner ditches paintings by Degas and Monet in order to save one of dogs playing poker.[10] And during the original run of the sitcom *Roseanne* (1988-97), two prints of paintings from the series appeared by the front door, deliberately connoting the blue-collar family's status.[11]

Was it Coolidge's purpose to satirize male behavior as somehow animal-like? Or was his target much broader, meant to incorporate the whole of the American middle and upper classes and their foibles? In their survey of American pop culture *Poplorica*, authors Martin J. Smith and Patrick J. Kiger speculate that Coolidge indeed intended the series as a satire. To support their argument they point out how "A Friend in Need" uncannily echoes Georges La Tour's 17th-century painting "The Cheat with the Ace of Diamonds" (mentioned in Chapter 2), a painting clearly intended to "expose the moral turpitude of the upper classes."[12]

Does such an allusion indicate Coolidge was using a commercial medium to make a similar pronouncement about middle- or upper-class America? If that were the case, America doesn't seem to have minded very much. Over the years the popular paintings have been widely reproduced in a variety of media, including as posters, figurines, needlepoint kits, ties and other clothing, clocks, coasters, and, most appropriately, on the backs of playing cards. At least a few among the upper class continue to like them as well. At an auction in 2005, a private collector from New York City purchased the originals of "A Bold Bluff" and "Waterloo" for $590,400. In 2014 the initial painting "Poker Game" sold in another auction for $658,000. Talk about fetching a lot of bones.

A Handy Volume for the Hearthside

Richard Simon (father of singer Carly) grew up in New York City where as a young man he had a burgeoning career as a salesman at a publishing company. In 1924 an aunt who liked crossword puzzles – first created about a decade before – asked him if there were any books available about her specific interest. Seeing an opportunity Simon partnered with Max Schuster to create a new publishing company, Simon & Schuster. Their first publication was a book of crossword puzzles. It was a huge hit, selling more than 100,000 copies, and they followed it that year by three more books of puzzles that also sold well. The following summer the company chose to publish a book devoted to another craze then sweeping the country, a "handy volume for the hearthside" explicitly targeting participants in home games called *Webster's Poker Book*.

The book's title shines the spotlight on the beloved cartoonist Harold Tucker Webster – better known as "H.T. Webster" or "Webby" – who contributes 50 poker-themed cartoons to the volume. Webster was the most famous American cartoonist of the first half of the 20th century, responsible for more than 16,000 cartoons, more than a dozen books, and even once appearing on the cover of *Time* magazine. But in truth the book is a collaborative effort, with a funny foreword by the columnist George Ade, stories and anecdotes by the pulp fiction author and screenwriter George F. Worts, additional material by the playwright and Algonquin Round Table member Marc Connelly, and an appendix with excerpts from R.F. Foster's *Foster's Complete Hoyle*.

A note early on advises readers new to poker to skip ahead to Foster's rules, "then the rest of the book will be more helpful – and more amusing."[13] Indeed, the book is equal parts educational and entertaining, evidence that by then there was not only growing interest in the game, but a considerable compendium of poker-related lore from which draw. As Ade writes in his foreword, "Euchre and seven-up have gone over the hill, but poker is still doing as much business in the winter as baseball does in the summer."[14]

Much humor in the book revolves around the battle of the sexes for which poker represents a familiar cause of conflict, in particular the efforts of husbands to discover ways to escape the notice of disapproving wives in order to play their favorite card game. An early chapter titled "Dealing with the Little Woman" jokes about failed excuses before offering more persuasive suggestions guaranteed to achieve positive results. One such recommendation involves lying about an unexpected visit to the office from the tax man, income taxes having only been introduced in the U.S. a little over a decade before. "The Income Tax, with all its disadvantages, has been a real help to poker players," goes the explanation. "Listen, hon," the reader is instructed to say. "The income tax man is up here in my office, and it's going to take me hours to straighten things out. I'll be home just as soon as I show him where his mistake is." This excuse "never fails," apparently.[15]

More evidence that poker was a game frequently played in homes can be found in chapters such as "Planning the Poker Party" and "The Etiquette of Poker." Naturally, most of the advice is delivered tongue-in-cheek. For those hosting games, recommendations regarding lighting and tables are provided, as are other items listed under "Clearing the Decks," including advice that "if the game is to be staged in one's own home, it is advisable to remove all rugs and everything breakable into another room."[16] As far as etiquette goes, we are instructed "when a glass is accidentally knocked from the table, it is quite proper to kick it into a corner with the foot and pay no more attention to it until the game is over." So, too, is it considered "unethical to empty an ash tray until about one-third of its contents has spilled onto the floor."[17]

There's more joking about remorse over losing (and hiding losses from wives), keeping games going when behind, and breaking away when ahead. Genuinely useful tips appear mixed in among the silliness, too, such as a recommendation not to play wild games too often and an argument outlining the advantages of playing for lower limits. The subject of cheating in poker is also broached in a chapter about "Poker Wolves" that includes warnings about players with "Educated Fingers" and other tricks involving marked decks, palming, bottom dealing, and collusion. Another chapter called "Playing Safe" offers advice to the "poker débutante" for how to play a tight, cautious style complete with rules to follow (including one stating "there are exceptions to every rule"). One more chapter lists "Fascinating Figures" with odds and probabilities for drawing five-card poker hands. Webster's humorous cartoons are a highlight throughout, poking fun at poker players' travails while sometimes illustrating genuine strategic insight. In his full-page panel "The Psychological Effect of a Big Stack," for example, the player with the most chips appears roughly four times the size of his opponent.

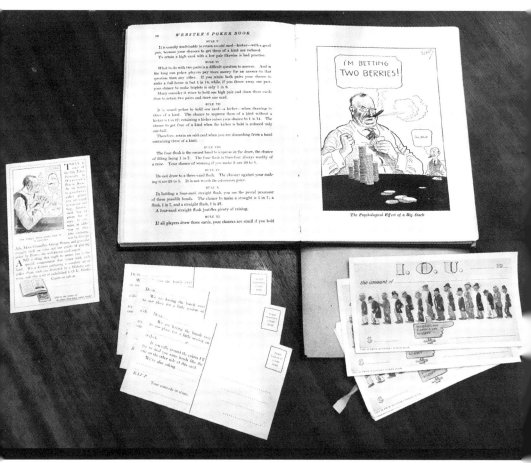

Webster's Poker Book (1925), with accessories including postcards and I.O.U.'s

Poker & Pop Culture

Further evidence of the growing popularity of home games is found in the several accessories included with the original hardbound edition of *Webster's Poker Book*. A tiny drawer is hidden in the back cover, containing several sheets of cardboard poker chips in red, white, and blue, each decorated with a cartoon by Webster. There are also postcards with which to invite friends to home games, and fill-in-the-blank I.O.U. notes to use at the end of the night. The book – the subtitle of which is "Glorifying America's Favorite Game" – could be regarded as a kind of memento of a cultural craze. It's also one of the first great coffee-table books about poker, ideally suited as a gift for home-game hosts.

Wild Cards and Women

If you are hosting a poker party, *Webster's Poker Book* additionally advises "it is wise to have your wife spend the night with some friend," once more suggesting poker's status as a game reserved for men.[18] This attitude is also adopted by the curmudgeonly Mr. Brush in James Thurber's memorable short story "Everything Is Wild," originally published in *The New Yorker* in 1932.

Thurber was a playwright, cartoonist, journalist and writer of fiction best known for his short story "The Secret Life of Walter Mitty" and its multiple adaptations. Much of what Thurber did went under the heading of "humorist" and he found a frequent source of laughter when noting differences between men and women and the conflicts such differences produced, especially in the domestic sphere. In "Everything Is Wild" Thurber cleverly sets up just such a clash when the hosts of a dinner party break out the cards after the meal and three couples gather around the table.

As an archetypal middle-class conservative highly critical of anything that upsets the status quo, Mr. Brush couldn't be less comfortable than to find himself taking hands in a poker game against women and less-than-serious men. Even before the first hand is dealt, Mr. Brush is in a sour mood. He doesn't much like socializing at all, especially with new people ("he never liked anybody he hadn't met before").[19] He becomes even more annoyed when the decision is made to play dealer's choice, and the others all insist on calling games with wild cards. "Seven-card stud," announces one of the women when it is her turn to pick a game. "With the twos and threes wild." The women, we're told, "all gave little excited screams" at the announcement of the wild cards. Meanwhile Mr. Brush, who picks "straight poker" when it is his turn, becomes increasingly exasperated.[20]

Finally he hits on an idea, and he announces they'll be playing "Soap-in-Your-Eye" when he's the dealer again. When the others say they've never heard of it, he notes the game is also called "Kick-in-the-Pants" before explaining the rules. "The red queens, the fours, fives, sixes, and eights are wild," Mr. Brush begins, going on to add how a player drawing a red queen on the second round "becomes forfeit," though "can be reinstated... if on the next round she gets a black four." He deals and keeps adding other options, including having to say "'Back' or 'Right' or 'Left' depending on whether you want to put [a card] back in the deck or pass it to the person at your right or the person at your left" and so on.[21]

Pretty soon everyone is so confused they *want* to play straight poker, but Mr. Brush insists on carrying the hand through to the end. Three of them end up with royal flushes, "but mine is spades, and is high" Mr. Brush announces. "You called me, and that gave me the right to name my suit. I win."[22] It's all a big ruse, of course, designed by Mr. Brush to amuse himself and get back at his wild-card loving opponents. When considering his conservative outlook and intolerance for change, it's clear that Thurber's title doesn't just refer to a poker game, but to the culture as a whole. It is Mr. Brush's angry response to a world in which "everything" seems as though it has gone "wild."

While Thurber's character is part caricature, Mr. Brush's stubborn op-position both to non-traditional poker variants and to progressive thinking about women's roles was common to the era, and continued to exist thereafter. Writing a few decades later in a 1963 essay titled "Poker and American Character," historian John Lukacs linked the rise of wild-card games to "the erosion of the American national character." He argues that games in which hands are routinely overvalued – and, importantly, in which the skill element is lessened – correspond to a society in which "inflation" occurs in other ways, too (e.g., everyone gets a college degree thus devaluing its worth, "the Great American Novel of the Generation" is published five times per decade, and so on). Sounding a lot like Mr. Brush, Lukacs believes a relatively new variant like Spit in the Ocean or even seven-card stud (the nuances of which he doesn't quite follow) represent "a form of immaturity, a strange kind of grown-up disorderliness covering up what is fundamentally an adolescent attitude."[23]

Also like Mr. Brush, Lukacs is unsettled by "the social acceptance of poker-playing women" which he believes "may well have had a bad effect on the game." Lukacs dates the phenomenon as coming shortly after women were given the right to vote in 1920, and also "around the time when smoking by women began to be generally accepted." Lukacs lists a couple of reasons for thinking the "introduction of the female element diluted the character of poker," summarily dismissing them as "notoriously bad gamblers" and thus ill-equipped to compete in a game with such "strongly masculine characteristics."[24] As with Thurber's character, Lukacs' resist-ance both to wild cards and to women playing poker are not unrelated.

"Marriage May Come and Go, But the Game Must Go On"
We'll revisit the subject of poker-influenced domestic strife in later dis-cussions of film, television and radio. But before leaving the topic of home

games, it's worth discussing one of the most famous examples in popular culture: the one imagined by playwright Neil Simon for *The Odd Couple.* First a play, then a film, then made by others into a hit television show, poker is of central importance to Simon's story. In fact, poker is really the only thing the two mismatched title characters have in common.

The original play premiered on Broadway in 1965 starring Walter Matthau as Oscar and Art Carney as Felix, with Matthau reprising his role for the 1968 film adaptation where he was joined by Jack Lemmon as Felix. The popular TV version with Jack Klugman and Tony Randall then ran from 1971-75. Simon's play and film are nearly identical in most respects, including much of the same cast and dialogue. Both begin with a weekly poker game hosted in Oscar's large New York City apartment where all of the play and most of the film is set, a game in which Felix, Vinnie, Speed, Roy, and Murray the Cop are regular participants.

Oscar, we soon learn, is a recently-divorced sportswriter and especially poor housekeeper. Simon's opening stage directions explain how "without the touch and care of a woman these past few months," Oscar's apartment has become "a study in slovenliness" with dirty dishes, empty bottles, unopened mail, and other items strewn about.[25] Roy even complains about the smell coming from a broken refrigerator. "Temper, temper," Oscar says in response. "If I wanted nagging, I'd go back with my wife."[26] The retort suggests a couple of ideas. One is the association of home-making and cleaning up with women, as the complaint is clearly one Oscar had heard from his ex-wife many times. The other is the idea that the poker game is no place in which to express such domestic concerns.

The game continues, although everyone is distracted by the fact that Felix has failed to show. In the play and film, Felix is a news writer, while in the TV show he's a photographer. A phone call from one player's wife reveals Felix and his wife have suddenly split after 12 years of marriage, and Felix didn't show up to work that day. In the film we've already seen him dejectedly wandering around New York, even renting a hotel room where he appears to prepare to kill himself though is unable to follow through. Meanwhile his poker buddies worry their overly sensitive friend may in fact be suicidal.

Eventually Felix arrives and not long after that the game breaks up, leaving Oscar to try to cheer up his friend. Each subsequently lists to the other his own faults, citing them as causes for their respective marriages having failed. "I'm a compulsive cleaner," confesses Felix, adding that his obsessive nature regarding home-making and bookkeeping likely drove his wife away. Oscar describes himself as inconsiderate, sloppy, and wasteful with money. From there comes the plan for Felix to move in with Oscar. They'll save money, Felix can cook and clean, and both can avoid having to endure living alone.

The pair immediately begin to drive each other crazy, with Oscar's boorish carelessness clashing with Felix and his desire for all to be neat, under control, and orderly. The rest of the play and film show their arrangement lasting all of three weeks before Oscar throws Felix out, the conflict building over three lengthy scenes. The first is another meeting of the weekly poker game, once more taking place in Oscar's now-immaculate apartment. Rather than take hands, Felix spends the entire time cleaning up while serving food and drinks. At one point he hesitates before delivering a glass of beer to Roy.

"Where's your coaster?" Felix asks. "My what?" asks Roy. "Your *coaster*, the little round thing that goes under the glass." Roy looks up. "I think I bet it," comes the reply. Oscar notices he has the coaster and tosses it over. "Here," he says. "I knew I was winning too much."

Soon it becomes apparent that fastidious Felix and his constant cleaning is getting in the way of the men's weekly gathering. Given the context, it's hard not to read the scene as showing something "feminine" having crept into what had been the wholly "masculine" sphere of the poker game. "In the last three hours we've played four minutes of poker," says an aggravated Speed while removing a cigar from his mouth. "I'm not giving up my Friday nights to watch cooking and cleaning." Roy agrees: "With the garbage and the smoke, it was better before."

Finally Speed gets fed up with Felix and his fussing about crumbs, coasters, and cleanliness. "I'm going out of my mind!" he yells, then gets up. "I'm going home... the day his marriage busted up was the end of our poker game." Soon after Roy begins sniffing. "What's that smell... disinfectant?" he asks. He then holds the cards up to his nose and his face quickly droops.

"It's the cards," he says, looking aghast. "*He washed the cards!*"

That revelation is enough to send Roy away as well, declaring "Nature didn't intend for poker to be played like that!" The whole scene furthers the idea that home-making is not "masculine" while poker is, and thus problems inevitably arise when the two are mixed. And even if our ideas of gender roles are largely shaped by cultural influences, Roy still thinks Felix's less-than-manly intrusions into their manly game somehow go against "nature."

From there Oscar arranges a double-date for the pair with two British sisters, Cecily and Gwendolyn Pigeon, who live upstairs in the same apartment building. The sisters begin the date all giggles, but Felix quickly ruins all when he cannot stop talking about his wife and kids. All smiles before, the sisters – both of whom had failed marriages, too – end up crying along with Felix about their pasts. It's another scene that marks thin-skinned Felix as somehow less masculine, and certainly different from the hyper-macho Oscar. The pair have a shouting match afterwards, ending with Oscar throwing Felix out of the apartment. The play then concludes by circling back to another poker game, where Oscar finds himself distracted worrying about Felix until he finally returns and the pair make amends. Oscar then asks Felix if he'll be coming to the following week's game.

"What about next Friday night?" Oscar asks. "You're not gonna break up the poker game, are you?" "Me? Never," Felix says. "Marriage may come and go, but the game must go on."

The Odd Couple clearly presents poker as a male ritual, associating it closely with Oscar's character and personality as the host of the games. In that final scene, one of the women from the double-date comes by and apologizes for disturbing the men. "So sorry to interrupt your bridge game," she says, suggesting that poker is something entirely foreign to women. In the play, the sisters even tell Felix to "invite your friends to play in our flat." The stage directions underscore the absurdity of moving the poker game into a non-male setting: "The five men stare dumbfounded at the door without moving."[27]

The later TV series (with which Simon wasn't involved) borrowed a few elements from the play and film, including remaking some scenes in early episodes. Much is different, however, including details of the characters' backstories as well as the fact that Oscar and Felix remain together as roommates for a much lengthier period. The poker returns, however, as do the same group of poker buddies. In fact, the very first episode reprises the double-date with the Pigeon sisters, with Oscar and Felix this time trying to figure out a way to have their date without interrupting the weekly game.

As Felix points out, the group has been playing "every Thursday night for the past four years. The guys lie to their wives, they get babysitters, they sneak out of work early. It's not a poker game anymore, it's a way of life!"[28] In other words, just like in the play and film, poker is still being presented as something that allows men to take refuge away from women. Only unlike in the story's earlier iterations, Felix in this instance is not interfering with the poker game, but rather trying to ensure it continues as a needed escape – a "way of life" for the men who play.

The show continued to use poker as an occasion to create humorous plots and dramatize differences between Felix and Oscar, although ultimately the game continued to be presented an activity essentially reserved for men. Twenty years after his original play, Simon wrote a new version in 1985 called *The Female Odd Couple*. It featured a similar story, but this time with two women roommates, Florence and Olive. And as if to emphasize even further the association of poker as a game for men only, he had the pair play a different game with their circle of friends.

What did they play instead? The name of the game seems like it might describe what some men might think of women's recreations, and what some women may well think of men playing poker: Trivial Pursuit.

10 Poker in the White House

America's most famous home is a 55,000-square-foot, 132-room mansion constructed during the final years of the 18th century and first opened in 1800. It has served as the residence for every U.S. president since John Adams – and it should come as no surprise that many of its occupants have been poker players, in some cases especially dedicated ones. Poker and politics are two of a kind, after all, and in this chapter, we look at the poker games played in and around the White House.

Similarities between America's favorite game and the running of the country are so obvious, in fact, it almost seems redundant to remark how one resembles the other. *Of course* politicians are always working on their images, using aggression, raising the stakes, exploiting edges by applying pressure to opponents, and "going all in" behind this or that cause. Politicians bluff, too. A *lot*. As a result, many have argued that being proficient at poker can be useful to those hoping to reach the nation's highest office. The opinion was held by Albert Upton, a college professor whose best known student, Richard Nixon, was one of many examples of poker-playing presidents. Upton once told a Nixon biographer he was "convinced that a man who can't hold a hand at a first-class poker table is unfit to be President of the United States."[1] Many others agree that learning poker helps teach would-be presidents, providing lessons in the ways of negotiation, diplomacy, and statesmanship.

That said, as has been well established thus far, cultural attitudes toward poker have always been divided, making the prospect of a poker-playing president a positive for some, but objectionable to others. In any case, the sheer volume of anecdotes of the country's commanders in chief enjoying America's favorite card game helps further the case for poker's centrality.

George Washington through U.S. Grant

None of the nation's first presidents played poker as such, the game's introduction having come a few years too late. Many were card players, however.

In a study of the contents of George Washington's library at Mount Vernon, Kevin J. Hayes notes how the first president owned a copy of *Hoyle's Games* (as did many of his generation), as well as other books on cards and gambling.[2] Further evidence exists to show Washington enjoyed playing whist, post and pair, and quadrille, and was even willing to bet small amounts on the games. Most notably, one of Washington's ledger books survives containing two facing pages titled "Cards – & other – Play" on which Washington impressively recorded all of his wins on one side and losses on the other right down to the penny. The account shows that from January 1772 to January 1775 Washington lost exactly £78.5.9 and won £72.2.6 for a total "Bal. against Play" of £6.3.3.[3]

John Adams, James Madison, James Monroe, and John Quincy Adams also played whist. Thomas Jefferson may have been an occasional player, too, though biographers have tended to dispute the claims. Andrew Jackson, who succeeded John Quincy Adams as the nation's seventh president, had an even greater reputation as a gambler, and there are numerous stories of his betting on cards, dice games, cockfights, and horse races. The most notorious ends with Jackson killing a man named Charles Dickinson in a duel in 1806 after a long disagreement that began with a disputed horse racing bet between Jackson and Dickinson's father-in-law. Later Jackson was among the early presidents commemorated in a lavish deck of playing cards produced by Philadelphia-based printer and publisher James Y. Humphreys to commemorate the First Seminole War (1816-19). Featuring four colors (blue spades, red hearts, yellow diamonds, and green clubs), the jacks showed different Indian chiefs while the kings featured Jackson (who was the war's Commander), Washington, Jefferson, and John Quincy Adams as the four kings.[4]

Writing in the 1890s, John F. B. Lillard shared as common knowledge that with just one exception (Rutherford B. Hayes) all presidents dating from the eighth, Martin Van Buren, "have been known to take a hand."[5] Even so, references to card playing come less frequently until later in the 19th century. There's a story of widower John Tyler serving as the 10th president and playing whist on a first meeting with Julia Gardiner, the woman who later became his second wife. However, Sarah Childress Polk, the wife of 11th president James K. Polk, forbade both dancing and card playing in the White House, a prohibition James Buchanan also instituted upon White House social events during his time serving as the 15th president.

Abraham Lincoln's biographers describe an awareness of card games though not much actual card playing by the 16th president. Carl Sandburg tells of Lincoln's trip as a young man down the Mississippi on a flatboat he helped build in order to transport cargo to New Orleans and his eye-opening stay in the Crescent City for three months in 1829. There Lincoln encountered a mix of races and nationalities, got his first significant exposure to the flourishing slave trade, and witnessed "no lack of gamblers with dice or cards."[6] He likely saw more card playing on a steamboat trip back up the river to Indiana.

Polk was in office when Lincoln first went to Washington in 1847 after being elected from Illinois to the House of Representatives. Biographer Benjamin P. Thomas describes how "a simple Western small-town lawyer of temperate habits scarcely had a place," causing Lincoln to be out of step with capital's social scene. "Favorite recreations of Congressmen were whist and bowling," Thomas continues, "and while Lincoln had no liking for cards" he would bowl now and then.[7] Doris Kearns Goodwin adds a later anecdote from a contemporary and friend noting that while others "in their hours of idleness have taken to the bottle, to cards or dice… [Lincoln] had no fondness for any of those."[8]

With Ulysses S. Grant come the first detailed stories of poker playing by the commanders in chief, including during his two terms as the country's 18th president (discussed in Chapter 6). From Grant onward, it became more likely than not for those occupying the office to be poker players.

Grover Cleveland and Theodore Roosevelt

Though of fighting age, New Jersey-born Grover Cleveland steered clear of the Civil War. Having been admitted to the bar in New York where he was serving as district attorney of Erie County, Cleveland took advantage of an option to pay someone else as a "substitute" to serve the Union Army in his place. It may not sound like the actions of a future presidential candidate, but Cleveland wasn't especially interested in politics as a young man, instead preferring to hunt, fish, drink, and play poker.

In his 40s, however, Cleveland began to cultivate an "outsider" image to win elections as a Democrat for mayor of Buffalo and then governor of New York, in part because of a divided Republican party's failure to produce viable candidates. Successful efforts opposing corruption and government spending as well as a willingness to stand up to the influential Tammany Hall helped his reputation as a hard-working representative. Cleveland nonetheless still found respite hosting 25-cent limit poker games each Sunday afternoon at the governor's mansion. "My father used to say that it was wicked to go fishing on Sunday, but he never said anything about draw-poker," Cleveland once joked.[9] Cleveland's popularity grew enough for him to become the Democrats' nominee for president in 1884. He went on to win the popular vote on three consecutive occasions, though is the only president to serve two nonconsecutive terms – he was the 22nd and 24th president – because Benjamin Harrison secured a majority in the Electoral College in 1888.

During his first term in office, Cleveland played a hand of poker that eventually affected the makeup of his cabinet once he was elected for a second time in 1892. In his autobiography, journalist Henry Watterson recounts a low-stakes draw poker game hosted by Secretary of Navy William Whitney, which featured the president alongside former Secretary of War Don Cameron, then Speaker of the House John Carlisle, and Watterson, who was longtime editor of the *Louisville Courier-Journal* and enjoyed a friendship with Cleveland despite delivering sharp criticisms of his presidency.

"Mr. Cleveland was fond – not overfond – of cards," Watterson explains. "He liked to play the noble game at, say, a dollar limit – even once in a while for a little more – but not much more." Perhaps taking advantage of Cleveland's risk-aversion, Watterson tells how he and Cameron "began 'bluffing' the game – I recall that the limit was five dollars – that is, raising and back-raising each other, and whoever else happened to be in, without much or any regard to the cards we held."

A hand arose in which Watterson was dealt a pat flush at the same time that Cleveland had a pat full house. Watterson and Cameron engaged in their pot-inflating once again, but this time couldn't squeeze Cleveland out of the hand. Carlisle also didn't fold, which meant four players lasted until the draw where Watterson and Cleveland kept their cards, Cameron drew one, and Carlisle surprised them all by drawing *four*. Then "after much banter and betting" they showed their hands. Incredibly, Carlisle had four kings to beat them all.

"'Take the money, Carlisle; take the money,' exclaimed the President. 'If ever I am President again you shall be Secretary of the Treasury. But don't you make that four-card draw too often."[10] Shortly after Cleveland began his second term, he kept his promise. While the appointment of Carlisle to the treasury was not viewed as eccentric as some of Cleveland's others, the "Panic of 1893" encouraged a negative estimation of Carlisle's financial acumen. (Perhaps Carlisle's knowledge of economics paralleled his uncertain understanding of probabilities in five-card draw.)

Theodore Roosevelt experienced a similarly rapid rise up the political ladder to the nation's highest office. As happens in poker, both skill and chance were factors helping Roosevelt to become the nation's 26th president in 1901 at the youngest ever age of 42. By then the Republican had already accomplished a great deal, including writing a dozen popular and influential books, serving as the Secretary of the Navy, leading the Rough Riders regiment to a decisive victory during the Spanish-American War, and serving a short term as governor of his native New York. Following the death of Vice President Garret Hobart in late 1899, Republicans

"Stand Pat!" pin from Theodore Roosevelt's 1904 campaign

tapped Roosevelt to join the ticket with President William McKinley for his re-election bid in 1900. After their victory, Roosevelt ascended to the presidency upon the assassination of McKinley 10 months later.

Roosevelt's skills as a poker player may well have played a role in facilitating his rise up the political ranks. In *Mornings on Horseback*, David McCullough tells how curiosity and a sense of duty had motivated Roosevelt to enter politics, though he employed some social wiles to negotiate his way into New York City Republicans' inner circles. The historian shares a note from the English social reformer Beatrice Webb's diaries in which Roosevelt reveals how he insinuated himself with those possessing political power. "I used to play poker and smoke with them," Webb records Roosevelt saying.[11] Poker not only helped Roosevelt build important relationships, but it also helped him complement his background as a cowboy, hunter, and soldier with an image as a bold, vigorous (and manly) leader with an understanding of how to measure risk versus reward.

During his initial three years in office, Roosevelt worked a poker analogy into a metaphor and catchphrase to describe his first and most famous series of domestic policies: the "Square Deal." As shorthand for legislation designed to protect consumers, regulate corporations, and conserve the environment (three "C's"), Roosevelt frequently used the term in speeches while advancing a progressive agenda in which egalitarian ideas of fair play were central. "All I ask is a square deal for every man," he said in one instance. "Give him a fair chance. Do not let him wrong any one, and do not let him be wronged."[12] Later he was even more explicit regarding the poker analogy. "When I say I believe in a square deal I do not mean... [it's] possible to give every man the best hand. If the cards do not come to any man, or if they do come, and he has not got the power to play them, that is his affair. All I mean is that there shall not be any crookedness in the dealing."[13]

At a time when poker games played "on the square" in private clubs and homes were increasing in popularity – specifically as an alternative to less secure games on steamboats and in saloons – Roosevelt's petition for fairness in the larger economic "games" of American capitalism resonated broadly with audiences. The poker theme continued during campaigning ahead of the 1904 election when Roosevelt implored the electorate to "STAND PAT!" The slogan appeared on buttons along with a poker hand of four aces representing "sound money," "expansion," "protection," and "prosperity." The kicker card was the image of Roosevelt himself. He was elected for four more years.

Taft, Wilson, Harding, and Hoover

Abiding by an earlier promise not to run again in 1908, Roosevelt backed his friend and Secretary of War, William Howard Taft, who defeated the

Democrats' nominee to become the nation's 27th president. Unlike Roosevelt, who carefully avoided conspicuous socializing with the era's business leaders, Taft was less adept at hiding such interactions. He played golf and poker with industrial giants like J.P. Morgan, Henry Frick, John D. Rockefeller, and Andrew Carnegie. During a game at steel magnate Frick's mansion in 1910, Taft is reported to have failed with a bluff in a hand versus Archie Butt, military aide to both Roosevelt and his successor. "How did you know I did not have four aces," Taft asked of Butt after the hand. "By your face," Butt replied, adding that when the president happens to pick up a good hand, "his face lights up with a smile which proclaims the secret to the whole table."[14] Taft sometimes drew similar criticism for his presidency. One commentator described him as "the blundering politician, the honest greenhorn at the poker table."[15]

Woodrow Wilson, the country's 28th president, who early in his second term took the country into the first World War, appears not to have cared much for cards. Novelist and journalist Clyde Brion Davis alluded to Wilson's lack of interest when speculating "I have always wondered if the results of the Versailles Conferences would have been different if Woodrow Wilson had been a poker player."[16]

By contrast, Wilson's successor Warren G. Harding, who died in office after only two-and-a-half years, was remembered as one of the most avid poker players ever to occupy the White House. Though Harding was popular, his administration was later found to be corrupt in numerous ways, notably over the Teapot Dome scandal in which his Secretary of the Interior Albert B. Fall received payments from oil companies in order to lease them Navy petroleum reserves at low rates. A subsequent cover-up compounded matters. Harding's Director of the Veterans' Bureau Charles Forbes also took bribes while embezzling more than $200 million from the bureau. Revelation of Harding's extra-marital affairs didn't help his lasting reputation, either, although as was the case with other scandals those didn't fully come to light until after he had succumbed to a heart attack in early August 1923.

During much of his time as the 29th president, Harding hosted poker games twice a week. The players included Fall and Forbes, among other members of his administration, as well as others from the infamous "Ohio Gang" of Harding cronies responsible for many of his administration's improprieties. The games began after dinner and lasted until after midnight, and were consistent enough to have earned Harding's administration the nickname the "Poker Cabinet." Players smoked and drank whiskey (despite Prohibition), with Harding insistent he not be treated any differently by virtue of his higher rank. "Forget that I'm President of the United States," he is quoted as having said to his fellow players. "I'm Warren Harding, playing poker with friends, and I'm going to beat hell out of them."[17]

"He was always congenial and enjoyed himself, but he took the game much more seriously than most realized – and he seldom lost," writes Harding biographer John W. Dean, himself a key figure in another scandalous administration as White House Counsel to Richard Nixon. "The risks he took were calculated and always conservative; he held his cards close to his chest, and he had a good poker face."[18]

However the most famous (and possibly apocryphal) account of Harding's card playing doesn't exactly endorse his skills as a gambler. According to the story, the wealthy socialite Louise Cromwell Brooks (first wife of General Douglas MacArthur) was a guest, and Harding played a game of "cold hand" with her – just a game of high-card – saying that whoever won could name the stakes. When Brooks won she chose as her prize the White House china, a set dating from the early 1890s and Benjamin Harrison's tenure in office. As the story goes, Harding had it delivered to her the next day.

Harding's vice president and successor Calvin Coolidge also enjoyed poker, although another member of his cabinet, his Secretary of Commerce Herbert Hoover, later the 31st president, assuredly did not. In his memoirs Hoover describes once being invited to the White House for the dinner "not knowing that a poker party was in prospect." After the meal the group convened in the study where Hoover saw a large poker table. "I had lived too long on the frontiers of the world to have strong emotions against people playing poker for money if they liked it, but it irked me to see it in the White House," Hoover writes. He soon found an excuse to depart early without taking a seat in the game. "Some time afterward Harding remarked that I did not seem to like poker; and, as I agreed, I was not troubled with more invitations," Hoover recalls.[19] Just as he escaped the game, Hoover likewise escaped being tarnished by the scandals of Harding's administration.

FDR and Truman

Hoover could not escape blame for the worsening economic conditions of the Great Depression, however, and after one term lost a reelection bid in a landslide to Franklin D. Roosevelt.

On his way to winning in 1932, FDR followed the example of his fifth cousin Theodore by employing a poker metaphor to describe his plan to help the country eventually to return to prosperity. "I pledge you, I pledge myself, to a new deal for the American people," Roosevelt promised upon accepting the nomination at the Democratic National Convention. Over the next several years his "New Deal" came to designate an ambitious series of reforms and programs that created numerous agencies, including the creation of both the modern Social Security system and what later became the modern welfare system. Not only did Roosevelt seek to ensure fairness to all, but to reset the "game" altogether, so to speak, with "rules" fashioned in such a way so as to ensure everyone equal opportunity and prospects for success.

Roosevelt also brought poker back into the White House while serving as the nation's 32nd president, hosting low-stakes games of stud several times a week among members of his administration and others. The reporter Walter Trohan, who sometimes played, wrote in his memoirs how "Nothing delighted him more than a successful bluff," noting as well how Roosevelt was "most unhappy when one of his bluffs failed, almost childishly so."[20] Robert H. Jackson served as U.S. Attorney General and on the Supreme Court during FDR's latter years in office, and in diary entries shares stories of having also participated in the games. Jackson states that he never won nor lost more than a few dollars, noting as well how the games routinely "ended one round after 10:00." Jackson likewise describes players frequently catching Roosevelt bluffing, though adds that while FDR usually started out sessions losing, "Invariably he made it up in the last three or four hands of the evening," inspiring others to joke how they "were going to arrange to have a fire call about four hands before the finish" in order to prevent such comebacks.[21]

The tendency for Roosevelt to be more successful the longer the night wore on features in one of the most often told stories of his poker playing. It concerns the annual game FDR hosted on the evening when a given Congress was scheduled to complete a year-long session. As Doris Kearns Goodwin explains, on that night players followed "the strict rule that at the exact moment that the Speaker of the House called the president to say that Congress was adjourning, whoever was ahead at that moment would win the game." On one occasion when such a call came from the Speaker, Roosevelt was down while his Secretary of the Treasury Henry Morgenthau Jr. was way ahead. "So Roosevelt just took the phone and pretended it was somebody else on the line," and the game went on for two-and-a-half more hours until Roosevelt had pulled ahead. That's when he arranged for an aide to bring him a phone, and FDR pretended to take the call from the House speaker signaling the game's conclusion. All was fine "until the next morning when Morgenthau read in the newspaper that Congress had adjourned at 9:30." Apparently Morgenthau "was so angry that he actually resigned his cabinet post until Roosevelt charmed him into staying."[22]

John Nance Garner, FDR's first vice-president, was a poker player as well. A reviewer of George Henry Fisher's *Stud Poker Blue Book* described him in 1934 as "one of the great American experts in stud."[23] However Garner (whose prickly personality earned him the nickname "Cactus Jack") did not receive invites to the president's games. A number of disagreements during FDR's second term cooled their relationship.

Besides opposing some "New Deal" policies as overly liberal, Garner was against Roosevelt's (ultimately unsuccessful) efforts in 1937 to expand the Supreme Court beyond nine justices as granting too much power to the presidency. For similar reasons Garner also strongly opposed the idea of presidents serving more than two terms, and when Roosevelt defied tradition by running for a third term in 1940, Garner split with FDR and ran himself. Historian Robert A. Caro describes fellow Democrats speculating over Garner's motives to run, characterizing some as thinking "the seventy-year-old poker player, having long bided his time, had at last found himself holding a royal flush and could scarcely contain his greed at the pot within his grasp."[24] But Garner's hand wasn't so strong, and with new vice-president Henry A. Wallace on the ticket, Roosevelt easily secured the party's nomination and was reelected by a wide margin.

Roosevelt won reelection once more in 1944, at a time when the country's engagement in World War II meant there was a desire for stability at the top. There was debate over who would be his vice-president, however, with Missouri senator Harry Truman earning the nomination following a contentious convention. Truman took office with FDR in January 1945. Two weeks later Roosevelt met with U.K. Prime Minister Winston Churchill and U.S.S.R. Premier Joseph Stalin at the Yalta conference, where the leaders discussed postwar reorganization in Europe. Two months after that Roosevelt died of a cerebral hemorrhage, and Truman – also a poker player – had suddenly been dealt into the highest-stakes game of his life.

Harry Truman playing poker in a club in Kansas City, Missouri

Truman's experience with poker harkened back at least to the end of the first World War. When captain of the American Expeditionary Forces in France, Truman (already in his early 30s) often played with other soldiers during the evenings. Later in Verdun after the armistice in November 1918, Truman had a long wait before being able to return home. "To keep from going crazy we had an almost continuous poker game," reports a friend of Truman's, a fellow Missourian with whom he was encamped.[25]

Once back home in Jackson County, Truman was a county commissioner during the 1920s, participating in a weekly game across the street from the county courthouse among a group of friends and fellow veterans. They eventually dubbed themselves the Harpie Club, and their game was usually five-card stud with a ten-cent limit and three raises. One player later recalled how Truman was an especially loose player. "He was a chump, in that he wanted to see what your hole card was, and knew anyone got a kick out of winning from him," he recalled. "And if he could whip you he got a big kick out of it."[26] Another of his friends was more charitable in his assessment of Truman as a skilled player who "liked to bluff and he did it on numerous occasions," especially enjoying "to chase me... out of a hand and then show me that I had him beat – that was worth a month's pay. And he did it all too frequently."[27]

There are more stories of Truman playing poker with army buddies over subsequent years, including during his decade-long tenure as a senator and his brief time as vice president. In fact, the very day of Roosevelt's death, another of Truman's army buddies, Edward D. McKim of Kansas City, was in Washington on a business trip and the pair had planned to play a poker game that evening at McKim's hotel. In an interview McKim tells of having arranged to have a green poker table moved into his room along with ice for drinks, then hearing the news of FDR's passing and getting a call from Truman. "Mr. President," McKim answered. "I guess the party's off," began Truman.[28] McKim was President Truman's first official White House visitor the next morning, becoming one of several friends Truman brought in to fill staff positions, a group dubbed "The Missouri Gang."

Less than a month after Truman took office came Adolf Hitler's suicide, Germany's unconditional surrender to the Allies, and V.E. day. Three months after that in early August, Truman was aboard the *U.S.S. Augusta* returning from the Potsdam Conference in Soviet-occupied Germany after having met with Stalin, Churchill and Churchill's successor Clement Atlee. Over the next few tense days final preparations were made for the dropping of the atomic bomb on Japan. Once more Truman filled long hours participating in stress-relieving poker games, this time with the traveling press corps. "Poker was his safety valve," reported legendary White House correspondent Merriman Smith, one of a few reporters invited to play in the games that lasted from mid-morning through to midnight, pausing only for meals.[29]

Smith tells how poker also served Truman in another capacity: keeping him apart from his Secretary of State James F. Byrnes. Besides being preoccupied by the military's plans in the Pacific, Truman genuinely sought respite from discussions of policies and programs with Byrnes. At one point Byrnes complained to Smith about the games occupying all of Truman's free time. "Why in the world don't you men leave the President alone?" Byrnes complained. "Give him time to do something besides play poker." Smith responded, "We don't start these games. He does." Smith jokingly characterized Truman as "running a straight stud filibuster against his own Secretary of State."[30]

Smith's account confirms Truman's loose playing style, his competitiveness regardless of the stakes, and his predilection for unorthodox variants. "Mr. Truman introduced us to an assortment of hair-raising games using wild cards," Smith notes. "One of his favorites was seven-card high-low with the lowest of the three hole or down cards wild…. It is played like regular seven-card stud, except that some players tend to go a little mad after a few hands." One morning the poker game was delayed as Truman "reviewed in great detail the development of the atomic bomb and the forthcoming first drop on Hiroshima. Once this graphic secret was told to us for later publication, out came the cards and chips."[31] There is one other bit of poker-related trivia associated with attack on Japan: two of the planes used for weather reconnaissance in advance of the bombings on Hiroshima and Nagasaki were named Straight Flush and Full House.

Truman played another famous poker game in March 1946, when he and Churchill sat down with cards aboard a train from Washington to Westminster College in Missouri where the statesman delivered his famous "Iron Curtain" speech. The event, along with Stalin's response, is often cited as the start of the Cold War. On Churchill's suggestion, the pair sat down for a poker game with members of the press and others, and for the first hour Churchill was a steady loser. During a break Truman reportedly instructed the others to start taking it easy on their guest, and so they did, allowing Churchill to finish the game a winner. While it is probably a stretch to draw too many deep connections between the poker game and the speech Churchill subsequently gave underscoring the alliance between the U.S. and U.K., it is tempting to give the Americans' "soft playing" against Churchill some symbolic significance.

The poker playing continued for Truman, though more often took place while sailing on the Potomac River aboard the *Williamsburg*, the presidential yacht, than in the White House. One of the regulars was Fred Vinson, Truman's Secretary of the Treasury, whom Truman later appointed as Chief Justice of the Supreme Court. Truman even had a special poker chip set made featuring the presidential seal. Meanwhile a sign reading "The Buck

Stops Here" appeared on Truman's desk. The slogan had poker-related origin, as the "buck" was an early term referring to the button when a buck-horn knife was used to designate the dealer's position. The sign had been given to Truman as a gift – from a fellow poker player, in fact – and he kept it as a way of underscoring his ultimate accountability as president.

Later Truman continued the Roosevelts' tradition of characterizing domestic agendas in poker terms by describing his legislative program as the "Fair Deal." However, as James N. Tidwell notes in a study of "Political Words and Phrases: Card-Playing Terms," the public's patience with such slogans had begun to wane and "any kind of dealing was beginning to be suspect." Sure enough, Dwight D. Eisenhower's deliberately presented himself as "a 'no-deal' man" during his successful 1952 presidential campaign.[32]

Dwight D. Eisenhower

The 34th president, Dwight D. Eisenhower, rose to prominence not through politics but as a five-star general and Supreme Commander of the Allied Forces in Europe during the Second World War. Eisenhower's poker education began while growing up in Abilene, Kansas where he heard tales from elderly neighbors claiming to have known Wild Bill Hickok during his time as marshal there.

In Eisenhower's collection *At Ease: Stories I Tell To Friends*, he fondly recalls a man named Bob Davis teaching him how to fish, shoot, sail, trap, and play poker. Despite being nearly illiterate, Davis well understood poker probabilities, and according to Eisenhower "dinned percentages into my head night after night around a campfire." Sometimes when his young pupil played a hand incorrectly, Davis would snap part of the deck across the youngster's hand "to underscore the classic lesson that in a two-handed game one does not draw to a four-card straight or a four-card flush against the man who has openers."[33]

As a result of such instruction, Eisenhower was a much more careful, informed player than Truman, "never able to play the game carelessly or wide open," and later at West Point routinely beat all comers. Eisenhower knew he was a winning player, too, since "the financial results of the games were always recorded in books with debts to be paid after graduation." He continued to play while working his way up the Army chain of command, once even purchasing a uniform with earnings from what he came to regard as his "favorite indoor sport."[34]

Eisenhower describes his first command of a unit stationed at Camp Colt near Gettysburg, Pennsylvania during the waning days of the First World War. He received a report of an officer who had been caught cheating at poker using marked cards, with those reporting the offense having brought Eisenhower the offending decks. Eisenhower called the man into his office and placed the decks on his desk. After asking the officer if he recognized the cards and receiving an unconvincing denial, Eisenhower had another question. "Well, I can show you exactly where you have marked them. Would you like me to do it?" Again the officer said no, and in response Eisenhower offered him a choice either to resign or be court-martialed. The officer chose the former, but familial connections with a member of Congress enabled the man to remain in the service.[35]

Another later story finds Eisenhower still in Pennsylvania, this time serving under General George Patton at Camp Meade where once again Eisenhower dominated twice-a-week games among fellow officers. Eisenhower discovered that one "uniquely unskilled player" was having to cash his family's war bonds in order to pay what he owed, so conspired with others to lose purposefully to the soldier in order to help him recoup his losses. "This was not achieved easily," Eisenhower explains. "One of the hardest things known to man is to make a fellow win at poker who plays as if bent on losing every nickel." After a long night of throwing hands the officer's way, however, they managed "to get the job done."

The next day Eisenhower met with Patton, and convinced the general to forbid card playing in the brigade. The episode served to make Eisenhower much less enthusiastic about poker. "I decided I had to quit playing," he said. "It was not because I didn't enjoy the excitement of the game – I really love to play. But it had become clear that it was no game to play in the Army."[36]

Long after his decision no longer to play with fellow officers, Eisenhower's skillful poker playing still earned him recognition while also increasing his popularity among the troops.

"Gen. Dwight D. Eisenhower's popularity has skyrocketed throughout the Fifth Army as a result of one of his recent pronouncements," reported the Associated Press just a few weeks before Eisenhower was named Supreme Commander in Europe. The pronouncement had nothing to do with calculating military strategy, but rather concerned a problem involving poker percentages. A soldier had written to Eisenhower, having "heard that the commander in chief has a hobby of mathematically computing odds on poker hands." The soldier asked him what the chances were of drawing *exactly* three kings and two jacks when dealt a five-card poker hand, and Eisenhower couldn't resist replying.

"Although I'm afraid my power of gauging percentages in filling poker hands is a bit overrated, I do like to figure them in my spare time," Eisenhower wrote in a letter dated October 19, 1943. "I haven't had time to go too deeply into the exact figures of your chances of drawing three kings and a pair of jacks – but I'd say they are about 1 in 1,082,900 times. Any mathematician will prove I'm completely wrong, but, anyway, don't count on doing it in a pinch."

The report continued: "Since then doughboys through Italy have been doing heavy pencil and paper work. Scores of them wrote letters to the Stars and Stripes declaring 'Ike' almost hit it on the nose with his estimate." (In truth, it appears Eisenhower may have added an extra zero to his answer, as the correct response is 1 in 108,290, or 24 ways to make three kings and two jacks among 2,598,960 distinct five-card hands.)

In any event, it clearly was a great morale booster for Eisenhower to have answered the letter so thoughtfully. The article concludes with a quote from one "doughboy" saying "I've always thought a lot of the general, but now he's tops on my list of great greats."[37]

JFK, LBJ, and Tricky Dick

John F. Kennedy reportedly enjoyed bridge while in the Navy, though was never much of a poker player. However his successor, Lyndon B. Johnson, was more partial to the game. In his multi-volume biography Robert A. Caro tells of Johnson learning poker from his father while growing up in Texas, and then possibly participating in Truman's poker games when he was a Congressman, either during the one time he rode aboard the *Williamsburg* or the two or three times he was invited to Fred Vinson's home.[38]

Johnson certainly knew poker, and also how the presidency sometimes demanded the decisiveness of a poker player. In *The Vantage Point*, Johnson's written reflections on his time in office, he recalls preparing his first State of the Union address following Kennedy's assassination and his determination to address the need for a civil rights bill despite the advice of staff members not to do so. Alluding to the then 95-year-old John Nance Garner, Johnson tells how Garner, "a great legislative tactician, as well as a good player, once told me that there comes a time in every leader's career when he has to put in all his stack." For Johnson, this was that time. "I decided to shove in all my stack on this vital measure," he writes.[39]

Another story suggests Johnson once won a sports car – the luxury Dual-Ghia, made from 1956-58 – in a high-stakes poker game from none other than Ronald Reagan. The story only appears in accounts of the rare automobile's colorful history and not in presidential biographies, however, and thus might safely be regarded as fabricated. Meanwhile poker pro Thomas "Amarillo Slim" Preston, also one never to shy from telling a tall tale, claimed in his biography to have played poker with both Johnson and his successor, Richard Nixon, of the latter claiming "he wasn't as tricky as advertised."[40]

There's no doubt Nixon, the nation's 37th president and the only one in its history to resign, was a poker player. In fact, Nixon was arguably the most studious poker player ever to hold the office, although there is disagreement over whether or not he might have been the most skilled and/or successful at the game. Historians disagree as well over when exactly

Nixon first played poker, with "Tricky Dick" himself not necessarily truthful about it. As the Senate Watergate Committee once asked of matters far more significant: What did he know, and when did he know it?

Nixon's Quaker upbringing would suggest he steered clear of gambling on cards during his youth. It is likely, however, Nixon first learned poker as a teenager during the two summers he spent in Prescott, Arizona visiting his mother (there nursing his ailing brother and other tuberculosis patients) and working odd jobs. One of young Nixon's jobs involved manning the "Wheel of Fortune" at a carnival called Slippery Gulch, part of the annual Frontier Days rodeo staged each Fourth of July in Prescott. At least one attendee with knowledge of the gambling-themed carnival attractions and high-stakes poker games played in "backrooms of cigar stores" has suggested Nixon "got his elementary education in gambling and poker at Slippery Gulch."[41]

In any case, Nixon certainly had played poker by the time he graduated from Whittier College and was attending Duke Law School. In the spring of 1937, a couple of months shy of completing his law degree, Nixon submitted an application to the Federal Bureau of Investigation for the position of Special Agent. That July he was interviewed in Los Angeles by the FBI, and among the interviewer's notes about Nixon's appearance, conduct, intelligence, and health is a short list revealing "What are his recreations and tastes?" At the time, Nixon said he enjoyed "Handball, swimming, movies, bridge, poker, dancing, reading."[42]

Nixon didn't get a job with FBI, and over the next few years passed the bar, got married, worked for a time in a Whittier law firm, then moved with wife Pat to Washington, D.C. where he took a position with the Office of Price Administration. In August 1942, when he was 29, he enlisted in the Navy, and the following year found himself a passenger control office for the South Pacific Combat Air Transport Command. Eventually he was promoted to lieutenant, and in January 1944 he and his detachment were reassigned to the *U.S.S. Bougainville,* a stop-off for pilots to and from battle missions. He also served on nearby Nissan Island, a.k.a. Green Island, until July 1944 when he was called back to the U.S. He remained in America for the rest of the war.

It was during his time in the Navy, most specifically when stationed in the South Pacific, that most Nixon biographers say he first played poker. In fact Nixon himself claimed as much. "I never knew what poker was until I joined the Navy," Nixon told Earl Mazo, who did not question the claim.[43] It's possible, though, that Nixon did not mean to refer to his lack of acquaintance with the game, but merely to his having yet to learn how to *win* at poker.

Nixon studied poker strategy with great earnest during his deployment, obtaining instruction from bunkmate Jimmy Stewart (not the actor) with whom he helped lead the SCAT detachment. "One day I noticed Nick lost in his thoughts," Stewart later recounted. "He was seemingly concentrating on some problem. Finally he asked: 'Is there any sure way to win at poker?'

I explained that I didn't know of a sure way to win, but that I had a theory for playing draw poker." Stewart's theory consisted of playing a tight game, "that one must never stay in unless he knows he has everyone beaten at the time of the draw." Nixon understood, and the pair "played two-handed poker without money for four or five days, until he had learned the various plays." Stewart concludes: "Soon his playing became tops."[44]

Other fellow officers later echoed the sentiment that Nixon was the most-skilled of the bunch. "He was the finest poker player I ever played against," said one. "I once saw him bluff a lieutenant commander out of $1,500 with a pair of deuces." Another claimed "I never saw him lose," adding Nixon "was consistent" and "might win $40 or $50 every night."[45] According to Nixon, his most memorable hand involved his having being dealt a royal flush in five-card stud and winning "a good pot" despite his multiple opponents folding to the tight player's final round raise.[46] As Nixon notes in his memoirs, he became so consumed by poker in the South Pacific he even once turned down a dinner with aviator Charles Lindbergh as he was hosting a game that night.

"My poker playing during this time has been somewhat exaggerated in terms of both my skill and winnings," Nixon later insisted.[47] It's impossible to pinpoint exactly how much Nixon won at poker as an officer in the Pacific, though letters to Pat reveal he sent money home with some regularity, and most biographers maintain he used at least some of those winnings to help fund his first Congressional campaign in 1946. In one of his later books, Nixon confirmed that prior to that first campaign he and Pat's "net worth was $10,000, a combination of what I had saved from my Navy pay, my poker winnings in the South Pacific, and Pat's job."[48]

In a 1983 interview Nixon outlined his poker strategy in great detail, largely echoing the tight strategy recommended by Stewart, although Nixon also spoke knowledgeably about the art of bluffing. "I didn't bluff very often," Nixon explained. "I just bluffed enough so that, when I really had the cards, people stayed in.... In order to win at poker, you must establish your credibility... that when you are betting you've got the cards."[49]

Such statements read ironically in retrospect, given how much Nixon later bluffed during Watergate, including well after the point when his credibility had been severely diminished. So does his statement about how best to determine if others might be bluffing. "I learned that the people who have the cards are usually the ones who talk the least and the softest," Nixon said. "Those who are bluffing tend to talk loudly and give themselves away." Of course, it was Nixon himself who ultimately talked loudly and gave himself away when Watergate investigators listened to recordings from his secret White House taping system.

Nixon continued to play poker as a member of Congress, as a senator, and occasionally when serving as Vice President under Eisenhower, though he never won as consistently as he did in the Navy. One of his opponents during those games was a young Congressman named Tip O'Neill (later to become Speaker of the House). O'Neill later insisted Nixon wasn't nearly as good a player as his reputation suggested, describing him as "just miserable at poker" and a player who "talked too much and didn't follow the cards." Once when O'Neill complained to Nixon about reading what a good player he was, Nixon responded: "I was pretty good in the Navy." For O'Neill, that was no defense. "Those were kids you were playing with," O'Neill said. "What did they know about poker?"[50]

Nixon played less poker during the 1960s, and even more sparingly after taking office in 1969. However he still talked about poker. On the thousands of hours of White House recordings – amid more sensational talk of payoffs, mysterious erasures, many expletives (deleted in transcripts), and the occasional "smoking gun" – there are several examples of Nixon mentioning poker.

The game comes up a few times both before and after a September 1971 speech in which Nixon declared "world trade was like a poker game," suggesting that in the past America had "generously passed out the chips" so that other nations could "play," but now should stop doing so.[51] Nixon and his staff can be heard debating the usefulness of the poker analogy, with Nixon insisting it not only made his point more understandable but helped him connect with a broader audience. "The poker analogy is very effective and dramatic," Nixon insists to Raymond K. Price, one of his speechwriters, who wonders that there might be "some people who would think it inappropriate to talk [about international trade] in terms of a poker game." Nixon argues to keep the passage, adding how "It would be inappropriate if Harry Truman did it, but it's not for me. Most people don't think I play poker."[52]

During a visit by two of Franklin D. Roosevelt's sons in September 1972, James and John, Nixon cannot resist asking the pair about their father's playing, including whether they recalled a game FDR was said to have hosted in the very San Clemente house Nixon himself then owned. "What did he play?" Nixon asked. "Did he play five-card or did he like wild cards?" Told that wild cards were occasionally used, Nixon calls "wild games... fun, but they're not poker.... When you've got the five cards, you know just what the odds are."[53]

Nixon also brings up his Navy poker games during phone calls with Henry Kissinger, urging his National Security Advisor to "use the poker analogy" during his secret negotiations in Paris with the North Vietnamese. In such instances, Nixon tries to link his poker prowess to a hard-line stance in which all threats are meant to be taken at face value. "You remember I told you about it?" Nixon says to Kissinger during one conversation on the eve of another meeting in early May 1972. "That in the South Pacific, the president as a young officer won $10,000 and he was one of the best poker players. And the mark of the president was that he *seldom* bluffed, but that no one can remember an occasion when he was called that he didn't have the cards.... That's the thing they got to remember. That that's the way I play the game.... I just don't play it in terms of, you know, huffing and puffing and backing down."[54]

Of course, Nixon did sometimes bluff at cards, and history would show he was bluffing here, too, even while claiming never to have done so. A month later the second break-in at the Watergate hotel was discovered, and the subsequent effort to cover-up the burglars' connection to Nixon's reelection campaign was itself a series of bluffs that might well have worked if not for the revelation of the recordings. As poker writer David Spanier concluded a few years later, "The bluff failed in the end because *the hands were recorded* in the form of the tapes."[55]

The recordings confirmed Nixon wasn't nearly as strong as he had represented himself to be, forcing the biggest fold in presidential history.

Gerald Ford through Donald Trump

Whether because of Nixon's ignominious downfall or by coincidence, stories of presidents playing poker become less frequent afterwards. In his autobiography, Gerald Ford tells of getting caught as a child playing penny-ante poker and being reprimanded for it by his stepfather, but offers nothing more regarding the game.[56] Despite the Dual-Ghia story with LBJ, Reagan appears not to have been much of a player, nor are there many stories of George H.W. Bush or Bill Clinton playing poker, although Clinton has made appearances at charity poker events. In *The Poker Face of Wall Street*, Aaron Brown recalls playing poker at Harvard in the mid-1970s including with students in the business school. "I learned later from some of the people I played with that George W. Bush was a regular at those games, and one of the better players," writes Brown, though he himself does not remember playing with "W."[57]

Poker was a favored pastime of 44th president Barack Obama, particularly during his climb up through the ranks of the Democratic party as an Illinois state senator, then as a U.S. senator on his way to his nomination and election in 2008. During his initial presidential campaign, stories surfaced about the low-stakes Wednesday night game Obama played with fellow lawmakers in the 1990s, dubbed "The Committee Meeting." Playing a tight style, Obama was said to have "studied the cards as closely as he would an eleventh-hour amendment to a bill," remaining mindful of odds and rarely bluffing. Indeed, an opponent once jokingly complained "Doggone it, Barack, if you were more liberal in your card-playing and more conservative in your politics, you and I would get along much better." While Obama is said to have often left the games ahead, "he reaped a bigger payoff politically" thanks to the building of relationships with colleagues of both his own party and the Republicans.[58]

Finally 45th president Donald Trump seems not to be a poker player despite his involvement in the casino industry. Trump owned three casinos on the Atlantic City Boardwalk at the time poker was legalized in 1993. Asked about his poker background during an interview at the 1997 U.S. Poker Championship at Trump Taj Mahal, he responded "I've never hand time to play seriously. I've been too busy to really focus on poker. But my life is a series of poker games. Ins and outs. Ups and downs. Highs and lows."[59] Later in 2004, *Bluff* magazine spoke with Trump about his casino's card room. "Poker and *The Apprentice* both are pop culture, both equally cool," he said, alluding both to the ongoing poker "boom" and his reality television show that debuted that year. As far as his own playing goes, Trump again referred to not having time to play. The interviewer persists, however, asking Trump to list six people in history whom he would invite to a poker game.

"Winston Churchill, Napoleon, Abraham Lincoln, Robert Moses, Leonardo da Vinci, and Amadeus Mozart," Trump replied. "Would I win...? Most likely."[60]

It makes sense that many who have sought the highest seat of political power in the US also gravitated toward poker. Possessing the ability to read situations and opponents, being able to adapt to changing circumstances, and having an oversized ego all often translate into success in both contexts. There is something analogous as well between a poker player building a bankroll while moving up in stakes from low to high buy-in games and a politician growing a constituency of supporters while ascending through party ranks.

Poker's legacy as a cheating game also helps encourage comparisons with politics. The point is emphasized by lyricist Sheldon Harnick in the song "Politics and Poker" from the hit 1959 Broadway musical *Fiorello!* about New York City major Fiorello H. LaGuardia's successful battle versus the Tammany Hall political machine. "Neither game's for children, either game is rough," sing a group of political hacks as they debate potential candidates. They list other parallels, too, including how both politics and poker require making decisions about "Who to pick, How to play, What to bet, When to call a bluff."

More than anything, though, the potential for corruption or unfairness in both realms invites the analogy, perhaps further emphasizing poker's unique status as emblematic of American culture and history (good and bad):

> *Politics and poker*
> *Politics and poker*
> *Playing for a pot*
> *That's mediocre.*
> *Politics and poker,*
> *Running neck and neck,*
> *If politics seems more*
> *Predictable that's because usually you can stack the deck!*[61]

11 Poker During Wartime

Metaphorical connections between poker and war are ubiquitous and clearly evidenced by the large overlap in vocabulary shared by the two forms of conflict.

Chips are "ammunition" with which players "fire" bets, actions also sometimes described as "pulling the trigger" or "taking a stab." Players hope to be dealt aces or "bullets," and sometimes, in a re-entry tournament, a player will "bleed" too many chips and have to fire multiple "bullets." In certain "cutthroat" games players might get caught in the "crossfire" between opponents trying to "whipsaw" them with their bets and raises. Occasionally such games involve "kill pots" (or perhaps a "half-kill"). A player might also play a hand "under the gun," go all in on the flop with a "gutshot," then be "drawing dead" by the turn.

That's before we even get into the many analogies between poker strategy and tactics employed on the battlefield. Poker player and author David Apostolico has written a couple of books exploring such connections, *Tournament Poker and the Art of War* applying Sun-Tzu's famous treatise to poker and *Machiavellian Poker Strategy*, which does something similar with *The Prince*. The no-limit hold'em tournament format especially invites the comparison, Apostolico argues, given how it "requires guts and killer instinct" while also emphasizing survival, strengthening one's position by accumulating chips, taking calculated risks, exploiting opponents' weaknesses, and adapting to constantly changing circumstances and goals. Being deceptive is also crucial in both poker and war, with bluffing the most conspicuous illustration.[1]

We've already seen how by the time of the Civil War poker's prominence in America made the game a significant part of soldiers' experience, as well as how the war itself actually helped facilitate the spread of poker throughout the country. We've encountered a few more relevant anecdotes as well of wartime poker among the stories of several poker-playing presidents. The subsequent history of America at war contains many more such stories and connections.

The Spanish-American War and the World Wars

Further evidence of poker during wartime has been colorfully chronicled in various decks of playing cards produced during or after the country's military conflicts. For example, during the Spanish-American War in 1898, soldiers were supplied with decks of cards by the New York Consolidated Card Company, with boxes shaped like little knapsacks and a "blanket" roll at the top of the package containing poker chips.[2] Once hostilities ended and a peace treaty was signed, Anheuser Busch produced special decks commemorating the war's heroes, with Theodore Roosevelt one of those recognized as the jack of spades in one deck and the jack of clubs in another.

When the Americans joined the First World War to fight alongside allies Britain, Russia, and France in April 1917, they again brought cards and poker with them. The Liberty Playing Card Company made a deck a couple of years earlier designed to encourage U.S. involvement, with the Joker showing Uncle Sam rolling up his sleeves in preparation to fight. Other decks featured flags and colors indicating who the Allied forces were, with some designed to further the U.S. soldiers' education. They included French phrases and song lyrics, introducing some basic vocabulary to the English-speaking men to help as they fought alongside the French and Belgians.[3] Several playing card companies produced First World War-themed decks after the war's completion, including one celebrating Armistice Day created and sold some years later by Melbert B. Cary, Jr., a publisher who

Soldiers in the 42nd Infantry Division ("Rainbow Division") playing cards (ca. 1915-20)

had fought with the 103rd Field Artillery on the Western Front. Cary's deck also commemorated the four different mademoiselles from the famous (and bawdy) song "Mademoiselle from Armentières" (a.k.a. "Hinky-Dinky Parlez Vous"), making them the four queens.

While U.S. involvement in the First World War also helped spread poker throughout Europe, many Allies were already well familiar with the game before the Americans arrived. Writing about life in the trenches in his diary, British soldier George F. Wear describes fighting in France in the summer of 1916 while enduring frequent German shelling and intermittent battles. Despite the difficult conditions and constant bombardment, he tells of "spending most of the night playing poker and vingt-et-un, drinking enormous quantities of whisky, cursing the War, and wondering if we should ever go on leave."[4] The Central Powers were plenty familiar with poker, too. The Germans produced a prodigious number of decks with cards depicting war heroes and generals, as well as unflattering caricatures of figures from the Allies' side including Russian Tsar Nicholas II, Serbia's King Peter, and the United Kingdom's First Lord of the Admiralty Winston Churchill.[5]

Poker & Pop Culture

"Aircraft Spotters" cards created by the U.S. Playing Card Company during the Second World War

Still more decks were produced during the Second World War, some of which served especially practical purposes. In 1941, Brown & Bigelow made a special "submarine deck" that featured the hearts and diamonds especially viewable through the dark red adaptation goggles submariners wore in dark conditions. Starting the next year, the U.S. Playing Card Company made a series of Aircraft Spotters decks featuring multiple views of aircraft to help with identification.

Most famously, the USPC's flagship brand Bicycle worked with American and British intelligence to create a deck of cards that peeled apart

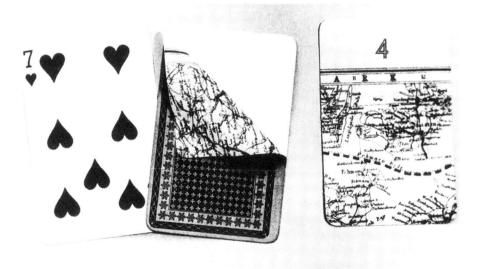

Photo of playing cards concealing an escape route smuggled into Colditz Castle, a German prisoner of war camp during WWII

when soaked in water to reveal segments of escape routes enabling POWs in Nazi camps to find their way back to Allied lines. The decks were delivered to captured soldiers in Red Cross Christmas parcels. The popularity of playing cards was so extensive that the items seemed innocuous to their captors. The decks reportedly proved key to helping a few dozen soldiers find their way to safety.

The Korean and Vietnam Wars

When North Korea's military, with Soviet support, crossed the 38th parallel in June 1950, a United Nations coalition led by the U.S. was quick to respond to help defend South Korea. Some considered the North's invasion as having been triggered by a speech by Secretary of State Dean Acheson early that year in which Acheson suggested America's "defensive perimeter" in the Pacific would not include the Korean peninsula, though Acheson and others later argued his comments had been misconstrued. Addressing the question, historian Bruce Cumings cites Richard Nixon in his 1980 book *The Real War* explaining the episode with "a metaphor from his favorite game, poker." As Nixon put it, "the North Koreans thought our intentions were face up on the board" with regard to what the U.S. would do should they invade. However, "It was a miscalculation by them, based upon a misrepresentation by us."[6] In poker terms, North Korea and the Soviets had misread the U.S. choosing not to bet on one round as indicating they were not intending to bet on a future round – *and* that the U.S. would readily fold should the Communists choose to act.

Three years later came the Armistice and division of Korea, after which Texas radio personality and songwriter Red River Dave McEnery marked the occasion with a novelty song titled "The Red Deck of Cards" (1954). A few years before in 1948 country star T. Texas Tyler had a hit with "The Deck of Cards," a spoken-word track with musical accompaniment telling the story of a soldier caught playing cards in church and facing punishment from a superior. The soldier pleads he wasn't about to deal a hand of poker, but was simply using the cards to reaffirm his faith. The ace, he explains, reminds him of the one God, the deuce the Old and New Testaments, the trey the holy trinity and so on. (Tex Ritter and future game show host Wink Martindale later enjoyed even bigger success with cover versions.) Red River Dave recasts the scene as taking place amid the last days of the prisoner exchange in Korea. A group of American soldiers are recovering in a Red Cross tent, and when one pulls out a deck to deal a game, another angrily swats the cards to the floor. He hates cards, he explains, since the "commies" used them to teach their doctrine. He then mimics the earlier song, matching each card in similar fashion starting with the ace that to the North Koreans meant their sole God, the state, with the deuce standing for Lenin and Stalin, the trey for the Soviets' desire to destroy the Catholic, Protestant, and Jewish faiths and so on. Moved by the soldier's words, the group together rip the cards into pieces before heading off to a nearby chapel to pray.

Later when the U.S. became increasingly involved in Vietnam, the prospect of any similar kind of resolution was unlikely when anchor Walter Cronkite famously surmised on the *CBS Evening News* in early 1968 that "the bloody experience of Vietnam is to end in a stalemate."[7] He made that judgment just over five years before America's withdrawal and more than seven before the North Vietnamese captured Saigon to end the war. While Cronkite was employing a chess metaphor to describe the situation, others likened America's prolonged and disastrous engagement to the stubborn refusal of a poker player to let go of a hand after having committed chips to the pot.

In the epilogue to *The Best and the Brightest*, a magisterial account of decisions made during the Kennedy and Johnson administrations that led to the escalation of U.S. involvement in Vietnam, journalist David Halberstam details the political turmoil swirling around Washington in the first half of the 1960s. In particular, Halberstam characterizes LBJ's win-above-all-else attitude in familiar fashion: "Johnson always liked to talk in poker terms and analogies; the more you put into the pot, the more you had to take out as a winner."[8] Much as Johnson had shown a readiness to go all in behind the civil rights bill the year before, he demonstrated a stubborn disinclination to fold with respect to Vietnam, despite mounting casualties.

As soldiers had done in previous American wars, many among the hundreds of thousands of American troops who served in Vietnam (around 2.7 million total, according to some estimates) carried playing cards. And poker was their favorite game. The cards took on added symbolic significance when American soldiers began leaving them on the bodies of dead Viet Cong, a custom later chronicled in Francis Ford Coppola's *Apocalypse Now* (1979). "Two of spades, three of spades, four of diamonds, six of clubs, eight of spades," calls out Lieutenant Kilgore (Robert Duvall) as he drops the cards on the bodies of dead enemy soldiers, his choice of cards seemingly directed by his estimation of the relative worth of those killed. "There isn't one worth a jack in the whole bunch," he declares.

The grim practice soon evolved to center on one card in particular: the ace of spades, believed by the Americans to represent a bad luck symbol to their enemies. The story earned national notice after the U.S. Playing Card Company began creating full decks in which all 52 cards were the aces of spades. They were useless for poker but more efficient for the type of psychological warfare they served. One September 1966 article in *The Corpus-Christi Caller-Times* tells how the card company shipped the decks for free to soldiers requesting them, coarsely adding that "whole units of card-carrying soldiers are shuffling through rice paddies like riverboat gamblers in jungle boots." However, the article also notes a lack of evidence regarding such beliefs, quoting a Vietnamese United Nations assistant pointing out: "We are a superstitious people... but not of playing cards."[10]

In Oliver Stone's Vietnam film *Platoon* (1986), a barracks poker game appears amid a short sequence of scenes depicting soldiers' efforts to escape the reality of war. Sergeant Barnes (Tom Berenger) is the big winner, his joke that "I ain't even cheating yet" indicating the relatively light mood. But his ability to enjoy the game is challenged by Sergeant O'Neill (John C. McGinley), who aggressively speculates which of them is going to "make it" and who isn't. Soon the daytime scene and country soundtrack of Merle Haggard's patriotic "Okie from Muskogee" (where "we don't burn our draft cards") cuts to night and Smokey Robinson's "Tracks of My Tears." The shift suggests the competitiveness of the game is perhaps uncomfortably analogous to the larger challenge to survive. Poker is replaced by dancing, a scene better resembling what the men have left back home.

Those thrown together in an environment as stressful as war often develop a camaraderie, as do veterans of different wars when given an opportunity to share their experiences. So, too, will poker players often develop a similar kind of fellowship despite the way poker necessarily pits individuals against one other. In a 2017 op-ed for *The New York Times*, Bruce Hobert neatly illustrates both principles at once in "Playing Poker with Veterans."[10] Hobert shares a story of playing in a low-limit cash game at the South Point Casino in Las Vegas, where the table talk happened to reveal that among his opponents were a 93-year-old veteran of the Second World War, another who had fought in Korea, and a third who had done so in Vietnam.

The trio and others at the table come to a couple of agreements, one being that the primary focus in war was "trying not to catch a bullet" (as the WWII vet puts it), something the Vietnam vet failed to do on a couple of occasions. Another concerns America's history as a country inviting to immigrants, as well as dismay over those with an interest in disturbing that legacy. ("Everybody comes from somewhere else," notes the WWII vet.) The story ends with Hobert reflecting how despite battling over pots for several hours, "no one said a hard word to each other," even when "Korea" had his full house beaten by the quad deuces of "Vietnam." "Who runs a puny deuce to the river?" Korea good-heartedly asks. "One's little. Four's battalion strength," cracks Vietnam in response.

The Cold War

Both the Korean and Vietnam Wars played out amid the context of the ongoing Cold War between the U.S. and U.S.S.R. The decades-long ideological standoff between the Second World War's victors began shortly after Winston Churchill's "Iron Curtain" speech in March 1946 – a speech that followed a famous poker game (discussed in Chapter 10) – and Joseph Stalin's denunciation in response, continuing until the Soviet Union's dissolution in December 1991. As it happened, poker played a crucial role in the Cold War, in particular in relation to the lengthy high-stakes "game" of nuclear brinksmanship played by the two superpowers.

Oskar Morgenstern, a German-born economist and mathematician, had been living and working as a professor in Vienna when Hitler's occupation of Austria in 1938 forced him to emigrate to the United States. He eventually joined the faculty at Princeton University where he met another academic émigré, the Hungarian-born mathematician John von Neumann, who in 1928 had published a study in German titled "Zur Theorie der Gesellschafsspiele" or "On the Theory of Parlor Games." Even before their meeting, von Neumann's article had been recommended to Morgenstern thanks to the pair's overlapping interests, and later the two collaborated on a book-length study titled *Theory of Games and Economic Behavior* (1944).

The book became a landmark publication, often heralded as having helped establish game theory as a new and distinct discipline. In a chapter titled "Poker and Bluffing," based in part on von Neumann's earlier article, the authors draw links between several "zero-sum two-person games" and other kinds of situations where two entities are pitted in opposition to one another. Thus heads-up stud poker is analyzed in comparison with, say, social contexts, political conflicts, financial transactions, and war.[11]

Later during the 1950s Morgenstern served as an advisor to President Dwight D. Eisenhower. Von Neumann did some advising of presidents as well, including during the war when he helped work on the Manhattan Project that produced the atomic bombs used in Japan. He also helped advise President Harry Truman about the bombs' use and the choice of targets. In fact, while Morgenstern was later advising Eisenhower, von Neumann was there as well providing guidance while serving as the chair of a secret Intercontinental Ballistic Missile Committee.

It was during this period that the idea of using mathematical models (including some derived from zero-sum games like poker) to describe various types of conflict gained increasing influence. One idea, credited to von Neumann, that often gets highlighted in discussions of these high-stakes Cold War "games" is the notion of "mutually assured destruction," sometimes referred to by its very suggestive acronym "M.A.D." The theory was introduced to explain the behavior of two sides engaged in a type of conflict where neither can win without both losing so badly they cannot "play" again. The certain annihilation that would follow an exchange of nuclear weapons between the two superpowers perfectly exemplified such a situation. If both sides recognized this reality (a key component of the theory), both would necessarily avoid engagement.

John McDonald's popular 1950 title *Strategy in Poker, Business & War* helped game theory and the idea of "Cold War Poker" reach the mainstream.[12] Derived from essays initially published in *Fortune* magazine, the book introduced to a much wider audience than von Neumann and Morgenstern's book how game theory could apply not only to business and economics, but also to politics and war. The book also managed to promote poker as a genuine source of knowledge applicable to everyday life, and not only as a worthwhile recreation for the intellectually inclined. McDonald explains how game theory provides the link between poker and other strategy-filled areas of our existence. He describes poker as "a kind of laboratory of man's experience."[13]

Moving into the 1960s and the start of John F. Kennedy's presidency, the Cold War continued to dominate headlines and op-ed pages, as did allusions to poker strategy's relevance to the question of nuclear conflict. In early February 1961, just a couple of weeks into JFK's tenure at the top, Morgenstern himself wrote an article for *The New York Times* titled "The Cold War Is Cold Poker." It specifically highlighted the parallel between poker strategy and ongoing diplomatic conflict between America and the Soviet Union.

"The cold war is sometimes compared to a giant chess game between ourselves and the Soviet Union, and Russia's disturbingly frequent successes are sometimes attributed to the national preoccupation with chess," Morgenstern begins. "The analogy, however, is quite false, for while chess is a formidable game of almost unbelievable complexity, it lacks salient features of the political and military struggles with which it is compared."[14] The main problem with the chess model, he explains, is the fact that it is "a game of complete information" in which "there is no possibility of bluffing, no opportunity to deceive." By contrast, he continues, poker "describes better what goes on in political reality where countries with opposing aims and ideals watch each other's every move with unveiled suspicion."[15]

Morgenstern argues that since "chess is the Russian national pastime and poker is ours, we ought to be more skillful than they in applying its precepts to the cold-war struggle."[16] Alas (in his view) that had not been the case by early 1961. He explicitly argues in favor of the country's leaders becoming more studious about poker strategy, particularly highlighting the need to learn how bluff effectively (and responsibly) and to learn how to recognize the Soviets' bluffs, too. "The problem of how, on the one hand, to make a threat effective and, on the other, to recognize a genuine threat by your opponent is one of the most fundamental of the day," Morgenstern writes. He then concludes by recognizing one obvious limitation of the poker analogy when applied to nuclear brinksmanship: "In poker there are always some winners and some losers; in power politics, both sides may lose. Everything."[17]

Not everyone agreed with Morgenstern. In a letter to the *Times*, journalist Louis Wiznitzer said the article's pro-poker position "sums up pretty much the essential reasons why the United States has been steadily losing the cold war in the last twelve years." He wrote: "Whereas the Communists are waging a game of chess, with moves as scientifically planned as possible, the Americans are improvising poker moves and bluffs, without a master plan or aim, and depending more or less on their last hand, or reacting to the enemy's bet." Since "politics is not a game nor simply an art" but rather a "science," Wiznitzer insists, the long-range thinking of chess is actually preferable to the overly reactive game of poker. "You cannot beat chess with poker," he concludes.[18]

It's an interesting response, and the failure of the Bay of Pigs invasion two-and-a-half months later, immediately recognized as a woefully shortsighted "play" with especially damaging consequences for the U.S., assuredly inspired still more doubt regarding Morgenstern's argument. The later Cuban Missile Crisis of October 1962 is more often discussed as an application of poker strategy to what was the most tense of all moments during the Cold War. It eventually ended with Kennedy finding a way to induce Nikita Khrushchev to "fold" and prevent a devastating "showdown."[19]

Stories of "Cold War poker" have been told repeatedly in popular culture as well, with both Sidney Lumet's somber drama *Fail-Safe* and Stanley Kubrick's dark satire *Dr. Strangelove or: How I Learned to Stop Worrying and Love the Bomb* alluding to game theory and poker. Both of the 1964 films depict in tonally disparate fashion an accidental U.S. nuclear strike against the Soviet Union and the frantic efforts of leaders to avoid Armageddon.

In *Fail-Safe* Henry Fonda portrays the president, shown toward the end discussing the situation with the Soviet premier while advisors debate the best course of action. One of them, Professor Groeteschele (Walter Matthau), is most often compared with RAND think tank strategist Herman Kahn whose game theory-inspired ideas of nuclear deterrence he articulates. The eccentric Dr. Strangelove (Peter Sellars) delivers a farcical version of the same figure in Kubrick's film, with the German (and ex-Nazi) Director of Weapons and Research Development also said to have been inspired by Kahn, von Neumann, and Nazi rocket scientist Wernher von Braun. Both are unique in their respective films in their espousal of winnable solutions to nuclear conflict and support of the idea of "M.A.D." as a deterrent.

In the 1962 novel from which *Fail-Safe* was adapted, co-authors Eugene Burdick and Harvey Wheeler describe the inner thoughts of Buck, the president's interpreter, as he handles the tension-fraught phone call with

Khrushchev. Unable to detect anything from the Soviet leader's "flat" tone, "Buck felt like a game of word-poker was being played through him."[20] Kubrick was likewise aware of the relevance of poker to the situation he was depicting in *Dr. Strangelove*, and in fact wished to allude to the connection on screen. The film's production designer Ken Adam later recounted how Kubrick explicitly asked that the enormous well-lit circular table in the War Room be made to resemble a poker table.

"Can you cover the table with felt?" Kubrick asked Adam. Apparently the large table around which two dozen men sit with the president was covered with green baize, although viewers cannot appreciate the color in the black-and-white of the film. "I want the whole film to be like a poker game," insisted Kubrick. "Like the general staff and the president and everybody is playing a game of poker for the fate of the world."[21]

More Wars, More Poker

For years following the Gulf War of 1991 the United States attempted to control Saddam Hussein with sanctions, a strategy *The New York Times* called "A Dangerous Poker Game With Iraq." *The Washington Post* reported in 2015 how "Afghan elites, grown wealthy on military contracts, calmly losing thousands of dollars in Texas hold'em" was one of many examples

The war room in *Dr. Strangelove* (1964).
"I want the whole film to be like a poker game," said Stanley Kubrick.

Poker & Pop Culture

of the "cultural imprint" the U.S. left on Afghanistan nearly 15 years after invading. Exactly two weeks before the March 2003 invasion of Iraq, President George W. Bush held a prime time press conference in which he was asked if the U.S. would be calling for a United Nations Security Council vote to authorize military action. "You bet," answered Bush, adding "It's time for people to show their cards, let the world know where they stand when it comes to Saddam." The response prompted *Time*'s Joe Klein to describe "The Poker Player in Chief."[22]

Another vestige of the initial invasion, and what became an eight-year commitment, were "personality identification playing cards" created by the U.S. military identifying 52 "Most Wanted Iraqis" with Hussein the ace of spades. Meanwhile the ongoing and wide-reaching war against the Islamic State militant group (ISIS), which began in 2014, has been variously described by participants and observers as a "high altitude 'poker game,'" "Moscow's game of poker," and "The World (War) Series of Poker."[23]

Likening war to a poker game can have the effect of minimizing the stakes of war, in some cases a deliberate intention of those who do. Meanwhile comparing a game of cards to war is one of many examples of hyperbole surrounding poker narratives, occasionally used to inflate the "stakes" of the hand or game being described.

Even so, when it comes to American wars, talk of poker is as common as a player with pocket rockets bombing the pot in the hopes of eliminating an opponent at showdown.

12 Poker in the Board Room

In early 1988, Warren Buffett wrote his annual letter to the share-holders of Berkshire Hathaway Inc., the multinational holding company for which he serves as chairman and CEO. It was an especially tense time in the investment world, just a few months removed from the "Black Monday" crash that saw markets plunge precipitously around the world. On that day (October 19, 1987), the Dow Jones Industrial Average fell more than 22 percent, the largest single-day decline in the history of the index.

Amid his analysis – by turns sober and bullish – Buffett conjures the image of "a remarkably accommodating fellow named Mr. Market," someone his investors were to regard as a kind of business partner. Mr. Market is mercurial and temperamental, and is really an *opponent* with whom the investor engages in something resembling a two-man poker game. If the analogy weren't already obvious, Buffett then makes it explicit.

"If you aren't certain that you can understand and can value your business far better than Mr. Market, you don't belong in the game. As they say in poker, 'If you've been in the game 30 minutes and you don't know who the patsy is, *you're* the patsy."[1]

Poker players instantly recognize the line, long part of poker lore and adapted as the memorable opening to the 1998 film *Rounders* ("If you can't spot the sucker in your first half-hour at the table, then you are the sucker"). For Buffett to evoke it is only to be expected, given that parallels between poker and the world of business and finance are so readily apparent. In America, a country in which capitalist ideology affects practically every aspect of society and culture, the analogy is all the more striking, with negotiations between self-interested players sitting around the table very much resembling – albeit in a sped up, stripped-down fashion – the transactions of profit-seeking individuals and entities engaged in trade and commerce.

Such comparisons date back to America's early history. Though not a gambler himself, Thomas Jefferson nonetheless once conceded how the work of merchants, land owners, farmers and others can be construed as "games of chance" in the context of describing such pursuits as "indispensible" and not inherently immoral.[2] We've considered as well how John Blackbridge, author of the 1875 book *The Complete Poker-Player*, began his defense of gambling in general and poker in particular by highlighting similarities between such "amusements" and socially accepted (and legal) forms of gambling that occur in the fields of banking, trade, investing, and insurance.

For Jefferson the analogy did *not* absolve games of chance that "produce nothing" (like card games that involve betting) from censure and legal proscription.[3] Blackbridge thought otherwise. "If social circles welcome the banker and merchant who live by taking fair risks for the sake of profit, there is no apparent reason why they should not at least tolerate the man who at times employs himself in giving and taking fair risks for the sake of amusement," argues Blackbridge (himself an actuary and lawyer).[4] Arguments supporting each of these opposing positions have appeared throughout poker's history. Even so, the debate hardly denies the existence of real affinities between poker and business, with Jefferson and Blackbridge's examples illustrating how the discussion often highlights such similarities regardless of the side being argued.

John McDonald also explored the connection in "The 'Game' of Business," another essay from *Strategy in Poker, Business & War* (1950). "Buyer and seller are the same as the players in a two-man poker game," he states, noting how "Each tries to 'maximize' his gain" and that "Each must take the other fellow's thoughts into account" while engaged in the pursuit of such profit. Immediately, however, the market provides examples that appear to expose limitations of the poker analogy. For example, oligopolies or monopolies exist in the business world that allow some "players" in the "game" to exert more influence than others, thereby distorting (or altering) the "rules." Coalitions are also frequently formed, requiring the creation of other models than one based on a game like poker in which such "teaming up" isn't typically allowed. Also relevant is the fact that "Unlike economics, games are nonproductive."[5]

The marketplace additionally tends to be an arena of immense complexity, despite the fact that a couple of major "players" often emerge to fight out "a kind of two-man game within the industry" for leadership.[6] McDonald addressed this "problem of large numbers"[7] in his essays about game theory and in a way, Buffett's "Mr. Market" works as a temporary solution to such a problem. It provides a theoretical reduction of the multi-faceted market to "two-man" competition conducted mainly for purpose of relieving the stress caused by trying to persevere in such an environment.

Being able to perform such mental maneuvers and see correlations others cannot is often a characteristic of the successful entrepreneur. More often than not, those who thrive the most in the world of business have demonstrated an appreciation of the game-like nature of their competition with others. Even though a game like poker is "nonproductive" (as Jefferson observed) and cannot involve on-table coalitions or partnerships (if played fairly), an understanding of how poker is played and the strategies that can produce profit are often both intriguing and genuinely useful to entrepreneurs.

There have been many examples of stock traders, fund managers, professional investors, and other varieties of magnates and moguls who have been drawn to poker, especially recently. Poker Hall of Famer Erik Seidel was a trader on the American stock exchange prior to his embarking on a successful and lucrative career in poker. Cliff Josephy, Dan Shak, Andy Frankenberger, Jason Strasser, Bill Chen, Rep Porter, Matt Glantz, James Vogl, Talal Shakerchi, Cary Katz and Steven Begleiter help form a long list of poker players who have similarly transitioned from the business world to poker (or who continue to straddle both). Many business leaders frequently turn up at the tables, especially in high-stakes cash games and "high roller" tournaments. Some of these games are spread especially to accommodate the deep-pocketed players anxious to test acumen honed in the business world against some of the game's best.

There are many others noted for their successes in the world of business who have found poker a favorite, sometimes serious recreation. Their examples and commentary help provide more reason to appreciate poker's influence in yet another area of American culture.

Turning Information Processing Into Profit

Starting in 1995, Microsoft founder Bill Gates began a more than 23-year run at the top of the *Forbes 400* list of wealthiest Americans. His net worth grew from $12.9 billion that year to nearly $100 billion in 2018, the year Amazon's Jeff Bezos surged past Gates and everyone else to the top of the list. For most of that period Gates also headed lists of the wealthiest people in the world. The story of Gates and his friend Paul Allen starting the company that would eventually evolve into such an immense fortune has been told many times, including by Gates himself in his book *The Road Ahead*. It should not be a surprise when it emerges in the book that Gates is a poker player.

Gates opens his narrative describing his first experience with programming and how he wrote his first software program – a game of tic-tac-toe – when he was 13. It was the late 1960s, and the early computer with which he worked didn't even have a screen. Instead it printed out its moves after a long processing delay. Gates tells how he and Allen started their own company in 1975, naming it "Micro-soft" (before soon dropping the hyphen) and funding it themselves. Allen contributed to the pair's start-up fund with money he had earned working for Honeywell, while "some of the money I had came from late-night poker games in the dorm," Gates says. "Fortunately, our company didn't require massive funding."[8]

Later in the book Gates provides more details regarding those Harvard poker games. He tells how like many college students, he skipped class a lot and crammed at the end just before exams, making it "a game – a not uncommon one – to see how high a grade I could pull while investing the least time possible." What did Gates do when not attending class? "I filled in my leisure hours with a good deal of poker, which had its own attraction for me."[9]

Looking back on his time at the tables, Gates readily notes the ways in which poker strategy overlaps with the tactics employed by successful entrepreneurs. "In poker, a player collects different shards of information – who's betting boldly, what cards are showing, what's this guy's

Founder of Microsoft, entrepreneur, philanthropist, and poker player Bill Gates

pattern of betting and bluffing – and then crunches all that information to-gether to devise a plan for his own hand," Gates writes. "I got pretty good at this kind of information processing," he continues, adding: "The experience of poker strategizing – and the money – were helpful when I got into business."[10]

Poker, Gates maintains, involves the kind of risk that can be managed and even minimized by those who are able to employ an effective, knowledge-able strategy. He differentiates poker from other gambling games in which the house always has a permanent edge. "I think of poker as mostly a game of skill," he says. "Although I play blackjack sometimes when I'm in Las Vegas, the gambling games that are mostly luck don't have a strong appeal for me."[11]

Managing Risk and Reward

Fund manager Jack D. Schwager has written numerous books about the industry, including several in his "market wizards" series of interviews with many of America's most successful traders. In *Market Wizards* (1989), Schwager spoke with Gary Bielfeldt who at the time was an especially suc-cessful trader of treasury bonds for his company, BLH, having entered the market at a fortuitous time.

A poker player from his youth, Bielfeldt talks about the importance of good starting hand selection ("You should play the good hands, and drop out of the poor hands") as well as how when "you have a strong hand… you raise and play that hand to the hilt." He then explains how both principles apply to trading. "I have always tried to keep the concept of patience in mind by waiting for the right trade," he explains, comparing that practice to folding bad starters. "On the other hand, when the percentages seem to be strongly in your favor, you should be aggressive and really try to lever-age the trade similar to the way you raise on the good hands in poker."[12]

Bielfeldt was reluctant to pursue the analogy too far with Schwager, not wishing "to contribute to the image of trading as a form of gambling."[13] However options trader Jeff Yass, one of the founders of the Susequehan-na International Group and also a poker player, was more eager to explore such parallels with Schwager for *The New Market Wizards* (1992).

Yass sounds a lot like Gates when recounting his own experience playing poker while in college. "My friends and I took poker very seriously," Yass says. "We knew that over the long run it wasn't a game of luck but rather a game of enormous skill and complexity."[14] For Yass, those games were more than just a fond memory; they provided the foundation of his training for a career as an investor.

Yass explains how understanding probabilities is a requirement in poker, but is only a first step toward being a winning player. "The really great poker players have an understanding of proper betting strategy," he says, again sounding like Gates as he talks about "information processing" in poker.

"What information do you get when your opponent bets? What information do you give up when you bet? What information do you give up when you don't bet? We actually use poker strategy in training our option traders, because we feel the parallels are very strong." As an illustrative example, Yass talks through a hand of poker in which a player doesn't bet his strong hand on the river, but checks and lets an opponent bet before check-raising as a means to increase the potential profit. "The basic concept that applies to both poker and option trading is that the primary object isn't winning the most hands," he explains, "but rather maximizing your gains."[15]

Yass says: "I learned more about option trading strategy by playing poker than I did in all my college economics courses combined."[16]

Investor and hedge fund manager Steven Cohen, founder of SAC Capital Investors with an estimated net worth of $14 billion, likewise grew up playing poker, as he explained to *The Wall Street Journal* for a 2006 profile. At the time Cohen's company's trading accounted for about 2 percent of the entire stock market.

The profile reads: "He began playing poker frequently as a high school student, he recalls, and would sometimes arrive home at 6 a.m. after an all-night game, hand the car keys to his father, then head to bed without saying a word." Cohen was a winner at those games, and quit a low-paying summer job "to concentrate on cards." His brother reports how he'd "look at his desk in the morning and see wads of $100 bills." Cohen continued to play in college four or five nights a week as he began to study and learn more about the stock market, and looking back affirmed that poker "taught me how to take risks."[17]

Speaking of risks and their potential impact on rewards, an insider trading scandal later dealt a setback to Cohen and SAC, costing the company a $1.8 billion settlement and forcing Cohen to the sidelines from managing outside capital for a couple of years.

Seeking Systems on Wall Street

In 2010, journalist Scott Patterson looked at a group of Wall Street hedge fund managers known for having successfully applied quantitative analysis investment strategies. His book's title gives the group a name while also signaling the scope of its story: *The Quants: How a New Breed of Math Whizzes Conquered Wall Street and Nearly Destroyed It.* The bestseller explores in detail the data-driven, math-centric investing strategy and some of its more famous practitioners. The story starts just before the 2007 subprime mortgage crisis that exposed some of the critical flaws of an approach guided by the idea that "The Truth" (with a capital "T") "was a universal secret about the way the market worked that could only be discovered through mathematics."[18]

The book draws comparisons between investing and card games, and early on highlights the influence of Ed Thorp, the math professor, writer, hedge fund manager, and (most famously) blackjack player who in 1962 wrote the groundbreaking *Beat the Dealer* that outlined for a mass audience how card counting worked as a means to overcome the house advantage in blackjack. Further reinforcing connections between poker and investing, Patterson's first chapter describes a celebrated event from spring 2006 – the "Wall Street Poker Night Tournament" that took place in a midtown Manhattan hotel. It's a way of introducing some of the book's titular characters, including Peter Muller, Cliff Asness, Ken Griffin, and Boaz Weinstein, all significant "players" on Wall Street.

All were dedicated poker players, too, some especially so. Some of "the guys... were *insane* about poker," Patterson explains, noting how Morgan Stanley's Muller in particular was consumed by the game, playing World Poker Tour events and elsewhere. "He played online obsessively and even toyed with the bizarre notion of launching an online poker hedge fund," Patterson writes.[19] The private, $10,000 buy-in tournament was played for charity, raising nearly $2 million to support math programs in New York City public schools. Poker pros T.J. Cloutier and Clonie Gowen also took part, as well as one of the more famous investor-poker players David Einhorn, who a few months later finished 18th in the 2006 World Series of Poker Main Event.

In the tournament, Muller and Asness make it to heads-up, with Muller ultimately coming out on top. The last hand was a preflop all-in in which Muller's king-seven outran Asness' ace-ten when a king spiked on the river. "Odds were against it, but he won anyway," Patterson states, adding a line to foreshadow the longer study to come.

"The real world works like that sometimes."[20]

Risk manager and financial author Aaron Brown is given a lot of attention in *The Quants*, too – as well he should as the author of *The Poker Face of Wall Street* (2006), a book that convincingly analyzes and explains the many ways poker strategy applies in the world of trading. "Poker has valuable lessons for winning in the markets, and markets have equally valuable lessons for winning at poker," Brown maintains, stating a thesis he then proves at length, covering both "poker basics" and "finance basics," then showing how often the risk-managing strategies of each intersect.[21]

In a similar vein, Michael Lewis' *Liar's Poker* (1989) thoroughly documents 1980s Wall Street from the perspective of a bond salesman in the heart of the action. The title comes from the gambling game Lewis presents as something of an obsession among many traders of the day. The game involves the serial numbers printed on dollar bills and players taking turns bidding on how often a particular digit appears among the players' bills until one challenges another's bid.

The game, maintains one such trader, "had a lot in common with bond trading. It tested a trader's character. It honed a trader's instincts. A good player made a good trader, and vice-versa."[22]

It's a game that can – and often does – involve bluffing, and Lewis says it forces players to ask "the same questions a bond trader asks himself," such as "Is this a smart risk? Do I feel lucky? How cunning is my opponent? Does he have any idea what he's doing, and if not, how do I exploit his ignorance? If he bids high, is he bluffing, or does he actually hold a strong hand? Is he trying to induce me to make a foolish bid, or does he actually have four of a kind himself?"[23]

Such questions are familiar to players of other kinds of poker, who constantly ask them as well.

Mapping Poker Variants Onto the Stages of Capitalism

In his 2011 book *Poker: The Parody of Capitalism*, Ole Bjerg carries the analogy even further, arguing not only "that contemporary financial capitalism does indeed resemble a poker game," but wondering "whether the equation of capitalism and poker is really a denigration of the former or perhaps a denigration of the latter."[24] A highlight among the many parallels Bjerg draws in the book is his attempt to map chronologically the historical evolution of poker variants from draw to stud to hold'em onto various phases of capitalism in America – that is, "to trace back in history the parodic simulation of capitalism performed by poker."[25]

Starting with original five-card poker without a draw (called "Straight Poker" in the *American Hoyle*), Bjerg focuses on how the betting action resembles haggling over the price for a product for sale, with players "underselling" or "overselling" their hands as they try to secure the most profit. Such negotiation thus detaches mere exchange value (determined simply by a hand's ranking) from use value (determined by the players' *idea* of what a hand is worth), a move Bjerg likens to the kinds of trade and commerce that took place amid westward expansion during the 19th century.

From there the introduction of the draw to poker increased the game's skill element, making outcomes even more greatly influenced by players' actions and strategies. According to Bjerg, "we can say that the evolution of poker from a game of chance to a game of strategy is comparable to the development of market-immanent mechanisms for the determination of exchange value in capitalist society."[26] In other words, as the nation evolved from an agrarian to an industrial economy and the market became more complex, so, too, did poker's complexity increase.

With the development of stud poker and especially fixed-limit seven-card stud, Bjerg notes the game adding additional challenges to players' attention and memory while also (in his view) becoming "a contest of approximating mathematically optimal play."[27] (Bjerg also suggests bluffing and targeting weak opponents to be less critical in seven-card stud than in draw poker, an opinion with which some players would disagree.) Here Bjerg evokes both Morgenstern and Von Neumann and game theory's efforts to calculate optimal moves as well as "the Fordist organization of the factory, the Keynesian regulation of the macroeconomy, and the market efficiency of modern finance" all finding ready expression in fixed-limit seven-card stud.

Finally comes hold'em with its fewer up cards, no "visible" differences between players' hands (as in stud), and "greater codependence in the development of hands" thanks to the shared community cards. All are important differences from stud, but for Bjerg the prominence of no-limit betting in hold'em creates the most significant break, with players' ability to go all in at any moment meaning "the entire mathematical structure of the game is upset and the nature of the game is transformed qualitatively."[28]

Again characterizing stud players as primarily betting their hands' true value ("representation"), Bjerg contrasts hold'em players being much less direct, so much so that "the betting action constitutes a virtual reality" that suggests value without necessarily actually representing it ("simulation"). That shift Bjerg suggests "corresponds to the difference between industrial capitalism in which the markets are representative and postindustrial capitalism "where financial markets tend to constitute a reality of their own."[29]

It's an esoteric allegory Bjerg draws, to be sure, though it contains enough points of relevance to support larger claims about poker's capacity to reproduce economic realities in sometimes uncanny ways.

The Good and the Bad

We could continue to withdraw from the bank of anecdotes and analogies, pulling out the story of business magnate Carl Icahn allegedly having won $4,000 at poker while in the Army, money he then used to make his first investment, a story echoing Richard Nixon's investing his first Congressional campaign with money won at poker as a Naval officer in the Second World War (discussed in Chapter 10). Or that of banker and businessman Andy Beal, the poker-playing star of both Michael Craig's *The Professor, The Banker, and the Suicide King* and multiple high-stakes poker games played for millions against a group of pros collectively described with the very business-like sobriquet, "The Corporation."

Instead, let's round out the discussion with the humorous aphorism attributed to the actor Walter Matthau whom we met earlier playing cards in *The Odd Couple*, one succinctly summarizing the connection between poker and business: "The game exemplifies the worst aspects of capitalism that have made our country so great."[30]

Poker & Pop Culture

The oft-quoted line highlights how poker uncannily reflects American culture and society, both the good and the bad. In particular the observation draws attention to how both poker and the American economic system necessarily requires individuals to rely on each other while also (paradoxically) forcing them to compete. Those who drill down further often emphasize the latter half of the observation, such as when Al Alvarez understands Matthau to be declaring poker to be "social Darwinism in its purest, most brutal form." Alvarez continues, "The weak go under and the fittest survive through calculation, insight, self-control, deception, plus an unwavering determination never to give a sucker an even break."[31]

Alvarez's conclusion evokes a W.C. Fields film title, and Matthau's line is itself Fields-like. The quote kind of sneaks up on you, beginning like some sort of sober truism and ending with an absurdist rim-shot.[32] It acknowledges there's something bad about the way both poker and capitalism pit us against one another. But it also celebrates such a flawed system (or set of rules) as having somehow, maybe even despite itself, produced something "great." Stepping back even further, the line could be said to evoke both the love-hate relationship some players have with poker and the similarly mixed feelings some Americans often have and express about their country.

It also reaffirms in yet another way – for better or worse – poker's inescapable cultural resonance.

Now I'll give you fifteen
minutes to raise the money,
or the pot's mine.

13 Poker in Folklore

Heard the one about the Chinese concubine who became an Old West saloon owner's bride after he won her in a poker game? Or how an election once ended in a tie and was decided by a hand of seven-card stud? Or how the king of Hawaii used three kings to beat three aces in a poker game, turning over his cards at showdown and then pointing to himself?

Delve deeply enough into poker's history and it doesn't take long to encounter certain stories that have been repeated over and again, many of them spun around accounts of individual poker hands. These famous and often imaginatively embellished hand histories not only help chronicle poker's story, but also shape the game's legacy. They highlight poker's ability to create memorable characters and situations, including fictional ones.

A hand of poker contains its own inherent dramatic structure, complete with an exposition, action building to a climax, and a resolution. Accounts typically start with the introduction of players involved, with relevant background regarding styles or tendencies supplied up front. The efforts of those "characters" to contest the pot is a built-in conflict generator, producing an antagonism sometimes reflected by the convention in hand histories to refer to those involved as "Hero" and "Villain."[1] Suspense is also a certainty, created by the hiding of information both from participants and observers, thereby tantalizingly obscuring the motives behind players' actions. The entire proceeding inexorably leads to *some* kind of dénouement as well (typically the awarding of the pot) which can either satisfy or defy expectations – *and* which can seem either comic or tragic, depending on where you're sitting.

In such stories, the structured order of play and repetitive nature of poker hands translate into something like generic conventions which tale tellers can either honor or violate. It is common in legendary (or mythical) hands from poker's history for there to be an element or elements far enough out of the ordinary that they become especially memorable. It is this that inspires the repeated retellings and the tale's entry into poker "folklore." In some cases the distance from reality is great enough to mark the hand as fanciful, betraying them as obviously fictional (though perhaps "based on a true story"). In others, figuring out what's true and what's false can be harder than reading the poker face of the most inscrutable bluffer.

Clay Calls With Ace-High, Webster Wins With Deuces
We'll begin with one much repeated story of a famous poker hand involving historically known figures – not always the case in these poker folk tales.

For more than 40 years Henry Clay represented Kentucky in both the U.S. House and Senate, including stints as both Speaker of the House and Secretary of State. Clay mounted unsuccessful presidential campaigns on five occasions from the 1820s through the 1840s, including making it to the general election three times. Throughout his public life, Clay's reputation as a gambler was common knowledge, with poker his favored game. In fact, his association with the game was so well known he was sometimes erroneously given credit for having created it.

The actor Joe Cowell in his 1844 memoir (discussed in Chapter 3) repeats that claim when he introduces poker to his readers as "exclusively a high-gambling Western game, founded on *brag* [and] invented, as it is said, by Henry Clay when a youth."[2] During one of his presidential campaigns, supporters of Clay's opponent distributed a pamphlet titled "Twenty-One Reasons Why Clay Should Not Be Elected" that included the charge that Clay "spends his days at the gaming table and nights in a brothel."[3] John Quincy Adams, who defeated Clay in the 1824 election and then named Clay his Secretary of State, similarly recorded in his memoirs how Clay's "armorial bearings" were then understood as "a pistol, a pack of cards, and a brandy bottle."[4]

In such a political climate, taking one more step to suggest Clay actually *invented* poker would not have been difficult, but no other evidence exists to corroborate such a claim. In fact, many stories of Clay's poker playing show signs of potential embellishment, including one of a hand he once played against fellow statesman Daniel Webster of Massachusetts. Like Clay, Webster served in both houses as well as Secretary of State on multiple occasions, and he also ran unsuccessfully for president three times. He enjoyed poker as well, and as fellow leaders of the Whig party (formed in 1834), the pair played on many occasions. These included in games with Robert C. Schenck during his time in Congress before his later service as the country's ambassador to Great Britain and authorship of the first book of draw-poker rules (discussed in Chapter 8).

The story finds Clay and Webster engaged in a hand of five-card draw, probably during the mid-1840s, and details of the hand are similar in all accounts. Picking up the action on the draw, Clay takes one card while Webster stands pat, then the pair engage in a series of raises until each had contributed $2,000 to the pot. The betting finally concludes when Clay calls Webster's last raise, at which point Webster is said to have laughed sheepishly while tabling his hand. "I only have a pair of deuces," he says, expecting to be beaten. "The pot is yours," replies Clay while showing his hand. "I only have an ace-high."

Over time the hand in which each player valiantly tried to bluff the other has been frequently connected to the political careers of both men. It is cited as an example of the courage and boldness both showed in other contexts during their ambitious careers and when negotiating historic compromises regarding slavery and how to treat new territories following the Civil War. It didn't take long, however, for doubts to arise regarding the story's veracity. In *A Game of Draw Poker* (1887), John W. Keller questions this and other tales promoting the pair as "redoubtable warriors in terrific Poker battles." Keller notes in particular how the hand concludes with Clay *calling* with ace-high, and that such a "play would indicate that he was ignorant of Poker." ("Poker players of to-day do not accept this story as true," Keller concludes.[5]) W.J. Florence in *A Gentleman's Hand-Book on Poker* (1890) similarly describes the same hand as "contrary to the probabilities... as well as to good play in general."[6]

There is another fantastic poker story involving Clay (also frequently told) that involves him drawing a pistol against an opponent he discovered to have unfairly secured an extra ace. After the player is sent away, Clay is said to have dramatically fired the weapon into the player's vacated chair. David Spanier later included both hands among "the classic myths of poker."[7]

Poker & Pop Culture

The "Looloo Story"

Another famous poker anecdote known as the "looloo story" first began appearing during the 1890s. Often included in compilations of poker anecdotes, the story emerged from a context including an earlier trick-taking card game from Britain and France called "loo" (occasionally referenced in Jane Austen novels) as well as other accounts of "looloo games."

A *New York Times* piece from 1893 describes New York senator Charles P. McClelland having once derisively described a rival lawmaker's bill as a "looloo."[8] Prompted for an explanation, McClelland was unable to respond, but another senator jumped in to tell the story of witnessing a riverboat poker game on the Mississippi some years before involving a group of black men. At the showdown of a hand of five-card draw, one player turned over aces full, but another claimed the pot after crying "I got a looloo!" while "throwing down five aces and a ten-inch bowie knife."

In yet another poker story emanating from the nation's capital, an 1894 *Indianapolis Journal* article describes Richard Bright, a senator from Indiana, inventing a new game "that may ultimately result in the overthrow in the West of stud poker, and of straight poker in the East."[9] Called the "loo loo game," rules for the five-card draw variant involve alternative hand rankings and use of the joker, plus a final, ultimate hand called a "loo loo" which requires a player to discard all five cards and then draw six. If the player happens to draw three pairs, that's a "loo loo" which beats everything, even five of a kind. If someone draws a loo loo, it is explained, "all that he has to do is to send his loo loo to the nearest bank – savings, national, or State – where it will be found as good as a government bond for obtaining money from the bank vaults."

The idea of a newly invented, unbeatable hand bears relation to the most famous "looloo" story – a story that also includes lawmakers discussing rule changes not just for America but for poker, too. The story first appears in a *Chicago Tribune* article in May 1893 and was soon after borrowed for inclusion in various poker story compilations.[10] (Eugene Ed-

THE LOOLOO
*can be played
but once a night*

A "looloo hand" as shown on the title page of *Jack Pots* by Eugene Edwards (1900)

wards thought enough of it to have a cartoon drawing illustrating the story on the title page of his 1900 book *Jack Pots*, where he also retells it.)

It usually begins in a gambling saloon in Butte, where a young stranger from the east – a "tenderfoot" – endeavors to take advantage of some miners in a game of five-card draw. After winning a few early pots, the stranger picks up four aces and, despite building up a pot, decides to keep the game friendly and only calls the last bet. "I don't want to bankrupt you so early," he says while showing his four aces and moving to scoop the pot. He's stopped, however, by the lone Montana miner left in the hand.

"I have a looloo," his opponent declares, showing a hand of five un-matched cards, three of which are clubs and two are diamonds. When questioned by the stranger, the miner explains how three clubs and two diamonds make up a looloo while jerking a thumb over a shoulder toward a sign hanging on the opposite wall of the saloon: "A LOOLOO BEATS FOUR ACES."

The game continues, and just a few minutes later the young stranger "began betting with his former vigor and recklessness." Meanwhile, we're told, it's at this moment "the barkeeper stopped in the midst of manip-ulating a cocktail, and hung up another card behind the bar." Finally the showdown arrives, and with great satisfaction the stranger shows his hand. "There's a looloo for you – three clubs and two diamonds!" he cries triumphantly. "Really, this is too bad," says his opponent this time. "You don't understand our rules at all. You certainly don't mean to tell me you play poker in such a slip shot way down East, do you? Why, look at that rule over there."

Directed to look over the head of the bartender, the stranger read with dismay: "THE LOOLOO CAN BE PLAYED BUT ONCE A NIGHT."

The story isn't that far removed from earlier tales of card sharps con-spiring with accomplices to facilitate hustles such those told by George Devol in *Forty Years a Gambler on the Mississippi*. It provides a template of sorts for comedic reiterations of the "poker trickster" story soon to be performed by W.C. Fields and others. It also helps chronicle the westward spread of both poker and the country itself, providing a wry commentary on the conflicts produced by the clash of disparate groups.

Using Cards as Collateral

Another oft-told story from the "Wild West" evokes that same idea of an unbeatable hand being "as good as a government bond." This one – of-ten titled "Good Collateral" or something similar – first turns up in sev-eral newspapers during the mid-1880s, then again in later books of an-ecdotes.[11] It is most often set in Denver or Chicago, though the locale changes depending on where the story appears.

It begins with a janitor arriving at a bank and noticing three men sitting on the steps outside. When the cashier arrives, one of the men says he wishes to take out a loan. The cashier asks the man for collateral, and he explains he's involved in a poker hand across the street with more than $4,000 already in the pot. He opens an envelope to show the cashier his collateral: five playing cards, consisting of four kings and an ace.

"This is certainly irregular," the cashier says. "We don't lend money on cards." The man is exasperated, explaining "we ain't playing flushes" which means his four kings with an ace kicker cannot be beaten by a straight flush or any other hand. But the cashier refuses and the three men depart.

Back on the street, they encounter the bank president "who was himself just from a quiet little all-night game." The men explain the situation once more, and immediately the president runs into the bank, grabs a bag full of twenty-dollar bills, and follows the group across the street. Ten minutes later he returns with the same bag plus "an extra handful of twenties" which he instructs the cashier to deposit in the bank's interest account. "Why I thought you had more business snap!" the president says to the cashier. "Ever play poker?" The cashier replies no, which the president already suspected.

"If you did you'd know what good collateral was," the president says. "Remember that in the future four kings and an ace, flushes barred, are always good in this institution for our entire assets, sir – our entire assets."

It's a hand that well evokes capitalist ideology and the sometimes uncanny ways investments in poker hands can resemble those made away from the table – despite the implausible conceit of pausing a poker hand long enough to settle a transaction at a nearby bank. The idea reappears as a major plot point in the 1966 western *A Big Hand for the Little Lady* (see Chapter 16).

The Endless Hand

Stories of poker sessions lasting days, weeks, or months are peppered throughout the game's history, but there aren't as many accounts of individual hands of especially long duration. However, another tale from poker folklore also dating from the 1890s seems determined to establish for all time an unbreakable standard for the longest poker hand ever played.

The story is sometimes attributed to James Stephen "Big Jim" Hogg, governor of Texas from 1891-95, who was said to tell "more good stories of the national game than any other public man in this section of the country" even though he was not a poker player himself.[12] It involves two neighbors living in Austin – Old Man Morgan and Major Danielson – "both enormously rich." The pair played poker nearly every night, occasionally losing significant sums although "the balance was generally pretty even."

On the night of June 15, 1853 at 8 p.m. – the story becomes conspicuously specific – a situation arose in game after dinner in which both players found themselves having been dealt big hands. (Given the lack of reference to a draw, they may be playing without one.) Danielson then bets and Morgan raises, and despite the action thereafter being described as "fast and furious" the raises stretch onward for another couple of hours until midnight. The pot balloons to about $10,000.

The betting continues for another couple of hours until both men exhaust all of their chips in what had originally been "a quiet little game of table stakes." They agree to lift that restriction, and after continuing to raise each other "the table fairly groaned beneath the weight of wealth." By dawn the table actually breaks, and the bets continue throughout the following day with the pair only pausing for meals. "Then they adjourned for six hours to sleep, and resumed the play again at midnight," Hogg says. "They kept it up all the rest of the week, and for the remainder of the year." By then each player "had invested his entire fortune – cash, bonds, stocks, live stock, land, houses, everything in that game," thereby attracting the attention of people from neighboring cities coming to Austin to witness the spectacle.

Some eight years after they had started "the war came along, but the game never stopped," and since both men were too old to fight they continued playing the hand. "Finally it became apparent that neither would ever call the other, so the hands were sealed up separately in tin boxes, and the rest of the deck was put in another one." The boxes were deposited at the bank in Austin, and the pair "went on with their betting," adding whatever income they made to the ever-growing pot.

Both men died in 1872, according to Hogg's account, having left instructions in their wills for their eldest sons to continue the hand. "The heirs did so for five years," until "one of them was killed in a railroad accident and the other went crazy." However *their* eldest sons – the grandsons of the original players – picked up the action from there, and "every time either of them gets a few hundred dollars together, he goes over to Austin and raises the other fellow out of his boots."

The story concludes with the teller explaining how as long as either of the men continues to earn an income, the hand will continue, and "the world will never know what sort of hands old man Morgan and Maj. Danielson drew on that balmy June evening forty-one years ago." Some versions add that the heirs know the hands, but are "sworn to secrecy."[13]

It is tempting to compare the story of the endless poker hand with later, realistic accounts of players unable to muster the strength to pull themselves from the table. In *The Biggest Game in Town* (1983), Eric Drache describes to Al Alvarez feeling as though he were "anteing himself to death" while spending the majority of his waking hours playing poker while think-ing, "I wonder where this is going to end."[14] Drache evokes the crisis David Hayano dubbed "the existential game" in his 1982 study, *Poker Faces: The Life and Work of Professional Card Players*. "To the full-time gambler time is not structured by clock hours and rigid routines but rather by the un-predictable flow and pattern in the fall of cards," Hayano writes. "Time is experienced as passing very quickly from game to game, with virtually no change in the physical surroundings," causing players to become gradually unmoored from the usual markers of temporal change and their effects. Along with other factors, such a circumstance "manifests itself in an exis-tential, if not socio-psychological, kind of imbalance."[15]

Jesse May explores a similar paradox in his 1998 novel *Shut Up and Deal* in which grinder Mickey Dane endeavors throughout to "stay in ac-tion" while also constantly wondering about the goal of a game in which "time stands still and there's no need to think in any terms other than up or down, aces and kings... a very pleasant place to spend eternity."[16]

That said, comparing Governor Hogg's yarn with these deeper pok-er-related inquiries into the human condition probably misses the point. Using deliberate hyperbole – not unlike the tales of legendary lumberjack Paul Bunyan that first appeared a few years later – the story of "the great Morgan-Danielson game" provides a humorous take on the extent to which poker had become an all-consuming obsession for many Americans.

Fixing the Fixer

Arnold "The Brain" Rothstein was best known as one of the likely architects of the infamous "Black Sox" sports betting scandal in which several Chi-cago White Sox players intentionally lost games to throw the 1919 World Series to the Cincinnati Reds. However, it was the manner of Rothstein's death in 1928, and its connection to "a stud poker game famed in the annals of Broadway" (as *The New York Times* described it), that assured the organized crime kingpin a place not just in baseball infamy but in poker folklore as well.[17]

The game began in the West Fifty-fourth Street apartment of Jimmy Meehan on the night of Saturday, September 8, 1928 and lasted until Monday morning. After losing more than $300,000 to multiple players in the game, Rothstein suspected his opponents to have cheated him and was reluctant to pay what he owed. After nearly two months, it appeared someone's patience might have run out as Rothstein was shot at the Park Central Hotel on Seventh Avenue and later died from his wounds. Evidence at the scene implicated one of the players, the gambler and bookie George "Hump" McManus who had served as host for the poker game and who had arranged to meet Rothstein on the night he was shot. Three weeks later McManus gave himself up, and a year after that he was on trial for Rothstein's murder.

Along with Rothstein, McManus, and Meehan, several other notorious gamblers were also present at the game. They included the legendary hustler Alvin Clarence Thomas, a.k.a. Titanic Thompson (on whom Damon Runyon later based his character Sky Masterson in *Guys and Dolls*), future Poker Hall of Famer Joe Bernstein, another notorious baseball game fixer Nate Raymond (rudely known then and afterwards as "N--- Nate"), and others. Everyone present had already earned notoriety of one kind or another for their gambling and/or criminal exploits.

A "parade of players" testified at McManus' trial, providing a few more details of the game. When Meehan was on the stand he explained how they had actually begun with bridge before switching to poker, using cash initially before slips of paper – IOUs from Rothstein – began to appear. Another player, Martin "Red" Bowe, was asked to explain how stud was played, a question that "plainly pained Mr. Bowe, who seemed unable to believe that the game of poker could be unknown to any one." Bowe explained how at some point before proceedings broke up Monday morning "the game got slow," and "so we began to bet on the high card." That's where other accounts suggest the night concluded with Raymond winning $40,000 from Rothstein on a single hand of high-card.

"I cut a card with him," Raymond testified. "Rothstein cut himself a deuce."

Rothstein left soon after. According to biographer David Peitrusza, Rothstein made known his suspicions to others before departing. "I think, my friends, that some of you play cards with more skill than honesty – I think I've been playing with a pack of crooks," he declared.[18]

In court Raymond was said to have won $219,000 from Rothstein, Bernstein "about $70,000," and Thompson "between $20,000 and $25,000."[19] Other reports offer additional (and different) figures, including some suggesting Rothstein's losses totaled nearly half a million. Just about everyone in the game came away winners except for Rothstein and, curiously, McManus. In fact, McManus apparently finished down $51,000. At the trial others confirmed how McManus would not have been bothered by the loss. "He was a good loser, the best loser I know," another attendee Sam Solomon (a.k.a. Sam Boston) testified. Also, McManus had paid his debts in full before leaving the game, including what he owed Rothstein.

Meanwhile Rothstein had only left IOUs. As the prosecution explained, he believed there had been the use of "some 'ring' whereby he was trimmed" – that is, a ring with a reflective surface used as a "shiner" to enable the person dealing to sneak peeks at cards as they were delivered. It was on November 4, 1928 that Rothstein had been called to a late night meeting with McManus at the Park Central Hotel. Rothstein staggered into the lobby soon after, having been shot in the groin. He died two days later on Election Day. Ironically, Rothstein had bet heavily on both Herbert Hoover to win the presidency and Franklin D. Roosevelt to become the governor of New York. Both did, meaning Rothstein would have won more than $500,000 had he lived to collect.

Rothstein had opportunities to finger McManus or whoever else had perpetrated the crime, having been asked repeatedly as he lay wounded who had done the deed. But he refused to identify his killer. McManus was acquitted owing to a lack of evidence, and the crime was never solved.

Decades later journalist Jon Bradshaw interviewed Titanic Thompson near the end of the gambler's life for a chapter in Bradshaw's 1975 book *Fast Company: How Six Master Gamblers Defy the Odds – and Always Win.* Thompson explained to Bradshaw how the night of the game Rothstein had actually approached him to suggest the two of them play "partners" against the others. But when Raymond arrived, Thompson changed his allegiances. "We knew all the angles, how to fix the cards and how to build 'em so they would come out like you wanted 'em to," Thompson explained, referring to himself and Raymond. "Nate was one of the really great fixers and connivers and I thought we might do a little business together that night."[20]

Bradshaw met with Bernstein as well, also near the end of his life and not long after he had won a World Series of Poker bracelet in 1973. (A long-time road gambler and poker player, Bernstein was posthumously elected to the Poker Hall of Fame in 1983.) He explained to Bradshaw how he believed McManus as host of the game felt "responsible for collecting the debts of the losers" and so had arranged the meeting with Rothstein to pressure him once more to settle his debts. Having gotten drunk beforehand, McManus had intended to scare Rothstein with the gun but accidentally shot him, Bernstein surmised.[21]

Such belated reflections don't answer all doubts regarding the game and Rothstein's fate, though they certainly add to the intrigue surrounding it.

More Canards About Cards
There is a durable story regarding Polly Bemis, the Chinese immigrant brought to the United States in 1872 who eventually became the wife of saloon owner Charlie Bemis in the Idaho Territory. However the suggestion of Bemis being won in a poker game was likely a fiction. While Ruthanne Lum McCunn's bestselling 1981 biographical novel *Thousand Pieces of Gold* includes the episode, Bemis herself, her acquaintances, and other local citizens all denied it ever happened.[22]

There are many examples throughout American history of close elections being decided by games of chance, including by dealing out hands of poker. In 2014, there were 35 states with laws stating tied elections must be resolved by games of chance such as drawing straws, coin tosses, or card games.[23] Usually if cards are involved the game chosen is simply high card, although in 1999 after a race for a magistrate judge seat in a New Mexico county ended in a tie, hands of seven-card stud were dealt face up to determine a winner (queens and fours beat a pair of aces).[24] There was even talk in November 2000 of New Mexico doing something similar to decide the extraordinarily close result of the presidential vote that year. "It's hardly likely we'll get Al Gore and George W. Bush back here for one hand of five-card stud," the director of the state Bureau of Elections said, and indeed it proved unnecessary.[25]

Finally, the story that some have shared of the card-loving King Kalahaua, monarch of Hawaii from 1874-91, declaring himself the fourth king to beat an opponent's three aces is not quite accurate.[26] The king did apparently take liberties when playing poker, with one visitor reporting how when playing five-card draw "he was accustomed to call for three cards, retain his discards, and match up a hand for himself out of the lot."[27] However in reality the "fourth king" story went differently, with a sugar plantation owner named Claus Spreckels, also the king's backer, making the declaration as a joke. While playing a Hawaiian card game (not poker), Spreckels noted how if they were playing poker, the three kings in his hand would beat another player's three aces because he was the "sugar king." King Kalakaua didn't appreciate the joke, however, and the hand signaled the beginning of the end of the pair's relationship.[28]

Like other poker folk tales, including Wild Bill Hickok's last hand in Deadwood, or the similarly uncertain one between Johnny Moss and Nick Dandolos in Las Vegas (covered in the next chapter), such tales contribute to poker's larger legacy as a game linked with trickery and deceit. Sometimes they are accompanied by wit and probity, other times by malice and fraud. After all, not only do some of the most memorable poker hands contain bluffs, but so do many of the best stories about them.

14 Poker in Casinos

While the players of the past might have played most of their poker on steamboats or in saloons, clubs, and private homes, the casino emerged during the 20th century as a familiar context for poker in America. For all that, poker's prominence within government-sanctioned gambling establishments has been somewhat muted when compared with other games, both historically and in cultural representations.

Las Vegas

When Las Vegas was founded in 1905 and then incorporated in 1911, it was little more than another small railway town. The line connecting Salt Lake City and Los Angeles ran through it, and the thinly populated desert city was merely a stopover for those traveling elsewhere rather than a destination in itself.

Gambling laws in Nevada had moved through several idiosyncratic iterations over the previous half-century, the most recent being a 1909 law prohibiting practically all gambling games. In 1913 some "social games" pitting player against player like whist and bridge were allowed, though poker and other games were still forbidden. By the time of prohibition there were many cardrooms operating across the state, the most popular of which offered outlawed games such as faro, roulette, slots, and poker while also serving alcohol. Recognizing such enthusiasm (while also taking into account economic hardship caused by the Great Depression) the state's lawmakers passed legislation in 1931 popularly referred to as "the wide-open gambling bill" that lifted all restrictions on gambling. Any establishment able to pay $25 for a license could spread poker and other "social games," while the license for bank games (player versus the house) was $50. A license to offer slots cost $10.[1] That same day, Governor Fred Balzar also signed into law another bill earning national notice, the so-called "six-weeks divorce act" that reduced the residency requirement for those wishing to dissolve a marriage, prompting the next-day headline "Gaming, Divorce Bills Signed."[2]

Also in 1931, construction began on the Boulder Dam Project on the Colorado River about 35 miles south of Las Vegas. At the time it was the largest federal public works project in the country's history. The construction employed thousands of people at a time when work was scarce, and boosted the Las Vegas economy all the way through to the dam's dedication in 1935 by President Franklin D. Roosevelt. (The dam was officially renamed the Hoover Dam after FDR's predecessor a dozen years later.) During these years there was nightlife to be found at several popular clubs in downtown Las Vegas, while a few miles away on Highway 91 those coming into the city encountered a couple of new establishments, the Pair-O-Dice Club and the Red Rooster, both of which had applied for licenses soon after the prohibition on casino gambling was lifted. Downtown the Las Vegas Club, the Boulder Club, the Northern Club, and the Exchange Club also obtained licenses. The end of prohibition in 1933 meant the end of raids some of these establishments had been routinely enduring. A renovated Pair-O-Dice became The 91 Club in 1938, then the El Rancho Vegas opened in 1941 as the first "resort"-style casino. The Last Frontier followed a year later and the Golden Nugget a few years after that.

As some of the club names suggest, many of these establishments borrowed "Old West" motifs and were consciously decorated with saloon-like paraphernalia. Along with the annual Helldorado Days festival and rodeo, which began in 1934, the theme helped lend a particular identity to the growing town. As Hal Rothman writes in his Vegas history *Neon Metropolis*, the theme was "one way that Las Vegas could stand apart from the multitude of similar towns," presenting itself as "a place out of time, left over from an older western past." The "frontier spirit" not only evoked especially American ideas of independence and liberty, but also contained some outlaw cachet or, as Rothman puts it, the "ribald." However, at a time when America was "quick to condemn aberrant behavior yet nostalgic for its lost roots, ribald could be packaged as individual freedom."[3]

It was into this milieu that the New York mobster Bugsy Siegel arrived. Landing in Las Vegas by way of Beverly Hills, Siegel had visions of building a hotel-casino of unprecedented grandeur on Highway 91, a mile south of The Last Frontier. From the point of view of popular culture, Siegel's entrance on the scene unambiguously signals the "birth" of Vegas glitz and glitter, although the true story is much more complicated. For one, the visions associated with Siegel actually originated with a developer named Billy Wilkerson, but they were commandeered after Siegel and his associates helped fund the majority of the project and forced Wilkerson out altogether. The project ultimately went way over budget, ballooning to $6 million – around four times its initial estimates – much of it paid for with mob money. Siegel named his building the Flamingo, and a grand opening took place near the end of 1946 despite the project not being complete. A month later the Flamingo closed again for further construction before reopening in March. By June 1947 the property had just begun to show a profit when Siegel was shot and killed at his Beverly Hills home by an unknown assailant. The murder case has never been solved.

Over the next decade more large scale hotel-casinos joined the Flamingo on Highway 91, soon to become known as "The Strip." The Desert Inn (1950), the Sahara and the Sands (1952), the Riviera and the Dunes (1955), the Tropicana (1957), and the Stardust (1958) eventually helped to create an impressive skyline. Several of the new resorts were similarly backed by mob money, which meant the influence and presence of the "underworld" continued in a different way the "outlaw" status that had already been accorded to Las Vegas. As properties changed hands amid frequent openings and closings, other notable additions to the Strip included Tally-Ho (1963), Westward Ho (1963), Casino Royale (1964), Caesars Palace (1966), and Circus Circus (1968). A population of just over 5,000 in Las Vegas in 1930 grew to more than 64,000 by 1960, and nearly doubled again to more than 125,000 by 1970. The centrality of gambling, still prohibited through much of the country during the century's middle decades, also helped perpetuate Las Vegas' global reputation as "Sin City."[4]

In truth, poker had only marginal standing in Las Vegas during this period. The game was often part of the broader casino scene but rarely the focus even well into the latter decades of the 20th century. Casinos' promotional material from these years – as well as the record of gaming licenses and casino revenue – confirms poker's relatively slight status. Booklets such as the *Eldorado Club Souvenir Gaming Guide* (printed in 1947) list the many games available to guests, including roulette, craps, 21, race horse keno, race horse betting, faro, bingo, slot machines, and sports betting. A brief note describing "the all-American pastime" of poker is included as well, with the rules for draw, stud, and lowball quickly summarized.[5] A similar pamphlet from the El Rancho Vegas recounts its early history and mentions a casino containing "70 slot machines, 2 roulette tables, several 21 tables and 2 craps tables," though makes no reference to poker. Materials from the El Cortez through 1969 all list "Roulette, Keno, Blackjack, Craps, and our ultra liberal slot machines," plus a bingo parlor, but no poker tables. Meanwhile The Last Frontier had a handful of poker tables in 1970 and as many as eight by 1985, though another "how-to" booklet for visitors from that time doesn't include poker among the games explained.

By the 1970s and 1980s the Golden Nugget was promoting poker a bit more enthusiastically than other casinos, and during those years hosted popular pro-celebrity tournaments and the Grand Prix of Poker series.[6] The casino's "how-to" flipbook likely produced around 1971 describes five-card stud, seven-card stud ("The most popular and best-known card game in America today"), and "hold'em stud" (i.e., hold'em), a game "re-

An advertisement for the Eldorado highlighting the table games poker and pan, among other offerings (ca. 1950)

Poker & Pop Culture

cently introduced at the Golden Nugget." Also on offer: "Razzle Dazzle" (six-card lowball) and "Low Ball Draw" (actually razz, but played with a 66-card, five-suited deck with a joker). By the 1980s most of the larger casinos had poker rooms with anywhere from a couple of tables to as many as 12 or 14, though it's worth mentioning that these rooms often spread the popular game of panguingue as well as poker. Better known as "pan," it is a trick-taking game with affinities to gin rummy in which players compete against each other rather than the house.

Surveys during these years show poker to have been gaining favor among the public (especially among men) though not yet exceeding other card games in popularity. A 1940 survey revealed rummy to be the best known card game and contract bridge the favorite to play among both sexes, with poker second among men and a distant sixth among women. A poll in 1947 still had bridge on top, then in 1957 another survey showed canasta having taken over the top spot ahead of contract bridge, pinochle, and poker. In 1974, gambling expert (and frequent survey-taker) John Scarne shared results from his survey of 25,000 American adults to discover poker had at last become the favorite card game of both men and women, edging just ahead of rummy for both sexes.[7] Even so, while poker was becoming America's favorite game to play at home or in other venues, in the casino other games proved more popular. This matched the casinos' preference too. "Bank games" (or "house-banked" games) like roulette, craps, and especially slots provided more significant and consistent revenue to the operators than poker. Such is still the case today, with slots being the favorite of more than 60 percent of those who gamble in casinos, compared with only 4-5 percent who name poker their favorite casino game.[8]

According to data compiled by the University of Nevada Las Vegas Center for Gaming Research, there were 86 poker tables in all of the state's casinos in 1963, a total that grew over the decades to more than 300 during the 1970s then peaked at 682 during the 1980s before falling back to a low of 373 in 2002. Then came the poker boom and by the late 2000s there were more than 1,000 poker tables, a figure that has receded to hover around 600–700 in recent years. The number of slot machines also steadily rose from 1963 to the 2000s before falling back following the recession in 2008. The ratio of slots to poker tables has fluctuated over the years, though today is almost identical to what it was in 1963 – close to 260 slot machines for every poker table.[9] It is worth noting as well that while the number of poker tables in the state has increased, the number of rooms has receded to pre-boom levels. In 2017 there were 71 rooms; in 1997 there were 77.[10]

Casino poker's relatively negligible status is reflected as well in Vegas-centric works of popular culture. The original *Ocean's 11* (1960), which takes place in five Las Vegas casinos (and is filmed in each), essentially disregards poker, although the 2001 remake does introduce an inspired sequence involving Brad Pitt's character teaching the game to a table of young actors playing themselves. Such scenes poke fun at once at celebrity vanity and mistaken assumptions about the relative importance of style and strategy in poker.

Elvis Presley lists poker among the games he's eager to play in the title song of *Viva Las Vegas* (1964), although none of the scenes shot inside the Flamingo and Tropicana for the film highlight the game. Neither is poker on Hunter S. Thompson's radar in *Fear and Loathing in Las Vegas*, although the drugs make it challenging at times for Raoul Duke and Dr. Gonzo to venture too far from their room in the Mint Hotel. In Mario Puzo's 1977 book *Inside Las Vegas*, the author of *The Godfather* more studiously presents a top-to-bottom study of the city's operation and those who inhabit it, folding in his own history as a self-confessed degenerate gambler along the way. Yet while Howard Chapnick's many great photos include several from the World Series of Poker, Puzo only occasionally references poker in his text, saying more about his own experience learning the game as a youngster than about its significance in the casinos.

Johnny Moss versus Nick "The Greek" Dandolos

Of all of the poker tales from the early days of the game in Las Vegas, one story in particular stands out. It involves a legendary heads-up match between Johnny Moss and Nick Dandolos thought by many to have been played at Binion's Horseshoe in either 1949 or 1951. Though much repeated and even celebrated as a famous early example of poker in casinos, the story as it is best known contains more fiction than fact, and arguably distorts the larger history of poker in casinos.

Benny Binion arrived in Las Vegas in 1946 shortly after the Golden Nugget had opened downtown. He had essentially fled Dallas where a checkered past of bootlegging, theft, illegal gambling and other more serious crimes (alleged and actual) had finally threatened to catch up with him. Binion soon became an investor in the Las Vegas Club, located downtown on Fremont Street in "Glitter Gulch," so named because of the many neon signs gaudily announcing the hotel-casinos' presence. In order to attract business, Binion offered higher limits than could be found elsewhere, raising the ire of other casino owners. In a 1973 interview he told of a player once being up $300,000 shooting craps, then ultimately losing $470,000 including $40,000 on a single roll.[11] Binion also describes the state tax commission refusing to grant him a new license when the Las Vegas Club moved across Fremont Street, a factor leading him to break with the casino's investors. Then in 1951 Binion purchased the nearby El Dorado along with the Apache Hotel, renaming it the Horseshoe and once again raising the limits higher than his competitors.

As Al Alvarez tells it in *The Biggest Game in Town* (1983) – an especially influential version of the story – a wealthy gambler from Crete named Nick "The Greek" Dandolos "arrived in Las Vegas looking for a high-stakes poker game" and not so coincidentally found himself in touch with Binion. "The Greek wanted to play no-limit poker, head-up with a single opponent," Alvarez writes, adding how Binion "offered to set up a game, provided it was played in public."[12] The story continues with Binion phoning his longtime friend Johnny Moss back in Texas, convincing him to leave his current game and come to Vegas to play Dandolos with a bankroll provided by Binion. Moss arrived and the two competitors squared off at the poker table as though engaging in an Old West duel over the baize.

In truth, Dandolos did not just show up at the Horseshoe like some mythical cardslinger seeking a challenge. By then he had been gambling in Las Vegas clubs and casinos for many years, just one of many locations in America and around the world where he had built his reputation as a high roller. The extent of his celebrity is proven in pop culture references, such as in the 1952 prison novel *Cast the First Stone* by Chester Himes in which inmate who runs a poker game jokingly says "Old Nick the Greek himself, that's me."[13] In fact, years before Dandolos had been one of the investors in the Las Vegas Club along with Binion.[14] There is also uncertainty regarding the date of the game, with Moss biographer Don Jenkins adding to the confusion in his 1981 book *Johnny Moss: Champion of Champions* by reporting the match began at the Horseshoe in January 1949 – in other words, two years *before* the Horseshoe opened.[15]

Jenkins colorfully describes the two combatants ignoring "the noises and blinking lights of the casino" as they played behind "maroon velvet ropes" with an "entranced crowd behind them." According to Jenkins the pair played for "four and five and six days at a stretch, stopping for sleep maybe once or twice a week," with other "drop-in players" occasionally joining for short periods as well. He relates two hands in particular, both involving Dandolos being lucky to win big pots off of Moss – a five-card stud hand in which Dandolos won more than $640,000 after pairing his jack in the hole on fifth street, and a deuce-to-seven hand in which "the Greek drew two to beat Johnny's pat 8-6 with an 8-5" to win another $250,000 pot. Ultimately, however, Moss overcame his opponent's good fortune to end as the big winner, Jenkins says, adding (with remarkable precision) how "nearly five months to the day after they began" Dandolos finally stood from the table to deliver "his classic statement": "Mr. Moss, I have to let you go."

Alvarez confirms all of those details with Moss, while adding a few more. He notes in particular how "the table, which Benny had thoughtfully positioned near the entrance to the casino, was surrounded by crowds six deep, drawn by rumors of the biggest game the town had ever seen." The gossip continued afterwards, too, regarding how big of a hit Dandolos had taken. "Precisely how much he hand lost is not certain; the rumor says two million," writes Alvarez.[16] Others infer how the spectacle of high-stakes match proved lucrative to Binion, having drawn customers into the Horseshoe where they subsequently gambled themselves. "Binion's subsequent fortune was founded on the dollars these same spectators then poured into his casino's coffers," writes Anthony Holden in *Big Deal* (1990).[17] "Noting how much the railbirds were wagering elsewhere in his casino, Binion called his new attraction 'the biggest game in town,'" adds James McManus in *Cowboys Full* (2009).[18]

It's a compelling story, rich in detail and of seeming importance both to the history of casino poker in general and also as an apparent introduction of high-stakes poker as a kind of "spectator sport." If it were true, that is.

According to Benny's son Jack Binion, Moss and Dandolos *did* in fact play poker with one another in 1949, although "it took place at the Flamingo and not in public," a quote Jack Binion attributes to Dandolos himself.[19] "There was a big game at the Horseshoe in the early 50s," Jack Binion explains, "but Nick didn't participate." The later game featured "multiple players" including Moss, who came and went as the game continued around the clock. Unlike the game at the Flamingo in 1949, the later one "was held in public." The confusion, he surmises, likely stems from Moss having participated in both games. But there was no heads-up match between him and Dandolos at the Horseshoe, nor did the pair ever engage in a high-stakes public poker duel.

Jack Binion adds another helpful point for those curious about the history of the World Series of Poker, which began as a humble gathering of players at Binion's Horseshoe in 1970 and eventually grew into an international extravaganza attracting tens of thousands of poker players from more than 100 countries. "The Moss and Nick the Greek game was not the inspiration for the WSOP," he notes, invalidating a connection many have made between the imagined earlier spectacle and the actual later one. He confirms how he and his father were present in 1969 for an event called the Texas Gamblers Reunion staged by fellow Texan Tom Moore along with Vic Vickrey at the Holiday Hotel and Casino in Reno. The gathering featured a series of high-stakes cash games, and afterwards the Binions asked Moore if he planned to run the gathering again the following year. Moore said he did not, describing it as a "loss leader." "Benny asked him if he would mind if they hosted an annual tournament based on the game," Jack Binion recalls. "He said he didn't mind, and the World Series was born."

One other entertaining – and also certainly apocryphal – part of the Moss-Dandolos story involves a particularly unexpected appearance from the Nobel Prize winning physicist Albert Einstein, who was in America at the time with the Institute of Advanced Study at Princeton University. The digression finds Dandolos spending a break from the action walking about Fremont Street with Einstein, showing the sights to the man who discovered the theories of general relativity and of special relativity while humorously introducing him to others as "Little Al from Princeton – controls a lot of the action around Jersey."

The story has its origins in another tale told by the journalist Ted Thackrey Jr. who in 1968 wrote about Dandolos in a series of newspaper columns called "Secrets of a Master Gambler." In one entry informing readers about differences between American and European roulette wheels and odds, Thackrey incorporates an anecdote about Einstein visiting Vegas where he accompanied Dandolos to a roulette table. It is there, claims Thackrey, the "little mathematician" declared no one can win at roulette "unless he steals money from the table while the croupier isn't looking." (Dandolos subsequently wins two straight spins betting on red then cashes out, as though to prove Einstein wrong.)[20]

Expanding the story for his book *Gambling Secrets of Nick the Greek*, Thackrey added more details, including a description of Dandolos employing the "Little Al from Princeton" line.[21] The episode is undoubtedly invented, and it is not the only instance of Thackrey taking creative license in his columns. An obituary writer described the journalist as "a throwback to an era when newsrooms were afloat in alcohol and reporters didn't let facts interfere with a good story."[22] To be fair, Thackrey's "Secrets" series and subsequent book focusing on Dandolos were clearly intended as at least partly fanciful. Even so, the Einstein cameo has persisted as part of the lore surrounding the mythical Moss-Dandolos match.

Thackrey also plays a role in the story of the birth of the World Series of Poker, having attended the inaugural event in May 1970 as a reporter for the *Los Angeles Times*. There he witnessed the series of cash games after the fashion of the gathering in Reno the year before, and the somewhat anticlimactic conclusion in which players voted Moss the "Best All-Around Player" he was awarded a silver cup.

"You gotta find some way to make it a contest," Thackrey said to Thomas "Amarillo Slim" Preston, a conversation Preston later recounted in his memoir. "If you want to get the press involved and turn the World Series into a real sporting event, you need to give it some structure, create some drama, and make it like a real tournament." Preston credits himself with the idea of making the no-limit hold'em tournament a "freeze-out," meaning eliminated players could not re-enter, sketching a portrait of himself, Thackrey, and Benny Binion "breaking bread" as they planned the following year's event.[23]

In 1971 six players paid $5,000 each to participate in a winner-take-all tournament, with Moss emerging again as the victor. The following year the fee was increased to $10,000, although Binion is said to have contributed the extra $5,000 to cover each player's entry. However, the added money was not enough incentive to attract some to play. As Doyle Brunson tells it in his autobiography, "there were twelve players signed up, but with the cash games so good only eight of us played."[24] However, the WSOP did become meaningful to the promotion of Binion's Horseshoe. As Benny Binion noted in 1973: "This poker game here gets us a lot of advertisement, this World Series of Poker." He added: "Last year it was seven thousand newspapers [covering the event]." Like stories of the Moss-Dandolos match, that too was hyperbole – the figure represented nearly four times the number of newspapers in America at the time.[25]

Such extensive reporting on the WSOP did eventually come, particularly after the event attracted television coverage and Main Event fields quickly swelled into the thousands during the first decade of the 21st century. But back in the 1970s, poker was still a minor element in casinos like Binion's Horseshoe where there wasn't even a poker room when the WSOP began. "The very profitable table games and slot machines were too valuable in the limited space the Horseshoe had to spread for the less profitable poker games," Brunson explains, adding how each year an area would be cleared for the period of the series, then the slots brought back out and reinstalled afterwards. The practice continued until 1988 when Binion's bought the neighboring Mint Casino, the expansion at last enabling the opening of a permanent poker room.

Atlantic City and Elsewhere

The launch of the WSOP came as Nevada was marking four decades as the only state that allowed legalized casinos. That unique status changed a few years later, however, when New Jersey citizens and lawmakers decided to get into the game.

The coastal resort city of Atlantic City had been the site of gambling well before legalization. Underground gambling games became prevalent soon after the city was incorporated in 1854 and the first hotels began to appear. Legislation passed in 1897 prohibited all forms of gambling in the state; however, the following decade a corrupt political leader named Enoch "Nucky" Johnson, first as sheriff then treasurer of Atlantic County, cooperated with crime bosses to help usher in considerable gambling expansion. Numerous illegal casinos were allowed to operate up and down the growing boardwalk. By the Prohibition era the city had earned the nickname "The World's Playground." The period is dramatized in the HBO series *Boardwalk Empire* (2010-14) that features among its recreations a scene of Johnson winning big versus Arnold Rothstein in a high-stakes poker game.

Johnson's period of influence finally ended when he was jailed for tax evasion in 1941. Then in the early 1950s a U.S. Senate Committee led by Estes Kefauver held hearings to investigate organized crime, bringing considerable exposure to many mob figures as well as prosecutions. One consequence of the hearings was the subsequent diminishment of gambling in New Jersey, one of a few factors leading to a period of decline for Atlantic City.

In 1939 the state began to permit racetrack betting, and during the 1950s other "amusements" like bingo and raffles were allowed. By the mid-1970s, and after a couple of attempts, proponents of legalized gambling were able to get a referendum passed by voters to allow casinos to operate in Atlantic City, and a couple of years later the Resorts International Casino Hotel opened in 1978. Following a slow start more casinos were built, with a peak of 12 reached by 1987. Revenues grew through the 1990s and into the 2000s, though it was not until 1993 that poker was legalized and casinos began adding rooms.

The Tropicana and Trump Taj Mahal were the most popular destinations in Atlantic City for poker initially, with the Taj Mahal hosting the United States Poker Championship in 1996 and again from 1998-2010. The poker room at the Taj Mahal garnered additional attention as the setting for a scene in *Rounders* (1998) where Mike McDermott and his cohort Worm describe profiting off tourists arriving each weekend like other "New York rounders." In voice-over during the scene, McDermott refers to the Mirage in Las Vegas as then occupying "the center of the poker universe." However after opening in late 1998 the Bellagio took over that title, with poker rooms at other major Strip properties such as the Venetian (which opened in 1999), the Wynn (2005), and the Aria (2009) also becoming well known poker destinations.

More importantly, casinos in Atlantic City followed the lead of those in Las Vegas by hosting high profile poker tournaments with large prize pools and televised coverage. ESPN covered the inaugural U.S. Poker Championship and did so again for several more years starting in 2003. That was the year the Borgata opened and immediately became the new focus of attention for Atlantic City poker players, hosting numerous World Poker Tour events. Like the WSOP, the WPT helped make casinos an increasingly familiar context for poker.

Laws passed in other states led to the opening of more legalized casinos, starting in Iowa and South Dakota (1989); Colorado, Illinois, and Mississippi (1990); Louisiana (1991); Indiana and Missouri (1993); and Michigan (1996). Meanwhile on Native American-owned lands bingo halls and other gambling establishments began to appear in earnest during the 1970s, prompting legal battles that eventually led to the passage on a federal level of the Indian Gaming Regulatory Act in 1988 that legalized tribal casinos while requiring compacts between states and tribes. By 2017 there were 24 states with legal, commercial casinos, with tribal casinos operating in 28 states and 40 states having one or both – a total of 460 commercial properties (including 347 land-based casinos, 63 riverboat casinos, and 50 racinos), and another 506 tribal gaming facilities.[26]

Many casinos around the country reflect the same trends exhibited in Nevada and New Jersey with an increase in poker tables and rooms during the 2000s followed by a sharp decrease thereafter. Poker currently enjoys greater prominence in some locations than others, especially in casinos serving as frequent stops for "mid-major" tournament series such as the World Series of Poker Circuit (begun in 2005), the Heartland Poker Tour (also launched in 2005), the Mid-States Poker Tour (begun in 2009), and World Poker Tour Deepstacks (started in 2012, with WPT partnering in 2014). Even so, poker consistently contributes a relatively small amount to overall casino revenue. In 2017 commercial casinos passed the $40 billion mark in revenue while tribal casinos also hit a new high at $32.4 billion.[27] Looking at Nevada as a sample, poker currently generates around 1 percent of the total revenue the state's casinos realize each year; for example, in 2017 the state's casinos enjoyed a total gaming win of about $11.57 billion, with just under $118.5 million from poker (or 1.02 percent).[28]

Perhaps unsurprisingly, feature films highlighting gambling in American casinos frequently tend to focus on games other than poker. In *The Gambler* (1974), the self-destructive title character bets on blackjack, craps, roulette, and baccarat in an illegal casino in New York and in several in Las Vegas (in addition to betting on sports illegally). In Albert Brooks' comedy *Lost in America* (1985), a couple's one-night stop at the Desert Inn in Las Vegas results in the gambling addicted wife losing their entire nest egg at roulette. Craps and roulette are the games highlighted in *Indecent Proposal* (1993) in which another couple's Vegas visit results in financial ruin. Blackjack is the game at which Clark Griswold loses his family's savings in *Vegas Vacation* (1997) and the same game is the focus of *21* (2008), the film adaptation of a significantly embellished account of the infamous MIT Blackjack Team. Characters on Las Vegas trips in *Swingers* (1996), *The Hangover* (2009), and *Last Vegas* (2013) also play blackjack. It's also the game used to explain synthetic collateralized debt obligations in *The Big Short* (2015).

As we will see, poker has been represented extensively in feature films, although most often in non-casino settings. Such is the case, generally speaking, for poker in American popular culture, where the game is much more likely to be portrayed in steamboats and saloons (when referencing the 19th century) or underground clubs and private homes (in the 20th and 21st).

15 Poker on the Newsstand

Starting in the late 19th century and especially throughout the 20th, magazines became an increasingly important aspect of American popular culture, often serving as a primary source of news and entertainment. While only a few weekly or monthly magazines enjoyed a national audience prior to the Civil War, many emerged in the years that followed thanks to the construction of railroads connecting the country, technological advances in printing methods to reduce production costs, federal legislation enabling lower mailing rates, and an overall increase in consumer goods. That in turn helped to make advertising an important revenue creator for publishers.

Historian Theodore Peterson notes that 70 to 80 percent of Americans aged 15 or older were magazine readers by the end of the Second World War with the average reader regularly following four or five magazines.[1]

At the beginning of the 20th century some of the country's most read magazines like *Harper's Weekly* enjoyed circulations between 100,000 and 200,000. A couple of decades later popular magazines like the *Saturday Evening Post* had more than 2 million readers per issue, and by the middle of the 20th century dozens of magazines could boast having that many readers. For example, in 1955 *Life* magazine had more than 5.6 million subscribers, with each issue reaching 27.75 million readers. At the time, that represented about one in five Americans aged 10 or older.[2]

Today the most widely circulated magazines in the U.S. still reach millions of readers with every issue, although like all print publications magazines have experienced declines as more readers move online. Throughout magazines' history those with the largest audiences typically fell into a few categories: "general interest" publications, news-oriented magazines reporting on current events, and "women's magazines," with other more specialized publications emerging especially after the Second World War.

It is revealing to review how mainstream publications have discussed and presented poker over the years. Many poker articles tend to highlight the game's social aspect or the fascinating "subculture" with its unique characters, terminology, and customs that often seem especially novel to an audience of non-players. Occasionally they delve into discussions of strategy, too, although often on a superficial level, just enough to confirm the game's skill component to the unaware. Meanwhile articles marveling at the amounts of money won and lost at poker generally don't appear until the boom of the mid-2000s, and even then only poker-specific magazines with limited audiences usually bothered to drill down to discuss particulars.

We've already seen how one magazine's influential profile of "Wild Bill" Hickok, another's publication of Frederic Remington's artwork, and another's sharing a James Thurber short story have contributed in different ways to the history of poker in popular culture. Here are more examples of America's favorite card game earning national attention via some of the country's widest read magazines, starting with a *Life* magazine article that provides an important source for anyone wishing to piece together a history of America's current most popular poker variant, Texas hold'em – an article that has been described as "Exhibit A for anyone investigating the origins of Hold'em."[3]

Life and the History of Hold'em

Founded in 1883, *Life* magazine's "classic" era began in 1936 after its acquisition by business magnate Henry Luce. The popular publication best known for its photography ran poker-related items on multiple occasions, including once reporting on the popular Hoyle Club in New York City in 1941 with an accompanying strategy article humorously explaining "How

Not to Play Poker." Later amid reports during the tumultuous summer of 1968 there appeared a four-page article titled "'Hold Me': a wild new poker game and how to tame it" by A.D. Livingston, author of numerous books including a few on poker strategy. The game Livingston calls "Hold Me" – short for "Hold Me, Darling" or "Tennessee Hold Me" – is Texas hold'em, and Livingston is most enthusiastic about the new game's prospects.

As Livingston explains, hold'em begins with each player dealt two "hole cards" face down followed by a round of betting. Five more "communal cards" are then dealt face up in the center of the table in three stages – first three, then one, then one more – with betting rounds after each deal. The game undoubtedly evolved from seven-card stud in which players also make their best five-card poker hands from seven possible cards. However, rather than each player individually holding an assortment of "up" and "down" cards as in stud, players in hold'em start with their two hole cards while sharing the five in the middle.

Many have surmised that hold'em resulted from a situation in which a group gathered for a game of stud discovered there were too many players to be accommodated by a single deck. With just two hole cards and five in the middle, hold'em theoretically could be played by more than 20 players (as many as 23, if dealt without burn cards), while in an eight-handed game of seven-card stud the deck can be exhausted prior to seventh street if enough players stick around to the end. In order to illustrate how hold'em could be played by a large number of players, a birds-eye photo of 12 men closely gathered around a poker table accompanies the *Life* article.

We've seen how initial references to poker in books by Joe Cowell, James Hildreth, and Jonathan Harrington Green describe what came to be called "Straight Poker" (without a draw) occurring in 1829, 1834, and 1835 (respectively), how Henry G. Bohn's 1850 book first describes draw poker, and how the 1864 *American Hoyle* provides the first mention in print of stud poker. But with hold'em references are less precise and more scattered. Much as the game itself begins with hidden cards followed by the gradual revelation of further information in the community cards, the origin story of hold'em begins in obscurity with certain subsequent pieces of evidence available for all to see, even if their significance is partially uncertain.

In his 2001 book *Poker: Bets, Bluffs and Bad Beats*, Al Alvarez sets forth that "Hold'em has been played in Texas since the end of the nineteenth century," albeit without concrete evidence.[4] In 2007, a native of Robstown, Texas serving in the state's legislature managed to pass a resolution declaring "The game's invention dates back to the early 1900s when it is traditionally held that the first hand of the popular card game was dealt in the city of Robstown," though again there exists no obvious support for such an assertion.[5]

In 1981, Poker Hall of Famer Johnny Moss told biographer Don Jenkins about his first acquaintance with hold'em, describing having played both fixed-limit and no-limit versions of the game in two Dallas clubs, the Elks Club and the Otters Club "around 1930."[6] When speaking with journalist Jon Bradshaw in 1974, Moss described himself initially working at a Dallas gambling house for $3 a day at the age of 16 (i.e., around 1923), then after "about three years" moving on to the "Elks Club 'cause there was some shrewd players in there who could learn me hold'em."[7] A 1986 feature for the *Houston Chronicle* by Evan Moore with the title "Poker: The National Game of Texas" also mentions Moss' recollections though pushes the origin of hold'em a little further forward and about ninety miles south. "It is said to have started in Waco in the early 1940s," Moore writes, adding, "and by 1946, it had spread through north Texas."[8]

Doyle Brunson's 2009 memoir *The Godfather of Poker* provides perhaps the most reliable first-hand evidence while recalling his experience playing in underground games on Exchange Avenue in Fort Worth, Texas. "Back in the early to mid-fifties, we played a lot of deuce-to-seven lowball, ace-to-five lowball, five-card stud, and five-card high draw – those were the main games," Brunson recalls. "Hold'em wasn't played yet; at the time, no one had heard of the game."[9] Later he explains how "Round about 1958, I first learned about a game called hold'em," adding that most called it "hold me darling" at the time and that it was explicitly introduced to him as a stud variation. "I suppose the game was spreading some because I started hearing of games" in other places, he recalls. "Some thought hold'em originated in Waco, although I've heard it said that hold'em might have begun in Corpus Christi.... I'm not really sure where the game began, but given that I'd never heard of hold'em before and I was playing games all over Texas and the South, I think the game must have started right about that time."[10]

Finally, for Brunson's 2005 strategy sequel *Super System 2*, Crandall Addington contributed an essay titled "The History of No-Limit Texas Hold'em" in which he recounts having been introduced to the game in San Antonio in 1963, crediting fellow Poker Hall of Famer Felton "Corky" McCorquodale as having led "a small group of Texans" chiefly responsible for hold'em's journey westward to Las Vegas a few years later.[11] (The phrase "Texas Hold 'em" first appeared in the *New Oxford American Dictionary* in 2005.)

All of these items appeared after the *Life* magazine article, and none had nearly the audience Livingston did when introducing "Hold Me" to his readers. While Livingston compares hold'em with stud, he doesn't speak of it as a stud variant. Rather he links "Hold Me" to other "widow" games, that is to say, earlier variants featuring something like "communal cards" such as Spit in the Ocean or Cincinnati. In Spit in the Ocean, each player is dealt four cards with a single card dealt face up in the middle to complete everyone's hand. There is a drawing round as well, enabling players to improve upon the four cards they are dealt. In Cincinnati, players are dealt five cards with five more dealt in the middle, turned up one at a time with betting rounds after each card is revealed. There, too, players make their best five-card hands from the cards they've been dealt and the shared cards.

"Exactly how widely Hold Me has spread is hard to determine," admits Livingston. "The reports I've had indicate that it has covered the country, though many purely social groups may not have heard of it." He concludes with a story of his having contacted "a poker man in Colorado" to ask if he knew about the game. "'Never heard of it,' he said. 'But a new game has really caught on. High Hold 'Em. Each player gets two cards down. You bet on 'em. Then three cards are turned up in the middle....'"[12]

Livingston's strategy advice for "Hold Me" is both tentative and self-admittedly limited. He's unsure about whether ace-king suited is a good enough with which to call a preflop shove, and describes himself folding the hand in just such a spot. He also thinks jack-ten suited to be a better starter than pocket aces in a 12-handed hold'em game, preferring to have aces when the table is just five-handed.

Livingston is undoubtedly right about one thing, however. "I believe the game is a major event in the history of poker," he writes, "and I predict it will replace stud for the rest of the century."[13]

It didn't happen right away. But with the arrival of the World Series of Poker a couple of years later and the adoption soon after of no-limit hold'em as the featured game in its Main Event, hold'em did grow in popularity over the next couple of decades to challenge seven-card stud as many players' favored variant. By the 2000s hold'em, and especially the no-limit variety, became the game most Americans thought of first when they thought of poker – as foretold years before in the pages of *Life*.

General Interest Magazines

The Saturday Evening Post was among the publications rivaling *Life* in popularity during the century's middle decades. We've already touched on Herbert O. Yardley's popular *Post* piece titled "How to Win at Poker" that previewed his 1957 bestselling strategy book. Poker frequently appeared in the *Post* both before and after, including in a 1942 cartoon by Fred Price depicting a five-man poker game in which the obvious big winner with many stacks of chips in front of him is speaking. "I think I'll quit, boys," he says, desirous to secure his winnings. "I find it impossible to concentrate on poker with the war going on."[14]

Fiction featuring poker occasionally appeared in the magazine as well, such as in a 1952 issue containing Ben Hecht's hard-boiled short story "Swindler's Luck." The story aligns poker with the underworld machinations of mobsters, featuring a character named the Sunset Kid whose danger-ous specialty involved cheating professional gamblers. The Kid's "signature" (and frankly, clichéd) move involved taking his victim for all he had in poker games, always coming up with four aces to beat four kings on the last hand of the night.[15] In a lighter vein, Maynard Good Stoddard's 1981 story "It's Called Poker" finds a male narrator complaining about participating in a dealer's choice poker game with his wife and other women in which the ladies indulge too heavily in wild card games like "Deuce, Low Hole, High Spade and After Aces" and "High Low, Criss Cross, Declare." When the nar-rator stubbornly calls five-card stud with no wild cards, the women are incredulous. "You call that *poker*!" one of them grunts.[16]

The "battle of the sexes" scenario occurring over chips and cards may sound familiar. It reprises the situation of James Thurber's story "Everything Is Wild" first published in a 1932 issue of *The New Yorker*. The literary-leaning weekly, founded in 1925, often featured poker-related fiction. Early examples include Robert McLaughlin's 1945 story "Let's Get Rid of the Ribbon Clerks" in which an army lieutenant plays over his head in a game with superior officers; Edward Newhouse's "Poker Game" from the same year in which cards create conflict between Air Corps officers; Robert M. Coates' "A Friendly Game of Cards" from 1952 telling of a poker game between strangers and suspicions of cheating aboard a boat ride to Brazil; and Robert Henderson's 1955 story "The Miser" in which anoth-er poker game between soldiers becomes the context for one to become parsimonious with his friendship.

By far *The New Yorker*'s most important presentation of poker to a mainstream audience came in 1983 with the publication in two lengthy parts of English poet, novelist, essayist, and poker player Al Alvarez's re-porting from the 1981 World Series of Poker, presented under the title "A Reporter at Large (Poker World Series)."[17] Published as a stand-alone volume shortly thereafter as *The Biggest Game in Town*, Alvarez's work represents a gold standard in poker reporting. Much more than just a com-prehensive account of the 1981 WSOP, Alvarez provides an illuminating portrait of America that transcends the card games and players at the heart of his narrative.

Beginning at Binion's Horseshoe, Alvarez initially lingers over the old sev-en-foot-high, million-dollar display that once stood right inside the casino's entrance like an ostentatious, garish shrine affirming Americans' devotion to the almighty dollar. The collection of $10,000 bills under glass strikes Alvarez as emblematic of "the perennial dream of the Las Vegas punter vis-ible to all, although not quite touchable."[18] From there Alvarez moves inside the casino to observe the rituals of the game as well as what he'll later call "the differing ordering of reality" recognized by those who play poker professionally and (often) at the highest stakes.[19] Many of them sat down with him for interviews, including Jack Binion, Johnny Moss, Jack Straus, Chip Reese, Eric Drache, Mickey Appleman, Doyle Brunson, and David Sklansky.

Alvarez also finds room to speak of both the artificiality and eclecticism of Las Vegas, "the logical conclusion of what is for the foreigner one of the eeriest aspects of America: the utter lack of continuity between the large towns and their surrounding countryside."[20] Alvarez has more to say about America and its values *and* how he sees those values illustrated in the oddly-formed, irregular landscapes of the country as a whole and Vegas in particular. It's not all flattering, of course, with certain "American" values of self-reliance and independence at times shading over into self-interest and even indifference. The many themes covered besides that "different ordering of reality" by high-stakes players include thinking of poker as "work" (as opposed to "play"), attitudes towards poker and gambling and the larger culture's acceptance (or non-acceptance) of the game, talk of the "straight world" or the "system" (and desires to escape it), and the many ways so-called "American" values can be said to be reflected by the game.

Alvarez reported again from the WSOP for *The New Yorker* a little over a decade later, this time including his own experience participating in the 1994 WSOP Main Event. A decade after that Kevin Conley followed in Alvarez's footsteps with a lengthy update from the world of tournament poker titled "The Players." Conley details the high-stakes lifestyles of Erick Lindgren and Daniel Negreanu while summarizing the recent rise of both the online game and televised coverage. The piece ends with an account of Negreanu's victory in the 2004 World Poker Tour Five-Diamond World Poker Classic at the Bellagio for better than $1.77 million, more than three times what Stu Ungar won in the 1981 WSOP Alvarez covered. A few days later Negreanu finds himself leaving a hotel in Toronto with three National Hockey League players, readying for a charity game at which Negreanu is to serve as a celebrity coach. Fans ignore the NHL stars to mob Negreanu instead, causing him to reflect "Wow, poker has arrived."[21]

Since its start as an scholarly journal in 1888, *National Geographic* has often focused on educating readers about geography, history, science, biology, and customs and cultures from around the world, with the magazine additionally known for its award-winning photography and inclusion of maps. During the Second World War it also featured many reports from correspondents, including by military personnel. Major Frederick Simpich Jr. delivered regular dispatches, including one from the South Pacific in 1944 where he discovered soldiers doing everything they could to recreate "the American Way of life" while stationed abroad. "They live by an American pattern true as that of our Southern States or in the open spaces of our great Southwest," Simpich reports. "There are baseball diamonds set in jungle glades to the specifications of Abner Doubleday, daily news mimeographs filled with the latest communiqués – from Hollywood, and bomb shelters on advanced bases with electric lights and poker tables – popular spots in the frequent raids!"[22]

There have been several versions of *Vanity Fair* dating back to the mid-19th century, a publication usually oriented toward popular culture, fashion, and stories about celebrities. Some earlier iterations of the magazine occasionally looked in on fashionable poker clubs in New York such as the Yellow Daisies where readers in 1915 were told: "The stakes are high, and the deuces in the pack always count as added jokers."[23] Alexander Woollcott, the critic who played in the Thanatopsis Pleasure and Inside Straight Club's poker game, wrote about it for a 1923 issue of *Vanity Fair*. The article reveals that he has quit the game (reportedly after losing too much to playwright George S. Kaufman) and predicts it won't survive without him. In his piece titled "The Passing of the Thanatopsis," Woollcott petulantly proclaimed in critic-like fashion poker to be "a preposterous waste of time."[24]

After nearly a half-century off the newsstands, the current and most popular imprint of *Vanity Fair* was launched in 1983 by the Condé Nast media company. Some time after a lengthy feature in the March 2005 issue reprised the theme of celebrity poker playing with an in-depth look at the many Hollywood home games popping up at the height of the poker boom. The article name-drops dozens of current and former actors, producers, and others involved in the film industry along the way.

One low-stakes outlier was a game hosted by former music agent Norby Walters that regularly drew A-listers such as Burt Reynolds, Sharon Stone, Alec Baldwin, Robert Downey Jr., and Dennis Hopper but featured a minimum bet of just $1. The buy-in was higher – $1,000 – at another game hosted by actor and World Poker Tour co-presenter Vince Van Patten, while it cost at least $2,000 to sit down in Tobey Maguire's game. Meanwhile the buy-in was at least $10,000 at another game in which Maguire and Leonardo DiCaprio were regulars. "Poker is the new golf," explains film producer Jon Landau, host of another regular game with a more modest $300 buy-in. "Both are very frustrating games. Both take a lifetime to master. Spouses who were tolerant of golf are now becoming tolerant of poker."

As the author points out, the fact that the star of the *Ocean's 11* remake George Clooney *doesn't* play poker "places him squarely in the minority in Hollywood these days."[25]

Since its debut in 1974, *People* magazine has also focused largely on celebrity gossip and entertainment news, and so similarly has concentrated on stories involving celebrities taking seats at the poker table. In 1985 *Peo-*

ple reported on *Kojak* star Telly Savalas' participation in that year's World Series of Poker where the actor described himself doing research for a role playing Nick "The Greek" Dandolos.[26] (The feature film never materialized.) In 1987, an item in the "Chatter" column reports on the "Gourmet Poker Club" that "meets three times a year and boasts a membership that includes Neil Simon, Chevy Chase and Johnny Carson." As club member Steve Martin explains, the night begins with a big gourmet dinner, then after playing for two hours everyone is tired and ready for sleep.[27] In 2003 Annie Duke appeared in a *People* article, titled "Cool Hand Duke," in which she talked about balancing motherhood and being a professional poker player.[28] Tournament successes by Ben Affleck, who won the California State Poker Championship in 2004, and Jennifer Tilly, who won a bracelet in the ladies event at the 2006 WSOP, also predictably earned notice in the magazine. In her profile Tilly describes her introduction to poker and its customs, including being "kind of shocked when I discovered that poker involved math." She also hilariously describes her attempt to emulate players against whom she found herself competing: "I try to do all the stuff that they do: become sleep-deprived, wear scruffy clothes, eat bad food."[29]

Not only did such items satisfy readers' desire for behind-the-scenes celebrity anecdotes, but they also served to introduce poker more broadly into the mainstream. They also provided encouragement to many to pick up the game themselves.

News and Sports Magazines
The most successful and influential news magazine of the 20th century was *Time*, started in 1923 and also originally part of the Henry Luce media empire. For much of the magazine's run poker only came up by way of analogy with politics, business, and international affairs, though *Time* has occasionally looked in on the game. In 1986 the magazine reported on poker professional Billy Baxter's victory in his lawsuit against the U.S. government from which he was awarded a $178,000 refund from the Internal Revenue Service. The IRS had tried to tax Baxter's gambling winnings (via poker) over a four-year span at the higher rate applied to dividends and interest, and not as though they were earned income. Baxter filed a suit, "contending that his winnings were the product of skill and hard work," and a U.S. district court in Nevada agreed. "Jack Nicklaus gets to file his prize money as earned income. Why not me?" Baxter said.[30]

Later came occasional reports from the Main Event, such "The Big Poker Freeze-Out" reporting Iranian-born Brit Mansour Matloubi's Main Event win in 1990, his participation helping demonstrate "Poker may be the most successful U.S. export."[31] In 2005, Francine Russo reported on the increased involvement of women in poker, particularly online and "away from the testosterone-fueled aggressiveness often aimed at women in casinos."[32] And a 2010 article reporting on the "Attack of the Math Brats" examines online poker's effect on tournament strategy, sketching in broad strokes a contrast between an older generation used to live poker and younger players weaned online. The conflict is generalized as the "old school" versus the "new math," with the latter's use of statistical data gathered from online play informing ostensibly unorthodox approaches. Meanwhile established players express doubts and hire a "mind-set coach" to help dispel "negative thought," an anti-math gesture meant to suggest the divide between the two camps to have been much wider than was actually the case.[33]

Time's primary competitor in the weekly news market has traditionally been the appropriately named *Newsweek*, which first appeared in 1933. Few references to poker appear in *Newsweek's* pages for much of its early run, although the magazine reported from the World Series of Poker from time to time. Sports writer Pete Axthelm went to the WSOP in 1979 and wrote admiringly of the pros.[34] Responding to David Hayano's book *Poker Faces*, Walter Goodman reflected both on poker's appeal and the Gardena poker rooms in 1982 in a piece titled "Poker as a Way of Life." While expressing measured skepticism of Hayano's academic approach to the Gardena "professionals," Goodman nonetheless finds the scene similarly intriguing while also recognizing the "prime appeal of the game is the testing of the qualities that are rarely exercised in the daily round." He seems to empathize with the players' hope to find an alternative to "punching in at some routine 40-hour-a-week job."[35] *Newsweek* wasn't so enamored by the poker in *Rounders*, however, and its scathing 1998 review, titled "The Bottom of the Deck," concluded: "Watching it is about as exciting as playing poker with all the cards face up."[36]

Like many other magazines *Newsweek* endured financial troubles in the 2000s, and in 2012 went to an all-digital format for a couple of years before returning to the newsstands in March 2014. Unfortunately by then the magazine's standing and influence had waned, a state of affairs that was not helped by a couple of cover pieces that drew criticism for their reporting. One purported to name the founder of Bitcoin, but was roundly criticized as lacking credible evidence. Another set out to describe "How Washington Opened the Floodgates to Online Poker, Dealing Parents a Bad Hand." It again earned censure owing to an incomplete presentation of current online gambling laws as well as the legislative history related to the subject.[37]

Poker found a more amenable home in *Sports Illustrated*. Easily the most popular sports magazine in America from soon after its debut in 1954 well into the 21st century, the rise of *SI* coincided with the fast-growing popularity of televised sports. With a largely male readership and the great majority of its coverage focused on men's sports, it's no surprise to find *SI* giving regular attention to poker and even sometimes covering the game as though it were a sport.

A profile of Johnny Moss published in March 1971 included "Tips from Johnny Moss on How to Win in the Office Poker Game."[38] Later, the magazine profiled pros including Bobby Baldwin (in 1979), Billy Baxter (in 1984), Phil Hellmuth (in 1994), Thomas "Amarillo Slim" Preston (in 2002), and published "Q&A" pieces with Chris Moneymaker and Greg Raymer (in 2004) and Annie Duke (in 2005). In 1977 reporter Edwin Shrake (who wrote several poker articles for *SI*) focused on amateur player "Cadillac" Jack Grimm and his quixotic effort to compete with the big boys at that year's WSOP. Shrake likened the millionaire oil tycoon's prospects to other "lost causes" that had captured his interest such as searching for Noah's Ark, getting the Loch Ness monster photographed, and finding Big Foot.[39] There were many more examples of sports-like reporting from the WSOP as well over the years, occasionally during the 1970s and regularly from the 2000s onward, as well as one in 1979 from the Amarillo Slim Poker Classic at the Las Vegas Hilton.

In many instances such articles romanticized gambling and poker, looking upon high-stakes players as existing in a distinct world from most readers. The impression was furthered by articles about poker players gambling at golf, such as Shrake's 1977 report from the three-day "Professional Gamblers Invitational" at the Sahara Nevada Country Club during which Moss, Baldwin, Preston, Puggy Pearson, Doyle Brunson and others gambled for more than $2 million among each other. Another from the three-day "Russ Hamilton Annual" followed in 2003, again marveling at amounts wagered by the high rollers.[40] That said, there is also a clear respect for top players' skill, with the work ethic and competitiveness of some fitting harmoniously alongside quotes from athletes and coaches in neighboring articles. As seven-card stud expert Rod Pardey tells Roger Dionne in a 1979 article about up-and-coming poker pros, "You've got to have the desire to be a winner, to be No. 1…. But poker is just another sport like golf or baseball…. It pays well if you work hard at it."[41]

Reports on poker games in other contexts appear in *SI* as well, such as Robert H. Boyle's inspired reporting for a 1963 article "The Poker in the Smoker" detailing card games among commuters aboard a New York train. "The idea behind smoker poker is to cram in as many hands as possible and yet have the pot as fat as possible," explains Boyle, given the generally short length of the trip for most players.[42] In 1971 A.D. Livingston reported on home games in Alabama and Kentucky being robbed, leading him to observe "the poker player's real concern is with the robbers, not the cops."[43] Following the path of Dick Miles reporting from the Gardena card clubs in 1967 (discussed in Chapter 7), Roger Dionne's 1985 visit to three different card clubs in Emeryville, California likewise gave readers a glimpse of the lowball games. As Dionne reported, the Oaks Card Club was thriving, the Key Card Club was busy with lower-stakes games, and the Sante Fe was struggling.[44]

During the 2000s *Sports Illustrated* reflected the explosion in poker's popularity with a number of articles. "The Prime-Timing of Texas Hold'em" in September 2003 followed up on the launch of the World Poker Tour's first season and ESPN's successful WSOP coverage that year, with Rick Reilly chiming in a year later to criticize such programming in a column titled "TV Poker's a Joker." A lengthy report on online poker's growth in 2005 – the only time in *SI*'s history when poker made the cover (as a corner "special report" announcement) – presented the phenomenon in cautionary terms, describing college students in particular being "Online and Obsessed." A shorter 2011 piece following "Black Friday" and the effective shutdown of the online game in the U.S. titled "Deal With It" also essentially marked the end of *Sports Illustrated*'s reporting on online poker.[45]

Music and Humor Magazines and Comic Books

Rolling Stone debuted in 1967 and for several decades was America's most popular music magazine by a wide margin, with articles often also covering other cultural (and countercultural) issues and trends. Incidental mentions of poker abound within the publication, such as in references to poker-related songs by the Everly Brothers and the Electric Light Orchestra, in a story about the Beatles playing poker with photographer Curt Gunther during their initial trip to America in 1964, and in profiles of card-playing musical artists such as Willie Nelson or Jay-Z who told about his predilection for the poker-like card game Guts (about which he rapped on his 2001 album *The Blueprint*).

A series on "College Life" in 1981 included companion articles about socializing between professors and students outside of the classroom, with drinking, smoking dope, and playing poker all part of the ritual. One article is by a professor who thinks of such get-togethers, including the "Student Poker Game," as an extension of his role as an educator. For him winning and losing isn't a concern, recognizing that he "is supposed to bring lots of money and be a Terrific Sport." The other article by a student also sees the gatherings as beneficial, and profitable, too, given that he tends to be a winner in the games. As he remarks, "my favorite professor was also a lousy poker player, and I could cover the cost of tuition and books just sitting across the table from him once a week."[46] The arguments for such fraternizing are dubious, though such student-teacher interactions (including affairs) were not nearly as out of place during the early 1980s as they would be today.

The mid-2000s poker boom brought a couple more items, including a 2005 feature on "The Crew," a group of bankroll-sharing "young guns" that included Russ "Dutch" Boyd and his brother Robert, Scott Fischman, David Smyth, Tony Lazar, Joe Bartholdi, and Brett Jungblut. Much like the "Math Brats" *Time* piece, an underlying premise of the *Rolling Stone* article is to suggest a sea change occurring in poker, especially tournament poker. The piece is fittingly titled "Poker's New World Order."[47] Boyd is credited with having "stitched together this loosely knit crew of savants" described as summarily crushing games both live and online. Most of the focus is on Boyd as the author discusses his bipolar disorder, his failed attempt to run his own online poker room (PokerSpot, see Chapter 21), and his deep run in the 2003 WSOP Main Event where he finished 12th. The story ends with "The Crew" drifting apart, their collective moment in the fleeting cultural spotlight having passed. Another 2006 series on "The New Vegas" also touches on poker's newfound popularity, though the pronouncement that "Poker chic has made gambling cool again" gets undercut by another assessment more mindful of the bottom line: "Poker might get all the buzz, but in truth, Vegas is all about the slots."[48]

Humor magazines have likewise occasionally reflected poker's place in American culture. Begun in 1881, the weekly satirical magazine *Judge* was quite popular for much of its run until circulation dropped off during the Great Depression and publication ceased in 1947. Poker references were occasionally sprinkled throughout the jokes, stories, and cartoons. Humor produced by married couples' conflicts was a common theme, with poker sometimes providing the context such as in an 1893 one-panel cartoon titled "Giving Himself Away." A wife asks her husband about the poker chips she's found in the pockets of a pair of slacks, and he responds uncertainly "I guess they are waiting for some darned fool to play them." The wife answers, "Then *you* do play poker?"[49]

Later in a 1922 issue of *Judge* journalist Heywood Broun (another participant in the Algonquin Round Table poker game) focused on poker for his "Sport Page." In a column titled "Just One More Round," Broun highlights the many ways he believes "of all American sports poker is preeminent as a character builder," arguing that it especially builds tenacity. In fact, there's never any reason to quit poker, he points out, since "the courageous player will never think of stopping while he is behind. The proud participant will scorn to quit as long as he is ahead. And the man who is just even, or almost so, will want to go on a little longer until something decisive happens." Broun jokes as well how poker is only "poignantly" played when the stakes are meaningful (played with "distress money"), and that it is potentially harmful to bottle up one's emotions while playing. "The player whose flush loses to a full house risks a nervous breakdown in later life if he does no more than remark pleasantly, 'You win, old chap!'"[50]

The guy who is always shy.

As Broun explains, the topic of his column was prompted by "Mr. Edison's latest questionnaire," a reference to an intelligence test Thomas Edison gave to prospective employees wishing to work at his plant. The questionnaire became public in 1921 thanks to articles in *The New York Times* for which test-takers supplied many of the questions they had been asked about history, science, art, geography, literature, and other topics. As a result of the questions becoming public, Edison revised his questionnaire, then in 1922 added more questions to another test for those applying to become his personal assistant. The tests were administered orally, with Edison asking the questions and interviewees shouting their responses (as he was hard of hearing). Some of those questions later became public as well, including the following:

"You have only $10 in the world and are playing poker with a man you have never seen before. On the first deal he holds a pat hand. You have three eights before the draw. There is 50 cents in the pot. He bets a quarter. What are you going to do and why?"[51]

In 1952 a new humor magazine appeared called *Mad* which soon began dominating that segment of the market. Starting as a comic book before developing a more wide-ranging satirical approach, the magazine's parodies of popular culture were often

The stony poker face.

Superfluous advice.

Somebody has to lose.

Cartoons accompanying Heywood Broun's "Just One More Round" for a 1922 issue of *Judge*

Poker & Pop Culture

directed toward a younger audience although equally appealed to adults. Other popular magazines joined *Mad*'s targets and it began referring to *The Saturday Evening Pest*, *National Osographic* and *Sports Inebriated.* During most of its run *Mad* mostly treated poker in a superficial way, such as in 1962 when featuring the gap-toothed mascot Alfred E. Neuman on the cover as the joker in a full house. However in 2005 *Mad* devoted several pages to a "Celebrity Poker Issue," including a multi-page skewering of the popular cable show *Celebrity Poker Showdown.*[52] "They're depending on luck over skill," remarks one observer, to which another responds "That's how most of them became celebrities in the first place."

A focus of the humor, and thus the commentary, is on the oversaturation of poker-themed content during the mid-2000s, a phenomenon for which a show like *Celebrity Poker Showdown* stood as a kind of emblem (see Chapter 20). Another spectator complains that he likes poker, "but between watching Celebrity Poker Showdown, ESPN World Series of Poker, Ultimate Poker Challenge and Poker Superstars, who has the friggin' time to actually play?" Elsewhere in the issue, a series of cartoons titled "Thanks to the Popularity of Poker…" offers various predictions regarding where the overabundance of poker-themed content is heading (e.g., poker players on Wheaties boxes, fantasy celebrity poker leagues). Another "*Mad* ad parody" pitches an instructional video, "Ben Affleck: The Art of the Poker Face," simultaneously poking fun at celebrity poker and Affleck's sometimes detached-seeming acting style. Rounding out the issue is a multi-page parody of the then-popular HBO drama *Deadwood* including a lament over the early death of the series' most charismatic character, Wild Bill Hiccup.

Poker has also found its way into comic books over the years, most famously in Marvel Comics' "Floating Superhero Poker Game" first introduced in a May 1979 Marvel Two-in-One issue in a story called "Full House - Dragons High." Taking place either at Avengers Mansion, the apartment of Ben Grimm (a.k.a. the Thing), or the Fantastic Four Headquarters, the game typically involves superheroes as well as human players, with the Thing, Captain America, Mr. Fantastic, Iron Man, and Wolverine among the dozens of participants. More often than not, the game appears as a kind of comic interlude before villains arrive to interrupt their play.

Men's and Women's Magazines

Popular men's magazines like *Esquire* and *Playboy* featured poker frequently as part of their male-centric content, often suggesting an aptitude at cards to be a requisite feature of modern masculinity.

From soon after its debut in 1933, *Esquire* often ran articles focusing on poker tips and strategy, and an early piece by humorist Rex Lardner (nephew of *The Cincinnati Kid* co-scripter Ring Lardner) self-reflexively comments on the very image of masculinity promoted by the publication in which he writes. In "Big Poker: The Only Game," Lardner blames magazines (along with movies and TV) for fostering the idea that the best poker payers are all "lantered-jaw, sleek, dark-bearded and rascally... feather-fingered, low-wristed deck rifflers." In fact, as Lardner points out, "some of the best poker players I have met... have been balding, bespectacled and paunchy." He proceeds to outline a dichotomy of sorts distinguishing unremarkable players of "little poker" ("normal people") from the most skillful who play "big poker" (the "maladjusted").[53]

Lardner's piece followed earlier ones such as Winston Hibler's "Dealer's Choice" from 1938 that shared more than a dozen odd variants for his "fellow maniacs" to introduce into their home games. These included "Legs" (in which "the pot stays on the table until any one player has won it TWICE"), "No Peek" (requiring a selective viewing of one's hand), "Pig" (combining stud and draw), and one called "Omaha" that is *not* the four-card hold'em variant later surfacing in the 1980s.[54] In a 1942 article "Playing Poker to Win," George F. Browne thoroughly explains poker probabilities (with tables), concluding: "If you can't win with all this information, I suggest you stop playing cards. I have."[55] Meanwhile during the 1940s Albert Ostrow challenged readers with a six-part quiz "on jack pots, stud and draw poker," then shared a version of the "cards as collateral" poker tale (discussed in Chapter 13) in "When Poker Was Poker."[56]

Later pieces provided *Esquire* readers an introduction to the life of a full-time professional ("Nine-to-Five Poker" from 1983), glimpses of home game shenanigans ("Jokers Wild" from 1986), an explanation of poker's relationship to politics ("The Poker Game" from 1992), and still more rapid-fire hints and suggestions ("How to Find and Play a Poker Game" from 2000, "The One-Minute Guide to Poker" from 2010).[57] The growing category of serious poker nonfiction found a home in *Esquire* as well, with contributions about the game by noted poker authors Peter Alson, Andy Bellin, and James McManus, as well as the publication of excerpts from the *Rounders* screenplay in advance of the film's premiere in 1998.

Playboy arrived in 1952, even more overtly promoting an image of the urbane and worldly libertine bachelor for whom the knowledge of poker was also deemed worthwhile, if not essential. In a short 1957 piece Max Shulman countered the argument of so-called poker "purists" that only five-card stud and five-card draw "can properly be called poker and everything else is an abomination." Calling that view "the veriest crap," Shulman posits newer split-pot games add "a whole new dimension in poker" (though he isn't a fan of wild cards).[58] That same year came a lengthy article titled "Playboy on Poker," supported by a cover image of a nude model adorned only by strategically placed playing cards. There strategy author John Moss (no relation to Johnny Moss) takes issue with Shulman in a measured way, suggesting many new variants were created for "the implicit purpose of reducing the amount of skill required to win." Focusing on stud and draw only, Moss delivers a series of specific tips about hand selection and betting strategies as well as more general advice about not playing for too long and developing a "philosophical attitude about the game."[59]

Later a nearly 50-page series of poker articles in the November 1974 issue of *Playboy* functioned as a kind of primer for anyone desiring an introduction to the game and/or its cultural relevance. There's a lengthy history of poker ("Who Dealt This Mess"), a series of basic beginner tips ending with a quiz ("How Not to Lose Your Ass") plus another ten-point list of tips ("Never, Never Fold"), some presidential poker trivia ("Full House at the White House"), the story of the Thanatopsis Pleasure and Inside Straight Club ("The Algonquin Games"), a fascinating and funny five-way conversation about poker between Jack Lemmon, Milton Berle, Elliott Gould, Walter Matthau, and Telly Savalas ("Table Talk"), plus reports on poker in Las Vegas and California.[60] Other poker advice continued to filter through *Playboy*'s pages from time to time thereafter, including tips on hosting games, plus a Mike Caro contribution in 2002 on "The Art of the Tell."[61]

Occasional poker-themed stories appeared on *Playboy*'s fiction pages as well, including an early highlight, Don Marquis' masterful "The Crack of Doom" from 1956, which was memorably adapted into an episode of *Alfred Hitchcock Presents* later that year. The story offers a gripping object lesson in which a player named Mason Bridges tells about the hand that caused him to swear off poker. His head swirling from drink, heavy losses, and a line-crossing decision to steal money with which to play, Bridges thinks he has four queens and wildly reraises multiple times against an opponent who certainly has four tens. As his opponent contemplates whether to call the last reraise, Bridges rechecks his hole card and to his horror sees it is a jack – he's misread it! His opponent finally folds, the bluff only getting through because Bridges hadn't realized he'd been bluffing. "My career, my fortunes, my future, my good name, the stuff of my honor itself, the sweetness of my life, had come back to me because my blurred eyes had misread one face-card for another," reflects Bridges, poignantly reflecting on the importance of the chance element in life itself.[62] By contrast, Richard Chiappone's 1995 story "Dealer's Choice" is much less edifying. It features a female protagonist playing in an after-work game with four male co-workers but ultimately provides little more than the context for a lurid male fantasy.[63]

The magazine also often featured nonfiction narratives about poker. Some add meaningfully to reflections about the game and its significance, such as David Mamet's 1994 piece "A Gambler for Life" which examines nuggets of wisdom from poker strategy texts in the light of their non-poker applications. "I recommend the literature," Mamet writes. "It will inform you to be humble, be aggressive and... be wary."[64] Others contribute very little, such as Joel Stein's superficial musings after *Playboy* bought him into a $10,000 World Poker Tour event played aboard a cruise in 2005. A newcomer to poker's subculture, Stein expresses a mix of incredulity and disdain throughout his report. He seems strangely surprised to "learn that poker players are all highly competitive people," somehow having gathered an impression that poker players "in the old days" were not. He jokes that everyone "seems to have Asperger's syndrome," his response to players enthusiastically discussing strategy ("poker minutiae are particularly boring"). In the end he claims to be "sad to leave the freak show that is the pro poker world" to return home and "never talk to these people again." Such wistfulness appears a half-hearted bluff.[65]

Profiles of poker pros have also appeared in *Playboy*, such as a short one of Cyndy Violette in 1987 in which Amarillo Slim Preston begrudgingly acknowledges her seven-card stud prowess while denying any general advancement in women in poker. ("She plays like a man, and that means darn good," Preston says.) A 2005 piece presented David Williams, fresh from his runner-up finish in the WSOP Main Event the year before, as a possible answer to the question "Is This Man the Future of Poker?" And in 2014 a feature on Phil Ivey mostly marveled at his gambling both on the felt and elsewhere via high-stakes prop bets and seven-figure business ventures. For Ivey (the profile suggests), poker is just one element of a larger risk-reward portfolio in which money is "a thing to be deployed, not savored when won or mourned when it's gone."[66] Meanwhile pictorials of poker players Jennifer "Jennicide" Leigh and Cindy Margolis in 2008 and *Poker After Dark* host Leeann Tweeden in 2011 highlight the game as part of the models' stories, reinforcing both poker's status as a form of "adult" entertainment as well as associations between poker and sex.

As might be expected, popular women's magazines discuss poker much less frequently than publications targeting men. When they do, the references more often than not avoid challenging the game's masculine legacy, often reinforcing poker as a "man's game."

Cosmopolitan has a long history dating from the late 19th century, covering a broad range of topics before narrowing its focus to women's interests and fashion during the mid-1960s. A 1979 article listing "30 Skills Every Cosmo Girl Must Master" leads off with "playing a mean game of poker." Put together with other items like "Jump-Starting Your Car" and "Throwing a Ball Like a Guy" the list might appear progressive, but such judgment is tempered by other listed skills like "Applying Lipstick Without a Mirror" and "Turbocharging Your Cleavage."[67] In fact, frequently when poker is mentioned the game is strip poker, coming up fairly often in horoscopes, "Cosmo quizzes," or articles imparting relationship advice ("Challenge him to a torrid game of Truth or Dare or strip poker").[68]

In a 2003 article titled "What Keeps a Husband Crazy in Love," *Redbook* advised its target audience of married women to take up poker, sharing a quick overview of rules for seven-card stud and hand rankings to help them get started. Like learning the perfect back rub and tying their husbands' ties for them, learning the game is primarily about supporting their spouses "so you can socialize his way for a change."[69] In 2004, younger readers of *Seventeen* were shown how to play hold'em, encouraged to do so because "celebs love to play poker."[70] Meanwhile in *Good Housekeeping* the emphasis on homemaking leads to articles advising how to make Father's Day collages from playing cards and refrigerator magnets from poker chips, though have little to do with playing the game.[71] When gambling games are discussed in *Good Housekeeping*, they represent a threat to the family such as in "A Husband's Secret Addiction" from 1997.[72] A year before readers of *Woman's Day* were similarly warned about growing numbers of women becoming addicted to gambling as more casinos open and more states introduce lotteries.[73]

An exception to the trend can be found in a 1985 issue of *Ms.* magazine, the feminist publication founded in 1971 as a deliberate alternative to mainstream media as well as to messaging about traditional gender roles being validated by other women's magazines. In an article "Deal Me In," psychologist Mary Parlee addresses why women might be less inclined to play poker and argues for why it may be in their interests to take up the game.

Taking as a starting point poker's history as "a game played by men" and "a masculine game," Parlee highlights both the game's bluffing element and the centrality of money as distinguished from other games women typically play. Citing psychological research and other arguments for women being "more likely than men to be cooperative rather than competitive, supportive rather than individualistic, egalitarian... rather than hierarchical," Parlee identifies all of these as "the opposite traits required of a good poker player."[74]

Why, then, should women learn poker? Referring to game theorists' likening of poker to business and war, Parlee suggests poker similarly reflects other types of interactions women encounter such as in families, in relationships, and in the workplace. Thus learning poker and its requisite strategies can serve as a kind of training for women. Knowing how to bluff can help a woman shape her strategy for negotiating a raise, Parlee explains. She also likens folding to ending relationships and calling others' bluffs to developing "habits of thought necessary to question and challenge others."[75]

Poker Magazines

Prior to the late 1980s there were few examples of magazines with a national reach focusing solely on poker. One early example was New York publisher Frank Tousey's *Poker Chips* from 1896. While other books, newspapers, and

The October 1896 issue of *Poker Chips magazine*

magazines published by Tousey targeted young male readers, his "monthly magazine devoted to stories of the great American game" aimed for a more mature audience. Some of the stories evoke the Old West ("The Old Settler's Last Game of Poker") and steamboat poker ("Baffled by Fate. A Tale of the Mississippi"). One titled "Mickey Finn Tells How Poker Was Invented" humorously invents a mythology concerning a "King Ingy" having ordered the game's creation, and in the original version he plays, kings beat aces. Among the contributors were a current U.S. Congressman (Amos J. Cummings) and a future one (Edward W. Townsend, then famous for his "Chimmie Fadden" stories). Joel Chandler Harris of "Uncle Remus" fame, as well as Stephen Crane, were advertised as contributors as well, although neither published stories in *Poker Chips*. After only six issues, *Poker Chips* changed its name to *The White Elephant* and for nine more issues followed the same format although the stories were no longer exclusively poker-themed.

In late 1988 *Card Player* became the first magazine of note to focus entirely on poker. Originally a 40-page black-and-white pamphlet produced in Las Vegas, *Card Player* grew in popularity and size, eventually becoming a twice-monthly glossy magazine containing features and columns about poker rooms and tournaments, profiles of players, strategy columns, and other items of interest to players. While paid subscription levels were modest, *Card Player*'s reach was extended via the magazine's placement in card rooms in Nevada, California, and (eventually) New Jersey and elsewhere, enabling players to pick up copies for free to read while waiting for a seat or when at the tables. The "boom" of the 2000s helped *Card Player*'s distribution increase to around 100,000 copies per issue.[76] Meanwhile other poker magazines began to flood the market to take up space on newsstands, with Atlanta-based *Bluff* magazine (started in 2004) emerging as *Card Player*'s most serious competitor. Following a similar model that included the free distribution of copies in card rooms, each issue of *Bluff* reached as many as 225,000 readers during its peak.[77] However following "Black Friday" (see Chapter 22), both magazines' circulation declined rapidly, with *Bluff* ceasing publication altogether in 2015.

Given their audience and frequent partnerships with casinos, poker rooms, and online poker sites (many of which provide a primary revenue source as advertisers), it is no surprise to discover poker magazines consistently adopting a "pro-poker" editorial stance. Even so, the popularity of such publications reflects the enthusiasm of those within the game's subculture, even occasionally serving to influence the mainstream conversations about poker.

16 Poker in the Movies

The representation of poker in films has had more to do with forming opinions about the game than has any other variety of American popular culture. One could argue that when it comes to shaping ideas about poker, John Wayne, W.C. Fields, and Paul Newman have exerted more influence than anyone who has played the game.

It's a point worth making, because even though poker can sometimes be exciting and satisfying to watch in the movies, the game is rarely presented in a convincing way, at least to those who actually play poker. A *Washington Post* article from 2017 listing the 25 best "profession-based movies" as judged by experts in the selected fields leaves off poker altogether. Such an omission might connote doubts about whether or not being a poker player should be regarded as a profession, although the list does include "chess player" and even "bank robber."[1] However it also could stem from a relative paucity of realistic depictions of poker on the silver screen. "Poker in movies never quite comes off," David Spanier once wrote, one reason being that in a poker hand "the drama is an interior one, consisting of what goes on in the players' minds" and is thus difficult to capture and present to an audience.[2] But even when the primary focus isn't on individual hands but on other contextual matters involving settings and players, those other elements are often also embellished, moving away from realism while reinforcing particular ideas about poker's significance.

While some filmmakers do endeavor to portray poker realistically, it is often a secondary concern to using the game creatively to advance plots, build characters, and/or underscore themes. In other words, unless the film is specifically *about* poker, the game's portrayal often serves other purposes than showing audiences how poker is *really* played. In westerns, such distortions frequently help support romantic visions of the Old West and its rough-and-tumble card-playing cowboys. In comedies, the rules, customs, and behavior-restricting etiquette of the game provide a ready context for the humorous upsetting of expectations. Meanwhile in dramas, poker has been used to color characters as reckless risk-takers, gifted polymaths, committed individualists, unprincipled degenerates, existential warriors, and a variety of other heroic (and anti-heroic) types.

Westerns

Poker and Violence in Early Westerns

The western holds a special place in the history of film criticism as it marks the start of "genre criticism" – that is, a variety of analysis that examines the movie principally in comparison with other, similar works. There were so many westerns made during the silent era and the first decades of sound film (up through the 1960s), that formal (or formulaic) similarities became readily apparent from film to film.

There are many reasons why westerns were so popular during these years. Most were set during the period following the Civil War, starting with the Reconstruction and lasting through the end of the 19th century, which was a period of continued westward expansion. Although individual westerns occasionally ignite debates about historical authenticity, most critics agree that the majority present a relatively idealized version of the Old West. They often highlight certain ideological values and ideas of national identity that helped make the films more commercially popular (as is often the case with mass market entertainment). In other words, these fictionalized accounts of the past were often presented with an eye toward satisfying contemporary audiences' most favored ideas of themselves and of America. To overgeneralize a bit, most westerns of the first half of the 20th century present an uncomplicated view of American progress and achievement, championing the advancement of the frontier – the "victory" of civilization over wilderness.

Poker appeared frequently. In some westerns, the use of the game is merely ornamental. Having characters play the signature card game of the Old West is akin to making sure they wear Stetson hats, ride horses, and carry guns. It's also part of the requisite scenery, like the vast landscape shots typically serving to segue one scene to the next. However, there are many examples of westerns that thoughtfully incorporate poker not just as a casual reminder of the Old West setting, but as an important element of the storytelling. Frequently the game is associated with violence, another way of highlighting hazards on the frontier. Poker also serves as a shorthand method of sorting heroes from villains in the fictional worlds these westerns create, often marked by a kind of "black and white" morality, a distinction sometimes even indicated by the color of Stetsons the characters wear. Poker games in westerns also become linked to efforts to restore order to among outlaws, or even provide the cause of more chaotic disruptions.

A film from 1899 called *Poker at Dawson City,* one of 1,200 or so films emanating from studios owned by Thomas Edison's companies from the 1890s through 1910s, is sometimes called the first ever "western." It might also earn the distinction as the very first "poker movie," even if its running time is less than it takes to play a single hand.

The title sets the game along the Yukon River in northwest Canada during the Klondike Gold Rush of the late 1890s,[3] although the film was shot in Edison's Black Maria studio in West Orange, New Jersey. The 20-second, single-shot silent film ostensibly shows the aftermath of a hand gone wrong, with gun-waving players brawling with each other around a card table while a bartender tries to cool tempers by spraying them with water. It's a suitable introduction to the topic of poker in the movies, where card playing and conflict are often two of a kind.

The association of poker with violence continued in other early silent westerns such as *Hell Bent* (1918) directed by John Ford. The film stars Harry Carey as Cheyenne Harry, a "saddle tramp" traveling from place to place as a kind of Old West nomad whom Carey portrayed in numerous Ford-directed films. Cheyenne Harry has many vices, including stealing, drinking, and cheating at poker, and often the stories feature him overcoming his wayward ways in order to serve as the story's hero.

Hell Bent introduces the character in a unique way, with the film opening on a novelist reading a letter from his publisher asking him to write a story about "a more ordinary man" than is typically found in novels featuring

A novelist draws inspiration from Frederic Remington's 1897 painting "A Misdeal" in *Hell Bent* (1918)

too-good-to-be-true heroes. The writer then gazes on Frederic Remington's painting *A Misdeal* showing the aftermath of a deadly game of cards in which a player scoops up the pot after apparently having killed several opponents (discussed in Chapter 5). The painting then comes to life (in the novelist's imagination), with the men not dead but recovering slowly from having been beaten. We soon see Harry fleeing the scene and getting rid of cards from his pockets — multiple handfuls, all of them aces. As in other Carey-Ford films, Cheyenne Harry ultimately becomes reformed into someone who can serve as the story's hero. In this case, his poker cheating is just one of the vices he must leave behind in order to do so. While Ford's film and the flawed character of Harry are designed to be more realistic than the typically romanticized version of the Old West, it still perpetuates ideas about poker's negative influence.

Hell Bent also heralds what will be a long cinematic tradition of Western heroes based on other fictional representations rather than on actual historical figures. Early examples of such adaptations include several of Owen Wister's influential 1902 western novel *The Virginian* (discussed next chapter). Both Cecil B. Demille's 1914 version and Tom Forman's from 1923 highlight an early scene from the book between the story's unnamed hero and his antagonist Trampas revealing how the pair's years-long animosity begins with an argument at the poker table. After being called a "son of a – – –" by Trampas, the Virginian coolly responds "When you call me that, smile."[4] The line survived into later popular culture, including being repurposed in many westerns. The better known 1929 adaptation, directed by Victor Fleming and with Gary Cooper in the title role, also retains a version of the verbal exchange while omitting the poker game. The link between poker and violence is reinforced later in the film, however, when Trampas finally challenges the Virginian to a duel. "I got you corralled now and I'm calling your hand," Trampas says, to which the Virginian testily responds, "All right, what do ya got?" – an angry prelude to a different kind of showdown.[5]

A poker game similarly brings about the story's central clash in the pre-Civil War silent western *White Oak* (1921) written by and starring William S. Hart. Introduced as "king of the River Dealers," Hart's character Oak Miller is a gambler entangled in a complicated plot involving his sweetheart, his sister, and a villainous character named Granger who poses a threat to both. Set in the early 1850s, hero and villain first meet while playing "the ancient and deadly game of stud poker" (as a title card describes it), a game that ends with Oak winning a big pot off Granger. After losing the hand Granger makes an offending comment about Oak's beloved. The third player in the game takes offense and throws the cards at Granger, who draws his pistol. Oak then fires a shot to quell the dispute. The game and situation prefigure the final scene of the film in which Oak tries to strangle Granger, but a third person – a Native American whose daughter Granger had treated badly – throws a knife into Granger's back to kill him.

William S. Hart (left) as Oak Miller in *White Oak* (1921)

Poker & Pop Culture

Card-Playing Cowboys in Classical Westerns

Moving into the sound era and the period of the "classical western," we've already mentioned Ford's landmark 1939 film *Stagecoach* and its unsubtle allusion to the "dead man's hand." For much of that film John Wayne's character, the Ringo Kid, is shown seeking vengeance upon the murderer of his father. When the murderer wins a pot with aces and eights near the film's conclusion, there's little doubt what will happen next. That same year came *Destry Rides Again* starring Marlene Dietrich and James Stewart in which the corruption at the heart of the Old West town of Bottleneck is revealed immediately by a crooked poker game at the Last Chance Saloon. A player bets his ranch on a hand of five-card stud only to have his ace in the hole swapped out for a deuce. When the sheriff comes to investigate he is promptly shot dead, setting in motion a plot that requires Destry (Stewart) to set things right. *The Bronze Buckaroo* also appeared in 1939 – one of several films by pioneering African American director Richard C. Kahn, with Herb Jeffries leading an all-black cast. The film is mostly a light-hearted affair with hijinks involving a ranch hand using ventriloquism to fool someone into buying a talking mule and the cast breaking out into song at regular intervals. However the merriment is suddenly interrupted by the sight of a player dealing himself seconds in a saloon poker game, upon which his opponent instantly shoots him dead.

In a similar vein came *Sunset Trail* (1939), one of more than 60 films featuring the character Hopalong Cassidy. Starring William Boyd in the title role, the film changes Cassidy from the rough-hewn wrangler of Clarence E. Mulford's original stories into a comically-chaste iconoclast who doesn't smoke, avoids hard language, and only drinks sarsaparilla. The character pokes fun at "masculine" traits associated with cowboys, but ultimately reinforces those traits by showing it's mostly an act and Cassidy is as tough as they come. The villain is a casino owner named Monte Keller (Robert Fiske) who begins the picture buying a ranch and 2,000 head of cattle from a local farmer, then shooting the farmer dead and keeping the cash. Cassidy arrives in Silver City to save the day, though comes disguised as a dandy with seemingly little experience riding horses and other ways of the Old West. He even responds with mock disgust at the sight of the casino, though nonetheless sits down for a high-stakes game with Keller. Continuing to act the part of a greenhorn, in one big hand of five-card stud, Cassidy pretends not to know hand rankings, asking if a full house beats a flush before raising on the last round. That's enough for Keller who folds his five spades, then Cassidy shows him he only had two pair. As viewers soon see, the poker game neatly functions as a kind of miniature set piece mimicking the larger plot in which Cassidy also successfully bluffs Keller.

John Wayne as Rocklin confronts Judge Garvey (Ward Bond)
with a suspicious deck of cards in *Tall in the Saddle*

The more serious *Tall in the Saddle* (1944) finds John Wayne as the independent Rocklin who like Cassidy plays an outsider coming to a lawless Old West town to restore order. On his way to Santa Inez, Rocklin has a conversation with the stagecoach driver Dave (played by frequent sidekick George "Gabby" Hayes) who makes an offhand reference to his boss being "too darn sane, believing in law and order." "What's wrong with law and order?" asks Rocklin in response. "Well, it depends on who's dishing it out," Dave answers. "I never was much on taking orders myself, and as for the law... heh... you'll find out what that means around these parts."

After arriving in Santa Inez, Rocklin joins a saloon poker game that includes several players, including Clint Harolday (Russell Wade), the stepson of Dave's boss, who has been the big winner. Soon Rocklin and Clint tangle in a contentious hand of five-card draw that ends with a dispute over the rules and Clint drawing his weapon before claiming the pot. Rocklin quietly leaves, walking up the stairs to his room above the saloon. As Clint gathers the money, it is reiterated to him by others how he should not have won the hand. "When anybody plays poker with me they play my game or not at all," Clint says. They warn Clint that Rocklin is coming back, but he doesn't believe it. But of course, Rocklin returns, now sporting a full holster, and when Clint immediately relents Rocklin gathers the bills and bids all a good night. The scene confirms Dave's earlier observation about "law and order."

There are rules, sure, but not everyone cares to follow them, and ultimately what really matters is whether or not someone is willing and powerful enough to enforce order. The scene also importantly positions Rocklin as willing to take on that responsibility, which becomes needful once he gets more deeply involved in the ranch wars happening in Santa Inez. In other words, the hand precisely foreshadows the larger story, with Rocklin the one having to bring order to the anarchic Old West town.

The 1950 film *Winchester '73* is in some ways an unusual western, although it still features easy-to-identify heroes and villains with good winning out in the end. The title refers to the Winchester Rifle Model 1873, which is the most coveted firearm among good and bad alike. The story opens on a shooting competition held in Dodge City where Marshal Wyatt Earp (Will Geer) presides. Two shooters emerge as the finalists, Lin McAdam (James Stewart) and Dutch Henry Brown (Stephen McNally), and after Lin wins Dutch Henry and his gang beat him up and make off with the prized Winchester. As it turns out the two men have a long history of bad blood and it is later revealed Dutch Henry killed McAdam's father. However we eventually learn that they are actually brothers, and Dutch Henry realizes that he killed his own father. On the way to that finale Dutch Henry plays a poker game with a cheater in which he gets swindled out of his money and the Winchester. He later manages to get the gun back, but it doesn't help him during the final shootout with Lin, especially after Dutch Henry impulsively uses up all his ammunition. Much as he showed a lack of perception and foresight when getting hustled in the poker game, a similar recklessness dooms Dutch Henry in his last heads-up confrontation.

Other westerns show poker upsetting the tenuous balance of frontier life, more often than not bringing harm to those who play and thus implicitly advancing criticism of the game as a source of trouble. *The Lawless Breed* (1953) provides a patent example of such commentary in its adaptation of real-life Old West figure John Wesley Hardin's self-aggrandizing autobiography. While Hardin mentions playing faro, euchre, seven-up, and poker in his memoir, the film makes poker-playing a central part of his character, positioning it as the first step down a dangerous path. Early in the movie, Hardin (Rock Hudson) earns his preacher father's wrath by his card-playing and leaves home. He had been studying law, but sells his textbooks for cash with which to gamble in a bit of heavy-handed symbolism. Soon Hardin manages to win a hand of five-card draw by outcheating an opponent trying to cheat him, afterwards drawing his gun faster and killing the man. A later game involves Hardin winning by cheating as well, furthering the impression of poker being a corrupt, morally-bankrupt game. The film goes on to superimpose a happy ending on Hardin's tragic real life, ultimately making him out to be the unjustly accused victim of circumstance with remorse over the gambler's life he's led.

"I got a different idea about gambling... I'm going to deal honest cards," insists Mark Fallon (Tyrone Power) as the title character of *The Mississippi Gambler* (1953). Fallon thrives at the steamboat poker tables, and even opens his own casino in New Orleans. But he endures hardship in battles with the less scrupulous, and even his triumphs at poker turn sour when a man he defeats for all of his money kills himself. Poker is more incidental in Howard Hawks' *Rio Bravo* (1959) starring John Wayne as the excellent-ly-named Sheriff John T. Chance struggling to maintain order in the Texas town of the film's title. There is a subplot, however, involving a woman player named Feathers (Angie Dickinson) being unjustly accused of cheating before being exonerated. "You could quit playing cards," advises Chance afterwards, suggesting avoiding poker altogether is a way to better one's chances of staying out of trouble. Poker comes up as well in the sprawling multi-part 1962 epic *How the West Was Won* in the character of a gambler named Cleve Van Valen (Gregory Peck). He gets a bumpy game going while riding a wagon train to California, but gets yanked out of the back of the wagon mid-hand by an angry wagonmaster unhappy about traveling with gamblers. Much later in the film, after Van Valen's death, his widow (Debbie Reynolds) continues to lament his predilection for poker and the strange "sense of honor" that compelled him to feel "duty-bound" to join a game.

Poker in Later Westerns
As the Golden Age of Hollywood cinema came to a close, westerns began to appear that not only upset genre expectations but also openly questioned the romanticized, conservative view of the Old West.

Fielder Cook's 1966 western-comedy *A Big Hand for the Little Lady* uses a single, inordinately lengthy hand of five-card draw to overturn conventional ideas about gender roles and poker being exclusively a man's game. The film is set in the late 19th century in Laredo, Texas, where a group of five wealthy businessmen meet each year in a hotel saloon to play a private high-stakes poker game. A family passing through on their way to a newly purchased farm in San Antonio has to stop to repair their wagon. As it happens, the husband Meredith (Henry Fonda) has a gambling problem, and while his wife Mary (Joanne Woodward) is at the blacksmith's with the wagon, Meredith can't avoid joining the game. When the men learn about Mary having made Meredith quit gambling (the "little woman make you give it up?"), they have a big laugh over the idea of *their* wives asking them to quit poker, such a challenge to their authority seeming unthinkable. The digs continue, such as later when Meredith shuffles and a player says he handles the cards "just like my old grandma used to." Even Meredith's name (also a woman's name), seems to underline his apparent lack of manliness.

The game is played using table stakes, although it becomes clear that rule isn't being strictly enforced. However the players are adamant about following "western rules," meaning a player is not allowed to "tap out" if he hasn't got enough to bet. In other words, if the betting gets too high and a player hasn't enough to call, that player must "bow out" of the hand and lose whatever he's put into the pot. Soon it becomes clear that Meredith is in over his head. He's sweating, growing increasingly edgy, and after losing yet another pot is talking out loud about his bad luck. Then comes a most curious hand in which, incredibly, all six of the players apparently have been dealt strong hands. Meredith, down to his last few hundred when the hand begins, finds himself bet out of the hand. Desperate, he gives his cards to his young son, then rushes up to their room to collect $3,000 more – the family's entire savings – with which he's allowed to buy more chips. (As noted, they seem to ignore the table stakes rule.) The betting resumes, but with all of the reraising Meredith again finds himself out of money and needing $500 more to call. And even if he does call, he can't close the betting. It is at this moment Mary returns, horrified to find Meredith in the game risking their nest egg. Overcome by the stress of the situation, Meredith falls to the floor, the victim of an apparent heart attack. While being attended to by a doctor, Meredith gives his cards to Mary, insisting that *she* play out the hand for him. She agrees to do so, and takes a seat at the table. First, though, she has a question.

"How do you play this game?" she asks.

From there the comically complicated story shows Mary receiving a quick poker primer, then having the idea to go across the street to the Cattle and Merchants Bank to attempt to secure a loan with the other players accompanying her. When asked what collateral she has by the bank's owner, she shows him her "big hand" – a situation resembling a famous story from poker folklore (discussed in Chapter 13). The bank owner is convinced and supplies her the needed funds, and after she puts in a big raise all five opponents fold their hands.

The behavior of the men afterwards shows them each expressing reformed views regarding women's inferiority, their former chauvinistic boorishness suddenly dissolving. As if everything weren't convoluted enough, a final twist reveals the entire plot has been a scam perpetrated by the family, the doctor, and the banker. Mary is not married to Meredith at all, but is instead Ruby, the banker's girlfriend and leader of the group of con artists. The film's final shot shows her dealing a hand of poker to a table full of men, hardly a typical western scene. The film upends traditional gender roles and ideas of women being inferior – whether in the Old West, at a poker table, or in modern America – showing that Mary (or Ruby) is no "little lady."

Henry Hathaway's *5 Card Stud* (1968) adapts elements of the traditional western into a kind of hard-boiled murder mystery, with poker the cause of trouble once again. A cheater in a card game is lynched as punishment, with only professional card player Van Morgan (Dean Martin) raising objections. Morgan leaves town in search of other games, and soon after the players from the lynch mob start to be murdered one by one. The mystery isn't terribly well hidden, however, as the killings begin soon after a new pistol-packing preacher named Rev. Jonathan Rudd (Robert Mitchum) arrives to town. The similarly violent *A Man Called Sledge* (1970), co-written and directed by Vic Morrow and starring James Garner going against type in the villainous title role, has higher ambitions artistically but fails to match the better Italian-made "spaghetti westerns" it tries to emulate. Heavy on atmosphere and even heavier-handed with its morality, multiple montages of poker games merely serve as a mechanism to deliver clumsy judgment against the destructive effects of greed.

Other revisionist westerns bring poker to the foreground more effectively when constructing their protagonists, even when those characters fail to meet the unrealistic ideals set by their fictional forbears. For example, Robert Altman's *McCabe & Mrs. Miller* (1971) begins like many westerns with the arrival of a mysterious figure to an Old West settlement, in this case "Pudgy" McCabe (Warren Beatty) to the oddly-named town of Presbyterian Church in Washington state. With Leonard Cohen's poker-themed "The Stranger Song" as the soundtrack, McCabe enters a tavern and immediately establishes himself by locating a blanket, fashioning a makeshift poker table, and dealing others into a game of five-card stud. McCabe's spell of community-building prefigures his taking over and running the town's brothel from which he similarly functions as a kind of "dealer" in charge of managing the town's inhabitants. His authority is only diminished by the arrival of an equally enigmatic Mrs. Miller (Julie Christie) who becomes his business partner.

It's clear from the start that McCabe's status as an Old West hero is partly built on a bluff, namely a rumor of dubious origin of his having once killed a man for marking cards in a poker game. Eventually he and Mrs. Miller's modest empire consisting of the brothel, an adjacent bath house, and "McCabe's House of Fortune" is threatened by a mining company desirous to buy them out, and after McCabe's mishandled attempt at negotiation falls through, hired killers are assigned to eliminate him. Prior to the shootout that ends the film, McCabe plays against type by revealing both emotion and vulnerability. He even cries. Then during the showdown, combatants display a further lack of heroism through their willingness to shoot each other in the back. By the end, McCabe's poker playing may well be the *only* trait he shares with traditional western heroes.

The Life and Times of Judge Roy Bean (1972) provides a similarly twist-ed take on the genre, featuring Paul Newman as the title character. It is a strange, uneven film that plays out like a fantasy, even though it is based on a true story. Like McCabe, Bean uses the force of his personality to ensconce himself in a leadership role in a frontier town, declaring himself a "judge" and frequently holding court over poker games. As the narrator explains, "I reckon poker had as much to do with winning the West as Colts .45 or the Prairie schooner." Indeed, poker is described as "more a religion, than a game," with Bean believing himself "a past master."

That said, the games in the film mainly show Bean to be a losing player, though nonetheless confirm his authority over his dusty kingdom. For ex-ample, after losing a hand to one of his marshals, Whorehouse Lucky Jim (Steve Kanaly), the Judge immediately charges Jim $25 for the next beer he orders. "That ain't sportin'," Jim complains. "What is a man supposed to do?" "Start losing or quit drinking," Bean declares. One last poker game precedes a final battle between Bean and a rival to his authority. As if to foreshadow the gunplay to come, the players use bullets for chips. "I open for a .38," says one. "I'll call the .38 and raise you two .45s." When the end finally comes for Bean, his demise is reported in fitting language: "The judge cashed in his chips."

Other latter-day westerns have also made certain to incorporate poker. In *Silverado* (1985), an homage of sorts to the classical western, a gambler named Slick (Jeff Goldblum) shows up midway through the story cheekily looking for an "honest game" of poker. Unsurprisingly, he turns out to be less than honest as the stock figure of a rambling, gambling man. *Maverick* (1994), an adaptation of the earlier television show (see Chapter 20) with Mel Gibson as the comic cowboy, fashions its plot around an anachronism – a poker tournament played aboard a steamboat. *Open Range* (2003), another throwback western directed by and starring Kevin Costner, begins with a slow-paced poker game among cowboys waiting out a rainstorm, one of many nods to generic conventions also serving as a light-hearted prelude to more serious conflicts to come. "A man's trust is a valuable thing," says the oldest of the group to the youngest. "You don't want to lose it for a handful of cards." Coming at the start of the film, the only meaningful context for the maxim are the century's worth of westerns that precede it.

Saloon poker becomes a requisite element in science fiction films re-imagining the Old West, such as the futuristic sci-fi thriller *Westworld* (1973), written and directed by Michael Crichton. The film imagines an adult-themed amusement park populated by robots enacting various his-torical periods and settings. In the Old West area of the park, the main characters sit in a saloon playing poker. Technicians overseeing the action on closed-circuit monitors call out "all right, let's start that bar fight," at which point one of the poker-playing robots yells "Cheat!" and a brawl ensues. The time-travel comedies *Bill and Ted's Excellent Adventure* (1989) and *Back to the Future Part III* (1990) are also both careful to incorporate poker (and bar fights) when reimagining the Old West. In the former, the dim-witted duo travel through time seeking help with a high school history project and visit a New Mexico saloon in 1879 where they play poker with the notorious outlaw Billy the Kid. The third *Back to the Future* installment similarly travels to a fictional California town in 1885, where among those sitting at the tables playing poker in the Palace Saloon are three veterans of western films: Dub Taylor, Pat Buttram, and Harry Carey Jr. (son of the silent film star). The bartender is likewise played by another frequent western actor, Matt Clark.

More recently, the neo-western *Hell or High Water* (2016) has fun with the genre's formula in several ways, including moving the action out of the Old West and into a contemporary setting. The film smoothly introduces a situation in which a pair of bank robbers choose to launder their ill-gotten gains at an Oklahoma casino located on a Native American reservation. One of the outlaws sits down at a poker table and battles with a Comanche over a hand of hold'em, and their tough talk parallels the light-hearted banter between the Texas Ranger and his half-Indian partner who are chasing the criminals. It also recalls the western's long tradition of using clashes over cards to complement broader battles for higher stakes.

Comedies

Poker in Silent Comedies

Poker serves a variety of purposes in film comedies, including as a tried and tested means by which to introduce a plot-driving complication into characters' lives. The trouble tends not to be as threatening as occurs in non-comedies, however, and generally does not interfere with the films' requisite happy endings. Often the humor generated from poker is derived from upsetting expectations, sometimes by disturbing the rules and etiquette of the game. Many examples of cheating at poker are often comically exaggerated in such films, while strip poker also frequently appears to add a risqué element and generate laughs.

We've already talked about the 1912 short *A Cure for Pokeritis* (discussed Chapter 7), which implies poker is a kind of sickness in need of remedying, and other silent comedies treat poker similarly. In *The Thousand-Dollar Husband* (1916), a romantic comedy starring Blanche Sweet as a Swedish maid named Olga, poker is a source of trouble early on when Olga's love interest discovers his father has lost his fortune then promptly loses everything he has in a poker game. *When Do We Eat?* (1918) is another five-reeler directed by Fred Niblo starring Enid Bennett as Nora, an actress who ultimately is able to use her dramatic chops to thwart a bank robbery. Along the way the crooks reveal their villainy by cheating a young man out of $300 in a card game, with poker used to liken one form of robbery with another.

Poker similarly creates trouble in *Dr. Jack* (1922) starring one of silent film's great comedians, Harold Lloyd, as the mild-mannered physician, Dr. Jackson (or "Jack" for short). Like other Lloyd films, *Dr. Jack* is full of great gags highlighting Lloyd's special brand of physical comedy. Halfway through the film comes a relatively lengthy poker scene, in which Lloyd is

Harold Lloyd as *Dr. Jack* (1922)

given another chance to engage in his typical antics. It also helps further establish his character as a doctor who is always quick to come up with unorthodox, creative "remedies" to those in need.

In a hotel lobby, Dr. Jack encounters a young woman asking for his assistance. Her father is upstairs playing in an illegal poker game, and she asks him to "get my daddy away" from the game since "he'll lose his paycheck... he always does." Dr. Jack goes upstairs to find four men playing five-card draw. Soon he notices a box containing several decks of cards, and quickly comes up with a way to break up the game. Procuring aces from a number of the decks, Dr. Jack surreptitiously supplies each of the players with cards needed for *all* of them to make four aces. All four put everything they have in the middle, including the young woman's father betting his paycheck. The showdown leads to pandemonium – and a nifty ride down the banister to safety by Dr. Jack – though the ruse nonetheless works to save the father from ruin. As in *A Cure for Pokeritis*, poker is presented as a kind of "illness" that Dr. Jack finds a way to treat.

W.C. Fields, the Comedic Card Cheat

One of the most iconic images of poker in mainstream entertainment is of W.C. Fields stealthily peering out from under a stovepipe hat over a carefully protected poker hand. There's a certain irony in the image, however. While Fields is the one looking wary, his opponents are really the ones who ought to be suspicious. After all, whenever *any* of Fields' characters played poker, it was pretty much a given the game would be crooked. As biographer Robert Lewis Taylor once noted, there is "something so blatantly felonious about the sight of Fields in a poker game that its humor was assured from the start."[6]

Fields had already made a mark in vaudeville and on the Broadway stage when he began his film career during the early silent era. By the 1930s he had become one of cinema's biggest stars, easily transitioning to sound in dozens of films until his death in 1946. Often Fields portrayed variations of a similar character, a hustling con man constantly putting one over witless others as the audience knowingly laughed along. In the 1923 musical comedy *Poppy*, Fields played a fraudster named Prof. Eustace McGargle, and one scene in particular, singled out by critic Alexander Woollcott, helped catapult Fields to greater fame. Woollcott wrote: "The stud game in which he manages to deal himself four fours and to win a thousand-dollar pot without having undergone the burdensome necessity of putting up any money himself is the most hilarious minor episode of the new season."[7]

According to Taylor, Fields claimed during rehearsals that he had put the scene together "from experience" fleecing skilled sharps. However when pressed for details about where he had gathered such experience, Fields cheekily avoided specifics. "Hither and yon," he said. Taylor notes that Fields shunned gambling for significant stakes, and in fact was highly averse to all forms of risk, avoiding investing in stocks and bonds (and thereby surviving the 1929 crash unscathed).[8] Fields portrayed a man losing money by investing in an oil stock in *The Potters* (1927), a now-lost silent film that also includes his first turn in film playing poker. Later in *Tillie and Gus* (1933), the first full-length talkie in which he had a starring role, Fields plays Augustus Q. Winterbottom whom we first meet in the film on trial for having shot a man during a game of draw poker. He defends his actions by explaining how during the game he had dealt himself four aces, only to find his opponent (and soon-to-be shooting victim) had drawn *five* aces. "I'm a broad-minded man, gents," he says. "I don't object to nine aces in one deck. But when a man lays down five aces in one hand... and besides, I know what I dealt him!"

Rather than toss him into jail as he deserves, the judge absurdly rules Gus must leave town, something he is more than glad to do once he receives a letter that his ex-wife's brother has recently died, leaving him part of his estate. As it happens, Gus finds himself reunited on the train with his estranged wife, Tillie, played by Alison Skipworth, who has received a similar letter. They further reveal themselves as con artists when Gus swindles a group of players in a humorous hand of poker in which his corrupt deal allows his four aces to beat his opponents' four kings, four queens, and four jacks.

Fields appeared in a film called *Six of a Kind* (1934) soon after, the title of which sounds like a poker reference. (It was called *Poker Party* when it was released in France.) However the film is more of a road movie featuring an ensemble cast including Skipworth again as well as George Burns and Gracie Allen.[9] The next year came *Mississippi* (1935), a musical comedy set on a steamboat starring Bing Crosby in which Fields plays a supporting role as the ship's pilot, Commodore Orlando Jackson. In another poker scene, Jackson deals himself five aces, and after discarding one reacts with frustration when he sees he's given himself another ace. He surreptitiously manages to discard and draw two more times, yet keeps picking up a fifth ace. Others are cheating, too, with multiple players also holding four aces. The showdown produces some comic violence, with Commodore Jackson bluffing once more by blowing cigar smoke into his pistols to suggest he had fired them when he had not.

Later Fields was paired with Mae West in the western spoof *My Little Chickadee* (1940), yet another film featuring a nonsensical plot mostly existing to provide opportunities for comedic ad-libbing. As Cuthbert J. Twillie, Fields again hustles a group of dupes in a saloon game in the scene from which comes the famous image of Fields peering over his cards. A little later in the movie Fields delivers one of the more memorable movie lines about poker when inviting a country bumpkin to play a game. "Is this a game of chance?" asks the victim. "Not the way I play it, no," comes the reply.

Poker Neither Good Nor Evil

Just as *My Little Chickadee*'s exaggeration of various western tropes pokes fun at the genre and at idealized versions of the Old West, Fields' many farcical scenes of cheating at poker similarly serve to diminish unreasonable fears about the game. Such scenes make poker appear more a context for harmless laughs than for real danger. There are many other examples of film comedies treating poker in a similarly playful way, not necessarily casting moral judgment one way or another.

The Lady Eve (1941) mixes romance and slapstick while telling the story of a father-daughter con artist team, "Colonel" Harrington (Charles Coburn) and Jean (Barbara Stanwyck), who on a transatlantic ocean liner target the naïve wealthy son of a brewery magnate, Charles Pike (Henry Fonda). After setting up their mark with an evening of bridge, they play poker the next night where the father uses his ability to "deal fifths" (saving the top four cards) and multiple extra decks hidden on his person to help win thousands from Charles. But Barbara falls in love with their victim, and she starts cheating for *him* by replacing her father's four-of-a-kind hands with poor ones. The fact is, Charles, himself an avid poker player (he calls himself an "expert") with seemingly unlimited means, cannot be hurt

Charles Coburn, Barbara Stanwyck, and Henry Fonda in *The Lady Eve* (1941)

that greatly by the game, nor can the film's many twists and turns avoid ending with Jean and Charles happily together.

Charles Coburn also stars in the comedy *Has Anybody Seen My Gal?* (1952), this time as a character who actually uses poker for "good" (so to speak). Coburn plays an elderly millionaire bachelor wishing to leave his estate to the descendants of a woman he had loved when younger, but who married someone else. He visits the family under a different name in order to get to know them before making them his beneficiaries, and one of the good deeds he performs on their behalf is to win money in a poker game to help one of the sons pay off a gambling debt. In *Roman Holiday* (1953), Gregory Peck's character Joe Bradley, an American reporter working in Italy, is introduced sitting at a poker table. At first it seems he's playing for significant sums, with bets of "500" and "1,000," but when the winner rakes in the pot he mentions it adds up to ten bucks – they're playing with Italian lira, not U.S. dollars. Joe's poker playing hardly reflects badly on him, other than to signify a kind of mundane existence preceding the higher "stakes" of the romantic adventure he soon falls into with Audrey Hepburn's wayward princess. Peck also stars in the romantic comedy *Designing Woman* (1957) as a sportswriter named Mike somewhat mismatched with a clothes designer named Marilla played by Lauren Bacall. The pair's differences are highlighted when Mike hosts his regular poker game on the same night Marilla has invited a group of theater friends to perform a play in the

Poker & Pop Culture

neighboring room. While a contrast is vaguely drawn suggesting poker to be a less refined recreation than the dramatic arts, there's no special judgment made against the game.

Other comedies continue this theme of avoiding judging poker too harshly, even when characters are cheating. *Kaleidoscope* (1966) is a flashy yet thin caper about an American criminal in Europe that features a novel method of cheating at cards. Barney Lincoln (Warren Beatty) manages to doctor the plates from which the Kaleidoscope brand playing cards are printed. Then using special (and amusingly conspicuous) thick-framed eyeglasses, Lincoln cleans up in several high-stakes Chemin de Fer games at a casino. He is eventually caught and subsequently agrees to help the authorities nab a crime lord in another big game of five-card stud. Only when the Kaleidoscope cards get replaced and Lincoln has to play without cheating does any minor tension arise. A short, inspired scene in the Bill Murray vehicle *Stripes* (1981) finds soldiers in basic training playing poker in the barracks, with the experienced player Ox (John Candy) taking advantage of the slow-witted novice Cruiser (John Diehl). Cruiser asks his opponent how to play his hand, and Ox convinces him to bet all he has with just a pair of fours. "Go on, bluff me!" says Ox, and when Cruiser does Ox promptly calls and shows a full house to scoop the pot. The comedy *Honeymoon in Vegas* (1992) similarly matches a far-fetched card game with a far-fetched plot. Jack (Nicolas Cage) and Betsy (Sarah Jessica Parker) travel to Las Vegas for a spur-of-the-moment marriage, though before the couple can get to the altar Jack loses $65,000 in a game of five-card draw to hustler Tommy Korman (James Caan). The big hand that sinks Jack – a jack-high straight flush losing to a queen-high straight flush – is improbable (and most certainly crooked). So, too, is it hard to believe the couple agrees to let Betsy spend a weekend with Tommy in lieu of paying the debt.

Such moral neutrality about poker in film comedies probably reaches a kind of apotheosis in *Oh God! You Devil* (1984) in which George Burns, starring as God in the third installment of the series, plays a hand of five-card draw for a person's soul against the devil, also played by Burns. The devil is dealt two pair, then improves to a full house on the draw while God draws two cards to his three to a straight flush. Then God puts in a big raise involving all the souls of those on his "list" (i.e., who have chosen him, not the devil). "If I lose, they're all fair game for you," God explains. "If I win, you can't touch them, ever, even if they ask for you." "Too rich for me," the devil says as gives up his hand, then cringes when God shows he's bluffed with ten-high. "Why did I fold?!" cries the devil. "I put the fear of me in you," God cracks.

It's clear enough that while individuals may choose good or evil, poker in and of itself is neither.

A Game for Guys

Burns plays poker as well in *Just You and Me, Kid* (1979), hosting a game among a group of old vaudeville buddies in a another setting familiar to film comedies – the home game among men. The 1968 film *The Odd Couple* (discussed in Chapter 9) provides the template for this sort of light-hearted setting for poker in which men are shown gathering in part to seek a respite from women.

The television film *Thursday's Game* (1974), written by famed sitcom creator James L. Brooks and starring Gene Wilder and Bob Newhart, is another example. Using the weekly poker game as a starting point, the film explores how competitiveness often arises when males relate to one another, thus making poker an especially fitting social activity. Players in a friendly home game decide one week to experiment with playing for higher stakes in order to make things more interesting ("We're playing cards, not poker," one of them complains, referring to the too-small pots). The experiment goes badly, with the night ending in heavy losses, physical altercations, and the permanent breaking up of the game. Two of the players, both married, decide to continue meeting, anyway, surmising they need the one night away from their wives. Though friends, the two men find themselves continuing to battle one another without chips and cards, especially after one loses his job as the other prospers.

Easy Money (1983), starring comedian Rodney Dangerfield, continues the theme. Dangerfield's character Monty enjoys a regular game with the guys as a favorite escape from the stress of work and family responsibilities. He constantly argues with his wealthy mother-in-law who strongly objects to what she regards as Monty's uncivilized "debauchery." She comes up with a plan, faking her death and leaving a will bequeathing her daughter's family an estate worth $10 million only if Monty can "reform" himself in one year by giving up drinking, womanizing, smoking, drugs, overeating, and gambling. The regimen aligns poker with other male "vices," making Monty's struggles to adhere to the will's terms seem a humorous form of emasculation. In the end, Monty gets everything, convincing his mother-in-law (who after a year reveals herself and her scheme) that he has reformed to earn the fortune while secretly carrying on with poker in the basement, as though the game is an undeniable requisite for manhood.

Often in comedies the game representing an escape from women becomes the context for men to think or talk about nothing else. In *Risky Business* (1983), the table talk among the high school males is all about how one of them lacked the courage to accept a woman's advances. In *Can't Buy Me Love* (1987), nerdy high schoolers about to start their senior year play their regular poker game, ongoing for two years and derisively styled by a young sibling as "a night of cards, chips, dips, and dorks," though one of them can't focus, his thoughts preoccupied by the coed parties happening elsewhere. The comedy *How to Lose a Guy in 10 Days* (2003) contrives a situation designed to highlight differences between the sexes. A writer for a women's magazine sets out to write a story about dating a man and losing him in 10 days using common mistakes made by women to ruin relationships, while the man she seeks out is an ad executive who happens to have made a bet with his boss that he can make any woman fall in love with him in 10 days. With those cross-purposes in place, the man's weekly poker game (his "boys night") arises, where the talk is about her – until she arrives to stage a series of comic interruptions to break up the game. And in *The 40 Year Old Virgin* (2005), the conversation among a group of co-workers at their poker game turns to R-rated tales of sexual exploits during which the title character is unable to bluff the others.

Strip Poker

The origin of strip poker is as hard to pinpoint as the beginnings of clothes-on poker. Most accounts suggest the idea of taking it off while taking a card probably first occurred not long after the game was introduced in early 19th-century America. Much as New Orleans is often identified as a starting point for poker in the United States, some have speculated that strip poker started there, too. Others have located the game in 19th-century brothels, introduced as a way to enliven even further the usual negotiations occurring in such establishments.

Cinematic references to strip poker date from the silent era. One of the more famous examples comes in the 1928 silent film *The Road to Ruin* starring Helen Foster as the wayward youth Sally Canfield. Blurring the line between educational and exploitative, the film was highly controversial in its day, banned in several U.S. cities yet apparently shown in high schools as a stern warning against delinquency's dire consequences. It was also one of the top grossing films of the year, earning $2.5 million at the box office. From the start, sweet Sally, her neglectful parents having failed to provide her proper guidance, falls in with the wrong crowd and swiftly slips into a downward spiral. Before her sad story concludes, it will involve smoking, drinking, drug use, premarital sex, prostitution, and abortion. She also joins a game of strip poker at a party, with the game clearly serving as further evidence of Sally's moral decline. The pre-Hays Code sequence reportedly featured nudity, too, thus prompting some exhibitors' objections. However, surviving prints feature an awkward jump cut which appears to have excised the offending images.[10]

Other strip poker scenes pop up during the early sound era, such as in the 1932 political satire *The Dark Horse* starring Bette Davis. That one begins with a party randomly choosing a woefully unqualified gubernatorial candidate, then finds his campaign manager struggling throughout to keep the candidate in line. On the eve of the election the rival party comes up with a plan – an "ace in the hole," they call it – to employ the campaign manager's ex-wife to lure the candidate to a remote mountain cabin for a game of strip poker. The low-budget melodrama *Mad Youth* (1940), a.k.a. *Girls of the Underworld*, also features strip poker being played by a group of teens while their parents are away at their bridge club, with some clever cross-cutting between the two card games affording a few grins.

Strip poker became increasingly popular in America during the 1950s and 1960s, appearing in popular culture with greater frequency along with other formerly forbidden fare as the nation embarked upon what would come to be called a sexual revolution. In was during this period that sexploitation pioneer Joseph Sarno produced a six-minute film *A Sneak Peek at Strip Poker* (1966). Much tamer than Sarno's feature work, the short functions as a kind of "how-to" demonstration for the curious. Strip poker found its way into experimental film as well in the 1965 Andy Warhol production *Horse* directed by Ronald Tavel. *Horse* is a plotless film featuring men dressed as cowboys acting out a variety of homoerotic scenarios, among them a game of strip poker. Meanwhile the adult sci-fi spy spoof *Zeta One* (1969) about a race of alien women visiting Earth begins with strip poker game – all of which sounds much more exciting than it actually is.

Before directing *One Flew Over the Cuckoo's Nest*, *Amadeus* and other acclaimed features, Czech director Milos Forman's 1971 comedy *Taking Off* comments on the period's cultural shifts while also incorporating strip poker into the story. After their teenaged daughter runs away from home, Larry and Lynn Tyne (Buck Henry and Lynn Carlin) meet up with other parents of runaways, eventually becoming encouraged by them to enjoy the newfound freedom they've been afforded. Eventually the Tynes and another couple find themselves at the end of an enjoyable evening – drunk, stoned and playing a card game called "Texas one-card showdown." In the game, each player draws a single card, with the one drawing the lowest having to remove an article of clothing. The game progresses, providing a kind of literal reference to the film's title, with Larry ultimately the big loser. He then delivers a rambunctious song in the nude, the performance having the others in stitches, when his singing is interrupted by the surprise return of their daughter. Awkward!

Further evidence of strip poker's popularity around this time is provided by the 1972 publication of *Playboy's Book of Games* which includes a detailed section describing the rules and game play. "This exciting game, though very popular in some circles, is rarely if ever discussed in card books," writes author and noted gambling expert Edwin Silberstang.[11] He goes on to present the game as a great way "to break the ice" at social gatherings. Among the many hilariously sober directives regarding the rules of strip poker, Silberstang insists only legitimate articles of clothing can be wagered, thereby excluding band-aids, eyeglasses, jewelry, and wigs or toupees. Further recommendations (drawn "from long experience and much study") include playing draw poker rather than stud, since the latter game will likely result in players running out of clothes too quickly.[12]

Strip poker faded from prominence thereafter, although if references in popular culture are an indicator, the game remains firmly in the public's collective consciousness. In the early 1980s, forms of strip poker were among the first games created for home computers, with players rewarded with static, monochrome images for winning hands, both crude and crudely-rendered. There was a short-lived game show called *Strip Poker* on the USA Network (in 2000-01), and another failed attempt by National Lampoon to produce a similarly-themed pay-per-view show in 2005. Unsurprisingly, Lady Gaga and her supporting cast play the game in her 2008 video "Poker Face." The *American Pie* franchise has alluded to the game more than once. And in the opening of *The Social Network* (2010) we see Harvard student Mark Zuckerberg busily creating and launching his "Facemash" site (a Facebook prototype) while students across campus party it up, with strip poker among their chosen activities.

Poker Parodies

Poker's sudden rise in popularity during the 2000s inspired still more comedic treatments of the game, including a couple of full-blown parodies poking fun at the phenomenon. Both *The Grand* (2007) and *Hitting the Nuts* (2010) are done in a "mockumentary" style with considerable improvisation from the casts. Both films also employed the trajectory of a tournament culminating in a winner emerging to shape their plots.

The Grand spoofs large-scale televised spectacles like the World Poker Tour and World Series of Poker, with a well known cast of celebrities, many of whom (Gabe Kaplan, Shannon Elizabeth, Ray Romano, Hank Azaria, Jason Alexander, David Cross, Cheryl Hines) were already known as "celebrity" poker players. Meanwhile *Hitting the Nuts* chronicles an illegal tournament in Indiana with unknowns filling the roles. Both enjoy intermittent success sending up poker clichés and other targets, although it wasn't too surprising neither made much of an impression upon the larger culture, given the niche subject matter.

Dramas

Poker in Early Dramas

Dramatic movies have presented poker in a wide variety of ways, more often than not reflecting negatively on the game. Many of these films associate poker with violence, lawlessness, and/or self-destructive behavior, although some present positive associations and even spirited defenses of the game.

Much like *A Cure for Pokeritis*, an even earlier one-reeler titled *The Last Deal* (1910) provided an object lesson against gambling, although in this case poker serves as a solution to a problem rather than the cause of one. Directed by D.W. Griffith for Biograph, the story begins with a man gambling on stocks with his employer's funds and losing. After confessing to his employer, he is given one day to recover the money. His wife agrees to allow him to pawn her jewelry, and with the money he goes to a gambling parlor to try to win what he can at the poker table. He wins at first, but then a newcomer to the game – a particularly skillful player – manages to clean out him and everyone else. The man is distraught and ready to commit suicide, but then discovers what the audience already knows: the card sharp is in fact his brother-in-law who gives him the money he needs to repay his boss. The man loses his job, but the brother-in-law promises to assist him going forward. "Whether the Biograph people sought to preach a sermon against gambling or not is uncertain, but that they have done so, and very effectively," judged one contemporary reviewer.[13] Even so, the message is mixed, with the brother-in-law's admonitions about gambling undercut by his own poker-playing success.

Other early dramas continued to advance negative associations with card playing. *The Gamesters* (1920) involves a love triangle being decided by a poker game between two men. The loser responds by kidnapping the woman and violence ensues. The suspenseful *Ace of Hearts* (1921), starring Lon Chaney, begins with members of a secret star chamber dealing out cards to determine who among them is to carry out an assassination. And poker and gambling are among several decadent activities intended to connote villainy in Erich von Stroheim's dark post-First World War drama *Foolish Wives* (1922).

Meanwhile poker provides a primary means for solving a murder in one of the first talkies to feature the game, *The Canary Murder Case* (1929). An early entry in a series of films featuring the crime-solving amateur detective Philo Vance, the film stars original flapper icon Louise Brooks as a showgirl known as "The Canary." Within 20 minutes we discover the Canary is involved romantically with multiple men and is scheming to blackmail all of them before turning up murdered. Enter Vance, here played by William Powell, who hits upon a novel method to figure out who among the many suspects might possess the craftiness and nerve to have carried out the crime. "A man's true nature always comes out in a game of poker," he says. "I know the type and the temperament of the man who murdered the Canary, and in a game of poker I believe that I can come pretty close to putting my finger on him."

Vance then arranges a game with all of the suspects. In one hand of five-card draw, a player demonstrates himself to be much too cautious to be a murderer when he only calls a small bet while holding three aces. In another, someone bets big with a nine-high straight flush, showing he only bets on a sure thing and is thus too timid to be the killer. Then comes a hand between Vance and an elderly banker named Spotswoode in which the latter raises predraw then stands pat. After Vance then draws the men exchange a series of raises. "I'm afraid I'm overcome by curiosity," Vance says as he calls the last raise, then watches Spotswoode sheepishly turn over a lowly pair of deuces. But he has bluffed with best hand as Vance only has ace-high, having called not to try to pick up the pot, but to pick up information. As Vance explains to the police sergeant later, for him the hand proves Spotswoode to be "the only man at the table with enough imagination to plan such a crime and with sufficient self-confidence and daring to carry it through." It's a bit contrived, the suggestion that bluffing with deuces makes one "psychological fitted," as Vance puts it, to plot and execute a murder. That said, the killer getting run over by a train in the next scene is perhaps even more improbable.

Other early dramas similarly connect card-playing with crime. *Smart Money* (1931) finds Edward G. Robinson as Nick the Barber, a small-time gambler with aspirations to play for higher stakes. After losing in a crooked five-card stud game to a group led by Sleepy Sam (pretending to be another famous gambler named Hickory Short), Nick gathers another stake and gets his revenge against Sam, bragging afterwards about having given him a "trimming" using "shaved cards." After busting the real Hickory Short, Nick becomes the most famous gambler around, opening an illegal casino before finally being taken down by the authorities. In a similar vein, the atmospheric crime drama *Dead End* (1937) shows the delinquent "Dead End Kids" playing poker for bottle caps, yet another nefarious activity along with spitting, using rough language, and failing to respect authority figures while being unduly influenced by the criminal "Baby Face" Martin (Humphrey Bogart). One contemporary article about *Dead End* makes special note of its inclusion of poker, suggesting how the boys' careful adherence to both the rules of five-card draw and even correct strategy "may be very beneficial for the game." Even so, the article explains that Sidney Kingsley who wrote the play upon which the film is based included the scene "as a sort of protest against a society that lets little boys gamble and fight and swear."[14]

The title of the 1940 film *Outside the Three-Mile Limit* alludes to the U.S. law against gambling on ships within three miles of either coast, and features a plot aboard a gambling ship filled with card-playing hoodlums and counterfeiters. Alfred Hitchcock's *Lifeboat* (1944) also depicts a poker game played on a sailing vessel, albeit under very different conditions. During the Second World War, an American freighter sinks after being attacked by a German U-boat. A group of passengers and crew members survive via a lifeboat and two survivors play a poker game with a deck created from memo pad pages. Alas, even in such extenuating circumstances the game creates conflict, with accusations of marked "cards" leading one player to attack another. A few years later Charlton Heston made his starring debut as the part-owner of an illegal gambling house in the noir *Dark City* (1950). The criminals are able to endure constant raids and inner turmoil, but it's only after they cheat a visitor out of thousands and the player subsequently hangs himself that their enterprise begins to crumble.

Men, Women, and Poker in *A Streetcar Named Desire*

One of the most notable uses of poker as both a plot device and a means to emphasize a film's themes occurs in the 1951 adaptation of Tennessee Williams' award-winning play *A Streetcar Named Desire* directed by Elia Kazan. A gripping domestic drama filled with sex and violence, the story conspicuously uses poker to emphasize the stark, conflict-causing differences that can sometimes exist between men and women. The play even carried the early working title "The Poker Night," a reference to a pivotal scene in which a poker game dramatically amplifies the contrast between the sexes conveyed over the course of the film.

By the time the scene arises the audience has already gotten to know the story's three primary figures: the muscle-bound factory worker Stanley Kowalski (played by Marlon Brando in the film), his newly pregnant wife Stella (Kim Hunter), and her visiting sister Blanche (Vivien Leigh). It's also already clear that Blanche's presence has upset the balance of the Kowalski household in their cramped apartment in the New Orleans French Quarter. "I understand there's to be a little card party here tonight, to which we ladies are cordially not invited," Blanche says to Stanley during the afternoon before the game. "That's right," Stanley answers, wasting no words to confirm the poker game is wholly off limits to the women. Stella understands the need for the men to be alone, and she and Blanche go out for the evening.

When they return late that night the game is many hours old. The men are drinking and smoking cigars, the room is darkly lit, and the atmosphere is claustrophobic. From upstairs comes banging and yelling from the wife of one of the players, impatient with the noise and wishing for the game to end. She threatens to repeat an action she's apparently done before to end their games by pouring boiling water through cracks in the floor.

Stella and Blanche hover over the game momentarily while a hand is dealt. "Poker's so fascinating!" Blanche says. "Could I kibitz?" she asks while reaching down to peek at one of the player's cards. "You could not!" Stanley yells and angrily pushes her hand away. Not coincidentally, Stanley has been losing, and soon after suggests the women should leave. They move to the neighboring room and the game continues, the card playing having literally segregated the sexes.

The sisters start to make noise of their own by laughing and playing the radio, prompting Stanley (not unlike the wife upstairs) to yell across for them to keep quiet. Eventually one of the men, Mitch (Karl Malden), leaves the game momentarily to talk with Blanche who turns the radio back on and begins dancing for him. In his absence a hand of Spit in the Ocean concludes with Stanley losing to a straight after thinking his three aces were best. Incensed, Stanley races into the next room, then grabs the radio and shockingly throws it through a closed window, the glass shattering in a loud explosion. Stella rushes in and an enraged Stanley begins to beat her, the attack ending only when one of the men knocks him unconscious.

"We should not be playing in a house with women!" Mitch pointedly shouts out amid the tumult. He repeats the line as Stanley, after finally coming to, throws everyone out, the repetition reminding the viewer of the game's apparent role in the fracas while reiterating the position that poker is a male-only province. The scene ends with a disoriented Stanley outside and alone, yelling for Stella who has taken refuge upstairs – the iconic "Stella!" scene everyone remembers from the film. Stella forgives him (this time) and comes back down.

There are a few possible reasons for Stanley's outburst, though the most pertinent seems his frustration at the poker game being disturbed. The women's intrusion seems to him a kind of threat to his authority as a man. Later on Blanche talks to her sister about Stanley, calling him an "animal" and "subhuman." Poker, too, becomes part of her argument when she refers to "poker night" as "his party of apes." Blanche tries to convince Stella she shouldn't stay with Stanley and thus "hang back with the brutes," but her argument isn't working. As the story's later, darker turn shows, Blanche's judgment about Stanley proves correct. The fact that the men reconvene to play one more round of poker at the end of the film seems to underscore how the divide between men and women has only widened by the story's conclusion. Here "poker night" ultimately appears designated as an arena in which men might readily indulge their most beast-like tendencies, a harsh judgment upon both men and the game.

Crime, Camaraderie, Cons and Other Connotations

Noir films of the 1950s and 1960s continued to include poker playing among the nefarious activities of their anti-heroes. Often the game appears as a small element in a broader sketch of criminality, such as in *Kan-*

sas City Confidential (1952) in which gangsters play cards, or the similarly-named New York Confidential (1955) where members of a crime family do the same. Meanwhile poker plays a more pivotal role in The Man With the Golden Arm (1955) starring Frank Sinatra and directed by Otto Preminger. An adaptation of Nelson Algren's gritty 1949 novel, Sinatra plays a drug addict named Frankie Machine who has managed to get clean after a prison stay. His efforts to start a new life as a jazz drummer are later thwarted, however, when he finds it necessary to resume his work dealing illegal poker games for an old acquaintance. The game requires Frankie not just to deal for long hours but to play as well with the house's money, and following a familiar causal chain he's hooked on drugs once again, triggering his life to spiral into disarray. The "golden arm" of the title thus alludes both to Frankie's winning ways as a dealer and intravenous drug taking, yet another illicit link in a popular portrayal of poker.

Along with The Life of Judge Roy Bean, Paul Newman appeared in a half-dozen films in which poker is played or mentioned, including starring in two of the greatest poker scenes in film history in Cool Hand Luke (1967) and The Sting (1973).[15] In Cool Hand Luke, Newman plays the rebellious and often self-destructive war veteran Lucas Jackson who gets sentenced to prison for the seemingly purposeless crime of drunkenly cutting heads off parking meters. He continues his stubborn ways as an inmate, losing badly in a fight with the prisoners' leader Dragline (George Kennedy), but a game of five-card stud among the prisoners soon helps Newman's Luke earn a certain status, as well as his nickname. In the hand, several apparently casual raises from Luke are interpreted as strength and his opponent folds his "pair of Savannahs" (sevens). Luke reveals his king-high – or, as Dragline gleefully crows, "a hand full of nothing." "Yeah, well," says Luke, pausing just a beat while opening a bottle, "sometimes nothing can be a real cool hand." In a single three-minute hand of poker, Luke's complicated character is comprehensively defined both to the other prisoners and to the audience as a heedless risk-taker always ready to bet on himself, even when it appears foolhardy to do so.

Newman is equally cool as the con Henry Gondorff in the Depression-era film The Sting, especially in a poker scene that takes place aboard the 20th Century Limited express train. The game serves as an initial stage in an elaborate plan devised by Gondorff and his partner Johnny Hooker (Robert Redford) to exact revenge against crime boss Doyle Lonnegan (Robert Shaw) for having had two of Hooker's accomplices killed. Pretending to be a bookie, Gondorff gets himself invited into Lonnegan's high-stakes game, successfully angering Lonnegan with his boorish behavior to the point that the mobster has a "cold deck" prepared to ensure Gondorff receives quad treys versus his own four nines. But Gondorff has an extra deck himself from which to draw cards, and when the betting concludes, he is the one who surprisingly turns over the best hand – four jacks – to the disbelief of Lonnegan. Even better, when Lonnegan goes for his wallet to retrieve the $15,000 he owes Gondorff he discovers it missing, as it was pilfered before by an accomplice of Gondorff's. "What was I supposed to do?" fumes Lonnegan afterwards to a lackey. "Call him for cheating better than me in front of the others?" Serving as "the hook" to catch Lonnegan in "the sting" to come (as the sequences are subtitled), the scene also hooks the viewer, neatly utilizing poker's legacy as a cheating game to augment the world of the con.

In the great character study *Five Easy Pieces* (1970), Jack Nicholson's Bobby Dupea plays poker with his oil rigging co-workers, alongside other recreations including drinking, bowling, and carousing. The game represents a non-meaningful yet benign pastime, providing temporary camaraderie to distract Bobby from deeper existential worries. Poker serves a similar function in *Silent Running* (1972), a low-budget science fiction film set aboard a spaceship orbiting Saturn. The film depicts a future in which the total colonization of Earth has caused the extinction of all plant life, with the ship's mission to carry specimens in forests preserved in climate-controlled domes, perhaps for reintroduction later. The four crewmen play a game of poker to pass the time, before an order arrives to destroy the domes and return to Earth. One of the crewmen, Freeman Lowell (Bruce Dern), resists and in the resulting conflict kills the other three and commandeers the ship in order to preserve some of the plant life. Alone and adrift in space, Lowell programs a couple of "drones" or robots to play five-card draw with him, and a light-hearted scene ensues in which one of the drones learns enough to win a hand. It's as though via poker Lowell gets to enjoy a simulation of the kind of "human" connection demonstrated in the earlier game.[16]

The Killing of a Chinese Bookie (1976), a hard-boiled noir written and directed by John Cassavetes, focuses on inveterate gambler and L.A. strip club owner Cosmo Vittelli. Even though Cosmo's gambling habit is central to his character (and the primary cause for the film's central conflict), we only see him indulge once early in the film when he visits a mob-run casino to play poker. There he embarrasses himself both with his play and behavior, ultimately coming away owing the owners a huge sum of money he doesn't have. In order to settle the debt, Cosmo must kill a crime boss (the bookie of the title). Just like in the poker game where Cosmo was ill-equipped to compete with the other players, here, too, he seems like he might be outmatched. Meanwhile in the big budget disaster film *Airport '77* (1977), Olivia de Havilland portrays an arts patroness whose character and standing is communicated quickly early on when she joins a game of five-card stud among a group of men aboard the plane, assuming the deal and declaring the rules like a seasoned pro.

In the 1986 film adaptation of Mark Medoff's Tony-Award winning play *Children of a Lesser God*, a game of poker in a social setting involving the story's deaf protagonist, Sarah (Marlee Matlin), subtly highlights prejudices against the disabled. Before the game a player alerts Sarah not to cheat, noting "I've seen deaf people cheat like bandits" by using "little signs that no one will see." The warning is delivered in a light-hearted way, but after Sarah wins the other players betray further insensitivity by commending her play as though she isn't present. They also congratulate her hearing boyfriend James (William Hurt) for having taught her the game even though it was explained beforehand she'd learned poker "out of a book."[17] Poker is more central to David Mamet's 1987 film *House of Games*, which uses a suspenseful hand in a backroom game both to introduce the audience to the story's world of con men and to reel in the story's main character (the cons' "mark"). Non-verbal communication at the poker table plays a role here too, with a player's supposed "tell" cleverly used to lead on the cons' victim. (More on *House of Games* in Chapter 17.)

More Mainstream Uses of Poker

Poker is an important element in Sydney Pollack's *Havana* (1990) starring Robert Redford, the story of which takes place during the last week of 1958 on the eve of Fulgencio Batista being driven from power by Fidel Castro. Redford plays Jack Weil, an American poker player whose interest in Cuba had up to then been solely focused upon the high-stakes games in Havana's casinos. Despite the increasingly unsettled political climate Jack shows little curiosity, even after one of the leading figures in the impending revolution, Arturo Duran (Raul Julia), suggests to him that his poker-playing skills might be useful to the rebels' strategic planning. "Oh no, I don't play cards for that," Jack says. "That's politics." "That's very American," Arturo responds, adding how he's fascinated by Jack's ability to avoid concerning himself with what is happening around him. Jack does ultimately get involved, though not before having to overcome certain character traits – including his independence – instilled in him by his experience both as a poker player and as an American.

Poker serves a particular purpose in James Cameron's 1997 blockbuster *Titanic*, affecting both the plot and helping introduce a thematic point about the importance of luck. At the start of the film Jack Dawson (Leonardo DiCaprio) and a friend are in a game of five-card draw at a Southampton pub near where the ill-fated passenger liner is about to launch. The pot contains coins, a knife, a pocket watch, and a couple of third-class tickets for the R.M.S. *Titanic*. After the draw Jack melodramatically announces "somebody's life's about to change" before revealing his winning full house. Grabbing the pot and tickets, Jack and his friend dash away to board the ship, Jack crying "we're the luckiest sons of bitches in the whole world."

The rest of the film doesn't show passengers playing poker on board, although it might well have done so. One Titanic survivor, René Harris, shared a story two decades after the ship's doomed voyage about a private poker game played in one of the Bridge Deck suites that featured a private promenade. Harris herself joined the game at one point in order for the group to squeeze out a suspected cheat, and reported she remembered coming away about $90 ahead.[18] In fact, a warning to passengers was posted in a smoking room identifying three known card sharps known to be aboard under false names. A newspaper story from May 1912, a month after the vessel's sinking, reported the trio survived the wreck by paying a steward already helping them maintain their cover to supply them women's clothing and hats which they donned before earning spots in lifeboats with other women and children.[19] Much later, following dives to the wreckage in 1985, both poker chips and playing cards were among the recovered artifacts.[20]

Poker continued to appear in crime films during the 1990s and 2000s, most often as a context for violence. In Martin Scorcese's 1990 crime drama *Goodfellas*, based on the story of real-life mob associate Henry Hill, two successive poker games are interrupted by the brutal behavior of gun-waving Tommy DeVito (Joe Pesci). In the first instance Tommy shoots the foot of the criminals' young apprentice, Spider, while he tries to serve the players. Then during a subsequent game Spider directs a profanity toward Tommy who responds by senselessly shooting him dead. *Menace II Society* (1993) sets the stage for the criminal life of one of its protagonists with an early flashback showing him as a child witnessing his father brutally kill a man over a disagreement about money owed during a poker game. In *Training Day* (2001), a Los Angeles cop finds himself in a poker game with gang members whom he gradually realizes have been paid to kill him. No one dies in the poker game in *2 Fast 2 Furious* (2003), the first sequel in the popular franchise in which illegal street racing is just one facet of a larger crime-ridden landscape. Still, it's almost expected that amid the over-the-top action sequences the character portrayed by rapper Ludacris wins a poker hand with a royal flush.

Some may argue that poker is an innocent bystander in these films — that like poor Spider in *Goodfellas* the game becomes collateral damage in the already violent worlds they depict. However doing so requires ignoring the long history of stories of violence in poker, both fictional and real.

"Poker Movies," Good and Bad
When it comes to "poker movies" — that is, films in which poker is the primary subject — there have been relatively few when compared with other games and sports, and even fewer that have managed to satisfy both au-

diences and critics. Besides the technical challenges associated with presenting poker in an interesting way to observers, the logistics of game play aren't always easily communicated on screen, especially to non-players. "I fear that Hollywood screenwriters of all eras, despite in many cases being poker players themselves, live in dread of the movie audience's ignorance of the ranking of hands," notes Anthony Holden while commenting on the paucity of good poker movies.[21] Even so, three films that have successfully negotiated both the challenge to depict poker dramatically and to tell compelling stories about poker players are *The Cincinnati Kid* (1965), *California Split* (1974), and *Rounders* (1998).

Adapted from a slight, 35,000-word pulp novel by Richard Jessup, *The Cincinnati Kid* tells the story of an up-and-coming poker player named Eric Stoner (Steve McQueen) who has aspirations to defeat the player everyone considers the best around, Lancey Howard (Edward G. Robinson). It's a plot somewhat resembling that of a sports film in which the hero is an athlete single-mindedly pursuing victory in a story-ending title bout. As a result, the film depicts poker as a genuine test of intellect and psychological resilience, distinguishing *The Cincinnati Kid* from earlier films in the way it explores the game and those who play it with genuine depth and discernment.

The film went on to establish the standard against which all future "poker movies" would be compared, but that achievement came in spite of early production troubles and the interests of some seemingly desirous to make *The Cincinnati Kid* about something *other* than poker. Producer Martin Ransohoff was said to be "interested in doing a gunfight with a deck of cards," believing "*The Cincinnati Kid* was almost a romantic western."[22] For that reason Ransohoff hired a director with experience directing westerns, Sam Peckinpah, but the pair clashed immediately over casting decisions and other matters.[23] Wishing to adopt a darker approach to the material than Ransohoff had envisioned, Peckinpah began filming in black-and-white. Within the first days of filming Peckinpah also shot a nude scene and another extraneous sequence portraying a riot by striking railroad workers involving 200 extras. With much fanfare Ransohoff fired Peckinpah and suspended production.

Norman Jewison, then a relatively new director with a background in television and comedies, was hired and filming resumed (in color). By then the script had gone through multiple changes as well with Paddy Chayefsky having written an initial treatment, then several other writers providing input before Terry Southern and Ring Lardner Jr. ultimately earned co-writing credit.[24] While Jessup's novel was set in contemporary St. Louis, the film moved the action back to the 1930s and shifted the setting to New Orleans, repositioning the story closer to poker's early history both temporally and geographically (given the important role of New Orleans to the game's introduction). The film also considerably alters the character of Shooter (Karl Malden) who in the novel provides significant counsel to Eric as a kind of father figure. In the film Shooter does offer advice to Eric, having once before challenged Lancey himself and lost, but is more friend than mentor. Shooter is also saddled with additional complications in the film not present in the novel, including owing a significant debt to a character named Slade (Rip Torn) and being mired in a loveless marriage with the vixen Melba (Ann-Margaret), both characters newly created for the adaptation.

The resulting film cleverly involves the viewer in Eric's ambition to defeat Lancey, a goal that supersedes all else for him including his relationship with girlfriend Christian (Tuesday Weld). The central characters' nicknames – Eric is "The Kid" while Lancey is "The Man" – highlight the coming-of-age aspect of the story and link Eric's ambition to a process of maturation. His gathering of experience at the tables contributes to his ascension up the poker ranks. As Eric explains to Christian, by playing and beating Lancey, "after the game I'll *be* the man, I'll be the best there is."

The juxtaposition of innocence and experience is paralleled elsewhere in the film, including in the repeated coin-pitching scenes between Eric and the shoeshine boy and in the contrast between the relatively naïve, blonde-haired Christian and the worldly, dark-haired Melba. There are several other examples of "heads-up" battles throughout the film that carry the viewer forward to the climactic duel between Eric and Lancey. In the opening underground game, Eric wins a hand of five-card stud then must make a hasty escape after being wrongly accused of cheating; Lancey crushes Slade in another preliminary game; Slade conflicts with Shooter over the latter's debt; and there's even a cockfight in which the combatants and surrounding crowd visually resemble the hotel room match that ends the film.

In the final game, Slade influences Shooter to cheat for Eric in exchange for forgiving his debt, an attempt by Slade to exact revenge against Lancey for beating him earlier. But Eric catches on and angrily confronts Shooter during a break in play, demonstrating his own integrity by declaring his intention to win the game fairly. That Eric then spends the rest of the break finally giving in to Melba's advances and sleeping with her (seemingly in response to his frustration with Shooter), thereby complicating the hero's moral standing. In any case the game resumes with a new dealer, Lady Fingers (Joan Blondell), and Eric wins a series of hands to appear on the verge of closing out the match. And then a climactic hand of five-card stud arises.

With the pot having ballooned to $11,000, Eric draws an ace on fifth street to complete a full house, (A♥)-10♣-10♠-A♣-A♠, and checks, then watches Lancey bet $1,000 with 8♦-Q♦-10♦-9♦ showing. Eric check-raises with the $4,500 he has left, then Lancey reraises another $5,000 on top of that, agreeing to allow Eric to raise the money later if he wishes to call. He does call, and Lancey dramatically shows the J♦ for a straight flush – the only card in the deck that could give him a winner. Post-hand conversation finds Lancey calmly acknowledging his good fortune after having raised with just a draw earlier in the hand. "Get's down to what it's all about, doesn't it? Making the wrong move at the right time," Lancey says while lighting a cigar. "Is that what it's all about?" asks a dazed Eric in response. "Like life, I guess," adds Lancey, who then points the still-lighted match in Eric's direction and with a devilish look delivers a final, devastating comment: "You're good kid, but as long as I'm around you're second best. You might as well learn to live with it."

Some have objected to the improbability of two players in a heads-up hand of five-card stud drawing a straight flush and a full house, with that unlikelihood necessarily undercutting any intended lesson learned by the Kid from his defeat.[25] The counterargument is that the extreme misfortune endured by Eric effectively delivers the point that having a goal and understanding what is required to achieve it is no guarantee of success. The world isn't necessarily going to cooperate with one's ambition, with a poker hand an excellent vehicle to show there are factors outside of a person's control that will affect his or her success. No one, not even "the Man," utterly controls one's fate in the world, a truth Lancey knew beforehand and still knows afterwards. Even though Eric fails to become "the Man," it is also clear he is no longer just a "kid."[26]

California Split is similarly effective in using poker (and other gambling games) to explore deeper truths about the human condition. Robert Altman's film tells the story of a temporary friendship between two gamblers with very different personalities, Charlie (Elliott Gould) and Bill (George Segal), who happen to meet at a poker table. While Charlie is utterly comfortable with the gambling lifestyle and the uncertainties it invites, Bill is much less at ease and instead appears to be experimenting with stepping away from the "straight" world in order to enjoy the adrenaline rush that poker and gambling can provide. In his memoir *Gambler on the Loose*, screenwriter and co-producer Joseph Walsh shares details from the considerable behind-the-scenes battles to get *Split* made, including how Steve McQueen had at one point shown interest in starring (and helped push the film) though ultimately backed out. The primary challenge, Walsh says, was to convince a studio to back a film in which the main characters "weren't heroes," but "just regular guys who needed to gamble to feel more alive – basically more victim than hero."[27] The finished film more than satisfies in that regard, presenting an entertaining and especially realistic portrayal of both gambling in general and poker in particular.

The opening scene in the California Club (discussed in Chapter 7) is complemented later in the film by another poker game, this one for higher stakes in a Reno casino, part of the end-of-film sequence of games played by Bill with the pair's money as they seek one last big score. Surveying the table ahead of time, Charlie provides for Bill hilarious and shrewd commentary on each player's style and skill level as indicated solely by his appearance. Among his reads, Charlie pegs a bald man with glasses as "a percentage player" against whom Bill should only play the nuts, a younger player as someone who "has seen *Cincinnati Kid* too many times," and an older player as a doctor who "would rather lose a patient than a hand." Eventually Thomas "Amarillo Slim" Preston, essentially playing himself, joins the game as well. Though only partly serious in tone, the scene cleverly gives voice to a poker player's inner monologue, including the kinds of prejudging based on stereotypes all players perform.

Bill plays stud in Reno, and while an early draft of the screenplay describes several hands in great detail none appear in the film. The California Club games do include such detail, however, when showing the pair play lowball, a game generally unfamiliar to audiences. Even so, director Altman and Walsh avoid the pitfall Holden describes, forgoing elaborate explanations of how lowball is played in favor of not underestimating the viewer's ability to follow the action. This was done despite pressure from the studio to change the game to something more accessible ("Can't you just make it four kings beating four queens?" Walsh recalls executives requesting).[28] There's no confusion about who is winning or losing hands, however, and the filmmaker's effort to show not tell adds further to the film's realism. The ending of *California Split* likewise offers no "Hollywood" moral to explain the letdown Bill experiences after his rush ends with the pair $82,000 ahead. They simply agree to part ways, a decision made in the same mercurial manner as their original union.

We've also already had occasion to reference *Rounders* (1998) and its story of an aspiring poker player dividing his time between law school and New York City underground games. After a strong opening weekend met by mixed reviews from critics, the film vanished from theaters quickly, though gained a considerable following over the next few years via cable television airings. For many *Rounders* served as an exciting introduction to the game of no-limit Texas hold'em, arriving as real money online poker games were starting to appear and just before televised poker became a cultural phenomenon. The film also convincingly depicts a variety of stakes and settings for poker in ways that further promoted the game's appeal. In addition to the organized games at the Chesterfield Club patterned after other NYC clubs and the high-stakes game at Teddy KGB's, the film shows separate home games involving elderly law professors and young adults, casino poker in Atlantic City at the Taj Mahal, another underground game played by municipal workers, and (on television) poker played at the WSOP in Las Vegas. Mike's friend Worm (Edward Norton) is also shown in prison dominating a game of hearts.

Rounders effectively invites viewers to contemplate the difference between those who choose a safe, reliable existence and others whose ambition to achieve something more encourages greater risk-taking. The two paths are represented by the different types of "rounders" portrayed in the film: low-stakes "grinders" such as Joey Knish (John Turturro) content to earn a small but steady income from the game, and those like Mike who wish to play bigger games and win larger pots. *Rounders* also overtly argues for poker's skill component with illustrative examples and an argument between Mike and his girlfriend, Jo, in which he makes the case. "Why does this still seem like gambling to you?" Mike asks. "It's a skill game, Jo."[29] As with *The Cincinnati Kid*, elements of all the poker scenes are certainly stylized, such as when Mike discovers the villain Teddy KGB's tell involving Oreos. (He eats the cookie when strong, but declines doing so when weak.) A cameo by two-time WSOP Main Event winner Johnny Chan in *Rounders* also parallels Amarillo Slim Preston's appearance in *California Split*, with protagonists of both films taking on the champions as a kind of test of their mettle. However unlike *California Split*, *Rounders* is not ambiguous about the meaning of the big win that punctuates the story, showing Mike immediately thereafter heading to Las Vegas to start a career as a professional poker player. This is certainly the most meaningful part of the film to the many real-life professional poker players who have cited *Rounders* as an influence.

In the wake of *Rounders*, and especially after the rapid rise in poker's popularity during the 2000s, came a spate of poker-themed feature films of uneven quality. The superficial and violent *Luckytown* (2000) is a dreadful drama set in Las Vegas starring James Caan as a gambler named Charlie Doyles. Though Charlie is described as "one of the all-time great poker players," the film provides no supporting evidence, as the one hold'em hand he wins requires hitting a two-outer on the river. Meanwhile a young aspiring poker player is told "you got what it takes" after winning in a session, though he seems equally dedicated to roulette for which he also believes he has some kind of gift.[30] Less awful though similarly unremarkable is the neo-noir crime drama *Shade* (2003) starring Sylvester Stallone as a legendary card cheat known as "the Dean." While the Dean's opening monologue challenges mistaken notions that poker is "a game of chance," he means to emphasize facility at cheating as comprising the real "tools of the trade," not the skill required to win fairly. Thus all of the underground poker games in the film involve cheating and collusion with most ending in violent gunplay. *Shade* also liberally lifts elements from previous poker films, in particular *The Cincinnati Kid*. Besides highlighting a young sharp named Vernon full of ambition to defeat the Dean in a climactic game ("Whoever takes the Dean becomes the Dean," he says), Vernon presents himself as from Cincinnati, with the Dean subsequently calling him by the city. After winning the Dean even lifts Lancey Howard's line, telling Vernon "you're good kid... but as long as I'm around, you're always going to be second best."[31] Much as *Shade* portrays poker as an elaborate mechanism for theft, so, too, does it suggest theft to be a requisite tool with which to construct a poker movie.

In 2006 came *Casino Royale*, the 23rd film to feature the British secret agent James Bond first introduced by Ian Fleming in his 1953 novel of the same name.[32] While an earlier film version of *Casino Royale* from 1967 was more of a parody of the character and series than a straightforward adaptation, the 2006 film starring Daniel Craig follows the novel's plot more closely. One of a number of alterations from the book, however, sees no-limit hold'em replace baccarat as the most significant casino game played by the characters. (Fleming was a poor poker player himself, something he once confessed in an introduction he wrote for a British edition of Herbert O. Yardley's *The Education of a Poker Player*.) The change might seem on the surface to have provided an opportunity for Bond's character to show off his famous wit as well as to demonstrate a spy's attention to detail. However the poker scenes in *Casino Royale* feature almost no table talk from Bond, nor do the hands show him to possess any special skill at the tables. In one Bond coolers an opponent with set-over-set (aces versus kings), while the climactic four-way hand in a $10 million buy-in tournament at the titular casino finds Bond luckily making a straight flush to clean out everyone including Le Chiffre, the story's chief villain.[33]

Neither *Luckytown*, *Shade,* nor *Casino Royale* aim for verisimilitude, either broadly speaking or with regard to poker. On the other hand, *All In* (2006), *Lucky You* (2007), and *Deal* (2008) seem to have had such ambitions, as well as a desire to promote poker as a skill game, though such efforts are hampered in each film.

All In misfires badly, presenting the story of a female medical student nicknamed Ace negotiating various challenges and tangential subplots to win the "All In Poker Championship." Along with several superficial howlers, the film betrays a deeper misunderstanding of poker by having Ace employ the talents of five fellow students to help her to victory, a seeming misapplication of the story of the MIT blackjack team to poker. The big-budgeted *Lucky You* goes to the opposite extreme, incorporating numerous lengthy sequences proving the filmmakers' familiarity with poker rules and strategy while telling the story of a young player's attempt to win the WSOP Main Event. Cameos by more than two dozen professional poker players (many playing themselves) and on-location shooting in Las Vegas (including at Binion's for the WSOP sequence) fail to offset a sluggish pace dragging the film over two hours. *Deal* also ends with a tournament, presenting an unconvincing mentor-trainee relationship that culminates in a World Poker Tour event – again at the Bellagio, and again with poker pro cameos. All three films end with protagonists purposely mucking winning hands to lose their tournaments, creating both unrealistic and unsatisfying endings. All three also awkwardly adopt an aesthetic modeled after televised poker that translates poorly to the silver screen. They were all panned by critics and failed spectacularly at the box office, indicating both the films' shortcomings and the public's lack of enthusiasm for fictionalized versions of tournament poker.[34] In their wake followed more poker-related action films with titles lifted from the game's terminology. Each also earned censure from reviewers: *Runner Runner* (2013) ("The actors hit the jackpot, but only in terms of their paychecks"); *Gutshot Straight* (2014) ("not thrilling, not exciting, not fun"); and *Cold Deck* (2015) ("Face cards have more depth of character").[35]

Mississippi Grind (2015) fares much better. It is a gratifying take on the "gambling buddies on the road" narrative that recalls *California Split* in several ways, including its authentic presentation of low- and mid-stakes live games and of poker players lying about their losses. The film also cleverly alludes to poker's history with the characters traveling south down the Mississippi River to New Orleans, hitting important port cities like St. Louis and Memphis along the way like modern day versions of George Devol and Canada Bill. The connection is evoked by one of the pair when he comments: "I had a dream we were on a steamboat and that river bandits took all our money."

Though critically acclaimed, *Mississippi Grind* failed to gain a wide audience. By contrast *Molly's Game* (2017), the big-budget adaptation of "poker princess" Molly Bloom's tell-all bestseller, earned both positive reviews and commercial success.[36] The film offers a glossy glimpse of celebrity-filled high-stakes underground poker games the setting for which is alternately described in the film as "the world's most exclusive, glamorous, and decadent man cave" and "a frathouse... built for degenerates." Heavy on dialogue and voice-over narration (most of which occurs away from the poker table), the film invites viewers to contemplate the relative power the sexes wield in American society, with Bloom's control over the game the men are playing earning special emphasis as a theme. That said, while the movie makes a hero of Bloom, it hardly aggrandizes poker. In fact, it does the opposite, presenting poker as a cutthroat and destructive game capable of causing grievous harm to those who play, not to mention a potential setting in which hedge fund fraudsters, those linked to organized crime, and others with bad intentions can operate. Even the best player in Bloom's game appears morally vacant. "I don't even like poker," he reveals to her. "I like destroying lives."

It's a cynical, even grim reflection on the game – just one of many different ideas about poker from the movies that have influenced how the game has been judged.[37]

17 Poker in Literature

Any game or activity as thoroughly embedded in a nation's culture as poker is in the United States is necessarily well positioned to inspire writers. Add to that the fact that each hand of poker is itself a form of storytelling – replete with characters, a readymade plot of inherent conflict, a setting with a rich back-story, and a built-in narrative arc with exposition (antes and opens), rising action (sometimes *raising* action), and a climax (a story-resolving showdown) – and it's no wonder poker so readily serves storytellers' purposes.

As America's favorite card game, poker not only fits harmoniously within a wide variety of invented contexts, its egalitarian nature allows characters of different classes and backgrounds to take part, another factor making the game useful for developing characters and plots. The rhythm of poker,

"BEEN LAYING FOR YOU DUFFERS."

John Harley's illustration of the climactic scene in Mark Twain's "The Professor's Yarn" (1883)

with frequent pauses both within and in between hands, readily accommodates narrative reflection and internal monologues. The game's significant psychological component makes poker an efficient and probing means to examine and reveal characters' identities. Poker necessitates conflict, with the success of one player (or character) requiring the failure of another. The essential element of money also tends to raise the existential stakes, so to speak, helping even a single poker hand to provide an occasion to explore the idiosyncratic ways individuals can make meaning of their lives.

Poker in Fiction: Cheats and Tricksters
Given the prevalence of cheating during poker's early history, it's not unexpected to find multiple early examples of stories in which cheating at poker provides a handy device to create entertaining narratives. Mark Twain's "The Professor's Yarn" (discussed in Chapter 4) in which the self-proclaimed "professional gambler" outcheats other cheaters aboard a 19th-century steamboat is the most notable early representative.

The topic surfaces more than once in popular humorist Samuel Adams Hammett's *Piney Woods Tavern; or, Sam Slick in Texas* (1858), a collection of frontier tales being passed around by visitors to a Texas tavern. In one a character named Uncle Billy recalls hoodwinking a quartet of French sugar planters by swapping in a cold deck to deliver each four aces. Another character named Milward follows that with a story of steamboat poker about a mysterious New Yorker traveling to New Orleans and repeatedly beating a group of sharps precisely because "so much of their attention being taken up by stocking the cards... their plans were defeated, being always annoyed and thrown off from their play." The story ends with the New Yorker outwitting them one more time, then revealing himself to be the governor of New York before banishing them to an island.[1]

The cheating conceit appears again in Benjamin Morgan's 1887 autobiographical novel *Shams; or, Uncle Ben's Experience with Hypocrites* in which the author comically highlights differences between "plain" country folk like himself and the "shams and sharpers" he encounters in big American cities. On a train from Buffalo to Cleveland he meets a group of "four highly educated and polished gentlemen from different states and nations," one of whom, named Mr. Smooth, invites him to join them in a poker game. Uncle Ben has to be taught the rules, then when antes are called for wonders aloud "What do you mean about bringing your aunt into the game...?" A hand soon arises in which Uncle Ben draws four aces, though the betting and raising suggests it's too good to be true and he's luckily pulled out of the game by his wife before committing all of his money. His innocence about poker saves him, much as the farmer's common sense and generous nature enables him to avoid the unending series of "shams" he encounters during his travels.[2]

In Somerset Maugham's 1929 story "Straight Flush" two septuagenarians who have each sworn off poker separately tell stories that differently warn against the ill effects of cheating. One says that as a young man he witnessed a man kill his brother after suspecting he had cheated during a drunken game. The other describes once being involved in a game for higher-than-comfortable stakes in Johannesburg, South Africa involving players about whom he believed "there wasn't a crooked dodge they weren't up to."[3] Dealt a pat queen-high straight flush in a game of draw, the man folded the hand rather than risk being cheated out of thousands, then saw to his dismay three sevens win the pot.

James Thurber's magnificent 1932 story "Everything Is Wild" (discussed in Chapter 9) involves a different form of poker trickery when the irascible conservative Mr. Brush, tiring of games with wild cards being called in a friendly home game among couples, invents his own hilariously illogical variant in which he cannot lose. Damon Runyon is another good source for slang-filled, colorful stories of New York City gamblers and hustlers, among them a few card-playing cons like Last Card Louie from the 1938 story "Princess O'Hara," so named because "the way he always gets much strength from the last card is considered quite abnormal, especially if Last Card Louie is dealing."[4]

Poker in Fiction: The Lure of Luck

A variety of fiction writers have seized upon poker's chance element when telling stories that emphasize the role luck plays in our lives. Like all gambling games, poker players have the freedom to choose whether or not they wish to play at all, as well as to decide how much they are willing to risk when they do. But even after the player sits down, the management of risk continues, with players' skill enabling them to exert *some* (though not total) control over how much they are willing to allow luck to govern their results. As such, poker fiction readily evokes existentialist themes as characters attempt to make meaning out of lives that on some level they understand and accept to be based on chance.

Bret Harte's story "The Outcasts of Poker Flat" presents an early example of a committed poker player demonstrating an acceptance of luck's significance. First published in the California-based magazine *Overland Monthly* in January 1869, Harte's story later became the basis for multiple film adaptations and even an opera. The story is set in November 1850 in a California town named Poker Flat and focuses on the hardships endured by a group of individuals judged by moral-minded citizens as "improper persons."[5] After two of the group are hanged, four more are banished including a thief, two prostitutes, and a gambler named John Oakhurst to whom (not coincidentally) many of the town's leaders have lost significant sums at poker. Oakhurst is described as receiving his punishment with "philosophic calmness," being "too much of a gambler not to accept Fate."[6] Oakhurst has learned at the tables to recognize factors he cannot control, and it's a character trait that surfaces again at the story's conclusion.

A couple of visitors join the group's encampment outside of town, including a young poker player Oakhurst has beaten before. Twin misfortunes suddenly befall the group, one natural in the form of a violent snowstorm, the other man-made as the thief among them takes off with their mules, leaving the rest stranded with 10 days' worth of provisions. "Luck... is a mighty queer thing," Oakhurst tells the young man as they assess the situation. "All you know about it for certain is that it's bound to change. And it's finding out when it's going to change that makes you."[7] The story ends tragically for the group as none survive. As others later discover, Oakhurst shot himself, selflessly shortening his life by a day or two in the hopes of extending those of the others. They also find he has pinned a playing card with a bowie knife to a tree on which he has written a note: "BENEATH THIS TREE LIES THE BODY OF JOHN OAKHURST, WHO STRUCK A STREAK

OF BAD LUCK ON THE 23D OF NOVEMBER, 1850 AND HANDED IN HIS CHECKS ON THE 7TH DECEMBER, 1850."[8]

The story ends enigmatically with the narrator referring to Oakhurst as "at once the strongest and yet the weakest of the outcasts of Poker Flat," although such a paradoxical character assessment can be explained. What distinguishes Oakhurst or makes him the "strongest" is his correct understanding of the way poker requires one to accept the influence of luck, both good and bad. In other words, as he understands it, poker is not an immoral game for "improper persons," but an activity for mature adults able to accept and withstand the game's inevitable ups and downs (something the town's leaders seem less capable of doing). Oakhurst is also the "weakest" of the outcasts for the same reason, his understanding of the situation having encouraged his noble self-sacrifice.

G. Frank Lydston's 1906 novel *Poker Jim, Gentleman* is also set in California not long after the initial gold rush, with Lydston even alluding to Harte's fiction while setting the scene. The story demonstrates Harte's influence as well, with the poker-playing title character resembling Oakhurst in several ways, including ultimately heroically losing his life while saving another. His demise is even described similarly when a character in the novel states: "Poker Jim hez passed in his checks."[9] The novel is narrated by a doctor from the east who early on tells of a wayward, poker-playing younger brother named Jim who ran away as a teen. After getting his medical degree, the doctor travels to California to practice, eventually meeting up multiple times with a mysterious gambler whom the attentive reader no doubt recognizes as the doctor's brother, spoiling the novel's not-so-surprise twist ending. Like Oakhurst, "Poker Jim" suffers from others' anti-gambling prejudices while coolly demonstrating his own acceptance of luck's role in our lives, supported by his reputation as one who unfailingly "plays a squar' game."[10] Poker Jim's perspective is summarized early by his counsel of a young player he's helped out of trouble: "In the first place, young fellow, don't gamble. If your blood is too red to heed this admonition, learn to play poker. It's a scientific game and a square one, usually – always so among gentlemen."[11]

Pulitzer Prize winning novelist and dramatist Booth Tarkington (*The Magnificent Ambersons*, *Alice Adams*) presents a decidedly less assured poker player named Collison in his 1923 story "One-Hundred Dollar Bill." During what should have been a regular penny-ante game, the lawyer and others start gambling for higher amounts over a supposedly lucky silver dollar, with Collison ultimately losing all of his own cash and most of the $100 he had collected from a debtor earlier in the day. As he walks back home after the game, Collison links the introduction of the so-called "lucky" silver dollar, along with his possessing the $100 bill, to his wife's frustration with their lack of money and his jealousy of the player to whom he lost – all of which motivated him to gamble. "What kind of thing *is* this life?" he wonders while "finding matters wholly perplexing in a world made into tragedy at the caprice of a little oblong slip of paper."[12] He then has an epiphany, recognizing in an instant how it wasn't merely luck but the foolish surrendering of his will to luck (chasing the "lucky" silver dollar) that caused his loss. It's a costly lesson, though results in his having "gathered knowledge of himself and a little of the wisdom that is called better than happiness."[13]

Influential German dramatist Bertolt Brecht takes on the theme as well in his darkly humorous and somewhat surreal "Four Men and a Poker Game, or Too Much Luck is Bad Luck" from 1926, one of several short stories by Brecht with American subjects and themes.[14] In the story, four swimmers returning by ship to New York from a competition in Cuba play poker initially for nickels, then for the highest-stakes imaginable including each other's houses, a piano, and one player's girlfriend. One called Lucky Johnny wins everything despite being the least skilled player of the group, though his good fortune turns sour when the others heave him overboard.

William Faulkner's pre-Civil War story "Was," which opens his 1942 collection of interlocking tales *Go Down, Moses*, presents a complicated pair of poker hands between quarreling slave-owning neighbors in which the stakes ultimately include money, a dowry, and ownership of two slaves. The latter is "bet" on the final round of a hand of five-card stud, forcing a fold that subsequently affects future generations of all involved. Faulkner's use of poker directly introduces a chance element into the larger narrative of his stories set in fictional Yoknapatawpha County, and invites readers to reflect on a world in which one race has the freedom to choose to allow luck to influence their lives while another does not.

James Jones likewise uses a well-sketched poker scene to highlight the romance of risk in his 1951 novel *From Here to Eternity* about Army soldiers (unluckily) stationed in Hawaii just before the attack on Pearl Harbor. On a monthly payday the main protagonist, a young private named Prew, chooses to risk his entire check in a stud game in an effort to earn enough to win the heart of a prostitute at a local brothel. As he watches the first hand being dealt, Prew thinks about poker in idealistic terms and how within the cards, "governed by whatever Laws or fickle Goddess moved them, here lay infinity and the secret of all life and death," which if accessible can allow a person to "penetrate the unreadability" of life, to "be shaking hands with God."[15] Prew wins, then loses, then borrows more money and loses again before leaving the game in disgrace. Along the way he marvels at his own change in attitude, having initially "played happily, lost in loving it, savoring every second," then later "with dogged irritation, not giving a damn, angered even at the time it took to deal."[16]

John Updike's short story "Poker Night" from 1984 uses the game to address the chance-based nature of human existence in a different, even more poignant way. The story presents an unnamed narrator visiting his doctor en route to a weekly low-stakes poker game he's played for more than thirty years. The doctor tells him that he has been diagnosed with cancer, and that his prospects going forward appear grim. The man proceeds to the game which provides him a kind of temporary escape, though thoughts of his mortality nonetheless occasionally surface in between hands. "The cards at these moments when I thought about it seemed incredibly thin," he explains, "a kind of silver foil beaten to just enough of a thickness to hide the numb reality that was under everything."[17] He finishes the night down five bucks, though tells his wife he broke even, a small equivocation that reflects the larger lie he'd been telling himself ever since getting the news from his doctor – namely, that somehow it wasn't as bad as it sounded, and that perhaps everything would work out even though he knows it will not. The story ends with the narrator recognizing in his wife's look that she's already contemplating life without him. The description sounds a lot like a player having finally noticed an opponent's tell, thereby learning something important about what might come next. "You could see it in her face her mind working," he says. "She was considering what she had been dealt; she was thinking how to play her cards."[18]

A man who dies of cancer sets in motion the plot of Paul Auster's 1991 novel *The Music of Chance*. A firefighter named Jim Nashe unexpectedly receives a large inheritance of $200,000 from his estranged and recently deceased father. From there springs a peculiar, absurdist story in which Nashe cuts all ties and drives aimlessly around the United States for a year with no plan, running through most of the cash until he randomly gives a ride to a poker player, John Pozzi (nicknamed "Jackpot"). The pair agree for Nashe to stake Pozzi in a private high-stakes game of seven-card stud against two eccentric lottery winners at their home. Though a skilled player, the cards don't go Pozzi's way and he loses all of Nashe's money as well as Nashe's car, and after one additional double-or-nothing gamble at high carding they owe the two multi-millionaires a debt they cannot settle. In order to pay off what they owe, Nashe and Pozzi take on a job building a wall out of stones from a 15th-century Irish castle, essentially becoming the lottery winners' captives until they can work off the debt. Though the work is difficult, Nashe strangely becomes accustomed to his life's new purpose, with the building of the wall serving as a metaphor for the way humans instinctively seek and impose order on chance elements. The work also uncannily parallels Pozzi's earlier explanation for how to play winning poker, when he suggests "The important thing is to remain inscrutable, to build a wall around yourself and not let anyone in."[19]

Poker in Fiction: A Dangerous Game

For some writers, poker operates as something more directly sinister than a mere emblem of chance. It can be a more direct, even malevolent force such as indicated by Twain's Professor when describing the professional card sharps aboard the steamboat he rides as "an evil and hateful presence."[20]

That notion is suggested in Owen Wister's seminal western novel *The Virginian* (1902) in which a dispute during a poker game initiates the central conflict between the villainous gambler Trampas and the unnamed title character. The book's narrator, who comes from the East and is nicknamed Tenderfoot owing to his naïveté regarding the Old West, marvels at how the Virginian readied for the poker game by rechecking his pistol and concealing it, *and* how no one else finds such behavior remarkable. "He might have been combing his hair for all the attention any one paid to this, except for myself," Tenderfoot says.[21] During the conflict at the game the Virginian does draw his weapon and Tenderfoot describes himself "learning gradually that stud-poker has in it more of what I will call red pepper than has our Eastern game."[22]

A short story by the New York-based fiction writer William Melvin Kelley titled "The Poker Party" (1956) similarly presents poker being viewed with trepidation and even terror, in this case through the eyes of a young African American boy. Now older, the narrator recalls an incident from his childhood involving one of his father's "poker parties" which the narrator confesses he never liked. Tucked into bed one Saturday night before the game begins, he describes himself imagining various horrors arriving with the poker players. "I was awake, the darkness soft and as close around me as my one soft blanket," he says, but the shadows outside his bedroom door frighten him. "I was afraid; each shape was a man in a long coat coming with a silver knife to slice my neck."[23]

The players are actually hardly to be feared. His mother and father both play in the game, as do an aunt and uncle as well as a family friend named Mister Bixby. On this night the boy wakes up and wanders out to watch, and his father allows him to do so (even though he has been losing steadily to Bixby). The mood turns sour, though, after Bixby wins another hand and suggestions of cheating lead to a game-ending argument, with the boy's incorrect belief that *he* caused his father to lose the hand compounding his alarm. Looking back, the narrator realizes the true importance of the incident. "For the first time in my life I was afraid of grownups," he explains, having "never *seen* them argue" before that night.[24] Here poker functions as an emblem of adulthood marking the end of innocence, a game capable of creating antagonism and hostility that introduces a child to feelings of fear and uncertainty.

Joyce Carol Oates' gripping 2007 story "Strip Poker" similarly features a young protagonist for whom poker represents "grownup" dangers. The

13-year-old Annislee one summer finds herself joining a group of older boys for a speedboat ride, lured by one who asks her to come play poker with him and his buddies. They arrive at an isolated cabin on the other side of the lake, and out come the cards and beers. Though new to the game (and to drinking), Annislee wins her first few hands to build up the money the boys gave her to start, then starts losing. Eventually Annislee runs out of money, at which point the boys declare the game is in fact strip poker. Things progress even more disturbingly from there, and at one point a couple of the boys insist she must strip because "that's poker."[25]

At a crucial moment, however, Annislee is able to turn the situation around, changing the game from poker to another card game named "Truth." "There's other kinds of stripping, not just taking off your clothes," she explains when introducing the game. "It's a little like poker, except you don't bet money, instead of paying a bet you pay in truth."[26] The boys are skeptical, but are utterly defeated by Annislee's first story, a frightening, violent yarn describing how her father had once treated another male predator who'd gotten too close to her. The tables are turned in a dramatic way, with Annislee playing the "hand" of her story perfectly – and devastatingly. The story seems to present poker as something dangerously risky, but perhaps not utterly to be avoided. One *can* learn the game. In order not to lose, though, a player has to keep one's wits and be able to shape and present the "truth" effectively.

Poker in Fiction: Professional Aspirations

Richard Jessup's slight 1964 novel *The Cincinnati Kid* (discussed in Chapter 16) more readily fits in the category of pulpy entertainments like the other 35 or so spy novels and westerns he authored than with the efforts of more literary-minded writers, although Jessup does successfully introduce to readers to the many trials of the aspiring poker pro. Two other substantial attempts by novelists to capture both the external and internal pressures faced by those seeking a livelihood from poker are Rick Bennet's *King of a Small World* (1995) and Jesse May's *Shut Up and Deal* (1998).

In his book (subtitled "A Poker Novel"), Bennet presents a wiser-than-his-years young gun named Joey "Pinocchio" Moore, a successful player in his mid-20s who mostly sticks to underground games and to the ones found in "charity" casinos throughout Prince George's County in Maryland. It's a "small world" where he does, at times, perhaps reign as a kind of "king," although over the course of the story he demonstrates an urge for greater challenges when taking his game to Atlantic City, Las Vegas, and elsewhere.

Poker both fuels the plot and contributes heavily to the novel's various themes, with Bennet drawing connections between the game and Joey's complicated life full of conflicts and relationships. We quickly discover how poker has put Joey in touch with a wide assortment of friends, foes, and few who could go either way. We also eventually learn how poker and gambling have aggressively shaped the value systems of both Joey and others, as demonstrated in their interactions – sometimes cautious, other times dangerously reckless.

With some trepidation Joey takes a job helping run one of the charity casinos, and Bennet does well filling out details of the technically legal but still sketchy world of the charity casino, where the rapid influx of money soon engenders a number of conflicts among those running the show. Additional complications in Joey's world include the pregnancy of an ex-girlfriend, relationships with a couple of other women, an ex-con living with his mother, and other (possibly nefarious) connections involving the casino owners.

These many obligations keeping Joey away from the tables invite meaningful introspection and commentary on the life of a full-time poker player or gambler. A trip to Vegas invites such thoughts as he describes the casino's efforts to arouse in visitors "The sense of life itself. Of drama. Of story. Of passion. Of love and fear. Of power and sex. Of a moment frozen, of existence beyond the mundane, of escape from all other problems because right now your attention is focused on the money you have on the line. If time is money and life is time, then money is life. And you're gambling for it."[27]

Bennet's novel presents a card-playing central character finding his way through a complicated, conflict-filled life in which poker provides him insight as he negotiates different types of risk and reward. May's *Shut Up and Deal* similarly presents a protagonist seeking to find meaning in his existence, in his case testing whether or not poker itself might be able to provide such meaning. May's narrator is a young poker pro named Mickey Dane who relates in episodic fashion the story of his ongoing struggles both at the tables and elsewhere, exploring in detail the many challenges he and his compatriots face as they all separately strive to "stay in action."

Just as Bennet drew from his own experiences for his novel, Mickey isn't that far removed from May himself, with many of the stories and characters drawn and shaped from the author's own poker-playing adventures. Like May, Mickey also started playing poker in high school, and also like the author the character finds himself in Atlantic City during the 1990s when poker was first spread in casinos.[28] While Joey's story concerns his literal survival in the face of various threats, Mickey's is first and foremost about survival *in poker*, with May showing how staying in action doesn't necessarily correspond with being the most skillful player. After all, Mickey notes, he's seen a number of world champions on the rail. "Poker is a combination of luck and skill," he explains. "People think mastering the skill part is hard, but they're wrong. The trick to poker is mastering the luck."[29]

May's non-chronological plot and narrative style, often edging into stream-of-consciousness, well suit the often repetitive, "timeless" experience of the full-time player whose life and relationships don't follow the same, recognizable patterns of "normal" people. As Mickey notes, "there aren't really hellos and good-byes so much as fade in and fade out."[30] His struggles as a player are especially well described, as are his many attempts to make meaning out of his existence, with success at the tables tending to help on both counts. "I maintain winning poker is the changing of chaos to order, of always perceiving order," Mickey says.[31]

That last qualifying statement is important, because Mickey realizes the order being imposed on the chaos is itself dubious, only perceived and not necessarily *real*. The plot resolves with a final, genuinely thrilling (and darkly humorous) climax involving Mickey going through a series of wardrobe changes amid a lengthy poker session as though trying to alter his real self via literal shifts in image. It's an inspired conclusion to a story that effectively examines poker's capacity to encourage reflection by disrupting preconceived ideas of self.

Poker on the Stage

We've already looked at what are arguably the two greatest examples of poker on the American stage. Tennessee Williams' 1947 play *A Streetcar Named Desire* expertly uses poker to accentuate the divide between men and women explored in the drama, while Neil Simon's 1965 comedy *The Odd Couple* presents one of the more famous fictional home games, similarly employing poker to comment on relationships between men as well as between the two sexes.

George S. Kaufman's 1926 one-act comedy *If Men Played Cards as Women Do* provides a context, in a way, for both *Streetcar* and *The Odd Couple*. Kaufman, who was a contributor to the Algonquin Round Table and a member of the Thanatopsis Pleasure and Inside Straight Club, also employs a poker game to highlight differences between men and women. As the title suggests, the four men who comprise the cast shun "masculine" traits like aggression and competitiveness, instead choosing to discuss each other's clothes and appearance, to swap recipes, and to gossip about those not present. Once the host finishes with his fastidious preparations – actions that prefigure those of Felix Ungar in *The Odd Couple* – cards and chips are produced though no one seems too motivated to interrupt their conversation by playing a hand. A question about stakes is quickly dismissed as unimportant (they play one-cent limit). Once cards are finally dealt the table talk evokes the era's prejudices, as well as *Streetcar*'s less amusing demonstration that women don't belong at the poker table. One player asks "Which is higher – aces or kings?" and another "Are these funny little things clubs?"[32] The men never do finish the hand.

Best known for her 1937 classic coming-of-age novel *Their Eyes Were Watching God*, Zora Neale Huston also wrote several plays including a short, one-act piece simply titled *Poker!* (1931). On the surface the play presents a familiar, uncomplicated scene of a home poker game in a New York "shotgun house," played by six black men. However the story ultimately offers a kind of allegorical comment on criminality and violence. The action begins light-heartedly with one of the men performing a song on piano in which he assigns symbolic significance to each of the 13 ranked cards. It's only in retrospect that the line "six spot means six feet of earth when the deal goes down" earns its resonance, with the six players' fates soon to be learned. Aunt Dilsey, the lone female character, interrupts a five-card draw hand briefly to admonish the men for gambling, warning that "all of you all goin' to die and go to Hell" before she leaves.[33] During her visit everyone produces extra cards from pockets and sleeves, and multiple players show down four aces, bringing razors and guns to the table. All concerned meet a violent end.

Pulitzer Prize winning playwright, screenwriter, and director David Mamet demonstrated his interest in poker in an insightful 1986 essay "The Things Poker Teaches," which gets to the heart of the game's revelatory properties. Mamet explains how (among other things) "Poker reveals to the frank observer something… about his own nature," the qualifier distinguishing players who pay attention from those who do not. Whereas good players are comfortable with learning about themselves, including their limitations, "bad players do not improve because they cannot bear such self-knowledge." Thus Mamet reasonably links becoming better at poker with becoming better as a person. Recognizing how others in his home game have improved as players, he concludes "improvement can only be due to one thing: to character, which as I finally begin to improve a bit myself, I see that the game of poker is all about."[34]

While teaching drama in Chicago in the early 1970s, Mamet is said to have played poker eight hours a day in a junk shop, an experience that helped inspire his early two-act play *American Buffalo* (1975) the entirety of which takes place in a similar setting. A poker game from the previous night serves as an important context for the story, as does the earlier sale of a Buffalo nickel by the shop's owner to a customer a few days before. We learn how Donny, the owner, sold the nickel for $90, though now suspects it might have been worth five times that. Those misgivings inspire a plot that initially involves young Bobby being employed by Donny to spy on the comings and goings of the customer who lives just around the corner. The original plan is to try and steal the coin back, but when Donny's poker buddy, Walter – a.k.a. "Teach" – gets involved, the idea broadens to a larger scheme to steal even more. (Mamet also earned the nickname "Teach" in the junk shop poker game he played.)

There is a regular poker game at Donny's shop, and talk about last night's game reveals another character named Fletch had been the big winner, taking away $400. Reflecting Mamet's idea that being good at cards is directly related to strength of character, Donny and Bobby speak admiringly of Fletch. "Fletcher is a standup guy... he is a fellow stands for something," insists Donny. "He's a real good card player," says Bobby. "This is what I'm getting at," Donny continues. "Skill. Skill and talent and the balls to arrive at your own *conclusions*."[35]

Donny's admiration of Fletch (who never actually appears in the play) alters his plans as he attempts to involve him in the robbery scheme. But the idea gets muddled when Teach alleges Fletch is a cheater, supporting his accusation with a story of his having witnessed Fletch cheat the night before in a hand in which Donny lost $200. The revelation also breeds suspicion that young Bobby might be keeping an alliance with Fletch hidden from Donny and Teach.

Bobby denies any such alliance, but is he bluffing? Is Teach bluffing about Fletch having cheated? Donny simply doesn't know, because he isn't a good enough poker player to figure it all out. Donny's confusion about the Buffalo nickel and what it might really be worth is similarly clouded by his inability to recognize his own limitations. He knows the prices listed in a coin book are only a starting point for negotiations. "The book gives you a general idea," he says. He also understands when Teach points out "you got to have a feeling for your subject" when it comes to applying that general idea to specific situations.[36] But Donny doesn't realize he *doesn't* have that "general idea" or "feeling" that someone with more experience and knowledge, like a winning poker player, would have – not with the coins, and not with the people with whom he's dealing.

American Buffalo was later adapted to film in 1996, with Mamet writing the screenplay. By then Mamet had written several screenplays, including *House of Games* (1987) with which he made his directorial debut, another story involving poker, bluffing, and how people deceive one another and fall for such deception time and time again. That story revolves around a psychiatrist, Margaret Ford (Lindsay Crouse), who through a patient gets involved in a world of high-stakes con men led by Mike (Joe Mantegna). Her fascination with them leads her to become romantically involved with Mike before realizing she herself is the mark.

Margaret's introduction to the world of the con men comes when she visits a backroom poker game in which a hand is expertly shown involving Mike and George (played by the magician and famous card-trickster Ricky Jay). As Mike explains to Margaret, George plays with his ring when he's bluffing, but George also knows Mike knows about his tell. A hand of five-card draw arises in which George makes a huge reraise after the draw and

Poker & Pop Culture

before deciding what to do, Mike leaves the table to use the restroom. In his absence Margaret sees George fiddle with his ring, and she informs Mike of this upon his return. Confident that George is bluffing she offers to cover the additional $6,000 if needed. Mike calls with three aces, George shows a flush, and Margaret loses her money.

The entire poker game is one big setup, it turns out, leading to another, much larger con as Margaret naively finds herself under Mike's spell. For much of the story she's not unlike Donny in *American Buffalo*, caught in a game she doesn't completely understand, with her own reluctance to realize her limitations as a "player" further impeding her ability to compete. However she does ultimately recognize and accept where she went wrong before, enabling her to compete more effectively against her "opponent" Mike. (*House of Games* was later adapted for the stage by playwright Richard Bean to mixed reviews.)

Literary Nonfiction: The "Poker Narrative"

Early collections of nonfiction poker stories like those by John F.B. Lillard, Eugene Edwards, David A. Curtis and others all possess certain literary qualities, as do autobiographical poker books like George Devol's *Forty Years a Gambler* and Herbert O. Yardley's *The Education of a Poker Player*, even if none are as concerned with the kinds of aesthetic achievement shown by most writers of fiction and drama. Later examples of nonfiction poker writing does demonstrate such literary aspirations, with some emerging from the categories of journalistic writing and especially poker tournament reporting.

We've had occasion already to draw from the writings of three British poker writers, all of whom happened at one time to play in the same north London home game: David Spanier, Al Alvarez, and Anthony Holden. Spanier was a foreign and diplomatic correspondent for *The Times* and later a reporter for other outlets, with a well regarded book about Britain's entry into the European Common Market among his credits. Alvarez's background was more directly literary, including time served as the poetry editor for *The Observer* while also writing his own poetry, fiction, nonfiction, and critical essays. Meanwhile Holden had worked as a reporter and classical music critic, translated Greek poetry and operas, and written biographies of artists and members of the British royal family. Having together participated in the same Tuesday night poker game, all three made important and influential contributions to nonfiction poker writing, their trio of seminal poker titles comprising an essential starting syllabus for others desirous to write about the game.

Spanier's 1977 collection of essays *Total Poker* provides a kind of "anatomy" of poker examining the game from multiple angles with essays about bluffing, the history of the game, poker in movies (where he rates *The Hustler* – a movie about pool, not poker – as the best "poker movie"), the psychology of poker and moral issues, and more. Spanier notes in the preface how writing the book enabled him to discover "how deep a subject poker is: one can't really ever get the boundaries of it; like exploring space, there's always farther to go." *Total Poker* ably demonstrates the point.

The critical and commercial success of Spanier's book is said to have encouraged Alvarez to pursue with his agent a deal allowing him to cover the 1981 World Series of Poker for *The New Yorker*, a trip that eventually resulted in a lengthy two-part report that later became the 1983 book *The Biggest Game in Town* (discussed in Chapter 15), regarded by many as the gold standard of poker reporting. In turn, *The Biggest Game in Town* inspired Anthony Holden to do something similar, although rather than just visit the WSOP and talk to poker pros about what they do, he chose to try out the life himself, ultimately chronicling his adventure in *Big Deal: A Year as a Professional Poker Player* (1990).[37]

Both Spanier and Alvarez appear in Holden's book, with Alvarez playfully reoccurring as the "Crony" alongside Holden's wife (the "Moll") and psychiatrist (the "Shrink") who help fill out the supporting cast in the narrative of his experiment. The 1988 and 1989 WSOP Main Events bookend Holden's story, necessarily more personal than either *Total Poker* or *Biggest Game* although Holden weaves anecdotes and episodes from poker's history into his own struggles as a player. He also provides several eminently quotable aphorisms about poker along the way, the most famous of which succinctly (and humbly) articulates poker's psychological component: "Whether he likes it or not, a man's character is stripped bare at the poker table; if the other players read him better than he does, he has only himself to blame. Unless he is both able and prepared to see himself as others do, flaws and all, he will be a loser in cards, as in life."[38] The same year Holden's book appeared, novelist and essayist Martin Amis provided a tongue-in-cheek version of the same sentiment to open a magazine article describing an especially literary poker game in which he, Holden, Alvarez, and Mamet were among the participants: "A man can find out a lot about himself, playing poker. Is he brave? Is he cool? Does he have any money left?"[39]

Spanier, Alvarez, and Holden's "Tuesday Night Game Trilogy" (as it could be called) greatly influenced later writers of poker nonfiction, with Holden in particular providing a kind of model for other literary "poker memoir" narratives. Alvarez himself contributed another one, in a way, with *Poker: Bets, Bluffs and Bad Beats* (2001) that among its additional reflections on poker includes the story of his own play in the 1994 WSOP Main Event. Journalist Andy Bellin's *Poker Nation* (2003) compiles essays about poker strategy and history, similar to Spanier's approach, and also includes interviews with high-stakes pros, after Alvarez. Furthermore he documents a personal journey that like Holden ends with a recognition that despite his strengths as a player he wasn't "ever going to be good enough to play poker professionally."[40]

Recalling Alvarez's earlier coverage of the WSOP for *The New Yorker*, novelist and teacher James McManus "wangled an assignment" from *Harper's Magazine* (as he puts it) to visit the 2000 WSOP and write about three different topics: the performance and progress of women poker players, the impact of strategy books and computer programs on the game, and the sensational murder trial in a Las Vegas courtroom that summer resulting from the death of Ted Binion of the Horseshoe-owning family.[41] From the start, however, McManus has an additional plan – to win entry into the $10,000 Main Event himself and play it, and this fourth topic eventually overwhelms the other three. McManus wins his entry in a one-table satellite, then improbably goes on to finish fifth of 512 entrants to win a prize of nearly a quarter million dollars. The fact that McManus is joined at the final table by poker pro T.J. Cloutier, co-author of one of the strategy books he had consulted as part of his preparation, provides a nifty symmetry to the story. Ultimately McManus managed to weave together all of those narrative threads effectively into a book, *Positively Fifth Street* (2003), that reached *The New York Times* best sellers list for nonfiction.

While no other poker writers have come close to equaling McManus' Main Event performance, others have nonetheless tried to challenge him with their own WSOP journey-narratives.[42] In *Take Me to the River*, author and journalist Peter Alson tells of playing in the 2005 WSOP, connecting his poker-related aspirations with a scheme to finance his upcoming wedding. Amis played in the 2006 WSOP Main Event at the height of the poker boom, producing a short essay afterwards in which he describes "the near-apocalyptic national upsurge in pokermania" then occurring.[43] Holden returned in 2006 as well, writing about his experience with the commercialized, hyped spectacle he mostly laments as the "rampant vulgarization of poker" in a sequel, *Bigger Deal: A Year Inside the Poker Boom*.[44] Later the website Grantland bought novelist Colson Whitehead into the 2011 WSOP Main Event, with his *The Noble Hustle* presenting an even less enthused, detached view of the proceedings signaled from the start by an inspired opening line: "I have a good poker face because I am half dead inside."[45]

The novelty of large cash payouts in poker tournaments has faded over recent years. So, too, has the originality of much written tournament reporting which today more often than not lapses into a formulaic presentation written primarily for a niche audience of poker enthusiasts. Even so, poker tournaments still continue to inspire occasional attempts to capture their "battle royale"-like structure creatively in nonfiction narrative, both in print and online.

18 Poker on the Radio

We've noted *The Cincinnati Kid* director Norman Jewison reflect how one of the challenges he faced when making the film was the fact that poker was widely regarded as a "totally uncinematic" subject.[1] However, as Jewison and others have shown, poker's inherent drama can in fact lend itself well to depiction on the silver screen, particularly in the hands of those with a talent for storytelling and a knowledge of the game. But what about *listening* to people play poker on the radio? Could that work? Thanks in large part to how familiar the popular card game had become to those tuning in, it absolutely could.

Wireless radio communication arrived during the last years of the 19th century, and the technology was further developed over the next two decades as radios were used to contact ships at sea and later for military purposes during the First World War. In 1920, KDKA of Pittsburgh became the first station to receive a federal commercial license to begin broadcasting. Few heard the initial broadcasts, but many more stations appeared over the following years as increasing numbers of Americans bought receivers.

Within another decade hundreds of stations and the first national and regional networks had been introduced. Surveys estimate two-thirds of American homes had at least one radio set by the mid-1930s, with the figure jumping to as much as 80 or 90 percent before the start of the Second World War.[2] Radios were not inexpensive, either, often costing roughly two weeks' worth of an average salary (and this during the height of the Great Depression). Most families shared a single radio, which meant many of the millions of sets had multiple listeners. While the broadcasting of news and weather reports were priorities early on, it didn't take long before entertainment programming also began to fill the schedules. The years from the late 1920s through the 1950s became known as the "Golden Age of Radio," a period during which the majority of Americans not only tuned in for news about the economy and overseas conflict, but also to hear plays, serials, soap operas, quiz shows, variety hours, children's shows, cooking programs, musical performances, call-in talk shows, and more.

During these years, radio served a role similar to the one fulfilled by television in the latter half of the 20th century and the internet in the early 21st, namely providing a steady stream of commonly-shared cultural productions that both reflected and responded to American society. America's favorite card game was not excluded during this peak era of radio entertainment, and poker often turned up with the same frequency as it appeared in film and other media. Such exposure not only further attested to the growing popularity of poker, but help shed further light on what values and ideas the game tended to signify to many Americans.

In radio westerns, poker functioned a lot like it did on the silver screen, adding color and an "Old West" flavor to the proceedings with encounters at the poker table often paralleling or standing in for gunplay or other more violent forms of conflict. In mysteries and detective shows, the intellectual component of the game sometimes fit neatly with the deductive work characters carried out in order to solve crimes, while other times the shows exploited the game's luck element as a means to heighten suspense. Meanwhile radio comedies more often than not presented their poker plots against the backdrop of the game's overwhelmingly male-centric history in order to stage light-hearted battles between the sexes.

Radio Westerns

As a dominant genre of film during the early sound era, westerns unsurprisingly enjoyed similar popularity on the radio. The shows frequently dot-ted station's daily schedules, often following tried and true formulas from western fiction and film, occasionally incorporating musical performances, and always supported by conspicuous advertising like all entertainment-based radio programs. There were anthology shows with rotating casts, juvenile adventures, "legends of the West"-type shows with stories of the frontier liberally mixing truth and fiction, and a few western soap operas aiming to capture the female audience. Populating the programs were many of the same enduring western characters also known from film, television, and comic books such Matt Dillon, Red Ryder, and Hopalong Cassidy, plus radio-only heroes like Hashknife Hartley, Hawk Larabee, and Britt Ponset.

The Lone Ranger radio show, with its theme song borrowed from Gioachino Rossini's *William Tell Overture*, is probably the most familiar of all of them. It premiered in 1933 and ran for nearly 3,000 episodes over two decades, well establishing the mask-wearing title character as one of the most famous fictional heroes of the Old West even before the later TV series and many films. Though not a poker player himself, the Lone Ranger occasionally encountered games during his travels such as in an episode titled "Gun Shy Gambler" from 1944. The story involves a character named Jeff Atkins having to defend himself against the brother of a man Atkins was thought to have killed in self-defense years before following a dispute in a poker game. The incident permanently frightens Atkins from using a gun, so he manages to convince his nemesis to duel him over cards instead. "My business is stud, not draw," he explains.[3]

The episode uncritically brings questions about masculinity to the foreground, with Atkins fretting over being a "coward" thanks to his distaste for guns, a weakness treated as a serious handicap in the Old West. In any event, his affliction makes more conspicuous the substitution of a poker game for a duel, a frequent occurrence in western stories that helped confirm the game's outlaw status to general audiences.

Cheating is either suspected or occurs in every poker game played in "Gun Shy Gambler." So, too, does cheating at cards lead to gunplay and a shooting at the start of "Poker Chip Draw," a 1957 episode of *The Cisco Kid*. The popular show very loosely based on a character from an O. Henry short story premiered in 1942 and appeared on various networks all the way through the 1950s. It featured a Mexican caballero as the title character (dubbed the "Robin Hood of the West") and his sidekick Poncho (more of a comic foil than Tonto is to the Lone Ranger). The episode finds the pair involved in a dramatic showdown between an untested marshal and a gambler-gunslinger duo who are making trouble in his small New Mexico town. Poker and guns meet once again in the story via the "poker chip draw" trick of the title, a maneuver in which a gunman places a poker chip on the back of his shooting hand, then turns the hand so the chip flies off, grabs his gun, and shoots the chip out of the air. Once more the disorder created by cheating and violence around poker tables must be resolved by those in authority, with the marshal predictably proving his mettle and handling the situation with some timely assistance from Cisco.

Speaking of poker games turning violent, we've already discussed how the story of Wild Bill Hickok and his fateful "dead man's hand" were dramatized many times over in various media. Hickok turned up in episodes of various fictional western series as well, including in an episode of *The Lone Ranger* in 1944, one of *Gunsmoke* in 1953, then again on *Frontier Gentleman* in 1958. The latter show's conceit involved a 19th-century Brit named J.B. Kendall reporting for the *London Times* while traveling through the Old West and encountering various figures, both historical and imagined. In "Aces and Eights" the reporter visits Deadwood, encounters Hickok, Calamity Jane, Jack McCall and others, and subsequently becomes a witness to Hickok's violent end. In fact, Kendall even takes a seat in Hickok's last poker game, enabling him to witness Jack McCall's fatal attack. A motive for McCall is supplied in the fictional recreation by talk of Hickok perhaps becoming marshal in Deadwood and deciding to banish McCall from town. The drunk killer is also encouraged by the idea that the reporter from overseas will tell the world the story of his shooting dead the famous gunslinger.

There was even an entire series devoted to the legendary lawman, *The Adventures of Wild Bill Hickok*, that ran concurrent to the television show of the same title during the 1950s and featured the same cast. A "cereal serial" sponsored by Kellogg's and aimed at younger listeners ("Hiya folks! Hold on to your hats and pass those Kellogg's Corn Pops!"), the real-life Hickok's tragic end was set aside in favor of other invented adventures with a comic sidekick named Jingles. While the Lone Ranger rode Silver and the Cisco Kid rode Diablo, Hickok's horse was named Buckshot while the horse Jingles rode had a card-playing name, Joker. One 1951 episode "Four Aces for Death" presented a skewed version of Hickok's deadly poker hand story, with a band of bank robbers drawing aces from a hat to determine the order in which each would successively try to take out Hickok. (The idea of teaming up to go after Hickok seems not to have occurred to them.) The fellow drawing the ace of spades tries first and fails, followed in turn according to suits' rank by the ones drawing the ace of hearts, the ace of diamonds, and the ace of clubs.

"Well, that fills our hand... we've got four of a kind," Hickok says upon capturing the fourth bank robber.[4] Even on these juvenile shows, poker hands and playing cards could be coded as dangerous or even deadly, a pattern evident in other radio dramas as well.

Radio Mysteries

Mysteries of various kinds, from detective-based dramas to horror-filled fright-fests, were also a staple of old time radio. Such shows typically targeted adult audiences, often airing at night and presented by sponsors selling cigarettes, beer and wine, automotive parts, razor blades, and the like. Poker was again frequently featured on these programs, more often than not aligned with the conflict-creating criminal activities around which such shows' plots often revolved.

One early example comes from the short-lived show *Nick Harris Detective* in a 1938 episode titled "Fatal Ace of Spades." A "true crime" show that drew on actual cases for its stories, in this episode a murder mystery is solved by the discovery of a deck of cards missing the ace of spades, a find that helps investigators implicate the killer following a deadly game of stud in a Los Angeles gambling house. The same card figures prominently in "The Case of the Poker Murders," a 1946 episode of the similarly named *Nick Carter, Master Detective*. A villain known as the "Ace of Spades" terrorizes a city with robberies and killings while leaving playing cards pinned to victims' bodies as "calling cards." The villain has a mob of subordinates who are all also named after cards, with the "Ace of Clubs" and "Queen of Hearts" his closest associates and some lower-tier henchmen named after the six through ten of clubs. More than once the hero detective Carter describes either the Ace of Spades' plans or his own counter efforts as going "according to Hoyle," with still more poker puns leading the listener up to the bad guy's capture and imprisonment – where, unsurprisingly, he plays solitaire.[5]

More than 500 episodes of the sometimes spooky, horror-tinged *Inner Sanctum Mystery* aired from 1941-52, including one in 1945 called "Dead Man's Deal" that begins with a genuinely gripping if improbable hand of five-card draw. The hand itself – four aces versus a seven-high straight heart flush – is certainly mathematically unlikely, though not atypical of many dramatized poker hands. But the circumstances of the betting is both unusual and hard to fathom, with the players involved agreeing after the draw that whoever loses the hand has to commit suicide. Upon realizing he has lost, the fellow holding the four aces chooses instead to shoot dead his opponent, then replaces the seven of hearts with the seven of diamonds in his opponent's hand to make it appear as though his quad aces had beaten an ordinary straight. Alas for him, the deal had been crooked, meaning the dealer-witness (and accomplice of the victim) knew his partner's hand had been altered. The story ends with the exacting of revenge against the killer, but not before the victim's friend spends some effort haunting him in Edgar Allan Poe-like fashion with the "tell-tale" seven of hearts.

An even scarier show was the popular *Suspense* that ran from 1942-62. An episode called "Hitchhike Poker" from 1948 stars Gregory Peck as a hitchhiker who plays "license plate poker," a game that involves making poker hands from license plate numbers, with a fellow who gives him a ride. Things remain fun and innocent until the driver tries to kill the hitchhiker. As it happens, the license plate poker game enables the remembering of a tag number, a key clue that helps solve the crime. *Escape* was another popular program which ran from 1947-54. The 1950 episode "The Ambassador of Poker," based on a short story by the pulp writer Achmed Abdullah, tells of a Virginian cast off a ship in Hong Kong for being too good at poker. He continues to play (and win) in his new locale before getting involved in an elaborate plan to recover a valuable seal worth a fortune, and uses his wits finely-tuned by poker to help him.

There are numerous other examples, with episodes of popular detective shows like *The Adventures of Sam Spade* ("The Hot Hundred Grand Caper" from 1948), *Pat Novak, For Hire* ("Jack of Clubs" from 1949), and *The New Adventures of Nero Wolfe* ("The Case of the Killer Cards" from 1951) all similarly marked by poker-centric plots. Such stories often exploited the game's early history as a favored pursuit of "outlaws," thereby further associating gambling on cards with criminal activity. For example, in "The Case of the Killer Cards" detective Nero Wolfe, the rotund hero of dozens of Rex Stout novels and short stories, is called from his armchair to solve another shooting death in a poker game. This time four co-owners of the Candy Club agree to deal out a single five-card hand, with the winner getting full ownership of the gambling den. "We're all crooks here, which sort of cancels out any funny business with the cards," one of them comments, underscoring the association between the game and criminality.[6] Some not-so-funny business follows, however, when the player with a pair of kings, the best hand, is gunned down.

One more later entry worth mentioning is the *CBS Radio Mystery Theater*, hosted by E.G. Marshall, which ran from 1974-82. Nearly 1,400 episodes of the show were produced, well after radio's "Golden Age," including the poker-themed "Come, Fill My Cup" from 1977. As is the case in a lot of the other poker-themed mysteries, the story presents the game as a risky, dangerous activity. A fellow named Don Jorgensen has played in a regular poker game aboard a commuter train for years, bothering his wife to the point that she's threatening divorce. Don decides to quit, but one of the other players, Jerry Garland, gets him to play one more time by offering to pay for any losses he might incur. Unfortunately for Jerry, it becomes the last poker game he'll ever play after he drinks from a cup of coffee laced with poison. Like some earlier poker-themed radio shows, it's an engaging whodunit in which an interesting parallel emerges between paying attention to details at the poker table and keeping an eye on details when plotting – or solving – a murder.

Radio Comedies

Finally, it's also unsurprising to find many popular comedies from the golden age of radio presenting poker-themed episodes. As is only to be expected, the game's many conventions and patterns, and the upsetting of them, serve as a ready means to generate laughs.

Duffy's Tavern was a very popular comedy show that ran on several different networks from 1941-51 – so popular, in fact, that a feature film spinoff appeared in 1945. There was also a short-lived TV version from 1954-55. The show might strike some as an early version of the TV sitcom *Cheers* with its

Ed Gardner as Archie from *Duffy's Tavern*

setting in a bar in the northeast (in New York City, rather than Boston), a cast of regulars, and numerous running gags including how the bar's owner, Duffy, never seemed to be around. Duffy's absence meant the manager Archie, played by Ed Gardner, was always left in charge. Similarities with the later show are not a coincidence: Abe Burrows, who co-created *Duffy's Tavern* with Gardner, was the father of James Burrows who co-created *Cheers*. *The Simpsons* also borrowed from *Duffy's Tavern* in the way its eponymous bar proprietor Moe answered the telephone declaring Moe's Tavern to be "where the elite meet to eat," the same line Archie rattles off to open every episode of the radio show.

One key difference between *Duffy's Tavern* and *Cheers* was the way the radio show leaned heavily on guest stars. An episode from 1949 titled "Playing Poker with Charles Coburn" finds the Academy Award-winning actor Coburn stopping by and getting roped into a poker game. The idea is to fleece him, but things turn out otherwise, as you might expect. Coburn and Archie agree to a game while denying profusely each has any knowledge of poker. Dim-witted bar regular Finnegan (Charlie Cantor), a true novice, joins in the game of five-card draw as well, with Archie advising him "don't go into a pot unless you have four of a kind." Eventually Finnegan excitedly opens a pot and only Coburn stays. Both stand pat, then raise each other repeatedly after the draw to build a big pot with Archie volunteering to back Finnegan knowing he must have at least four of a kind. At the showdown Coburn turns over an ace-high straight, at which Archie chuckles as he tells Finnegan to reveal his hand.

"10-4-2-7-J... Finnegan, where's the four of a kind?" asks an exasperated Archie. "There they are... four spades!" answers Finnegan.[7]

A number of other popular radio comedies of the day involved familiar, domestic settings with married couples at the heart of the shenanigans. In fact, most long-lasting radio comedies featured poker-themed episodes at some point during their run, helping to highlight the familiar "battle of the sexes"-type stories that often inspired much of the humor. Some of these shows feature husbands eager to play poker going through various machinations to get away from their wives to play, often keeping their poker-playing secret in order to avoid their wives' wrath. Sometimes the wives played poker themselves, usually coming out victorious to the comical chagrin of the men.

Fibber McGee and Molly was one of the longest-running, most popular radio shows ever, starring real-life husband and wife Jim and Marian Jordan and airing from the 1930s through the 1950s. An episode from 1943 simply called "Poker Game" revolves around Fibber trying to plan a night of poker without Molly finding out. "Poker is pretty much of a man's game," the announcer declares when introducing the story. "Trying to get out of the house for an evening to play poker is also a man's game." The subsequent show involves one extended bluff by the aptly named Fibber as he poorly lies to Molly that an evening Elks Club meeting is for the businessmen to discuss labor issues and not play poker. "They all want to see if they can get some good hands... you know, to *work* in the factories and stuff," he explains. "Everybody's going to lay his cards on the table. We're going to try and see that everybody gets a square deal." Molly responds by telling her husband she's proud of him for taking part. "Aw shucks," says Fibber. "It's nothing that any good red-blooded American boy wouldn't do."

Of course Molly knows her husband is lying, and in fact has plans of her own to play bingo while he's out. The show ends with the wife revealing to her husband she knew all along Fibber was playing poker. "I knew you would have more fun if you thought you were getting away with something," she says.[8]

The Burns and Allen Show was another much loved program, running for nearly two decades and also starring a husband-and-wife team, George Burns and Gracie Allen. An episode from 1944 with guest star Alan Ladd similarly concerns George trying to play a poker game and Gracie not letting him, with Ladd giving George grief for not being able to exert his influence over his wife. Unlike Fibber, George doesn't lie to Gracie about the game, but she's dead set against it. "It won't stop with a poker game, you'll probably all wind up at a burlesque show," she insists. Rather, George spends the show coming up with made-up stories to tell the men to cover why he can't play. Eventually, despite boasts from Ladd insisting men are the "stronger sex" (playing off his tough-guy image from his film roles), it comes out that the other men, including Ladd, are likewise struggling to convince their wives to let them play.[9] Ultimately the convoluted plot concludes with Gracie, not George, playing and winning a pot off the men.

My Favorite Husband followed a similar theme through more than 120 episodes from 1948 to 1951. The show starred Lucille Ball, and served as the basis for the groundbreaking *I Love Lucy* television show that debuted just after the radio show ended its run. An episode from 1950 titled "Be a Pal" featured Ball as Liz Cooper looking for ways to enliven her marriage with her husband George, played by Richard Denning. She attends a ladies' luncheon where a professor billed as an authority on marriage is the featured speaker. He encourages the women to "be a pal" to their husbands – that is, to "learn to like the things *he* likes, be interested in *his* hobbies... for this way lies peace and happiness in marriage."

"Why is it always the woman who has to give in?" asks Liz. "A very interesting question, and the answer lies in my book which will be sold at the door as you leave," answers the professor.

Pursuing the "be a pal system" leads to Liz joining George's poker game, despite not knowing the first thing about how to play. Dealt a hand of five-card draw, she cannot avoid giving away her cards. "Oooh... a queen," she says. "Oooh... there's her sister!" When it comes time to draw, it has to be explained to Liz that she should keep her best cards while discarding her worst ones. "Which ones should I throw away?" she asks in response. "The two queens or the three fives?" The experiment proves exasperating for George, and his poker buddies aren't crazy about it, either. Afterwards George apologizes to one of them who sarcastically consoles him. "That's all right," he says. "I was honored to be present on such a memorable occasion. I can always tell my grandchildren that I was there the night poker died."[10] (As discussed next chapter, the "Be a Pal" story was redone by Ball and her husband Desi Arnaz as one of the first episodes of *I Love Lucy*.)

Comic plots like these remind us how poker's legacy is not only primarily male-dominated, but how poker has for much of its history been coded as a "masculine" game in which knowledge of both the rules and skillful play is associated with manliness. Thus while Molly professes to like poker and complains "I think it's pretty selfish of the men to want to play by themselves all the time," she's ultimately more interested in playing bingo with other women than competing against men at poker.[11] Along the same lines, when Gracie and Liz sit down with men to play, and actually win, their presence at the tables is regarded as mostly farcical. It hardly challenges traditional gender roles or ideas about poker being a "pretty much of a man's game."[12]

Besides its utility in quickly generating conflicts – the kind that can, conveniently, be resolved in 15 minutes or a half-hour – poker worked on radio programs in large part because of the audience's familiarity with the game, with even non-players able to follow the machinations of hands and understand poker references in the context of the stories. That said, whether to increase suspense or for comic effect, the poker played in such shows was only rarely intended to seem realistic. More important to scriptwriters was poker's historical cachet as a forbidden or "outlaw" activity, thus making it useful to color characters quickly as Old West villains, modern day urban-dwelling criminals, or mischievous individuals amusingly seeking low-stakes escapes from everyday routines and responsibilities.

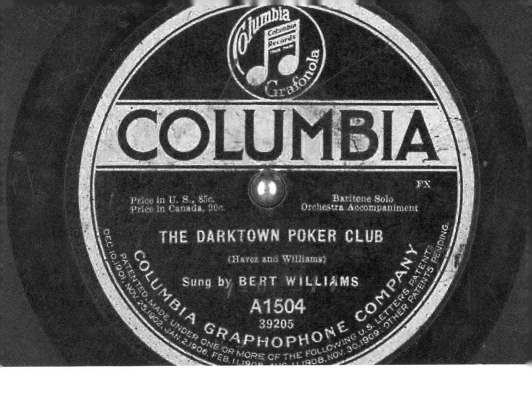

19 Poker in Music

Poker's central place in American culture is well supported by its frequent appearance in popular music. There are numerous examples from practically every genre in the American songbook of musicians addressing poker directly, with some celebrating the game's many pleasures and thrills and others ruefully lamenting poker as the cause of ruin.

Musicians have used poker as a context for storytelling in much the same way as writers and filmmakers. Songwriters have also frequently exploited the game's colorful and familiar terminology for metaphorical purposes, figuratively alluding to poker actions to address the role chance plays in our lives, generally speaking, especially when it comes to love and romance.

Charles MacEvoy's "That Game of Poker" (1878)

Early Poker Stories in Song

One of the first mentions of poker in popular song comes via a 19th century Chicago music teacher named Charles MacEvoy, whose Ireland-themed traveling show MacEvoy's Original Hibernicon earned him national fame. The show featured original music performed before scrolling panoramas of Irish subjects. In 1878 MacEvoy wrote and published "That Game of Poker," a song celebrating the game while introducing it to those who are unfamiliar. Dedicated to a New York City poker club (the "Home Club"), the song begins with a singer presenting himself as "a man of the world" before telling of his own experiences playing five-card draw while explaining various terms ("rake," "kitty," "jack pots"). Much as John Blackbridge did in *The Complete Poker-Player* (1875), MacEvoy delivers advice about bankroll management and the need to be vigilant when watching for card cheats: "Unless you are wealthy, pray be not too rash / And cut the cards always, 'twill save you your cash." Ultimately MacEvoy champions the game ("I like it… you all do!"), adding to the already considerable evidence of poker's growing popularity.[1]

Another popular poker-themed song from 1883 similarly recalls other poker tales of the day. Richard A. Saalfield, a.k.a. Richard Field, was born in the U.K. and had a background that included contributing to musical productions in London as well as operatic work before coming to New York in the 1880s where he began writing and publishing popular songs.[2] In Field's "Poker; or, That Queen," he presents a game of cards between a pair of old friends, a judge who "played on the square" and a colonel who "could play a more difficult game" that included occasionally giving himself an unfair edge. Too evenly matched at poker, they decide to play euchre, but then a hand arises in which both players are dealt cards that would be strong in poker. So they agree to switch the game back. The listener suspects what's coming, though, as when "the Judge turned a moment his head" the colonel had slipped in a stocked deck while shuffling, "And the Judge cut a cold one instead." In this case the judge has drawn four kings, then the colonel offers that if he can be allowed to add the current upcard to his hand – a queen – he'll be willing to play it as five-card draw. Thinking "that queen" can't help the colonel top his four kings, the judge readily agrees and they build a big pot, only for the colonel to show four aces to win.[3]

The mid-hand game switch was a common ruse recounted many times in poker stories of the era. Eugene Edwards explains how the trick was a favorite of sharps traveling in teams on trains. "Two or four men would be playing euchre, and the cards would be worked around until the victim found himself with a hand containing three aces," Edwards explains. That's when one player would innocently say "I wish I was playing poker," with the mark holding three aces often responding by eagerly agreeing to the change. "Nearly every time the man with three aces would fall into the trap" after an opponent drew to a flush or some other better hand.[4]

The first popular recording of a poker song likewise had a connection to contemporary poker stories: "The Darktown Poker Club" recorded in 1914 by Ziegfeld Follies performer Bert Williams. The singer, dancer, and comedian was the first black American to star on Broadway, often appearing alongside partner George Walker during his early career and later sharing the stage with W.C. Fields. Among his many standout stage routines was one in which he performed a pantomime of a poker game in which he deals out a hand and loses, a skit Williams first introduced in *Bandanna Land* (1908) and reprised later in the two-reeler *A Natural Born Gambler* (1916). The routine became one of his most famous, with audiences so receptive they reportedly would not let Williams end shows without performing it and also singing his famous theme song, "Nobody."[5]

"The Darktown Poker Club" enabled Williams to build upon his audience's association of him with poker. Williams co-wrote the music with Will Vodery (a pioneering African American composer), with novelty songwriter Jean Havez providing lyrics directly inspired by Henry Guy Carleton's popular Thompson Street Poker Club stories (discussed in Chapter 7). The song is delivered from the point of view of a character named Bill Jackson who complains about cheating going on in a game, the scene neatly mimicking the tone and vibe of Carleton's stories. Jackson lays down his own rules for the game – e.g., "Keep your hands above the table when you're dealing, please, and I don't want to catch no aces down between your knees" – all while threateningly sharpening his razor. "Not gonna play this game no more according to Mr. Hoyle, hereafter, it's gonna be according to me!" he concludes. Comedian and singer Phil Harris covered the song again in the 1940s, then country star Jerry Reed also released a version titled "The Uptown Poker Club" that proved a hit for him in the early 1970s.

In 1919, two other stars of the stage took turns performing another poker-themed song when Fanny Watson and Al Jolson each separately recorded the historically fanciful "Who Played Poker with Pocahontas (When John Smith Went Away)?" Written for the hit Broadway musical *Monte Cristo Jr.* by Joe Young and Sam M. Lewis (lyrics) and Fred Ahlert (music), not only does the song wholly invent a Jamestown colony affair between the English explorer Captain John Smith and the Native American Pocahontas, but also has Smith teaching Pocahontas poker some two centuries before the game's introduction. The tune is notable, nonetheless, for providing an early example of poker-inspired sexual innuendo in song. It describes John's suspicions about Pocahontas' faithfulness being aroused since "every time that John came back, he found her with a larger stack." That same year another song titled "The Four Flushers" tried to seize upon both poker's popularity and the current foxtrot craze, warning listeners how "all your bluffing may fail if it lands you in jail." With music by "I. Bluffem-Hall" and words by "Ura Nother," it appears the songwriters had some experience with bluffing themselves.

One other early poker ditty came via vaudeville star Frank Crumit, composer of a string of novelty hits during the 1920s and 1930s before becoming a popular radio quiz show host. (Crumit's "Buckeye Battle Cry" is still used as a fight song by his alma mater Ohio State University.) Though he often accompanied himself on the ukulele (an instrument he helped popularize), Crumit's 1928 song "Dolan's Poker Party" features him before a small orchestra singing about a friendly six-handed game of draw that begins peacefully but ends in a brawl. The turning point in the narrative comes when one player, Dolan, discovers the pot short after he wins a hand. It's a comedic take on the game's violent history, with Crumit's relaxed delivery humorously conflicting with the overturned stove, smashed pictures, and broken noses resembling roses.

Looking for Love in the Cards

There is ample evidence of poker's popularity among African Americans throughout the game's history. In the late 19th century, the fictional Thompson Street Poker Club had plenty of real-life counterparts from which Henry Guy Carleton drew inspiration. So, too, was Bert Williams' poker pantomime borne from the game's popularity among both blacks and whites. The African American businesswoman and arts patron A'Lelia Walker, sometimes called the "hostess of the Harlem Renaissance," also hosted regular afternoon poker games. Most famous for throwing hundreds of high society gatherings during the 1920s at which gathered many of the great artists and writers of the day, Walker was known to both play poker and stake others in the games.[6] By the time gambling was legalized in Las Vegas in 1931, there were already multiple African American poker clubs and other underground games run out of barbershops and cafes, as was the case in many American cities.[7] And in 1942, one of the longest-lasting poker clubs in America was started by black professionals in Washington, D.C. where faculty from Howard University and others gathered on a monthly basis at the Brookland Literary and Hunting Club.[8]

Several early blues recordings by African American artists further attest to poker's popularity among blacks, most of which associate the game with romantic liaisons. For example, Arthur "Blind" Blake's "Poker Woman Blues" from 1929 is sung from the perspective of an inveterate gambler who has grown to accept wild swings of fortune. Accompanied by Blake's unique strumming style mimicking a ragtime piano, the gambler even tells of winning a woman in a poker game, then losing her, before finally finding another whom he decides he won't gamble away. A couple of years later a family group from Bolton called the Mississippi Sheiks recorded "Bed Spring Poker," a song denouncing the ruinous "game" of men being unsatisfied with their current mates, vainly drawing and discarding women as though they were trying to improve their hands in five-card draw. Also prevalent during the period are examples of singers boasting their prowess as lovers by associating themselves with playing cards. Blues pianist Peetie Whitestraw declares himself the "King of Spades" (1935) and guitarist Buck Turner calls himself the "Black Ace" (1937) in a song later included on a compilation titled after an explanatory line from the song, *I'm the Boss Card in Your Hand*.

A number of early blues singers recorded the traditional folk song "Jack o' Diamonds," sometimes titled "Jack of Diamonds (Is a Hard Card to Play)," with Blind Lemon Jefferson the earliest to popularize it in a 1926 recording. Thought to have originated with Texas railroad workers and sometimes dated as far back as the Civil War, many versions personify the card itself as villainous: e.g., for Jefferson the card takes his money and clothes; for Sippie Wallace, a.k.a. "The Texas Nightingale," who also recorded it in 1926, the card becomes a cruel and untrustworthy man; and for Henry Townsend, who recorded it as "Jack of Diamonds Georgia Rub" in 1931, the card takes his woman away. Later recordings by John Lee Hooker, Odetta Holmes, and Mance Lipscomb describe vainly attempting to play the card versus other cards in the deck (against the deuce it's no use, etc.). The song was popular among many early white recording artists as well, starting in the late 1920s with recordings by Ben Jarrell, Jules "The Singing Cowboy" Allen, and Tex Ritter, with dozens of cover versions following thereafter.

Delta blues guitar legend Robert Johnson also famously sang about a playing card in his 1937 recording "Little Queen of Spades." Johnson recorded only 29 songs over the course of a couple of years before he died aged 27, yet his influence over subsequent blues and rock is immense. His early (and mysterious) death later helped to fuel Faust-like fables of his having struck a "crossroads" deal with the devil, with the lyrics of several of his songs providing myth-makers with support. In "Little Queen of Spades," Johnson describes how he is among the men to become spellbound by a devilish-seeming gambling woman. Obliquely casting his relationship with her as a card game, the "little queen" appears to enjoy an advantage both via supernatural means (her "mojo") and perhaps more directly by a propensity to cheat (by "trimmin' down" the cards). He nonetheless can't quit the game, continuing to hope he might become her king.

Like Johnson, Memphis Minnie grew up in Mississippi though ran away to Memphis when she was a teenager. Eventually the guitarist began a lengthy recording career stretching from the late 1920s through the 1950s. In her 1941 song "Don't Turn That Card," she casts doubt over a long-term relationship by describing it in four-year intervals (1930, 1934, 1938, 1942) while assigning a single card to each verse – the ace of clubs, a black deuce, the queen of hearts, and the ten of spades. With each card she begs the dealer (or fortune teller?) not to turn over another, as though worried either about what five-card hand she'll ultimately complete (or, perhaps, the hand coming to a conclusion). In any event, the song ends before the fifth card appears.

The popularity of country and western music grew significantly during these years, and the genre's affinity with the Old West inevitably brought poker into the songs. One humorous example from 1950 is the single "Wild Card" by Tex Williams and His Western Caravan. Co-written by Bonnie Lake and the actor Buddy Ebsen, the fast-paced number swings through the story of a hapless steamboat traveler losing repeatedly to a card sharp who always seems to draw a wild card. The traveler then loses even more to the charms of the sharp's female friend, a different kind of "wild card" to torment him. The moral? Avoid poker, especially when traveling, and instead just play solitaire. In a similar vein, one of the first songs Patsy Cline recorded, "Turn the Cards Slowly" (1955) by Sammy Masters, employs an upbeat, cheerful sound while inveighing against a poker cheat, in this case one whose double-dealing and stacking of the deck represents unfaithfulness.

Influential blues guitarist T-Bone Walker of Texas had a string of releases covering nearly half a century from the late 1920s until just before his death in 1975. Among them was a rendition of Albert Deroy Burghardt Jr.'s "You're My Best Poker Hand" for his 1953 album *Classics in Jazz*. Up against an opponent holding three aces, Walker describes himself drawing a single card in the hopes of improving his hand, suggestively singing how he needs a queen like his beloved to improve. Sure enough, he gets his queen – of hearts – to complete a winning flush. Providing a contrast that same year was Ray Charles with "Losing Hand," the B-side of one of his first singles that would eventually appear on his self-titled debut LP. Written by Jesse Stone (as Charles E. Calhoun), the slow and soulful blues number uses the poker metaphor to describe a relationship on which the singer has incorrectly gambled.[9]

Rocking Road Gamblers and Cardslinging Singers

The phrase "fading the white line" was used to describe poker players from the 20th century's middle decades who drove from city to city both to seek out games and avoid the heat invited by a lifestyle dependent on illegal gambling. The trio of Doyle Brunson, Thomas "Amarillo Slim" Preston, and Sailor Roberts are among the best known such players, "road gamblers" who often traveled together from game to game with a shared bankroll while dodging the authorities. The phrase might also apply to many of the touring bands of the 1960s and 1970s, a period during which several more folk, blues, and rock artists found inspiration from poker, often either evoking America's frontier past or the more immediate travails of touring as contexts for their songs.

Blues-rock pioneer Bo Diddley drew on multiple western themes for his eclectic 1960 album *Bo Diddley Is a Gunslinger*, the song "Cheyenne" in particular featuring an ornery cowboy having to fend off a tinhorn wanting to fight him in a poker game. Singer-songwriter Bob Dylan similarly found both the Old West and poker stimulating areas of inquiry, most memorably in "Rambling, Gambling Willie," first recorded in 1962 as an outtake during sessions for his *The Freewheelin' Bob Dylan* LP. In it Dylan introduces the character Will O'Conley, a veteran of poker games in so many different locations – on the Mississippi, in the Colorado mountains, even in the White House – his career almost functions as a capsule summary of poker's history in America. Willie's death even evokes poker's most famous hand, his prodigious winning streak coming to an end after being shot in the head during a poker game while clutching aces and eights. By comparison *Bonanza* star Lorne Greene's 1966 single "Five Card Stud," written by Wally Gold of "It's My Party" fame, presents little more than a poker short story with a twist ending. A mysterious stranger joins a saloon poker game and in the climactic hand strangely folds a hand containing three aces (two up, one in the hole) against an opponent's three kings before departing, the final lines revealing he was playing against his son.

In 1971 Grateful Dead leader Jerry Garcia opened his self-titled solo album with "Deal," sung from the perspective of a seasoned gambler ostensibly drawing on his experience with card cheats to advise his listener to watch the deal carefully and thereafter to play with caution. That same year folk-blues artist Townes Van Zandt recorded the mini-epic "Mr. Mudd & Mr. Gold" for his album *High, Low and In Between*. It is a surreal song describing a hand of five-card stud between the title characters in which the players' cards are personified as though waging an apocalyptic battle, with Mr. Gold's four wicked kings ultimately falling to Mr. Mudd's four angelic aces.

The Eagles dominated FM radio during the 1970s, with their second LP *Desperado* (1973) and accompanying tour helping confirm their status as leaders of the folk-influenced soft rock being produced by many of their contemporaries. The album comprises several Old West-themed tracks, with the title song telling of a weary card-playing cowboy whose tribulations seem to mirror that of a road-exhausted band. Another track titled "Out of Control" even more directly references poker, specifically a saloon game in which a cowboy weighs risks associated both with the hand he holds and a flirtatious barmaid. Not coincidentally, the Eagles themselves were dedicated poker players, and when not on the road lead singer and guitarist Glenn Frey hosted weekly games at his Laurel Canyon home in Los Angeles, eventually dubbed the "Kirkwood Casino" after its location on Kirkwood Drive. Among those regularly joining the game was singer-songwriter Joni Mitchell whose "Song for Sharon" from her 1976 album *Hejira* included a reference to her being able to remain cool at poker but not so much when love was involved. Frey even invented a new poker variant called Eagle Poker, one involving players betting on whether or not a third card's value would fall in between the ranks of two other dealt cards. The game is commemorated indirectly in Cameron Crowe's film *Almost Famous* (2000) in which a character based on Frey plays blind man's bluff.[10]

The Flint, Michigan rock group Grand Funk Railroad also enjoyed peak career success during this period, with their first number one single on the Billboard charts, "We're An American Band," the title track from their 1973 album. The autobiographical song written and sung by drummer Don Brewer chronicles happenings from the road, with highlights including lots of boozing, partying with groupies, and encountering an agreeable hotel detective. Brewer also makes reference to the favored card game of blues guitarist Freddie King who had opened for the band during the previous year's tour. As Brewer tells it, King "would, every night, have a poker game in his room and he'd make his band play cards with him and he'd win all his money back."[11]

Other rock acts of the era embedded poker in album tracks as well. Though most of the members hailed from Canada, The Band often evoked Americana both through their lyrics and a sound that combined country, blues, and early rock 'n' roll. A track co-written by band member Robbie Robertson and Van Morrison for their 1971 album *Cahoots* titled "4% Pantomime" compares the rigors of touring to a poker game in which the performers are being bottom dealt by money-grubbing managers – a no-win situation in which even though they play before a "full house" everyone turns out to be a loser. Southern rockers Lynyrd Skynyrd opened their 1975 album *Nuthin' Fancy* with an anti-gun track "Saturday Night Special" that associates poker with violence. Among the song's characters is a whiskey-drinking poker player named Big Jim who handles suspicions of cheating Old West-style, using the .38 caliber weapon of the title to gun down his friend. Electric Light Orchestra's 1975 album *Face the Music* included a song simply titled "Poker," a heavy, driving rocker filled with oblique references to jokers, aces, and high cards. Less vague with its poker references was "The Jack" by Australian rockers AC/DC from their 1975 album *T.N.T.*, a song that became a live show highlight for the band as they grew a significant audience in America over subsequent years. While the lyrics superficially suggest a poker game, the double-entendres eventually overwhelm a narrative in which the singer realizes the object of his desire has given him the sexually-transmitted disease for which the song's title is an Aussie euphemism.

"The Gambler," Poker's Theme Song

Undoubtedly the single most famous poker song ever recorded, "The Gambler" is the title track of the 1978 album that not only helped catapult

Kenny Rogers to iconic status, but thrust poker into the mainstream as well. The song tells the tale of a chance meeting aboard a train between a younger man and an older gambler in which the latter passes along pok-

Kenny Rogers sings "The Gambler" at the 1979 World Series of Poker.

er-inflected life lessons. It was an immediate hit, eventually winning awards both for Rogers and songwriter Don Schlitz. Decades later "The Gambler" remains not only a signature tune closely identified with Rogers, but a kind of theme song for poker, selected for preservation by the National Recording Registry in 2017 for "its indelible place in popular culture."[12]

Schlitz was a struggling songwriter in his early 20s when he wrote the song in 1976, recording it himself and achieving modest commercial success. By then Rogers was already an established country star, having recorded more than 15 albums and having had several country hits both in bands and as a solo artist. Rogers had also begun to enjoy some crossover success, most notably the year before with "Lucille," a song that not only topped the country chart but reached the top 10 of the Billboard Hot 100. Eventually "The Gambler" was presented to producer Larry Butler who recognized the song's potential and brought it to Rogers. At the time Butler was also producing Johnny Cash's new album, *Gone Girl*, and Cash, too, recorded "The Gambler" one day before Rogers did. However Rogers' recording, released a month ahead of Cash's with a slight tweaking to the lyrics and an increase in tempo, was destined to become the definitive version.[13]

While Rogers' gruff baritone perhaps best suits the character of the old poker player, "The Gambler" is actually told from the point of view of the younger man to whom the old-timer imparts his wisdom. Poker players instinctively recognize the gambler's advice to be mostly well founded, highlighting several elements of the game that may well escape novices. The gambler discusses physical tells and being able to read others' hands by their expressions, as well as how any given hand can be a winner or loser depending on the situation. The chorus then includes a couple more important guidelines for players – that understanding when to leave the game is a crucial skill for ensuring profitability, and that chips on the table are still in play and thus should not be considered otherwise.

The poker tips all have figurative meaning as well, together comprising a kind of general philosophy about the "game" of life and how best to approach (and accept) its potential risks and rewards. Schlitz, not a card player himself, describes the song as not so much about poker as "about discretion... and the choices you make."[14] That message – along with the infectious, sing-along chorus – helped ensure the song's broader appeal.

The song's references to "hold 'em" (and knowing when to do so) are actually generic, referring not specifically to Texas hold'em – still about a quarter-century away from becoming America's favorite poker variant – but rather to the decision in *any* poker game to hold onto one's cards and not to fold. Even so, it was especially fitting when Rogers appeared at Binion's Horseshoe in May 1979 to perform the song prior to the Main Event where the featured game was no-limit hold'em. Later that year Rogers performed the song

Poker & Pop Culture

again on *The Muppet Show*, humorously passing cigarettes and whiskey to the puppet character accompanying him. The following spring Rogers then starred in a television movie titled *Kenny Rogers as The Gambler*, the first of five popular films in which he portrayed a 19th-century gambler named Brady Hawkes who takes on a younger poker player as a protégé. It was a much admired throwback to earlier western heroes romanticizing both poker and the Old West – and made a prediction by the song's producer come true. "I got a funny feeling," Butler reportedly told Rogers before the recording of the song, "that if you do this you will become the Gambler."[15]

Later Poker Hits

Around this time several British rock bands with poker references in their songs were earning both commercial and critical success in America. With their acclaimed double-LP *London Calling* (1979), original punk rockers The Clash expanded their sound to incorporate a wide variety of genres and subjects. One track, the ambitious, piano-driven "The Card Cheat," maps an Old West poker game ending in the violent demise of a cheater onto all of human history with allusions to ancient, medieval, and modern wars. A year later the art rock band The Alan Parsons Project released *Turn of a Friendly Card*, a concept album with multiple songs addressing different gambling games including poker. Both *London Calling* and *Turn of a Friendly Card* went platinum in the U.S., selling more than a million copies.

Another English rock band, Motörhead, released the most popular single of their career – "Ace of Spades" – in 1980. The roaring speed-metal track sung from the perspective of a fearless gambler with a self-destructive streak was the title song from the band's album of the same year and effectively served to introduce the band to American audiences. Having co-written the song with two other band members, lead singer Ian "Lemmy" Kilmister later explained how even though he wasn't much of a card player, the subject matter required references to the title card and the joker, a directive to "read 'em and weep," and a very conscious allusion to Wild Bill Hickok's last hand. "I used gambling metaphors, mostly cards and dice," Lemmy wrote in his autobiography. "When it comes to that sort of thing, I'm more into one-arm bandits actually, but you can't really sing about spinning fruit, and the wheels coming down."[16]

Following Kenny Rogers' lead, other American country acts subsequently enjoyed mainstream success with poker-themed songs. Originally recorded by Welsh pop rocker Dave Edmunds, Juice Newton's "Queen of Hearts" reached number two on the Billboard Hot 100 in September 1981, a catchy toe-tapper written by Hank DeVito whose upbeat rhythm belies a story of heartache. On his way to becoming one of the best-selling recording artists of the 1990s, Garth Brooks reached number one on the country charts in 1991 with "Two of a Kind, Workin' on a Full House," which as the title suggests describes a well-matched couple looking to start a family. Indie rockers O.A.R. also included a lengthy, nonsensical country-tinged song "That Was a Crazy Game of Poker" on their 1997 debut *The Wanderer*. It was an anthem-like hit at college frat parties that earned a wider audience amid poker's sudden growth in popularity a few years later.

Several successful hip-hop artists have also used poker terminology and imagery in their songs. The influential East Coast group Wu-Tang Clan's track "Back in the Game" from the 2001 album *Iron Flag* incorporates multiple poker references, particularly in a verse by GZA in which the rapper repurposes several poker and blackjack terms to support the collective's broader challenge to other MCs. Fort Minor, a side project of Linkin Park frontman Mike Shinoda, concludes their 2005 album *Rising Tied* with "Slip Out the Back," the message of which essentially is to avoid unnecessary risk, especially in situations where it might seem less than heroic to avoid conflict. Poker provides a ready analogy to illustrate the point, with Shinoda indirectly evoking strategy advice from "The Gambler" about recognizing when to fold a losing hand. More recently, Joey Bada$$ released his politically-charged "Land of the Free" on the date of Donald Trump's inauguration in January 2017, the second single from his album *All-Amerikkkan Badass*. While Trump gets name-checked in a critical way, the song more broadly addresses continued racial injustice in the United States. In the repeated bridge, Bada$$ makes reference to the "full house" he and others have been "dealt" as represented by the stylized spelling of "Amerikkka" in which the two A's and three K's evoke the lingering, destructive influence of the Ku Klux Klan.[17]

While all of these songs earned varying degrees of renown, the only other poker hit to provide a genuine challenge to "The Gambler" as a cultural phenomenon has been Lady Gaga's synth-pop smash "Poker Face" from her 2008 debut *The Fame*. With sexually-charged lyrics and an earworm chorus, the dance track helped make Lady Gaga an international star, topping the charts in more than two dozen countries and remaining among the Billboard Hot 100 for forty weeks. Alongside its numerous innuendo-filled references, the song's title and theme apply poker players' efforts to remain "unreadable" at the table to romance-related mind games between partners. As Lady Gaga's own fame rapidly grew in the wake of her blockbuster debut, it was hard not to recognize how her obvious awareness of the significance of image creation in popular music (through interviews, photos, concerts, videos, and via the fast-growing platform of social media) uncannily related to the importance of image at the poker table. The artist herself seemed often to make a "game" out of others' efforts to "read" her, complementing her provocative declarations with fashion choices that to some seemed outrageous.

Much as poker seems to yield endless possibilities when it comes to hands and ways to play them, so, too, does it appear that when it comes to different ways of singing about poker there is no limit (pun intended).

20 Poker on Television

"Since the major part of the story concerned itself with a poker game, I was very much afraid that because of its static nature and because of the difficulties involved in shooting a group seated around a table the play would lose its drama and excitement when translated to twelve inch screens."[1]

So wrote Dan Petrie, director of *The Billy Rose Show*, one of several anthology drama programs from the early days of American television. Petrie was referring to staging and shooting the very first episode of a new weekly series, a live "teleplay" broadcast on October 3, 1950 called "The Night They Made a Bum Out of Helen Hayes." He was faced with the challenge of televising poker players sitting around a table playing a hand in a way that would neither confuse nor bore viewers, never mind ensure they remain engaged.

Poker & Pop Culture

The series debuted on ABC, the last of the "Big Three" national networks to launch during the 1940s, along with NBC and CBS. The 1950-51 season was the first in which each network filled all of the "prime time" hours from 7-11 p.m. with programming, Sunday through Saturday. The early schedule was a mixture of variety shows, comedies and dramas (many adapted from radio), music and talk shows, a bit of news and sports (including wrestling and roller derby), and other anthology drama series such as NBC's popular *Fireside Theatre* against which *The Billy Rose Show* competed Tuesday nights at 9 p.m.

Such programs were performed live – the use of video tape did not emerge as a standard in television until the late 1950s and only a small number of early shows were shot on film. As Petrie points out, most early television screens were quite small with the 12-inch size most common. "We had to shoot in close, concentrating on faces, and by a judicious use of cutting, dollying, and panning we were able to create an illusion of pace and movement," Petrie explains.[2] It was a challenge combining limitations faced by both filmmakers and theater directors, with the new medium requiring a different kind of resourcefulness from the show's producers.

The show's host Billy Rose was a popular entertainer and lyricist whose nationally-syndicated column "Pitching Horseshoes" supplied a few of the stories later adapted for the program, including the one for "The Night They Made a Bum Out of Helen Hayes." The 30-minute show revolved around a high-stakes card game in a New York hotel room to which a young actor named Danny Dowling gets himself invited. The seven-handed game is bigger than he's used to, and in fact forces him to risk the entire $2,000 savings he shares with his fiancée, Myra (also an actress). Near the end of the show a huge hand develops in which Danny raises with all he has showing 10♦-9♦-8♦-7♦, then his lone remaining opponent, a high roller named Sport, raises another $5,000 on top of that showing A♥-J♠-J♣-Ax. Danny animatedly says he's calling that raise and reraising another $3,000 more, though he'll need to phone someone to obtain the money, and Sport allows it. It's Myra who arrives to deposit her engagement ring in the middle as a raise, all of which is enough to make Sport fold his hand. Before the couple leaves, Danny's hole card is revealed – the 5♠. It was all a bluff, with the two actors having together helped pull it off.

"Come on, Honey," says Danny to Myra as they leave. "Tonight you made a bum out of Helen Hayes," referring to the famous actress of stage and screen.[3]

There's a final twist, however. As Sport explains, he *knew* it was a bluff, since he had the J♦ in the hole (for a full house) and, as confirmed by the meticulous stage directions in Edward Chodorov's script, he'd noticed another player who had folded on third street had been dealt the 6♦. The fold was made out of pity, not because he believed Danny had him beat. "Don't ever bring those crummy kind of people around here again," Sport complains to the player who had invited Danny, referring to the kind of desperate risk-takers Danny and Myra represent. From Sport's perspective, such players unreasonably skew the spirit of a regular game otherwise untroubled by pangs of conscience.

It was no doubt the first televised poker hand shown in such detail, right down to all seven of the players' upcards. But when it comes to showing poker on television, the ingenuity described by Petrie regarding the logistics of production is only part of the overall picture. So, too, have TV storytellers demonstrated many other kinds of inventiveness and creativity when presenting their poker-related plots, both fictional and real-life, as a result further shaping public opinion about the game.

Fictional Poker on TV

TV Westerns

At the time *The Billy Rose Show* debuted in 1950, there were not quite 4 million television sets in use in America in about 9 percent of households. By the mid-1960s that total jumped to more than 50 million, with more than 90 percent of American homes having a television. The TV was the primary entertainment and news source as well as advertising medium.[4] During that period westerns dominated American television screens, often occupying at least half of the top 20 spots in the ratings. As ever, poker was commonly part of the stories.

Shows like *The Life and Legend of Wyatt Earp* (1955-61) and *Bat Masterson* (1958-61) recast Old West legends in digestible half-hour stories delivered weekly, with poker once again a constant source of trouble. In an early first season episode of *The Life and Legend of Wyatt Earp* titled "Trail's End for a Cowboy," an untested rancher's son tasked with selling 500 head of cattle is shown being unable to negotiate a desired price for his father. He then worsens his circumstances by joining a saloon poker game with a mind to run up the money he had obtained. Of course he loses it all, and as Sheriff Earp (Hugh O'Brian) explains the young man was similarly in over his head at the poker table, "played for a sucker" by two gamblers colluding against him.[5] Meanwhile poker was a constant throughout *Bat Masterson*'s run, starting with the first episode "Double Showdown" in which competition between two casino owners is supposedly resolved with a hand of five-card stud dealt face up. Bat (Gene Barry) wins the hand with a pair of jacks versus ace-high, but the loser has a backup plan and gunplay ensues, with Bat drawing his weapon first much as he outdrew him at cards.

The Texan (1958-60), starring Rory Calhoun, was another western series in which poker-generated conflicts created storylines. In the second episode of the series, "The Man With the Solid Gold Star," an ex-lawman loses big at poker, then turns thief and becomes a fugitive after robbing the stockmen's association. In the end both he and the avaricious winner of the poker game end up dead. Poker is also part of the environment of *The Rifleman* (1958-63), starring Chuck Connors as rancher Lucas McCain, where again the game serves both as a source of trouble and the object of censure. In the episode "Tinhorn" losing at poker ruins a friend of Mc-Cain's who suspects he was cheated, and McCain decides to play against the winner in order to determine if his friend's suspicions are correct. Not knowing the reason for his participation in the game, McCain's poker playing creates a scandal both within his family and throughout North Folk. As one person tells him: "The whole town's calling you a tinhorn gambler."[6]

As central as poker is to Old West storytelling, poker was often only a tangential (and frequently negative) element in the worlds portrayed by televised westerns. Multiple episodes of the longest-running western *Gunsmoke* (1955-75) associated poker with murder, although one near the end of the series titled "Whelan's Men" involved Miss Kitty saving the Marshal Matt Dillon from an outlaw gang by beating them at poker. In *Bonanza* (1959-73) plots occasionally incorporated poker, often with characters coming away with unusual, story-generating winnings such as a Kentucky thoroughbred racehorse ("The Hayburner"), an old ore processing mill ("Queen High"), and even a Chinese slave girl ("Day of the Dragon"). Sometimes in these shows poker was associated with gambling addiction, such as in an episode of *Have Gun - Will Travel* (1957-63) called "The Poker Fiend" in which the central character Paladin is hired to extract a wealthy man from a months-long poker game he cannot make himself leave.

A significant pro-poker exception among TV westerns, however, was *Maverick* (1957-62) starring James Garner as the Old West poker player, Bret Maverick. Created by Roy Huggins with a conscious intent to spoof other "straight" western series like his own popular *Cheyenne* (1955-63), *Maverick* featured a humorous hero decidedly unlike the standard rough-hewn model of masculinity. A *Life* magazine article from 1959 marveling at the show's popularity considers how the unique approach to the genre helped *Maverick* stand out from the 32 westerns on television at the time it premiered. "It's 'hero' is a lazy, sneaky, poker-playing vagrant, the black sheep of the cattle country," observes the commentator. "On any other western he would be taken for the heavy, or least for a personification of human frailty." The article points out how the character dislikes gunplay, doesn't drink, prefers to run from conflict than to face it, and isn't even especially intelligent, usually being more lucky than good – all evidence to support the idea that "as western heroes go, Maverick is singularly unheroic."[7]

As the series progressed other Mavericks were rotated in and out of starring roles. A poker-playing brother, Bart (Jack Kelly) was introduced partway into the first season, then after Garner left the show following the third season a cousin Beau (Roger Moore) and later another brother Brent (Robert Colbert) were added. While poker wasn't always the focus of episodes' plots, it was nevertheless a constant subtext, with Maverick's identity as an archetypal 19th-century itinerant gambler (albeit with a modern sense of humor) helping present the game in a more favorable light than was the case in other TV westerns. Sometimes his poker playing was carefully integrated into episodes' plots, such as in the very first, "War of the Silver Kings," in which Maverick beats a silver baron in a game, thereby becoming an endangered target. (He manages to escape unscathed.) Another early episode, "According to Hoyle," finds Maverick playing poker aboard a steamboat and getting beaten repeatedly by a Southern belle who it turns

James Garner as Bret Maverick and Jack Kelly as Bart Maverick
from the Maverick TV series (1957-62)

Poker & Pop Culture

out is exacting revenge against Maverick for having defeated her father in the past.[8] Other times poker is a means to inject humor, such as in "Relic of Fort Tejon" when Maverick unwittingly wins a camel in a poker game. In all cases the game functioned as an meaningful element of the show, with Maverick's wit and craftiness at the tables seamlessly translating to the ingenuity he displays when away from them.

One of the most memorable uses of poker in the series comes in the episode titled "Rope of Cards" in which Maverick serves on a jury in a murder trial. He has to convince a holdout juror that reasonable doubt requires a not guilty verdict. In order to prove to the fellow juror (also a fellow poker player) both that a "sure thing" isn't always as it seems and that "your judgment can be wrong," Maverick gets him to agree to a wager that from 25 randomly dealt cards he can produce five "pat hands" – i.e., hands ranked as a straight or better. The fellow juror believes the odds of doing so to be 100,000-to-1 against, but after being dealt 25 cards Maverick is able to arrange them into four flushes and one straight quite easily. In fact, the true odds are something like 98 percent – or as Maverick says, "practically every time" before naming the demonstration "Maverick Solitaire."[9]

Show creator Huggins later observed that the day after "Rope of Cards" was broadcast, stores across the country sold out of decks of playing cards as everyone who had watched wanted to try out "Maverick Solitaire" themselves. It's true that the show's popularity genuinely helped encourage more to take up the game, sparking a surge in interest in poker.[10] The show inspired series tie-ins like the paperback strategy guide *Poker According to Maverick* (written anonymously by Huggins), a run of comic books featuring issues adapting episodes' plots, *Maverick* holster sets and toy guns, and even children's costumes. Other series both contemporaneous and later repurposed elements from *Maverick*, and the show itself spawned a couple of belated reboots (also starring Garner) and a feature film in 1994 in which Garner played a supporting role to Mel Gibson's Bret Maverick.[11] All the imitations and iterations shared the same playful approach to the character and concept, making Bret Maverick more comedian than cowboy. That a western series purporting to parody the genre would be the one to provide the most consistently positive portrayal of poker perhaps says something about the game's often contested place in the larger culture.

Mysteries, Horror Shows, and Science Fiction on TV

Other early genre shows employed poker in a variety of ways, sometimes associating the game with crime and vice, though occasionally finding other creative uses. The popular anthology series *Alfred Hitchcock Presents* (1955-62) occasionally involved poker in its mysterious crime-filled plots.

In "The Big Switch," a gangster tries to use a heads-up poker game as an alibi while he commits a murder elsewhere, though in a final surprise the player who was supposed to cover for him accidentally shoots himself and the gangster gets wrongly blamed for the killing. "Crack of Doom" adapts the great Don Marquis short story discussed in Chapter 15 in which a troubled gambler explains why after luckily surviving a heedless risk he gave up poker for good. Another episode, "A Night With the Boys," adapts a different poker-related short story that also first appeared in *Playboy*, this one concerning a man losing more than he can afford in a poker game with his boss. He then lies to his wife that he was mugged and the money was stolen from him, then surprisingly learns the mugger has been caught. Even later, he learns that the mugger's victim was his boss, the winner in the poker game.[12]

The science fiction anthology series *The Twilight Zone* (1959-64) included several memorable gambling-themed episodes with stories often delivering moral judgments. In "The Fever" a man is possessed by a haunted slot machine and "A Nice Place to Visit" a gambler who wins every bet he places eventually discovers such a "paradise" is in fact hell, not heaven. In "The Trade-Ins" an elderly couple interested in trading in their old, broken down bodies for young healthy ones can only afford the procedure for one of them, leading the man to try to double his money in a poker game. The foolhardiness of the risk in the game is implicitly compared with the larger gamble the couple is contemplating. In another episode titled "The Lonely" about a convict sentenced to solitary confinement on an asteroid millions of miles from earth, poker and other social games appear to connote humanity and/or social interaction. Visited only four times a year by a crew bringing him supplies, we see the convict desperately wanting to play cards, yet his visitors haven't enough time to do so. Meanwhile in "Third from the Sun," two couples secretively planning an escape from a planet on the precipice of nuclear war play a low-stakes poker game as a cover for their plotting, with a potential informant who could ruin their plan describing their gambling on cards in a way that hints at knowledge of their larger risky scheme. A later revival of *The Twilight Zone* (1985-89) also included a Wes Craven-directed episode titled "Dealer's Choice" in which one of the players turns out to be the devil.

Other sci-fi series incorporated poker in curious ways. An episode of *The Outer Limits* (1963-65) titled "Fun and Games" begins with voice-over narration describing humans' fascination with games and conflict, with a montage of games resolving upon a starkly-lit, high-stakes seven-card stud game that ends in a murder when a player is caught bottom dealing. One of the players tries to escape the scene, but after opening a door oddly finds himself having been "electroported" to another planet with a female acquaintance. Bored aliens them pit them in a fight to the death versus a couple from another planet, a somewhat murky attempt to deliver judgment on our fascination with games like poker.

An episode of the original *Star Trek* (1966-69) titled "The Corbomite Maneuver" memorably evokes poker strategy as well as Cold War brinksmanship. Facing a threatened attack that will destroy the *U.S.S. Enterprise*, First Officer Spock (Leonard Nimoy) compares the situation with chess, adding that "when one is outmatched, the game is over... checkmate." Captain Kirk (William Shatner) is not satisfied with the analysis. "Not chess, Mr. Spock... *poker*," Kirk says, suggesting it provides a better strategic model. Kirk then informs the commander of the threatening ship that a substance called "corbomite" present on the *Enterprise* will cause a "reverse reaction" that will ensure the destruction of any attacking ship. It's a bluff, but it works, earning a "well played" from Mr. Spock.[13] (As it turns out, the attacking ship was bluffing, too.) In another episode, "A Piece of the Action," Kirk again shows inspiration in a situation where he and his crew are held captive in an alien city (surprisingly patterned after 1920s Chicago) with their guards biding time playing poker. Kirk calls poker a "child's game," challenging the guards instead to play "Fizzbin," a nonsensical card game the rules of which Kirk makes up as he goes along, successfully distracting the guards and enabling them to escape – another successful bluff![14]

Poker was even more meaningful to the franchise's next series, *Star Trek: The Next Generation* (1987-94), which featured a new *Enterprise* and a new staff. Punctuating the fresh crew's adventures was the weekly poker game, which came to provide an important, recurring motif upon which various character traits and thematic messages were frequently sounded.

An early episode titled "The Measure of a Man" focuses on whether or not the "sentient" android Data (Brent Spiner), though on some level a "machine," should be regarded as human, with the theme introduced by a poker game. Having recently learned how to play, Data's first impression is that poker is "exceedingly simple." In a five-card stud hand Data folds three queens after being raised by Commander William Riker (Jonathan Frakes) who has four hearts showing, and when Riker shows his hole card – the 2♠ – Data is incredulous. "It makes very little sense to bet when you cannot win!" he exclaims. "But I did win," Riker explains. "I was betting that you wouldn't call."[15] The main plot follows in which a decision must be made regarding Data's status, with the lesson the android learns in the poker game helping bolster the argument for his humanity.

Riker is established as a top player, his skills coming into play in "The Price" in which he's tapped to represent the Federation in negotiations due to his poker prowess. A later episode titled "Ethics" highlights the VISOR (a Visual Instrument and Sensory Organ Replacement) that Lt. Geordi La Forge (LeVar Burton) wears. His kit enables him to see through the backs of cards but he insists that he doesn't take advantage of such an edge during their games. Another episode called "The Outcast" explores the significance of gender roles after the crew encounter an androgynous species called the J'naii that was once male and female, but has evolved in such a way as to remove the distinction. A game of dealer's choice involving male and female crew members finds Counselor Deanna Troi (Marina Sirtis) calling a game with wild cards and Klingon Lt. Commandor Worf (Michael Dorn) objecting by saying "that is a woman's game." The comment draws censure from Dr. Beverly Crusher (Gates McFadden), who notes how the prejudice it evokes is made all the more stark in the context of the J'naii they have encountered.[16]

"Cause and Effect" features a clever, complicated plot in which the ship gets caught in a "temporal causality loop," something the crew only gradually realizes after repeating the same sequence of scenes over and over, with the details of the poker game proving a key aid to discovering what is happening. Data shows his game has improved in "Time's Arrow" when he slips through a time portal and winds up in late 19th-century San Francisco where he is able to start his progress back to the Enterprise and the 24th century at the poker tables. "The Quality of Life" features another men-versus-women discussion over cards, while the two-parter "Descent" finds Data playing a kind of virtual reality poker game with Albert Einstein, Sir Isaac Newton, and Stephen Hawking (playing himself) on the holodeck. When Newton asks why they are playing "this ridiculous game," Data says: "When I play poker with my shipmates, it often appears to be a useful forum for exploring the different facets of humanity. I was curious to see how three of history's greatest minds would interact in this setting."[17] Hawking wins the hand of five-card draw. (One of the later episodes, "Lower Decks," reveals there's an ongoing game among the junior officers on the *Enterprise* as well.)

As if to confirm the significance of poker on *The Next Generation*, the final episode of the series titled "All Good Things…" concludes with one last poker game. In this two-parter, Capt. Jean-Luc Picard (Patrick Stewart) suffers a neurological difficulty called Irumodic syndrome, causing him to move wildly back and forth through time. After much strife, it is discovered near the end of the episode the entire ordeal has been caused by the recurring character named "Q" (John de Lancie) as a kind of test of Picard. In the episode's final scene, the senior staff is shown gathering around the poker table one last time. Picard then arrives and surprises the crew by asking if he might join the game, and they offer him a chair and invite him to deal.

As he shuffles the cards, he stops and gazes around the table. "I should have done this a long time ago," Picard says. "You were always welcome," says Counselor Troi. It's a genuinely moving moment, coming after an episode in which Picard's sense of self has been challenged considerably. Much as the poker game functioned in earlier episodes to help clarify certain ideas about what constitutes life and humanity, gender roles, relationships, and other matters, here the game is clearly connected to the idea of friendship, helping to confirm a final message of the episode and of the series.

"Five-card stud, nothing wild," says Picard, announcing the game. "And the sky's the limit."[18]

Crime Shows on TV

Courtroom dramas, detective shows, police procedurals, and other television programs focused upon criminal activity have been popular throughout television's history. Among the many different (and often creative) ways crimes and murders are plotted, executed, and solved by the shows' protagonists, poker's proximity to illegality makes it a frequent context for such stories.

For example, *Perry Mason* (1957-66), starring Raymond Burr as the titular criminal defense lawyer, incorporated poker games and clubs into several episodes. In "The Case of the Dangerous Dowager," the owner of a California poker club is murdered, with a woman to whom the victim had written a large number of I.O.U.'s the initial suspect. "The Case of the Garrulous Gambler" involves a faked murder at a poker game in which cheating is the ostensible cause for the killing. "The Case of the Singing Skirt" involves another California poker club called The Big Barn, where a high-stakes poker game kicks off a complicated murder plot. A notable plot point in the episode centers on the fact that the game wasn't draw poker (then legal in California), but an illegal game of stud.

Later the stylish *Mission: Impossible* (1966-73) followed the exploits of a covert team of government agents given a mission each week to stop the work of criminals and their organizations, including foreign dictators and corrupt foreign governments. Here poker becomes a mechanism for high-stakes transfers of money, with the trickery and deceit inherent to the game fitting well with the team's elaborate schemes. In "The Psychic" the team must stop the illegal sale of stock in a company that supplies weapons to NATO. One part of the ruse involves a team member playing a hand of five-card "showdown" (a simple deal of five cards, face up) against the villain for the stock. In "The Emerald" the team has to beat an enemy agent to obtain a precious stone, currently in the possession of an arms dealer. (Some microfilm attached to the emerald contains plans for devaluating Western currency.) The target is coerced into playing a high-stakes game of five-card draw for the object, with the team employing a number of gadgets to prevail. The technology includes glasses through which to communicate information to a player as well as a specially-designed table with sensors enabling the reading of cards. It is a kind of proto-version of RFID tables and cards used many years later for televising real poker games. "The Merchant" recycles the same table-and-glasses formula to target an arms dealer, though after the table malfunctions the agent has to play the game straight (and wins).

Other crime shows have occasionally featured poker in ways that could again be interpreted as associating poker with unlawful activity. An episode of *Magnum P.I.* (1980-88) called "Texas Lightning" finds the private investigator getting hired as a bodyguard for a woman hosting a high-stakes poker game aboard a yacht, though the game turns out to be a cover for an attempted burglary. An episode of the police drama *T.J. Hooker* (1982-86) called "Raw Deal" involves a cocaine dealer recruiting debt-ridden losers at his poker club to help him deliver drugs. More notably, the Mafia crime drama *The Sopranos* (1999-2007) incorporated a number of poker games throughout its run. Sometimes the games added lightness to contrast with the frequently serious subject matter, though other times the games descended into the same sort of violent conflict that frequently occurred in the series.

Early on mob boss Tony Soprano (James Gandolfini) organizes the "Executive Game," a high-stakes private game once hosted by his deceased father. It represents part of the process of Tony assuming the patriarch's role as the "executive" of the family's business. Meanwhile made man Eugene Pontecorvo (Robert Funaro) runs a low-stakes game as part of his duties for the crime family. In one instance the game is held up, with the robbery ending in a shootout and deaths. Another member of the crime family, Richie Aprile (David Proval), likewise hosts a regular game, as does Christopher Moltisanti (Michael Imperioli), Tony's protégé. A subplot related to the Executive Game involves one of Tony's friends joining and losing more than he can afford. That story is echoed by a parallel subplot in which one of Chris' friends, a successful TV screenwriter, joins his game and subsequently endures a downward, life-destroying spiral caused by his gambling addiction. Near the end of the series, in an episode titled "Remember When," Uncle Junior (Dominic Chianese), previously the de facto head of the family until his confinement in a mental health institution for dementia, organizes a forbidden poker game among the patients. Using buttons for chips, the game is an obvious though somewhat parodic attempt to recreate the mobsters' lifestyle within the ward. Throughout the series, the element of risk and illicit nature of the poker games is presented as of a piece with the perilous world the mobsters inhabit.

An early episode of *Breaking Bad* (2008-13) called "Crazy Handful of Nothin'" uses a poker game to highlight the massive bluff high school chemistry teacher Walter White (Bryan Cranston) runs throughout the series. After being diagnosed with lung cancer, Walter uses equipment from the school's lab to create and sell crystallized methamphetamine in order to raise funds to provide for his family after his death. In the episode, Walter plays poker with his brother-in-law Hank, a DEA agent, who boasts over a hand of hold'em of an arrest he made that day all while having no clue of the crimes Walter is committing. In the hand Hank asks Walter questions with potential double-meanings ("You hiding something?"), then when Walter goes all in on the river with four hearts and two aces on the board, Hank calls him a "bad, horrible liar" before folding his ace-king for trip aces.[19] Walter wins the pot with seven-deuce and no heart, illustrating an ability to bluff he proves time and again away from the poker table.

Other recent crime shows fit murder plots into the context of televised tournament poker, such as in an episode of *Lie to Me* (2009-11) titled "Fold Equity." The show features experts in reading facial expressions and body language (i.e, in a poker context, "tells"), and in the episode the experts use those skills to analyze players at the final table of the "2009 Poker World Championship" after they become suspects in the murder of the coach of one of the players. Another example is "Last Woman Standing" from the long-running, franchise-launching series *CSI: Crime Series Investigation* (2000-15) in which players from the final table of the "1997 Palermo Poker Classic" (another WSOP-like event) are murdered one by one. It is all part of an elaborate revenge plot investigators connect back to cheating at that final table. The gruesome murders are all related to the five community cards dealt in a particular hand, in one case the playing card itself being used as a murder weapon.

TV Sitcoms

The situation comedy was another staple of early American television, with many shows featuring familiar, domestic settings that tended to reinforce "traditional" ideas of family life, including conventional roles for men and women. As noted, a frequent source of humor in the sitcoms of the 1950s and 1960s were scenarios in which the men's authority was momentarily challenged – when, say, the father in *Father Knows Best* (1954-60) actually *didn't* seem to know best. Even so, more often than not the established household hierarchy would be restored in time for the closing credits. As a popular recreation in particular among men, poker frequently turned up in such programs to instigate these good-natured conflicts between the sexes.

We've seen this pattern already in comedic films and radio programs in which the "masculine" setting of a poker game serves as a ready device to poke fun at traditional gender roles, if not to challenge them too seriously. The early TV comedy *I Love Lucy* (1951-57), starring Lucille Ball as Lucy and her real-life husband Desi Arnaz as Ricky Ricardo, was by far the most successful during the era. It often topped the first Nielsen ratings and was television's top-ranked show for four out of its seven years. *I Love Lucy* evolved from Ball's radio show *My Favorite Husband* with early shows adapting some of the same stories. One of the earliest episodes recreated the "Be a Pal" story in which Lucy follows a marriage expert's advice to take up her husband's hobbies, including poker. The scene (discussed in Chapter 18) is a riot, although hardly helps much with Lucy's dilemma as it only serves to make her husband angry with her before a rapidly-delivered kiss-and-make-up ending concludes the show. While played for laughs, poker nonetheless is presented here as wholly a "man's game," with the thought of a woman taking the seat at the table itself a source of comedy.[20]

The Honeymooners (1955-56) existed in several iterations as sketches on variety shows hosted by star Jackie Gleason before becoming a half-hour sitcom in its own right. Gleason portrayed a boisterous bus driver named Ralph Kramden living in a Brooklyn apartment with his wife Alice (Audrey Meadows). They frequently socialize with the neighboring couple upstairs, with the husbands-versus-wives dynamic serving as a recurring theme. As on *I Love Lucy* the game of poker is used as a kind of humorous conflict-creator between the men and women, and the men's efforts to get away from the women and play often became a parallel "game" in its own right. The men even belong to a lodge, the "Raccoon Lodge" or the "International Order of Friendly Sons of the Raccoons," which primarily serves as an excuse to escape from the women in order to play poker. In one episode ("A Dog's Life"), Ralph explains to Alice how he has to get over to the lodge for "another emergency meeting," and a suspicious Alice complains they just had an "emergency meeting" the night before.[21] One of the earlier extended sketches ("The Man in the Blue Suit," from 1952) similarly features Ralph playing poker without Alice's knowledge. The fact that he came away the big winner increases the urgency of not letting her find out and take away his earnings. Ralph hides the money in an old suit Alice subsequently gives away to a visitor from the Needy Society, sending Ralph on a wild chase to recover it. As it turns out, the man from the charity returned the money to Alice while Ralph was trying to get it back. That causes the episode to resolve into a kind of bluffing game between Ralph and Alice in which both know the other's "hand" but can't reveal that they do.

The Adventures of Ozzie and Harriet (1952-66) starred the real-life family of Ozzie Nelson, his wife Harriet, and their sons David and Ricky. The Nelsons presented a somewhat idealized version of a "typical" happy family, with poker again frequently coming up as a favorite entertainment of the men. One notable early episode featured guest star John Carradine joining the family in a reading of *Hamlet* before playing poker with Ozzie and others (and proving himself a surprising shark). The episode involves an attempt to extricate Ozzie from the family activity by neighbor Thorny (Don DeFore) who humorously champions poker as a preferable alternative to Elizabethan drama. "You're gonna miss out on a very interesting evening," Thorny says when Ozzie insists he has to honor his family obligation to read *Hamlet*. "Playing cards, jokes, laughs, good fellowship. You're not gonna let William Shakespeare come between you and culture, are you?"[22]

Later in "Harriet's Dancing Partner," Ozzie hosts a game, but soon finds his fun disturbed by a growing awareness that his poker-playing could perhaps be interpreted as his neglecting his wife. In another episode, "Hayride," Harriet and other wives organize a romantic outing, but Ozzie and the men are planning a Saturday night poker game. It starts as a seemingly minor disagreement, but the stakes get higher after it grows into a larger men-versus-women clash. A variation on the same idea occurs in "Rick and Kris Go to the Mountains" when son Ricky (now married) plans a poker game with his buddies at his in-laws' mountain cabin, but his wife Kris mistakenly thinks Rick is planning a vacation for the two of them, their first since the honeymoon. "He even gave up a poker game," Kris tells the Nelsons of the plans. "Sounds like you've got him trained pretty good there," says Ozzie.[23] As in all of these shows, the conflict is resolved without too much drama, though again the story positions poker as a cause for antagonism between the sexes.

An episode of *The Dick Van Dyke Show* (1961-66) titled "A Nice, Friendly Game of Cards" counters the trend by featuring Rob (Dick Van Dyke) and Laura Petrie (Mary Tyler Moore) hosting two other couples for a night of poker. As the episode title suggests, the social aspect of the game is promoted, with the choice to play poker described as "a good way of getting to know each other." Despite the penny-ante stakes, the men's competitiveness distinguish them from the women. "Don't take it so seriously, it's just a game," one of the ladies says, to which her husband replies "There's no other way to take it."[24] A marked deck Rob uses for magic tricks accidentally gets introduced into the game. When Rob coincidentally begins winning, the discovery of the accidental substitution threatens to make the game a lot less friendly, with the men (again) finding it all much more concerning than the women.

The general observation that poker provides an effective method to get to know others is more broadly relevant to the use of the game on TV sitcoms. Poker generally requires individuals to interact with one another, and thus a poker game is obviously a great way to introduce characters who tend not to change or develop very much from show to show. In sitcoms especially, conflicts tend to be resolved by the end of each episode, essentially returning the characters to where they were at the start. (Such resetting is useful for later syndication when the shows are often viewed out of sequence.) In a way, traditional TV sitcom series – that is, those made before the phenomenon of online viewing and "binge" watching – are themselves like weekly poker games featuring the same players over and again, with no one winning or losing *too* much and everyone always able to "stay in the game," so to speak.

The poker episode of *I Love Lucy* was only the second in the series, appearing when audiences were just getting to know Lucy and Ricky Ricardo. *The Odd Couple* (1970-75) television series (discussed in Chapter 9) similarly dived straight into the weekly poker game in the very first episode as part of a general strategy to introduce both the main characters and supporting cast. Such is typical of poker-themed sitcom episodes, with the game not only offering writers the chance to introduce numerous characters, but also to distinguish them by highlighting traits and features exaggerated by the setting.

For instance, poker games in early episodes of *Sanford and Son* (1972-77) helped flesh out characters and provide the backstory of the widower junk dealer Fred Sanford (Redd Foxx) and his son Lamont (Demond Wilson). In one called "The Card Sharps" Lamont wants to host a card game though Fred objects, citing his dead wife's description of a deck of cards as "fifty-two devils in Satan's army." The game goes on nonetheless, and when Fred correctly suspects one of the players is cheating, he manages to outhustle the hustlers with a marked deck of cards and some special sunglasses. Afterwards he paraphrases scripture: "Deal unto others as they have dealt unto you."[25] The episode fits well with others in which the pair engage in money-making schemes while attempting to better their situation. It also illustrates one of the show's recurring plot devices wherein the son doubts the father's acumen and decision-making abilities, but Fred ultimately proves himself more worldly and wise. Other poker-related episodes in the series included another early one called "The Kid" in which Fred plays with a 9-year-old boy from the neighborhood, and a later one titled "The Stung" featuring another poker night and another set of villains against whom Fred and Lamont must scheme.

The long-running series *M*A*S*H* (1972-83) about a medical unit during the Korean War also employed poker early on as a means to help introduce characters. Spun off from Robert Altman's 1970 film of the same title, the show in fact lasted many years longer than the Korean War itself, remaining popular right up until its farewell show, at the time the most watched television episode in history. Again showing the importance of poker to those serving in the military during wartime (discussed in Chapter

11), it's no surprise to find *M*A*S*H* making poker kind of a running motif.

The first season especially featured numerous poker games involving chief surgeon Hawkeye Pierce (played by Alan Alda, the actor whose name is sometimes used to refer to pocket aces), surgeon Trapper McIntyre (Wayne Rogers), Colonel Blake (McLean Stevenson), Corporal Klinger (Jamie Farr), and others. In the show's fifth episode ("The Moose"), a visiting sergeant arrives with a Korean girl servant he has improperly "bought." In order to restore the young woman's freedom, the men invite the sergeant to play in the poker game where – with a little help from Corporal Radar O'Reilly (Gary Burghoff) spying the sergeant's cards with a telescope and relaying the information – Hawkeye cleans him out, including having him give up the servant. In "The Long-John Flap," also from the first season, Trapper loses a much coveted pair of long johns to Radar in a poker game. And another first-season episode called "The Sticky Wicket" opens on a poker game in which a player has fallen asleep at the table with cards in his hand, with Hawkeye joking that he's been alternately losing and winning with the cards as the others continue.

The second-season episode "Deal Me Out" cleverly uses poker to highlight the chaotic nature of the mobile army surgical hospital, showing a game being constantly interrupted by various emergencies though amusingly remaining a high priority. Another titled "Payday" finds the men putting their paychecks in play, including the unit's chaplain, Father Mulcahy (William Christopher). Radar chimes in at the end asking if anyone wants to play Go Fish or Old Maid. In "The Novocaine Mutiny," Major Frank Burns (Larry Linville) is given temporary command of the unit and takes the opportunity to outlaw the poker game, a situation that swiftly escalates to his filing mutiny charges against Hawkeye. In "Lt. Radar O'Reilly," Burghoff achieves W.C. Fields-levels of hilarity as Radar chuckling and laughing as he draws a full house. "The Merchant of Korea" similarly deals with poker tells, when the group invite Major Charles Emerson Winchester III (David Ogden Stiers) to play while under the impression he's a novice. He spends several hours crushing them until the others figure out his whistling of classical melodies gets much louder whenever his hand is weak, a habit Captain B.J. Hunnicutt (Mike Farrell) calls "Rhapsody in Bluff."[26] Much as the show often dealt with wartime themes with grins rather than grief, the poker games on the show are usually played for laughs, although Hunnicutt does play some cutthroat five-card draw in a later episode, "Wheelers and Dealers." He stands pat on ace-high and successfully bluffs with a huge bet that includes his wedding ring. Finally, in "Your Hit Parade" the gang play the made-up game Double Cranko – a combination of checkers, chess, poker, and gin rummy in which the rules seem to change constantly according to players' whims ("Bishops are jacks!" "Checkers are wild!").[27]

Set in a Boston bar and featuring an ensemble cast, *Cheers* (1982-93) likewise used poker games to highlight character traits of cast members. A good example is found in the first-season episode "Pick a Con... Any Con" which presents a complicated plot centered on the character of the bartender Coach (Nicholas Colasanto). Coach's (alleged) friend George has hustled him out of thousands playing gin. With the help of the recurring character Harry (Harry Anderson), himself a con, the gang sets up a poker game with the hustler to try to get back what Coach has lost. In one hand Norm (George Wendt) moves to raise, saying "Lord hates a coward," but when someone suggests he's bluffing he instantly folds, confirming his character's general disinclination to leave his comfortable seat at the end of the bar and entertain risk. Ultimately the gang's plan works and they do recover Coach's money. During the game, the waitress Diane Chambers (Shelley Long), a newcomer to the group whose intellectual-mindedness often clashes with the less erudite bar patrons, raises an interesting question regarding the scheme. "Why *poker*?" she asks. "Why not crazy eights? Why not chess?" Her questions go unanswered, though it's obvious poker is a much preferred means to get back the money (not to mention further highlight characters' traits).[28] A later episode ("License to Hill") finds bartender Woody (Woody Harrelson) cleaning up in a game in which the contrast between his rural background and that of the Bostonians earns some laughs, especially when he suggests they play "Five Blind Piglets and One Full Teat."

Other ensemble comedies like *Hogan's Heroes* (1965-71) set in a German prisoner of war camp during the Second World War, *Taxi* (1978-83) featuring a group of cab drivers, and *Night Court* (1984-92) set in a Manhattan municipal courtroom similarly featured poker games that relocated characters from their typical environments in order to place them in different comic situations. Similarly latter-day family-based sitcoms used poker to pull the father temporarily outside of the familial context. For instance, in the show *Married...with Children* (1987-97), part of a wave of "dysfunctional family" TV comedies that appeared during the late 1980s and early 1990s, embattled shoe salesman Al Bundy (Ed O'Neill) is constantly mocked and disrespected by his wife and two children. A first-season episode titled "The Poker Game" shows Al earning some esteem in the only place he can when he wins $300 off his neighbor in a poker game. Al subsequently enjoys even more leverage over his neighbor when advising him how to lie to his wife about his poker losses. Similarly, during the original run of *Roseanne* (1988-97), a regular low-stakes game involving the father Dan (John Goodman) and his buddies served to connote both the family's blue-collar status and poker being the province of men, although for a couple of seasons the opening credit sequence showed the whole family playing poker for pretzels and marshmallows. (During the series' brief reboot in 2018 the poker game returned though with only women playing.)

Many popular sitcoms have featured special one-off "poker episodes," with the shows tending to serve one or more familiar purposes. The first season of *Friends* (1994-2004), which featured a cast of three single men and three single women, included what almost seems a requisite episode titled "The One With All the Poker." All six of the characters play multiple games, in which the men win repeatedly, and while Rachel (Jennifer Aniston) claims the last big pot from Ross (David Schwimmer), it is clear his crush on her has caused him to let her win. On an episode of *NewsRadio* (1995-99), the radio station's owner Jimmy James (Stephen Root) plays in an annual poker game with other station heads where he gambles away equipment and even staff members, part of the farcical character's detached and distracted form of leadership. When challenged about his authority to do so he reminds staff about the "act of God" clause in their contracts and the additional definition that "Jimmy James will hereafter and for the purposes of this contract only be referred to as God."[29] The third episode of *30 Rock* (2006-13), titled "Blind Date," similarly uses a poker game to define the relationship between arrogant network VP Jack Donaghy (Alec Baldwin) and the creators of the fictional TV show over whom he has authority. Donaghy crashes the staff's weekly poker game, gleefully upping the stakes and stating how he is "interested in seeing my new employees under that kind of pressure."[30] The boss is also the butt of the joke in an episode of the American version of the workplace comedy *The Office* (2005-13) called "Casino Night" in which the cast play a variety of games with each other, including poker. Along the way the always inept Regional Manager Michael Scott (Steve Carrell) loses miserably at the table, afterwards repurposing poker pro Phil Hellmuth's famous line, "If luck weren't involved, I would always be winning."[31]

Other modern TV sitcoms incorporate poker more meaningfully into the "situation" that helps enable the "comedy." For example, in *The Bernie Mac Show* (2001-06) the stand-up comedian plays a reluctant father figure, having been thrust into the role when he and his wife agree to take care of Bernie's sister's children while she goes through drug rehab. There his regular poker games with the guys provides an important vestige of the life from which he's had to step away. Similarly, *My Boys* (2006-10) presents a female sportswriter who finds herself constantly surrounded by men both at work and otherwise, a circumstance that ironically negatively impacts her dating life. In that case, the character's participation as the only woman in a regular poker game with the guys helps demonstrate her unique status relative to the opposite sex.

In such shows, poker provides an integral, ongoing context for characters' interactions and the development of larger themes. More often in TV sitcoms, though, a game of cards works as an occasional, efficient way to bring in conflicts and allow audiences to get to know unfamiliar characters – as though inviting them to a seat at the table with the cast.

Actual Poker on TV

During the early 1970s, Dean Martin had his "Rat Pack" pal Joey Bishop as a guest on his variety program, *The Dean Martin Show*, and the pair performed a skit called "The Bar." Sitting at a table, Bishop invites Martin over to play some "imaginary poker." Bishop explains his wife made him promise not to gamble, leading him to devise this new way of enjoying the game with imaginary cards, chips, and money. They play a couple of fun hands, raising each other unmercifully and "showing down" royal flushes.

Until then practically all of the poker shown on American television had also been "imaginary," so to speak, featuring only within the context of fictional programs. That would begin to change, however, thanks in large part to the promotional efforts of Thomas "Amarillo Slim" Preston following his victory in the 1972 World Series of Poker Main Event. On June 16, 1972, a month after his victory, Preston was invited to appear on *The Tonight Show with Johnny Carson*. By then Carson had hosted the popular late-night talk show for a decade, increasing its audience considerably thanks largely to his amiable personality, quick-wittedness, and a special capacity for steering clear of the spotlight to let his guests shine. It was a perfect fit for the gregarious Preston, dressed in colored suits and cowboy boots with a wide-brimmed, ten-gallon Stetson as though he were an Old West gambler stepping out of the 1870s into 1970s living rooms.

Preston's homespun one-liners and anecdotes about various prop bets got him invited back on *The Tonight Show* again in August and multiple times thereafter. Meanwhile the "Amarillo Slim" Preston publicity tour continued elsewhere on America's television screens, with a profile on *60 Minutes*, guest spots on more talk shows including *Good Morning America*, *The Mike Douglas Show*, and *The Tomorrow Show* (along with Benny Binion), as well as appearances on several game shows such as *I've Got a Secret*, *To Tell the Truth*, and *What's My Line?* As Preston later explained it, while such efforts were no doubt self-serving, he saw himself as helping Binion and "several other casino owners [who] asked me to help change the image of poker." He concluded: "I became sort of a touring ambassador for the sport."[32]

Preston's spot on the revived version of *I've Got a Secret* in early August 1972 is meaningful in the way it reveals what was then a very modest status for poker and high-stakes players in American culture. Following the show's format, Preston appeared as a guest with celebrities asking him questions in order to guess his secret, which in his case was having once lost $190,000 in a single night of poker. The panelists (Alan Alda, Betty White, Richard Dawson, and Pat Carroll) are unable to discover Preston's secret, with his clothing and hat causing them to wonder if he might be a western singer or perhaps someone working with the rodeo. When his secret is revealed, host Steve Allen reports how Preston had recently won the World Series of Poker – that, too, being largely a "secret" insofar as few then were aware of the WSOP at all. During a short interview after the guessing game, Preston's status as a high-stakes poker player proves intriguing, and Allen asks him how it came to be that a player who could win the WSOP could also lose such a large sum at the tables. "Occasionally the lamb slaughters the butcher, you know?" Preston replies, earning laughter and applause.[33]

In retrospect, one can regard Preston as engaging in what was then a nascent effort to "normalize" poker for mass audiences, presenting the full-time poker player as a legitimate (if novel) occupation. Sports commentator and Las Vegas bookmaker Jimmy "the Greek" Snyder also took up the cause a year later when he helped arrange for CBS to broadcast an hour-long documentary of the 1973 WSOP Main Event. The program aired during the *CBS Sports Spectacular*, a sports anthology program that often featured less frequently covered sports like track and field, gymnastics, bowling, fishing, and the like. Narrated by Snyder, the show delves into the players' personalities with Preston among those featured, explaining along the way the logistics of no-limit hold'em and tournament poker so an audience unfamiliar with the game might be able to follow the action. Snyder's commentary shapes the contest as a sporting event, with boxing the most-employed analogy as he describes the competitors as vying to earn the "pride and prestige of a heavyweight king" and the spectators as unwilling to give up a "ringside seat" to watch.[34] The show culminates with Puggy Pearson's victory over Johnny Moss for the winner-take-all $130,000 first prize.

While the show was compelling to those with an interest in poker (and in retrospect fascinating to see in light of what the WSOP would later become), CBS declined to air any other WSOP coverage over the next five years. Meanwhile as the WSOP continued its slow growth the daytime talk show *The Merv Griffin Show* devoted an entire 90-minute program in January 1976 to poker and the WSOP. Binion appeared alongside Johnny Moss, Jack Straus, and actor Jack Klugman (the poker-playing star of TV's *The Odd Couple*), with sleight-of-hand artist John Scarne joining for some card tricks as well.[35]

An episode of The Merv Griffin Show from January 1976 featuring Jack Klugman, Benny Binion, Merv Griffin, Jack Straus, Johnny Moss

CBS later tried again with the WSOP, when Snyder once more co-hosted half-hour programs in 1978 with Brent Musberger and in 1979 with Frank Glieber (both sportscasters). Then during the early 1980s ABC attempted something similar with famed sportscaster Curt Gowdy hosting WSOP specials on a couple of occasions before the network abandoned the idea. In their history of the WSOP, Jonathan Grotenstein and Storms Reback note how all of the major American networks (as well as one from Canada and another independent network) were on hand to cover the Main Event in 1983, but an especially long final table "strained not only their patience, but their budgets, as they had to pay overtime to their crews."[36] Perhaps as a result, several years passed before the WSOP was televised again, this time by ESPN.

The cable sports network aired its first edited, one-hour shows about the WSOP Main Event in 1988, continuing to do so nearly every year for

Poker & Pop Culture

the next decade. Sportscaster Chris Marlowe, tournament director Jim Albrecht, and poker-playing actors Dick Van Patten and Gabe Kaplan served as commentators. From 1999 to 2001, WSOP Main Event specials were aired on the Discovery Channel, with ESPN coming back in 2002 to create a two-hour show hosted by sportscaster Lon McEachern alongside Kaplan. However such examples of televised poker were only occasional, a small slice of programming coming once per year (if that) and tucked away amid other shows on cable networks to which not every American home even subscribed.

During the 2002 final table broadcast, Kaplan was prescient when drawing an analogy between the poker game being shown and the relatively new phenomenon of "reality TV." Referencing the highest-rated show on TV at the time, Kaplan tells his co-host McEachern: "This is *Survivor* with cards, Lon. Someone is going to stay on the island and someone is going to leave very soon."[37] That 2002 broadcast was forward-looking in another way, too. It revived an earlier experiment of revealing the players' cards *before* the showdown, albeit via after-the-fact editing. Doing so enabled viewers to follow the action more effectively and to create genuine suspense via the dramatic irony of the audience possessing information the players did not.[38]

The result simulated in a less immediate way the "under-the-table" hole card camera that had already been employed to great effect on the groundbreaking U.K. show *Late Night Poker* (1999-2002). Producer Rob Gardner and Nic Szeremeta had together conceived the idea to film a made-for-television poker tournament, with satellites ensuring some variety among the players – i.e., a well-known professional, a woman, a foreigner, a player who would "who would create either action or trouble," and so on.[39] The tournament was shot and re-edited, with Jesse May and Szeremeta's commentary helping add to the game's drama, as did the considerable charisma and adroitness of the first season's winner, the stylish David "Devilfish" Ulliott. Despite airing after midnight on Channel 4 (whose viewing share was then far below the leading networks), viewership rose during the first season from 16 percent of viewers to 30 percent by the end. According to Szeremeta, an incredible 1.7 million viewers tuned in for the final show.[40]

Nowhere near that many watched the WSOP on ESPN in 2002, but everything changed the following year, thanks both to a new approach adopted by the network in its coverage and the emergence of another, equally popular televised poker series featuring final tables from the new World Poker Tour. Beginning March 30, 2003, the Travel Channel aired a two-hour show in prime time every Wednesday night, each of which culminated with the tournament's winner taking away a six-figure first prize.

Winners often took away more than half a million and in the case of the season-culminating championship a $1 million-plus prize.

The shows were directed by Steve Lipscomb who had previously created the Discovery Channel WSOP shows and who co-founded the WPT with poker player Lyle Berman. Unlike the earlier documentary-like shows, the new WPT programs more closely followed the model of *Late Night Poker* with clever editing, enthusiastic commentary from Mike Sexton and Vince Van Patten, and the showing of player's hole cards, this time with a new "lipstick" camera for which toy inventor and poker player Henry Orenstein had obtained a patent. Players squeezed their cards in front of tiny lenses fitted around the sides of the table in order to give viewers a glimpse of what they were playing. Such technology plus the ability to spend eight months selecting and editing hands ("Working ten to fifteen hours a day, seven days a week," reports Lipscomb[41]) meant not having to deal with many of the challenges faced by the makers of *The Billy Rose Show* a half-century before. Unlike earlier poker on American TV, these shows were watched by significant audiences, with the season finale in late June 2003 attracting more than a million viewers. Repeats thereafter drew even larger audiences, making it the most-watched series in the fledgling Travel Channel's history.[42]

While the WPT shows were first airing, a Tennessee accountant and amateur poker player with the too-good-to-be-true name of Chris Moneymaker was winning the 2003 WSOP Main Event, topping a record field of 839 players to win a $2.5 million first prize. Like "Amarillo Slim" Preston three decades before, Moneymaker was a guest on a late night talk show a few weeks after his victory, appearing for a short segment on *Late Night with David Letterman* on June 10, 2003. As was the case with Preston, however, relatively few viewers then knew anything at all about Moneymaker or the WSOP, with most no doubt having stayed up to see the show's other guest that night, actor Bruce Willis.

Those circumstances would change, however, once ESPN began airing weekly one-hour shows presenting an edited version of the WSOP Main Event over seven weeks starting on July 15, 2003. With commentary from McEachern and sports columnist and poker player Norman Chad and (importantly) the use of hole card cameras,[43] the programs began with early action from the five-day tournament, thereby documenting Moneymaker's unexpected journey to the title almost the entire way. While his name had initially piqued the attention of ESPN producers looking for potential storylines to follow, Moneymaker also drew a seat at the table of two-time WSOP Main Event champion Johnny Chan to start Day 2. That fortuitous seat assignment ensured Moneymaker was followed on that day, and his surprise elimination of Chan – "like Buster Douglas knocking out Mike Ty-

ESPN commentators Lon McEachern and Norman Chad at the World Series of Poker

son," according to Chad – ensured ESPN tracked him thereafter. On August 26 the exciting final table was aired, ending with the novice Moneymaker heads-up versus seasoned poker pro Sam Farha. A table-talker with Devil-fish-like allure, the finely dressed and tanned Farha with slicked-back hair and unlit cigarette dangling from a Cheshire cat grin could not have provided a more stark contrast to the close-mouthed, baseball-cap wearing Money-maker hiding behind mirrored sunglasses. That Moneymaker managed to pull off a bold bluff against Farha in a key heads-up hand only supplemented fur-ther the David-versus-Goliath narrative ending with his surprising triumph.

The original shows averaged nearly a million viewers each week, peak-ing at 1.67 million for the finale.[44] Almost all who watched were unaware beforehand Moneymaker had won, thus aligning the viewing experience very closely with "reality" shows like *Survivor* and *American Idol* (for which audiences also increased steadily until each season's finale). And as the Travel Channel was discovering with its repeats of WPT shows, ESPN soon realized viewership hardly declined at all when the WSOP shows were re-aired across its several networks, becoming an inexpensive way for the network to fill one-hour gaps in programming while guaranteeing ratings.[45]

Such success rapidly inspired what would become a new subgenre of game-show styled reality television as so-called "poker programming" began to appear up and down the channel listings. By the end of the year the WPT was already producing new content with a special "Ladies Night" show and a "Hollywood Home Game" in anticipation of starting its second season. For Thanksgiving 2003, Fox Sports Net aired six back-to-back episodes of "Showdown at the Sands," another made-for-TV event. In early December the Bravo Network debuted *Celebrity Poker Showdown* featuring entertainment stars playing one-table tournaments, with more than 1.5 million tuning in for the premiere and 1.7 million watching the finale in January – a total exceeding the viewership of the initial 2003 WSOP Main Event broadcast.[46]

On February 1, 2004 while the Super Bowl pregame aired on CBS, NBC chose to show as counter-programming the two-hour "Battle of Champions" in which Season 1 winners of the WPT competed for a $250,000 prize pool and retired Air Force captain Ron Rose beat out several poker pros for the title. Soon a deluge of made-for-TV poker tournament shows appeared such as the *Poker Superstars Invitational Tournament* (Fox Sports Net), *Poker Royale* (Game Show Network), the *National Heads-Up Poker Championship* (NBC), and the *Ultimate Poker Challenge* (syndication), along with cash game shows like *Poker After Dark* (NBC) and *High Stakes Poker* (Game Show Network).

Another consequence of poker programming was the creation of a new kind of pop culture persona, the "poker celebrity." Any player who appeared frequently on such shows became a recognizable figure, by default also becoming the same sort of "ambassador" "Amarillo Slim" Preston saw himself as before. Thanks largely to the efforts of the shows' producers to create compelling narratives (and in some cases players' own desires to self-promote), the most famous players almost resembled characters in an ongoing drama, each fulfilling specific roles sometimes suggested by memorable nicknames like "Kid Poker" (Daniel Negreanu), "The Professor" (Howard Lederer), "The Magician" (Antonio Esfandiari), "The Grinder" (Mike Mizrachi), "Jesus" (Chris Ferguson), "The Prince of Poker" (Scotty Nguyen), "The Robin Hood of Poker" (Barry Greenstein), "The Orient Express" (Johnny Chan), "The Great Dane" (Gus Hansen), "The Mouth" (Mike Matusow), and the "Poker Brat" (Phil Hellmuth). Along with Moneymaker – whose given name precluded the need for a descriptive moniker – these players and others such as Doyle Brunson, Phil Ivey, Erik Seidel, Annie Duke, and Jennifer Harman were promoted to a status resembling that of famous athletes, suddenly conspicuous among the cultural landscape as emissaries demonstrating poker to be not just a game of skill, but a genuinely entertaining "spectator sport" as well.

One could argue (and some did) that much "actual poker" shown on television during the mid-2000s and afterwards in fact contained elements of fiction – that like "reality TV" there was enough editing and manipulation of the story to carry what was shown beyond the scope of what some believed "real" poker to be. Author and 1983 WSOP champion Tom McEvoy once described tournament poker as "hours of boredom and moments of sheer terror"[47] but by necessity, the new poker programming excised the boredom and highlighted the terror. It edited out less exciting, small-pot hands and focused instead on dramatic preflop all-ins. As a result, the shows often gave the impression of tournament poker being much more consistently exciting than is actually the case – in other words, not unlike how other, fictional TV shows often portrayed the game. For those making such an argument, the fact that some of the most popular poker shows featured actors playing the games (and demonstrating wildly varying degrees of skill when they did) further supported their case that much poker shown on TV was not "real."

There was, of course, one other important factor helping to increase the popularity of these shows – in fact, another variety of poker also viewed with disdain by poker purists, though one making it easier than ever for Americans at home to jump in and try the game themselves.

These were now the days of online poker.

21 Poker on the Computer

In the 2012 documentary *All In: The Poker Movie*, historian Doris Kearns Goodwin notes that the rapid increase in popularity of televised poker in the mid-2000s helped foster a wider sense of kinship among all poker players. "When a game is shared on television, especially something like poker, then people feel when they are playing themselves in their own communities, that they are part of some larger network that's also magically playing all across the country, and they are part of some national phenomenon instead of just themselves," Goodwin says.

During the years that poker emerged as a "spectator sport," another phenomenon was taking place that enabled poker players to think of themselves participating in one big communal game. Many of those watching those poker shows were also playing poker – some for the first time – on

Poker & Pop Culture

their computers for real money and against opponents from around the world. In other words, Goodwin's idea of poker players feeling as though they belonged to a "larger network" when watching others play poker on television wasn't just being imagined or "magically" occurring. It literally was taking place thanks to the advent of online poker, a truly global phenomenon to which players in the United States contributed significantly from its inception in the late 1990s until early 2011.

Poker-Playing Programs

The story of poker being played on a computer begins several years before. In 1961, computer science educator Nicholas V. Findler revealed that he had been working on a project to develop a poker-playing computer program, publishing his progress to a small audience of readers of an "electronic computers" journal. As represented in part by a somewhat involved flowchart, Findler expressed confidence at being able "to have the machine adapt itself to the character of the opponent" while also employing a random number generator to help obscure its own patterns.[1]

Over the next two decades Findler continued to pursue the idea with his students while publishing further progress reports. In a 1978 article for *Scientific American*, Findler described his progress to a wider audience (again with some complicated decision trees and other formulas) in an article titled "Computer Poker." There Findler expressed confidence that "computer programs can model the human approach to decision-making" to such an extent that it might one day be possible that humans playing poker against such programs would not be able to tell if their opponent was another human or a computer. In fact, even then Findler believed that in experiments in which "a human player is seated at a computer terminal and... asked to play poker against a number of opponents," that unless the human was especially versed in the programs and also an experienced poker player, "he will not be able to differentiate between machine and man in a statistically significant number of cases."[2]

Findler's work heralded that of others who similarly attempted to create poker-playing programs, including poker player and author Mike Caro. Using an Apple II computer and programming in Pascal, Caro spent two years in the early 1980s creating a program first to play fixed limit hold'em, then the no-limit version of the game, calling the program "ORAC" (his own name spelled backward). ORAC was made public at the 1984 World Series of Poker where games were staged between a computer running the program and WSOP Main Event winners Tom McEvoy and Doyle Brunson, earning coverage in several national magazines. Another match between ORAC and casino owner Bob Stupak was staged at Vegas World (later the Stratosphere) with half a million dollars on the line. The match was televised nationally on the ABC show *Ripley's Believe It or Not*, with Stupak winning (albeit aided by a mid-match computer crash).[3]

Academics continued with similar programming efforts over subsequent decades, with the creation of increasingly sophisticated and nuanced computer "players" paralleling advances in machine learning and artificial intelligence. In 2007, a competition dubbed the "First Man-Machine Poker Championship" took place at an annual meeting of the Association for the Advancement of Artificial Intelligence in Vancouver, Canada. It was a heads-up, fixed-limit hold'em match pitting professional poker players Phil Laak and Ali Eslami against Polaris, a poker-playing program created by the Computer Poker Research Group at the University of Alberta's Department of Computing Science. The humans won that round, but a year later a second match was staged at the 2008 World Series of Poker between Polaris 2.0 and another team of four poker pros in which the computer won. That breakthrough earned notice in several national, non-academic publications, including *Wired*, which ran a graphic novel-like spread to share the news ("Ante Up, Human: The Adventures of Polaris, the Poker-Playing Robot").[4] Jonathan Schaeffer, the chair of Alberta's Computer Science department, predicted: "One of these days – within 5 to 10 years – two-person, limit hold'em will be solved."[5] Ahead of schedule and with a new poker-playing "bot" called Cepheus, the Alberta team announced in a publication of their research in 2015 that "heads-up limit hold'em is solved."[6]

Among other teams working in a similar vein was one at Carnegie Mellon University who in 2015 saw its program Claudico lose a two-week long no-limit hold'em match against human opponents. Then in January 2017, another 20-day NLHE match was staged between four poker pros and a new CMU program called Libratus. The AI won handily thanks in part to the program's greater success both at bluffing and sussing out the humans' attempts to bluff. While stopping short of claiming no-limit hold'em to be "solved," the professor of computer science Tuomas Sandholm, who co-created Libratus with doctoral student Noam Brown, described the win as indicating an important advance for AI. "The best AI's ability to do strategic reasoning with imperfect information has now surpassed that of the best humans," Sandholm said, adding how Libratus' algorithm for problem solving "can be used in any situation where information is incomplete, including business negotiation, military strategy, cyber security and medical treatment."[7]

Such research applications remind us of something already demonstrated in our survey – namely, poker's relevance to multiple areas of American culture. We have seen the game's strategy compared with and even applied in the worlds of high finance, politics, and warfare. By contributing to the progress of AI research, the achievements of those developing such poker-playing programs will have enormous relevance to life in the 21st

Electronic draw poker machines at the Stardust Resort and Casino, Las Vegas (ca. mid-1970s)

century. Even so, their accomplishments have yet to earn much notice in mainstream America, mostly limited to articles passed around social media with titles like "Time to Fold, Humans: Poker-Playing AI Beats Pros at Texas Hold'em."[8] Meanwhile for the majority of Americans – depending on their age – the idea of playing poker on a computer came initially via "video poker" machines first developed in the late 1970s, by rudimentary games designed for home computers during the 1980s and 1990s, or by online poker in the 2000s and after.

Video Poker, Home Computers, and Game Consoles

A businessman from Mississippi with a background in pinball machines and jukeboxes named William "Si" Redd moved to Nevada in the late 1960s to work with the Bally Distributing Company. By the mid-1970s Redd had founded his own company, and with the involvement of engineers such as Logan Pease (whose background included elevator safety) oversaw the development of "Keno" and "Twenty-One" machines that utilized a TV-like screen with a computer processing unit inside, essentially built from already obsolete Pong machines.

A video poker machine

From those early units came the first video poker machines, a revolutionary development for Nevada casinos upon their introduction in 1979. The games proved so popular that the upright machines were soon supplemented by "bartop" models that took up even less valuable floor space.[9] "The person could sit there while he's drinking, deposit his quarters or dollars, have his fun, and if he did win the money, it would come shooting right out into a pan while he was sitting there," Redd reflected. "The poker was just sensational. People would play it that don't play slot machines."[10]

Unlike actual poker or poker played against computer opponents, video poker is a single-player game in which the player is dealt a five-card poker hand, selects cards to discard in order to draw new ones, then either loses or earns a payout linked to hand rankings. The rarest hands like royal flushes or four of a kind yield the highest returns. Video poker rewards those with an understanding of poker probabilities who know which cards to keep and which to toss away, making the games attractive to poker players otherwise disinclined to gamble on slots. It also enables those who enjoy home poker games but are intimidated to play in casinos or clubs to play a version of the game that does not require interacting with others. The same factor also later proved meaningful to the growth of online poker.

Also part of the story of people playing poker on the computer were games developed for early home computers and home video game consoles, all of which tended to run (often simple) card games with bitmapped graphics. Owners of the original Atari VCS (later the Atari 2600) who picked up the "Casino" cartridge could play either five-card stud or poker solitaire, games that were also available on the "Poker Plus" cartridge. Those who bought the competing Intellivision system, which appeared in 1979, received "Las Vegas Poker & Blackjack" for free, which meant nearly 2 million copies of the game were distributed over the next few years. The game included both five- and seven-card stud as well as seven-card draw, and featured an animated dealer-opponent with black dots for eyes that shifted back and forth and facial expressions reacting to wins and losses.

While "Space Invaders" and "Asteroids" were of greater interest to younger players, the card games attracted older players otherwise uninterested in arcade games. The Apple II's "Draw Poker" game, introduced in 1981, enabled users to play against two types of computer opponents, Player A ("Very consistent and deliberate player") and Player B ("A bit more caprecious [sic]––was known to bluff once"). In response to the mostly older male demographic to whom new home computers largely appealed, crude strip poker games were also developed and sold for practically every platform. The first, Artworx's "Strip Poker" for the Apple II, appeared in 1982, followed by versions for the Commodore 64, Atari, and other systems.

Though essentially made for entertainment purposes, such early poker-playing programs prefigured later, more sophisticated software developed and marketed during the 1990s and 2000s. These games included the Wilson Turbo Series, which offered genuine educational value. The games' popularity also parallels that of more recent free-to-play offerings for mobile devices such as Zynga Poker, a game that by 2010 was being played by 37 million players worldwide each month.[11]

Poker Over the Internet

The 1983 film *WarGames*, in which a teen hacks into a NORAD supercomputer and unwittingly brings the U.S. to the brink of World War III, includes a nod to such early computer games. Poker appears along with bridge, chess, and checkers as games the hacker passes over in order to play the more intriguing Global Thermonuclear War.

The film not only captured burgeoning interest in video games and technology, but also introduced to many the concept of a network of computers able to communicate with one another. Though hardly mainstream, by then text-based communication via modems had been developed and employed for several years, with early adopters participating in discussion groups like Usenet and playing text-based "MUD" (Multi-User Dungeon) role-player games against one another. As the internet continued to develop, the first internet chat network, Internet Relay Chat (IRC), went online in 1988. IRC not only allowed users to communicate with one another via instant messages passed from their computers through a third-party server, but also made it possible for users to write and execute their own scripts within the program. Then by the early 1990s came the first commercial dial-up internet service providers, the first web pages, and soon the first graphical browsers and web-based email services.

In 1994, a researcher at Carnegie Mellon University's School of Computer Science named Todd Mummert, along with colleague and code-writer Greg Reynolds, created a program that enabled IRC users to play poker against one another. Upon connecting to the poker server, users could join different "channels" each of which offered a unique poker variant, including many types of stud, draw, hold'em, and Omaha games plus a few others, as well as rudimentary tournaments. Users received 1,000 chips per day, and were able to play hands against others by entering commands ("check," "bet," "call," "raise [amount]," "fold," etc.).

Even though the games did not involve real money but rather "etherbucks" or play chips, the quality of play was reportedly quite high. An updated leader board helped keep things competitive, and the games were also primarily populated by skilled players already part of early online strategy discussion groups, in particular the Usenet newsgroup rec.gambling.

poker.[12] "The participants in these games were mostly computer geeks with a passion for poker," recalls Michael Maurer, author of a program that logged more than 10 million IRC poker hands played through 2001. "Many were serious students of the game, armed with the analytical skills needed to understand the mathematics, and all other aspects of advanced poker strategy."[13] One IRC poker player was Chris Ferguson, a computer science Ph.D. who went on to win the 2000 World Series of Poker Main Event. Games were played at various "stakes," with players needing a minimum number of chips to graduate from fixed-limit to no-limit, dubbed "Hold'em Hell" (the limit games where those with fewer chips were "banished") and "No-Limit Heaven" (the NL games where those with larger "bankrolls" could play).[14]

Though intriguing to some, these developments primarily took place on the far edges of American culture, essentially unknown to most. Even within the poker community, only a small percentage of ardent enthusiasts were even aware of the possibility of playing poker on the computer against other human opponents. That situation, however, was soon to change.

The First Online Poker Sites

In early 1995, an astronomer and educator named Clifford Stoll wrote what would turn out to be his most referenced article. Published in *Newsweek*, the one-page piece shared the central argument of his forthcoming book, *Silicon Snake Oil*, namely, that the still nascent "Internet" wasn't nearly as impressive or potentially significant as Stoll's contemporaries were making it out to be.

While others excitedly described the many ways the new World Wide Web would soon impact education, government, business, the media, and other areas of everyday life, Stoll was having none of it. "Baloney," he wrote. "Do our computer pundits lack all common sense?" Among Stoll's many howlers that have since been rendered hilarious are his comments about "cyberbusiness" and its future prospects. "Even if there were a trustworthy way to send money over the Internet – which there isn't – the network is missing a most essential ingredient of capitalism: salespeople." Indeed, informing just about all of Stoll's cynicism is the impersonal nature of online communication. "What's missing from this electronic wonderland?" he asks. "Human contact."[15]

Though decidedly against the grain at the time, Stoll wasn't the only one skeptical about the willingness of consumers to send real funds from their bank accounts to online merchants. Nor were his thoughts regarding the relative lack of human interaction available online without justification. However, when it came to the early days of online poker, those taking part were not inhibited too greatly by the prospect of electronically delivering cash to the sites in order to play the games. Nor were players much bothered by the relative lack of social interaction online games offered when compared with live poker – in fact, for many, that aspect proved a positive.

The same year as Stoll's article, both Amazon and eBay launched what would prove to be hugely popular online marketplaces, followed soon after by the mainstreaming of online banking as well as the introduction of third-party payment service sites like PayPal (1998), Neteller (1999), and Moneybookers (2001). As American consumers swiftly became comfortable using their credit cards to make purchases online, so, too, did gamblers begin to find and make use of the many so-called "offshore" sports betting sites and online casinos that began to appear. Over the course of 1997 alone the number of such sites ballooned from around a dozen to more than 100, with one research firm determining that after earning less than $100 million in 1996, "Internet gambling industry's revenues grew from $445.5 million in 1997 to $919.1 million in 1998."[16]

Such rapid expansion drew the attention of news reporters who, during the summer of 1997, wrote about American gamblers willing not only to risk betting on the outcomes of sporting events but also to hazard uncertainty surrounding sending funds to gambling sites hosted by operators located on Caribbean islands, in Central America and Europe, in Native American territories in Canada, and elsewhere (e.g., "Wagering on Web is risky business").[17] It also drew the attention of lawmakers, including U.S. senators of both parties who that year jointly introduced a bill called the "Internet Gambling Prohibition Act of 1997" designed to prohibit Americans from placing bets on the sites and to require internet service providers to block their access. (More on such legislative efforts next chapter.) In other words, much as was the case in early 19th century America when poker was first introduced into an environment already saturated with suspicions about gambling and a lack of legal clarity, so, too, were the first real money online poker games played by Americans contested in an especially ambiguous and uncertain context.

In late 1997 a systems engineer from Alberta with a background working for the Royal Canadian Navy named Randy Blumer launched a site called Planet Poker. With servers located in Costa Rica running software written by a programmer from Atlanta, the site initially offered play money games, then on January 1, 1998 began spreading real money games, starting only with $3/$6 limit hold'em with a $30 minimum buy-in. Owing to slow dial-up connections, graphics were kept simple with an overhead shot of the table surrounded by players' avatars and minimal animation. Even so, the appeal to some was immediate and significant. "Straight out of the gate, you could see this was going to be the crack cocaine of gambling," Blumer

Lobby for the first online poker site, Planet Poker

recalled. "Some players were playing 10 to 12 hours straight even before we converted to real money."[18]

Players initially had to mail in checks to deposit to their accounts, with credit cards only accepted after a few months. Despite frequent site outages and player disconnections, soon tables were running around the clock. Higher limit games were added, though the increased volume made crashes even more common. The site suffered another setback when it was discovered the random number generator being used by the software was flawed in a way that caused it to produce considerably fewer combinations of dealt cards than it should. The error was corrected, and thanks largely to Planet Poker being the only (virtual) game in town, the site continued to grow over the next year-and-a-half.

Competition arose, however, to push Planet Poker to the online poker periphery. Paradise Poker, launched in 1999 by another Canadian group, featured better, smoother-running software with visually-appealing animation. Offering even higher-stakes games and non-hold'em variants (though still limit only), Paradise soon eclipsed Planet to take over the majority of the still-modest online poker market. Another site called Poker-Spot, based in Antigua and launched by California poker pro Dutch Boyd, became popular thanks in part to introducing multi-table tournaments as an option for online players. However, problems with a credit card processor led to the site operating for an extended period without funds on hand, eventually leading to PokerSpot's shutdown in 2001 with many of the site's players reportedly losing hundreds of thousands of dollars.

A chapter on "Computers, Casinos, and Cardrooms" included in the 2000 title *Poker for Dummies* foresaw just such a possibility. Alerting readers to the fact that playing poker for real money online put them in "a gray area of the law," the chapter's author Kathleen K. Watterson noted: "If an overseas-based casino goes bankrupt, you could lose any money you have on account without recourse." She advises keeping no more on the sites that a player could afford to lose while also encouraging them to check rec. gambling.poker to find out which sites players recommended as trustworthy. Watterson also recommends players "be alert for collusion" occurring among their opponents while acknowledging many players (especially less experienced ones) might have trouble detecting "unusual betting patterns" indicating something might be amiss.[19]

The games nonetheless continued, and continued to grow. Player pools swelled, funneling increased rake into the online rooms' coffers. And as Americans soon discovered, there would be no lack of the "salespeople" Stoll described as essential to capitalism turning up to help encourage more poker players to open accounts and join the fun.

Explosion

Dozens of online poker sites appeared during the early 2000s, with UltimateBet (2000), PartyPoker (2001), PokerStars (2001), Pacific Poker, soon rebranded as 888 Poker (2002), Absolute Poker (2003), Bodog (2004), and Full Tilt Poker (2004) eventually emerging as the industry's major players. High-functioning, improved software and faster connection speeds considerably increased traffic at all of them, as did a wide variety of cash game and tournament options at stakes ranging from the "micros" to the "nosebleeds." Most significantly, a variety of easy-to-use options for depositing and withdrawing funds emerged to help make each of these sites – all owned and operated by companies located outside of the U.S. – ready options for American poker players seeking to play online.

The complicated stories of these sites' histories could each fill books of their own. An early chapter in the story of PokerStars would tell how Chris Moneymaker, playing under the username "Money800," entered an $86 satellite on the site, winning entry into another $650 buy-in satellite in which the top three finishers would receive packages to play in the 2003 World Series of Poker Main Event starting one month later.[20] That the amateur player indeed earned his Main Event seat there, then went on to win the $2.5 million Main Event first prize not only helped spark the ensuing poker boom, it also brought attention to online poker as a place where others might follow his remarkable path to become moneymakers themselves.

The story would proceed from there to relate how the 2004 WSOP Main Event winner, a patent attorney lawyer named Greg Raymer, also won his entry via PokerStars, and how a former chiropractor named Joe Hachem who won the Main Event in 2005 likewise became a "sponsored pro" for the site. With other online poker sites also providing satellite entries into the WSOP Main Event, the number of entries skyrocketed from 839 the year Moneymaker won to 2,576 in 2004, 5,619 in 2005, and 8,773 in 2006 when a Hollywood talent agent named Jamie Gold won the $12 million first prize. On his way to victory, Gold sported a baseball cap with the Bodog logo, one of five different online poker rooms represented at the final table as sites routinely "patched up" players to represent them when playing in all televised events. Full Tilt Poker assembled a large team of sponsored pros against whom players could regularly play, part of the site's successful "Learn, Chat, and Play with the Pros" promotional campaign. Among those representing Full Tilt were some of the most seen players on American television, including Phil Ivey, Howard Lederer, and Chris Ferguson, while UltimateBet was represented by similarly well-known players Annie Duke, Phil Hellmuth, Antonio Esfandiari and others.

Meanwhile PartyPoker remained the most popular online poker site around the world and among American players, its profile significantly enhanced through frequent television commercials on the World Poker Tour starting with the show's 2003 debut. Pro player Mike Sexton, who co-hosted the WPT shows and who was an original spokesperson and co-owner of PartyPoker, recalls how within a month of the PartyPoker commercials airing "we multiplied our business by 10 and never looked back... becom[ing] the number one online poker site in the world – due primarily to those TV ads."[21] By June 2005, PartyPoker had captured more than 50 percent of the online poker market share, at which point PartyGaming launched an Initial Public Offering on the London Stock Exchange that saw the firm valued at approximately $8.5 billion. It was the largest float in years on the LSE and at the time a greater market capitalization than British Airways.[22]

Research conducted in 2005 by the Media and Entertainment Consulting Network revealed there were "over 200 online poker websites, housing 1.7 million online poker gamblers with that figure increasing approximately 10% every month." Barely five years after the first room went live, $170 million was being wagered worldwide each day on online poker sites. Approximately $60 billion was wagered in 2004, with the United States accounting for almost 50 percent of the total market.[23] Online poker had arrived.

On the surface, the online version of the game might appear to reduce poker to its basic elements, replacing all the nuances of face-to-face interaction and the physicality of handling cards and chips with impersonal mouse clicks and occasional chatbox messaging. In fact, as site developers began to demonstrate, there was much that could be done online that could not possibly happen live, with innovations helping make poker on the computer into something not just different but (for some) preferable to the "brick-and-mortar" game.

Hands could be dealt more quickly online, on most sites at least twice as fast as could be done live. The ability to "multi-table" was also an online-only option, with many players opting to take virtual seats at multiple tables at the same time. Online card rooms could spread a greater variety of games, too, freely offering heads-up and short-handed tables along with "full ring" games without having to sacrifice floor space or pay extra dealers. Games of practically any stakes were possible, with $0.01/$0.02 hold'em games as easy to offer as those with stakes of $500/$1,000 or even higher. An ever increasing variety of games could be spread as well, including "sit-n-gos" that began the moment the required number of players had registered as well as traditional multi-table tournaments of different kinds, including those with massive fields comprised of tens of thousands of players that would be hardly feasible live. Online-specific poker variants were eventually created as well, such as "fast-fold" games that involved a large player pool constantly changing tables with every hand and players able to fold undesirable cards immediately and join a new table without even waiting for the previous hand to finish. The online game also enabled players to collect text-based "hand histories" that could be entered into other data-crunching programs calculating statistics regarding players' tendencies and styles, revealing in an instant how loose or tight they are, how aggressive or passive they play, and a whole host of information accessible even as the games were ongoing.

Also, and perhaps most importantly, like everything else on the internet, online poker games *never stopped*. Anyone wishing to join a game could do so at any time of day or night, instantly, without having to shower or dress.

While online poker players didn't have to worry about bottom dealing, stocked decks, or marked cards, playing poker on the computer did present a new set of cheating methods specific to the online game. As noted, collusion is always a possibility when playing online, much easier to commit with cell phones or other messaging programs than is the case with live poker. Multi-accounting likewise arose as another way to gain an unfair advantage, whereby players registered under multiple accounts with which they could all by themselves occupy multiple seats at the same table (and collude with themselves, as it were). "Ghosting" could involve an online player receiving coaching while playing or even letting another, more experienced player take over and play hands instead, say, when deep in a tournament.

Eventually so-called "poker bots" or poker-playing software programs not unlike the ones being developed by academic researchers began to infiltrate the online game as well. Sites incorporated into their "terms and conditions" rules designed to forbid all of these cheating methods, and in some cases endeavored to counter them by employing security experts to monitor the games. The sites also built into their clients preventative measures disallowing the simultaneous running of certain programs that might facilitate cheating. Minimum age requirements were also included in TOCs, though there, too, policing presented a challenge to online sites decidedly greater than that faced by live poker rooms.

There always also existed the possibility of site owners themselves cheating their customers via so-called "superuser" or "God mode" programs enabling the viewing of hole cards. Most who played online poker during the first decade of its existence tended to doubt an operator would attempt something so brazen. After all, the sites were so immediately and consistently lucrative, to risk some sort of insider cheating scandal seemed akin to killing the goose that kept laying golden eggs. (As we'll see, in some cases such trust turned out to be misplaced.)

The Biggest (Virtual) Game in Town

In terms of both players' strategic knowledge and cultural perception, the many differences between online and live poker initially tended to relegate the online version of the game to a lesser status as somehow less "real" than traditional poker. On early poker television, pros were sometimes designated as strictly "live" or "online" players, though such distinctions eventually began to dissolve as live pros found themselves tempted to dip into the large online player pools full of novice players.

As more money poured into the online poker "economy," the biggest games grew to mind-boggling levels, with seven-figure swings by individual players becoming not just possible but somewhat commonplace. On November 21, 2009 with thousands of virtual "railbirds" looking on, a heads-up hand of $500/$1,000 pot-limit Omaha played out on Full Tilt Poker between a Finnish pro named Patrik Antonius and a relatively new Swedish player named Viktor Blom (at the time known only by his username, "Isildur1"). The hand resulted in Antonius winning a pot worth a staggering $1,356,946.50. Blom, whose account showed profit of nearly $5.5 million in his first month after appearing in October 2009, ended the year down about $2.2 million. All of that in just three head-spinning months online.[24]

In late March 2011, a *New York Times Magazine* profile of 21-year-old online player Daniel "Jungleman" Cates highlighted the enormous amount of money being passed back and forth at the virtual poker tables while also introducing to a mainstream audience the life of a full-time online grinder of high-stakes games. Writer Jay Caspian Kang introduces Cates multi-tabling from his Orlando, Florida condo, his $5.5 million profit in 2010 more than a million clear of the year's next-winningest player, making Cates "online poker's big winner." Cates' casual attitude toward the six- and seven-figure swings he had endured recalls the "different ordering of reality" Al Alvarez once described high rollers experiencing in *The Biggest Game in Town*.[25] However unlike those players whose ability to remain unfazed seems the result of learning taught by experience, the boldness exhibited by Cates and others like him appears informed more so by naïveté. "Most of us young kids who play at nosebleed stakes don't really have any clear idea about the actual value of the money we win or lose," Cates confirms, adding that many "see the money more as a points system" than units representing real-life value.

The reference recalls Cates' background in video games, an arena in which he is said to have developed a "dexterity" (both "mental" and "manual") enabling him to think quickly while multi-tabling. Fairly or otherwise, Kang also draws attention to Cates' idiosyncratic social skills, suggesting that for high-stakes online players like him, "the greatest benefit borne from a life spent playing video games lies somewhere in the strange, disconnected relationship between what is simulated and what is real."[26]

The piece reports Cates having played "145,215 hands in 2010 alone," comparing the achievement of such prodigious volume to what could be accomplished playing at the relative snail's pace of live poker. "If an 18-year-old online whiz can play 12 hands at once," writes Kang, "then by his 19th birthday, he is no less experienced than a career gambler who has sat for a dozen years at the big-money table at the Bellagio." In truth, the number of hands Cates played wasn't nearly the highest among online players in 2010, not even half the 296,725 hands another "poker prodigy" from New Jersey named Tom "durrrr" Dwan reportedly played that year on his way to earning $3.6 million in profit.[27]

That summer Dwan appeared on the popular poker show *Poker After Dark* that aired each weeknight at 2 a.m. on NBC, and on one episode he and Poker Hall of Famer Doyle Brunson had a conversation about which of them had played the most hands of poker. On one side of the discussion was a 23-year-old who had been playing online for a few years; on the other a 76-year-old with more than a half-century of experience playing live. The answer was genuinely difficult to determine. In fact, as the top online players gained more experience and strategic knowledge, many found it increasingly profitable to join higher-stakes live games to play against those whose skills weren't advancing at the same rapid pace.

By the spring of 2011, online poker's prominence in America had led to several high-profile partnerships being tentatively agreed to between major casino operators and the sites. In March, 888.com and Caesars Interactive Entertainment reached an agreement subsequently approved by Nevada regulators for the site to provide a online platform for Caesars to market the WSOP brand online. That month Full Tilt Poker struck a similar partnership with Fertitta Interactive whose owners also owned the Nevada-based Station Casinos, as did PokerStars and Wynn Resorts, with all of the deals said to be contingent upon future federal legislation regulating online poker.[28] A *Forbes* article appearing in early April 2011 shared background to the Wynn-PokerStars relationship, quoting casino mogul Steve Wynn expressing uncertainty about what lawmakers might do next, but confidence that whatever was to come, Americans were going to keep right on playing poker online, regardless.[29] "The point is millions of people are playing poker," says Wynn, "and they are going to continue to play poker legally or illegally."

At the time, it was an easy assumption to make. About as easy as sitting down for a hand of poker on the computer, one might say.

22 Poker Under Siege

It has long been a paradox of poker in the United States that such a quintessentially "American" game enjoyed by millions regularly invites enough scorn and censure to be judged by some as unacceptable, thereby inspiring efforts to restrict or prohibit the game altogether. Practically every time and place America's favorite card game has achieved significant notice, forces have arisen attempting to stop poker's spread. A result of this phenomenon is a crazy quilt of inconsistent laws pertaining to poker, often inconsistently applied, that differ from state to state.

The situation parallels what occurs when a poker player wins *too* much, thereby causing opponents to leave and the game to break up. If an appropriate balance isn't found in which all participants remain satisfied enough to continue playing, the game's existence becomes imperiled. Similarly criticisms of poker in the wider community often surface just when the game appears to be prospering the most, thereby presenting a different, external threat to the game.

We've already discussed the non-linear history of poker in California, going back to the mid-19th century gold rush and accompanying appearance of hundreds of gambling houses where poker was among the many games played. Both the state and cities licensed the houses in order to earn revenue from them, and during the early 1850s San Francisco in particular became the undisputed gambling capital of the country, taking over the distinction from New Orleans. But the tide of public opinion turned against gambling and especially the "professional," with laws soon enacted to curtail its spread and "Committees of Vigilance" using violence and even lynchings to convey their disapproval.

Prohibitions against banked games led to the closure of many houses, but gambling games persisted and for a time there was a mini-boom in stud poker. By the 1880s the city's Chief of Police was routinely complaining to the city's board of supervisors about frequently having to break up stud poker games. In July 1884, the Chief wrote an editorial that was reprinted throughout the country titled "The Evils of Stud-Horse Poker" in order to publicize his grievances.[1] "I desire to call your attention to the prevalence of a game known as stud-horse poker, which is extensively played for money in saloons and other public places in this city," the Chief writes. "It is not less injurious and demoralizing than faro and other games that are prohibited by law." He goes on to describe "the magnitude of the evil which has resulted" from the game, which in his view "fosters idleness, and tempts many young men of weak resolution to steal from their employers." The argument was convincing enough to prompt lawmakers to attach an amendment to a previous anti-gambling statute, adding "stud-horse poker" to the list of prohibited games. The move caused more than a hundred years' worth of headaches for those desirous to play stud in the state.[2]

Of course, California poker players still played stud despite the law. Such has been the case throughout the country where many – indeed, most – poker games have been technically illegal for much of the game's history, with applicable laws in many cases dating back to the early 20th or even the 19th centuries. Adding to the confusion, there has also almost always been a divide between theory and practice when it comes to the policing of poker in the United States. There have been exceptions, but generally speaking it is only when the games get bigger, drawing too many players or involving stakes that are too high, that they have become too prominent for the authorities to allow them to continue unchecked. Even then, however, the penalties levied are frequently adjusted to fit with current societal judgments regarding the significance (or lack thereof) of the crimes being committed. The punishments often serve more as a nuisance than a deterrent to those hosting and playing the games.

Writing in the late 1980s, gambling law expert I. Nelson Rose described the ongoing growth of gambling in the United States and what he believed to be an inevitable clamping down to come. Recognizing similar responses to gambling's growth earlier in U.S. history, Rose predicted "the pendulum will swing back," since "in America, gambling eventually self-destructs" by becoming too big for its own good.[3]

During the early months of 2011, the continued growth of online poker in the United States meant more players were playing the game than had been the case at any time over the previous two centuries. By April 2011, the number of Americans playing poker online for real money had been "estimated variously at between 1.3 million and 15 million."[4] Poker in America had never been more popular. Nor more conspicuous. In retrospect, it is unsurprising to think such a situation would not continue much longer.

Post–UIGEA, Online Poker Becomes the Virtual Wild West

The rise of online gambling began to attract U.S. legislators' attention during the 1990s. The proposed Internet Gambling Prohibition Act of 1997 sought a draconian response to the situation, looking not only to force ISPs to block Americans' access to online gambling sites but to penalize any U.S. citizen who placed an online bet with a $5,000 fine and a year in jail. That bill died in committee, though a couple of years later another similar one targeting site owners and providers (and not the bettors) was passed by the Senate and nearly made it through the House before failing as well. That bill's defeat was brought on in large measure by the lobbying efforts of Jack Abramoff, soon destined to become the center of an enormous corruption scandal involving White House officials, Congressional aides, and other lobbyists. He pleaded guilty to multiple felonies and served time in prison. Needless to say, Abramoff's subsequent notoriety didn't exactly help the cause for subsequent opponents of anti-online gambling efforts.

Further iterations of an anti-online gambling bill continued to be revived over the next several years, ultimately coalescing into a new version called the Internet Gambling Prohibition and Enforcement Act. It was aimed at neither sites nor bettors, but more specifically at third-party "communication facilities" that enabled the transport of funds between the two. That bill passed the House in July 2006 by a 317-93 vote, but lingered in the Senate for the next three months. Efforts arose in late September to pass a modified bill called the Unlawful Internet Gambling Enforcement Act of 2006 that again focused on prohibiting "financial transaction providers" from transferring money to and from online gambling sites. After one failed attempt to attach the UIGEA to a defense spending bill, Republican Senate Majority Leader Bill Frist of Tennessee succeeded in appending it to another ostensibly unrelated piece of legislation called the SAFE Port Act, a post-9/11 bill designed to improve maritime and cargo security at U.S. seaports. The SAFE Port Act, with the newly-added UIGEA, was passed by the Senate by "unanimous consent." Then shortly after midnight on the evening of September 30, the last night before the 109th Congress was scheduled to adjourn prior to that year's elections, the bill was passed by the House by a 409-2 margin.[5] Two weeks later on Friday, October 13, following a short speech outlining the bill's provisions to increase port security and without any mention of online gambling, President George W. Bush signed the SAFE Port Act and thus the UIGEA into law.

It would take a couple of years for the UIGEA's final regulations to be formulated. In fact, it wasn't until January 19, 2009 (the last full day of Bush's presidency) that the regulations went into effect and not until June 1, 2010 before compliance was required of the banks and other financial transaction providers. Even so, in October 2006 there were a few significant consequences for online poker players in America. The most dramatic arose when PartyGaming immediately chose to suspend all real money business with U.S. customers, which meant Americans could no longer play on PartyPoker, at the time the world's most popular online poker site. Other publicly-traded online gambling companies such as 888 Holdings, SportingBet (which owned Paradise Poker), and Bwin Interactive Entertainment (owners of the Ongame Poker Network) likewise withdrew from the U.S. market, removing other online poker sites as options for Americans. Players were additionally affected when popular online payment processors like FirePay and Neteller, previously used to deposit and withdraw funds from the sites, also stopped serving Americans.[6]

However other sites continued to serve the U.S., with some issuing statements maintaining the UIGEA's passage did not affect the legality either of sites offering games to Americans or to Americans playing them.[7] The sites that chose to remain quickly surged ahead of PartyPoker to claim the greatest global market share. PokerStars (the new leader) and Full Tilt Poker (moving up to second) became the most popular sites both globally and in America, the online poker equivalent of Coca-Cola and Pepsi. In July 2008 two other sites that stayed, UltimateBet and Absolute Poker, joined together as the Cereus Network to enable the combining of player pools. The impetus for the move was ostensibly competitive, with a press release at the time describing the partnership "instantly making Cereus the third-largest online poker network." However, to those who were paying attention, another less innocuous motive seemed apparent. At the time of the merger, both Absolute Poker and UltimateBet had experienced significant "insider" cheating scandals eventually to become the largest and most damaging in online poker's short history.

The cheating at Absolute Poker was the first to be discovered. Players' suspicions about unusual betting patterns first surfaced in August 2007. Then on October 12, an unknown player with the username "POTRIPPER" won a $1,000 buy-in tournament on Absolute Poker in questionable fashion. Most notably, in the final hand the player made a big, improbable heads-up call on the river with just ten-high to win the event.[8] The tournament's runner-up, a poker pro named Marco Johnson, was curious to review hands played at the final table, and requested the site send him hand histories. The site complied with the request, but soon Johnson discovered the Excel spreadsheet he had been sent revealed all players' hole cards (not just his own). It enabled him and others to discover many other instances of suspect play by POTRIPPER, all suggesting the player could see what everyone else was holding. The spreadsheet additionally contained other information connecting the account to one of the site's owners, Scott Tom, and eventually to the site's director of operations, A.J. Green. Two weeks later Absolute Poker admitted a software breach had occurred, and that the site intended to issue refunds to affected players totaling $1.6 million. The Kahnawake Gaming Commission, the regulatory body located in the Mohawk Territory of Kahnawake that had issued Absolute Poker its license to operate, launched an investigation. It identified multiple cheating accounts, and in January 2008 the KGC fined the site $500,000 though allowed it to keep its license subject to future audits. Curiously, the KGC did not publicly identify who had perpetrated the cheating.

That very month similar suspicions arose regarding the activity of several accounts at UltimateBet, including abnormally high win rates being exhibited by a player named "NioNio." Another more extensive round of sleuthing by players eventually caused the site to admit publicly in early March that a large scale cheating "scheme" had been discovered. In late May the site issued a statement confirming that six different accounts (several of which had employed multiple screen names) had been involved with "fraudulent activity" taking place from March 2006 to December 2007. The site also began delivering refunds totaling $6.1 million to affected players. The Kahnawake Gaming Commission (from whom UltimateBet also had received its license to operate) once more investigated, hiring Frank Catania, a former New Jersey gaming official, to assist. Catania concluded cheating had taken place over a much longer period of several years with about $20 million having been taken from players. He recommended the site's license be suspended. But as with Absolute Poker, the

KGC chose not to take away UltimateBet's license, instead fining the site $1.5 million while also giving UltimateBet two months to refund all players adversely affected by the cheating. In this case, one individual was named as having perpetrated the cheating: one of the site's original owners, 1994 World Series of Poker Main Event champion Russ Hamilton. The KGC said Hamilton had used several accounts to cheat players from May 2004 to January 2008.

The creation of the Cereus network, then, was clearly part of a re-branding effort by Absolute Poker and UltimateBet. The purpose became especially clear once the mainstream news media began reporting on the cheating scandals in earnest during the second half of 2008, with a major exposé appearing in *The Washington Post* and a *60 Minutes* report airing on CBS in late November. Besides encouraging negative sentiment about both poker in general and online poker in particular, the scandals addition-ally served to heighten fears among some regarding the overall trustwor-thiness of the games. The scandals also highlighted the apparent lack of recourse available to players should they find themselves victimized by cheaters. The sites' repayments hardly assuaged concerns about owners potentially using such "superuser" programs to cheat their players, nor about the efficacy of offshore regulatory bodies operating independently of United States laws.[9]

Post-UIGEA, Americans playing online poker were entering a legal gray area. Whether they liked it or not, they had to accept the fact that U.S. laws ensuring fair business practices did not apply to their games, which meant the players wholly relied on the sites themselves to provide reme-dies should complaints arise. Additional online poker scandals did little to help the game's reputation. Other reports focused on "superuser" accounts being used on smaller sites; high-profile "ghosting" and "multi-accounting" incidents in cash games and major online tournaments; the use of "data mining" tools in violation of sites' terms and conditions; and other instances of sites shutting down and making off with players' funds. The circum-stances were not unlike those faced by poker players taking their chances aboard steamboats or in saloons during the 19th century. Even if they could prove the game was unfair, there was no obvious authority to whom they could petition to adjudicate. As John Blackbridge wrote in 1875 con-cerning card sharps and the threat they posed, "In such a case there can be no umpire."[10]

Online poker nonetheless continued to be promoted during these years on American television, albeit less overtly than had been the case pre-UI-GEA. Commercials for online poker purported to advertise free-to-play "dot-net" sites rather than the real money "dot-com" analogues (e.g., full-tiltpoker.*net* instead of fulltiltpoker.*com*) as a cursory acknowledgment of the legislation. The World Series of Poker stopped accepting satellite entries from offshore U.S.-facing sites, which in turn halted the upward surge of Main Event entrants. Player numbers fell from 8,773 in 2006 to fewer than 6,400 the following year. However players continued to wear site patches at WSOP Main Event final tables and elsewhere on television, including on site-sponsored shows like *Poker After Dark*, *High Stakes Poker*, *Face the Ace*, *PokerStars Million Dollar Challenge*, and *PokerStars Big Game*. For a time Fox Sports Net aired two shows sponsored by Ultimate-Bet, one a "poker news" show called *Poker2Nite*, and the other a "poker reality" show, *The Best Damn Poker Show*, in which the site's primary spokespersons Annie Duke and Phil Hellmuth coached teams of aspiring poker players to compete against one another.

Duke, the sister of Full Tilt Poker co-owner and professional player Howard Lederer, could frequently be heard defending the efforts of UB (as UltimateBet became known after another rebranding in November 2009) to rehabilitate its damaged reputation, giving interviews to poker-related outlets explaining the site's new management and direction.[11] Duke also made several appearances on mainstream television, starring in a short-lived game show *Annie Duke Takes on the World* on the Game Show Network, appearing as a guest on talk shows including *The Colbert Report* and *The Ellen Degeneres Show*, making appearances on the game shows *1 vs. 100* and *Deal or No Deal*, and most famously competing on *Celebrity Apprentice* from March–May 2009 where she finished runner-up to Joan Rivers. It was on *Celebrity Apprentice* that Duke occasionally tried to defend poker and poker players, with Hellmuth also making cameos during her run.

Duke likewise defended online poker on a couple of occasions on Capitol Hill, testifying before House committees on behalf of the Poker Players Alliance, a pro-online poker lobbying group. In 2007 Duke appeared before the House Judiciary Committee to speak against the UIGEA, then in 2010 she testified before the House Financial Services Committee in support of new federal legislation to legalize and regulate online poker. In the latter appearance, Duke specifically alluded to the cheating scandal at UB and how "under a U.S. regulated system players would have legal recourse should they feel they are harmed and regulators would be able to penalize licensed companies that breach the regulatory standards."[12] (Both Duke and Hellmuth left UB at the end of December 2010.)

Following the UIGEA's passage, Representative Barney Frank, a Democrat from Massachusetts who at the time was Chairman of the House Financial Services Committee, more than once proposed bills such as the one Duke spoke in support of in 2010. Late that summer Frank appeared as a guest on *The Tonight Show with Jay Leno* where his online gambling bill was among the topics discussed. While Frank argued in favor of allowing adults to be able to decide for themselves about playing poker online, Leno espoused an opposing view. "To me, Vegas works because you have to go to the desert to get there... you have to make an effort," Leno said. "You go to the desert, you lose your money and you come home. You can't go to the desert again unless you get more money. If you're sitting at home and you're up late at night and you got your little credit card, next thing you know... it's like a mini-bar. You're not going to eat the potato chips unless they are in the mini-bar."[13] Frank reiterated his point about individual liberty and how government needn't prohibit citizens from gambling online if they wished. Even so, the position espoused by Leno, at the time the host of television's highest-rated late night talk show, perhaps more closely corresponded to the mainstream view of online poker.

In any case, there was certainly general confusion about online poker's legality. During his appearance Frank himself spoke of Americans then being "prohibited" by current law from playing poker online. Appearing on another late night talk show in February 2009, *Late Show with David Letterman*, comedian Steve Martin told a humorous story about playing online poker after having taken an Ambien, then waking the next morning to discover he'd won a thousand dollars without any memory of having done so. When introducing the story, Martin explained how "for a while I played internet poker... when it was legal," the qualification indicating again that for many Americans (including poker players), it wasn't at all clear whether or not playing online was something they were allowed to do.[14]

Black Friday

On Friday, April 15, 2011, Americans who played online poker received clarity regarding the status of online poker in the United States. And how.

That was the day the U.S. Department of Justice dramatically unsealed a 52-page indictment against top executives of the largest online poker sites in the world – PokerStars, Full Tilt Poker, and Absolute Poker – as well as a civil complaint against the sites. The individuals named in the indictment faced years in prison while the civil complaint sought $3 billion in assets from the companies owning the sites. The charges included violating the UIGEA as well as bank fraud, money laundering, and illegal gambling. The latter offenses were the result of sites having employed illegal funding methods for players once the UIGEA had succeeded in closing off previously available mechanisms for Americans to deposit and withdraw. Adding to the shock, the sites' domains had been seized, replaced by solemn black text on a white background describing the crimes and outlining the penalties, the twin seals of the Federal Bureau of Investigation and Department of Justice humorlessly hovering up above.

This domain name has been seized by the F.B.I. pursuant to an Arrest Warrant in Rem obtained by the United States Attorney's Office for the Southern District of New York and issued by the United States District Court for the Southern District of New York.

Conducting, financing, managing, supervising, directing, or owning all or part of an illegal gambling business is a federal crime. (18 U.S.C. § 1955)

For persons engaged in the business of betting or wagering, it is also a federal crime to knowingly accept, in connection with the participation of another person in unlawful Internet gambling, credit, electronic fund transfers, or checks. (31 U.S.C. § § 5363 & 5366)

Violations of these laws carry criminal penalties of up to five years' imprisonment and a fine of up to $250,000.

Properties, including domain names, used in violation of the provisions of 18 U.S.C. § 1955 or involved in money laundering transactions are subject to forfeiture to the United States. (18 U.S.C. § § 981 & 1955(d))

The domain seizure notice visitors to PokerStars, Full Tilt Poker, Absolute Poker, and UB discovered on April 15, 2011

Unlike with the UIGEA, the effect upon American online poker players was both instantaneous and comprehensive. By mid-afternoon U.S. players were blocked from real money games on PokerStars, then from the games on Full Tilt Poker a few hours after that. That evening both sites released statements explaining that while Americans could no longer play and they would continue to serve those outside the U.S. By dinner time both Fertitta Interactive and Wynn Resorts had announced the tentative alliances they had recently struck with the sites were no more. ESPN stopped running online poker-related advertising altogether on its WSOP repeats, and live site-sponsored tournament poker series the North American Poker Tour (PokerStars) and the Onyx Cup (Full Tilt) were immediately cancelled. The national news media reacted swiftly with articles reporting the sudden change to the online poker landscape appearing under metaphor-laden headlines such as "Prosecutions Turn Online Poker Into a Shaky Bet," "Odds Aren't Looking Good for Online Players," and "U.S. Prosecutors Not Bluffing With Shutdown of Poker Sites."[15] Such headlines contained a certain irony, given how they pointed to how ingrained poker is in the American vernacular at the same time that they described the game's prohibition.

Subsequent reporting from *The Wall Street Journal* revealed how the many online poker site-sponsored shows were a significant factor motivating the feds' crackdown even before the UIGEA had been passed. The article "TV Helped Drive Traffic to Online Poker Websites, Irking Justice Department" tells how the DOJ had sent a letter to media companies in June 2003 warning them not to accept advertising from "offshore sportsbook and Internet gambling operations since, presumably, they would not run advertisements for illegal narcotics sales, prostitution, child pornography or other prohibited activities." The article also notes the FBI had seized $6 million from Discovery Communications Inc., previously the owner of the Travel Channel on which the original World Poker Tour appeared, for having aired the PartyPoker ads during WPT episodes.[16]

Five days after what quickly became known as "Black Friday," the dot-com domains were returned to PokerStars and Full Tilt in order to facilitate U.S. players' withdrawals of funds from their accounts. Within 10 days PokerStars players in America were already receiving their money, but such was not the case for those with Full Tilt Poker accounts. Meanwhile the two Cereus sites stubbornly kept allowing U.S. players to play for a full month until finally reaching an agreement with the DOJ to stop doing so and begin facilitating player withdrawals. However, it did not bode well when the parent company to the two sites filed for bankruptcy and dismissed the sites' sponsored pros. As a belated aftershock, 10 more sites allowing Americans to gamble had their domains seized by the DOJ in May on a day later described as "Blue Monday." That sweep meant two more online poker sites (including one previously associated with Poker Hall of Famer Doyle Brunson) were no longer available to American players.

By the end of June 2011, it had become increasingly apparent Full Tilt Poker players were not going to be able to withdraw their funds. The Alderney Gambling Control Commission suspended the site's license to operate, and 10 weeks after Americans had been shut out of the games on Full Tilt the site went dark worldwide. Soon it was discovered Full Tilt Poker had not segregated player funds and had instead used deposited money to fund advertising and promotion (including sponsoring television shows) as well as to pay owners. In response, the Department of Justice amended the earlier civil complaint to add further charges that the site had defrauded its players, owing them $390 million (including $150 million to U.S. players) while having only $60 million on hand. The amendment also notably added the names of poker-playing sponsor-owners Howard Lederer, Chris Ferguson, and Rafe Furst to the list of the accused. With astonishing specificity, the amendment alleged that "Between April 2007 to April 2011, Full Tilt Poker and its board distributed $443,860,529.89 to board members and owners." In an accompanying statement, U.S. Attorney for the Southern District of New York Preet Bharara declared "Full Tilt was not a legitimate poker company, but a Ponzi scheme."[17]

"Poker Site Stacked Deck" read the headlines thereafter, with more national coverage including large-font, "front page" reports on CNN, Fox News, MSNBC, and other news websites.[18] The Alderney Gambling Control Commission revoked Full Tilt Poker's license altogether, and *Poker After Dark*, which had still been airing new shows well into September, abruptly went off the air. While the "Ponzi scheme" reference seemed not entirely accurate, it was nonetheless obvious to all the site had not been run with the kind of oversight a licensed and regulated gambling operation should. Nor had the Cereus sites, as their players soon discovered they, too, were unable to withdraw from their accounts as the money had all been otherwise spent.

The legal fallout continued for years. In July 2012, PokerStars settled its case with the DOJ, forfeiting $547 million to the U.S. government, an amount from which the DOJ then drew to refund American players what they were owed from their Full Tilt Poker accounts. PokerStars agreed as well to acquire Full Tilt Poker and refund another $184 million to players outside of the U.S., a process that took a couple more years to complete. (Eventually PokerStars reopened Full Tilt to the rest of the world, combining the sites' player pools.) Later a different agreement eventually resulted in players on Absolute Poker and UB also being able to recover their funds starting in the fall of 2017, although a year after that some were still awaiting payments.[19] When commenting about the settlements, U.S. Attorney Bharara reiterated the firmness of the federal government's stance against anyone – offshore or otherwise – attempting to allow Americans to gamble online illegally. As he explained, the "settlements demonstrate that if you engage in conduct that violates the laws of the United States, as we alleged in this case, then even if you are doing so from across the ocean, you will have to answer for that conduct and turn over your ill-gotten gains."[20]

In the United States, April 15 is known to all as the day on which federal and state taxes are due to be paid each year. As months and eventually years passed, it was clear that from the government's perspective its actions that became public on April 15, 2011 had represented the start of a process in which payment for past transgressions would be collected.

Aftermath

Two poker-themed documentaries released shortly after Black Friday tell the story of the day in greater detail. Both consciously connect poker to the "American dream," explicitly associating the game and its potential rewards with ideas of the United States being a "land of opportunity" while lamenting its online version having become essentially unavailable to Americans.

All In: The Poker Movie was in post-production when Black Friday occurred, prompting the filmmakers to shoot additional interviews and reshape its narrative of poker's history. The final version of the film contains a montage of poker pros and others involved in the industry sharing their raw reactions to the wholly unexpected thunderbolt of online poker in America being instantly razed to the ground. Some even evoke the assassination of John F. Kennedy in the way that every poker player can recall where he or she was when first learning the news. Less hyperbolically, others reflect on the seeming incongruity of Americans being prevented from playing the nation's favorite card game, among them *Rounders* star Matt Damon. "Why are you cracking down on poker?" Damon wonders. "This is like cracking down on baseball."

A year later *Bet Raise Fold: The Story of Online Poker* (2013) chronicled the remarkable rise and precipitous fall of the game in the United States. Like *All In*, *Bet Raise Fold* had begun production prior to Black Friday, then saw the trajectory of its story similarly altered by the events of that day. Focusing in particular on the stories of three full-time online poker players, the film foregrounds the game's skill component while arguing for the legitimacy of poker as a profession, thereby highlighting the trauma of training for and becoming successful at a job that suddenly becomes obsolete. "This was my livelihood, it wasn't just a game," says pro Danielle Andersen in the film's opening, using the past tense to indicate grimly that her chosen occupation is no longer available to her.

A small number of Americans relocated outside the U.S. to continue playing online, while a similarly small percentage of U.S. players took their chances on the few "rogue" offshore sites that continued to risk serving them. In late 2011, a memo from the Department of Justice, written in response to a question about states being able to sell lottery tickets to residents not physically located within the state, included a clarification of the Interstate Wire Act of 1961. The clarification suggested that when it came to online transactions, the Wire Act only applied to sports betting and not other forms of gambling, a change of sorts from the DOJ's prior stance. That opinion helped pave the way for individual states to begin considering online gambling legislation, and over the next few years Nevada, Delaware, New Jersey, and later Pennsylvania all passed such laws. In April 2013, the first regulated online poker site launched in Nevada. Online poker arrived in Delaware and New Jersey later that year, and starting in May 2018 the three states arranged a compact to allow the sharing of player pools. Even so, the total number of Americans playing legal, regulated online poker remained only a small fraction of the number playing before Black Friday – in the hundreds rather than the hundreds of thousands.

In January 2019 the DOJ made public a new opinion delivered a couple of months before maintaining the 2011 memo had misinterpreted the Wire Act and that in fact it does apply to all forms of online gambling. This development seems to make it less likely other states will try to pass online gambling legislation in the near future, and further suggests the revival of online poker in America might be slow to come.

Poker in America survived Black Friday, just as it has survived other efforts to combat its spread throughout the game's tumultuous history. Despite the dire predictions of some during the days that followed, the 2011 World Series of Poker did not experience a steep decline in players taking part, and in fact overall attendance at the WSOP has continued to climb every year since. Other tours, including the WPT, the WSOP Circuit, the Heartland Poker Tour, and the Mid-States Poker Tour continue to thrive as well, as do cash games in poker rooms and casinos across the country. Poker continues to be played in clubs, including in an untold number of illegal ones. Since the late 1980s and early 1990s, a vestige of steamboat poker continues to exist off the coasts of a few states on the modern riverboats.[21] During recent years "bar poker" games and leagues (also called "pub poker" and "tavern poker") have also become popular. And, of course, home games of all kinds, many of which were started by players who first learned and became excited about poker by playing it online, continue to be the type of poker most players enjoy.

Today online poker's impact on the game in the U.S. is dramatically muted when compared with the decade preceding Black Friday – much less popular, and thus much less prevalent in American popular culture. A handful of offshore sites continue to serve Americans, and there even exist illegal "underground" online games operated within the U.S. for which the risks to players resemble the ones faced when playing in unregulated, unlicensed live games. Again, though, only a very small percentage of Americans participate in such real money games online, with most either unaware of them or purposefully choosing not to seek them out. Even within the poker community, the online game is considered by many to be distinct from the type of poker most Americans play, a game Americans *used* to play and that now only poker players in other countries do. Like smoking on airplanes or driving without seatbelts, playing poker online for real money is now most often evoked as an activity once permitted though now prohibited.

Unlike those other activities, there always remains the possibility for the pendulum to swing back in online poker's favor. In any case, it is safe to say that during the country's "online poker era," millions more Americans became acquainted with the game than would have been the case otherwise. That in itself is a significant factor helping to ensure the game's continued prominence in American culture.

23 Poker in the Future

"I spoke of our American climate. It was a potent drug, I said, for millions to be swallowing every day.... Our American climate, I said, had worked remarkable changes... it has given our whole race the habit of poker."

Owen Wister, *The Virginian*[1]

In 1929 a playwright and fiction writer from New York named Percival Wilde published a collection of short stories titled *Rogues in Clover*. The stories feature a poker-playing central character named Bill Parmalee, introduced initially as a card sharp familiar with all of the techniques employed by the many "mechanics" preceding him.

"He had learned to play the American game well – more than well," we are told, then became even more unbeatable after being "introduced to the various devices with which misapplied ingenuity has endeavored to hamstring the legs of chance."[2] Bill initially appears unrepentant, a modern-day George Devol with zero misgivings about his ethically dubious craft. However, a quarrel with a disapproving father in the book's opening story has the effect of reforming him, and thereafter Bill spurns cheating at cards in favor of applying his skills in a positive way, using them primarily to catch other card sharps.

Resembling detective mysteries or crime fiction, the stories are fun and full of light humor, typically concluding with an enjoyable twist or revelation – not unlike some poker hands. One titled "The Poker Dog" finds Bill helping his friend Tony catch a card cheat in the act, with Bill using a dog to help him expose the cheater. Bill suspects the cheater to be employing a hold-out device operated by pulling a string that runs down inside his clothes, out through a seam in his pant-leg near his knee, then fastened to the other knee. Pulling his knees apart under the table causes the device to shoot out of his sleeve and deliver him the cards he needs, while bringing his knees back together draws the hold-out back up inside of the cheater's sleeve. Bill then plays in a game with the suspected cheat. After having the player sit in a particular chair near where the dog lies, at a crucial moment mid-hand Bill gives a whistle and the dog runs through the player's legs, causing him suddenly to separate his knees and shoot three cards out onto the table.

The explanation of the hold-out device doesn't come until the end of the story, leaving both Tony and the reader in suspense until the final scene. The delay thus makes an earlier scene in which Tony and his wife buy Bill a dog initially appear a *non sequitur*, with Bill's strange desire for a pet not given any obvious explanation at the time. All is revealed, however, once the dog – picked because of its immediate affinity with its new owner – dutifully responds to Bill's whistle, thereby helping to blow the whistle (so to speak) on the sharp.

The dog Bill chooses is a mutt, and his friend isn't very enthused by his selection. "Tony surveyed the curious beast with disapproval. The head was mostly collie, though adorned with most un-collie-like prick-ears; the coat – what there was of it, for the animal had suffered from mange – was reminiscent of the traditions of the Airedales; yet the shape of the body was that to be expected in the ancient and honorable order of Irish wolf-hounds."[3] Tony asks Bill what is the dog's breed.

"It's much easier to say what his breed isn't," Bill responds. "A product of the great American melting pot; a true cosmopolitan. I'm going to invent a new variety, and call him a poker dog."[4]

It's an inspired metaphor, and ranks alongside Cassius M. Coolidge's famous card-playing canines as one of the more creative links between dogs and poker. Poker is assuredly a most "American" game, which means it is an amalgam of many different elements, much like Bill's mutt. As we've seen, besides being a "melting pot" game descended from a mixture of other games bred elsewhere, poker has a number of different significances,

Poker & Pop Culture

both good and bad. Indeed, Bill's own transformation from a card sharp to someone using his poker skills for good mirrors poker's past in a way, given its early history as a game dominated by cheaters and later evolution into something different and (for many) relatively more favorable.

As demonstrated by the many cultural representations of poker over the past two centuries, the game has produced markedly varying responses despite its enduring popularity. Some look upon poker disapprovingly, much as Tony judges Bill's "curious beast." Others celebrate the game, in some cases their attraction made even greater by the aversion of others having accorded the game a romantic, "outlaw" status. Some echo Jonathan Harrington Green's early judgment of poker to be "a game that is immensely destructive."[5] Others side with Lou Krieger's opinion that poker is "a microcosm of all we admire about American virtue."[6] Still others, including many of the game's most ardent enthusiasts, fall somewhere in the middle, recognizing that much like the country whose values and ideals poker has always reflected, poker possesses both positive and negative qualities.

Looking ahead to poker's future in America, there will no doubt continue to be divided opinions about the game's worth and significance. But it also seems certain that a game so popular and well established will remain so in the years and decades to come. Such will likely continue to be the case outside of the U.S. as well, where in many countries the game has never been as popular as it is today. Poker booms are ongoing in Brazil and Russia, while countries in Asia and elsewhere are likewise showing an increasing affinity for America's favorite card game. Meanwhile the online version continues to attract new players in dozens of other countries, re-exporting poker all over the globe two centuries after America first created the game out of elements from card games imported from abroad. The continued prosperity of poker outside of America will no doubt have some impact upon the game's future in the U.S.

That said, there are three primary factors that will affect just how many people play poker in the U.S. going forward and thus how prominent the game continues to remain in American popular culture: the economy, legislative decisions affecting when and where poker can be legally played, and poker's ability to adapt and innovate in order to attract and retain new players.

Since money is an essential element of the game (along with cards and bluffing), poker's popularity will always depend in part on the health of the nation's economy, with the relative level of Americans' discretionary income directly affecting how full poker rooms remain, how big tournament fields become, and how often home games are hosted. Much as consumer spending on entertainment, travel, dining out, and other hobbies and sports goes up during times of prosperity, so, too, will more people play poker when there is more money available to them with which to play. Such has always been true. Poker boomed in California during the mid-19th century Gold Rush; in port cities along the Mississippi before and after the Civil War; in several Old West settlements during the mid-to-late 19th century and after; in many major American cities following both World Wars; and throughout the country during the era of post-recession economic expansion that began in the late 2000s.

Legislative decisions regarding gambling games will also directly affect poker's popularity. Economic factors often exert the greatest influence those decisions, notwithstanding the moral objections frequently raised by lawmakers and lobbyists who oppose gambling. The spread of state lotteries during the past half-century provides the most obvious example of gambling legislation being influenced primarily by budgetary concerns. In 1969 only three states had legalized lotteries. In 2019 there are 45 that have them, and in every case lotteries were introduced only after a sufficient percentage of legislators were convinced of their ability to produce revenue.[7] Recent arguments on behalf of legalizing and regulating online gambling tend to evoke the potential for economic benefits as well, with proponents sometimes describing money generated as a "sin tax," a concession to those who liken gambling to other activities deemed harmful to individuals and/or society.

Economic arguments tend to fare better than ones attempting to distinguish poker from other gambling games due to poker's skill component, although there have been occasional courtroom rulings favoring that position. In 2009 a county court in Pennsylvania ruled poker to be a game of skill and therefore not "illegal gambling" as described by state law, though the decision was later overturned on appeal.[8] A federal judge similarly ruled in 2012 that the operator of a New York poker room was not guilty of illegal gambling because "poker is predominated by skill rather than chance," though again a federal appeals court overturned the ruling a year later. It decided "the question of whether skill or chance predominates in poker is inapposite to this appeal" – i.e., irrelevant to legal definitions of poker as gambling.[9] Others will no doubt continue to try to emphasize poker's skill component when challenging legal prohibitions against it. Even so, while individual judges may entertain such arguments and even rule favorably to confirm them, the cumbersome process required to change existing laws or pass new ones will more likely be set in motion by arguments about fiscal benefits that don't try to distinguish poker from other forms of gambling.

Finally, poker's unique ability to adapt to players' changing desires and predilections spurred its growth in the past, and that same ability will no doubt help to ensure the game's future survival. Historian John Lukacs once characterized poker as "a game of a thousand unwritten rules," by which he was referring not only to the game's capacity to admit variations, but also to the way poker uncannily responds to the "social standards and codes of behavior" of those who play it. "People play poker in the way they want to play it," Lukacs explains, which means in turn "it is a game based to a large extent on free will."[10] Starting as a 20-card game played without a draw (retroactively described as "Straight Poker"), poker evolved in response to player preferences, with full deck draw poker and stud poker variants proving most popular during the 19th and most of the 20th centuries, then Texas hold'em with no-limit betting becoming the favored game in the late 20th and early 21st centuries. Within those larger categories have arisen hundreds of other related types of "open" (with some cards up) and "closed" (with all cards down) poker games, including the many wild card games and unique home game variants, all of which satisfy creative and competitive desires of those who invent and play them. The introduction of tournament poker and its continued development and refinement similarly reflects both current proclivities of poker players as well as larger cultural trends like the increased "gamification" of American life as found in marketing, education, health, employment, and politics.[11] Just as poker in the past could be regarded as an expression of Americans' "pioneer spirit" connoting foundational ideas of individual liberty, freedom, independence, self-reliance, and the pursuit of happiness, in the future the game will continue to evolve and adapt to accommodate other aspects of American culture and to reflect those aspects by the way the game is played.

Of course, poker not only can be *played* in many different ways, but as this book has demonstrated, poker can be *portrayed* in many different ways, too. As we've seen, the game extends into a whole host of contexts as an incredibly complex and versatile emblem for all sorts of ideas and messages, all of which might be said in one way or another to reflect the diversity and richness of the American experience. We've seen how artists, fiction writers, dramatists, musicians, filmmakers, radio and television show creators, and storytellers of all kinds have discovered in poker a fertile setting in which to advance plots, to introduce and develop characters, to create conflict, and to further themes. We've seen how poker strategy can provide meaningful, revelatory analogues to business, economics, politics, and war. We've seen as well how the game can provide an avenue by which to pursue broader areas of inquiry such as psychology, sociology, anthropology, and even philosophy.

Poker is all of these things, and will continue to be all of these things and more. Indeed, like Bill's mutt, poker reflects so many different aspects of American life, it's almost easier to say what it isn't.

Notes and References

Introduction

1. Tocqueville, 326.
2. As discussed in Chapter 4, this quote comes from a July 31, 1877 speech delivered by Twain prior to the performance of a play he co-wrote. The best known version of the speech appears in Merle De Vore Johnson's revised edition of *A Bibliography of the Works of Mark Twain, Samuel Langhorne Clemens* (140), which is based on a report of it in a New York publication called *Tid-Bits* (20 Dec. 1884). Other, more contemporaneous articles recount the speech differently, including his comments about poker. For example, a version published just a few days later in the *St. Louis Globe-Democrat* (4 Aug. 1877) reports Twain as having said "The game of poker is all too little understood in the higher circles of this country. Here and there you find an Ambassador that has some idea of the game; but you take the general average of the nation, and our ignorance ought to make us blush. Why, I have even known a clergyman, estimable, pure-hearted man, and most excellent husband and father, who didn't value an ace full above two pair and a jack. Such ignorance as this is brutalizing."
3. Crane, 263.
4. Edwards, 36-37.
5. Carleton, 30. In other words, "that's the way with cards," since "gambling is uncertain."
6. Lukacs, 57.

Chapter 1: Poker in the Past

1. Alvarez, *Poker*, 22.
2. Green, Jonathan Harrington, *An Exposure,* 95.
3. Childton, 772.
4. Harte, 41, 47.
5. Bierce, 258.
6. Jewison.
7. Thompson, Howard, 48.
8. "Mixed Deal," 136.
9. Rosenbaum.
10. Tucker.

11. Scarne, *Scarne's Guide to Modern Poker*, 2.

12. Goodman, Walter, "About Men," 54.

13. Hayano, 138.

14. Reilly, 156.

15. Maher, 53.

16. "Right Guard, Right Way Out," *Celebrity Apprentice*, season 8, episode 9, NBC, 26 Apr. 2009.

17. Gaul, A1.

18. United States Attorney's Office, Southern District of New York, "Civil Complaint Amended."

19. Koppelman, "The Beauty of Black Friday."

Chapter 2: Before Poker

1. Qtd. in Stevenson, 76.

2. Milton, *Paradise Lost*, Book IX, lines 651, 779, 781-84.

3. Schwartz, *Roll the Bones*, 6-9.

4. Culin, 128.

5. Wilkinson, 61.

6. Another game similar to poque and much closer to the first version of 20-card poker called *as nas* from the Middle East is sometimes listed as a precursor to poker. The great games authority R.F. Foster once confidently declared "the game of poker, as first played in the United States... is undoubtedly the Persian game of *as nas*" (*Foster's Complete Hoyle*, 207). Herbert Asbury in *Sucker's Progress* also speculated that as French settlers in Louisiana played poque, as-nas "is believed to have brought to New Orleans about the time of the American occupation, when the city began to develop an extensive foreign commerce, and was probably introduced by sailors" (22). However, detailed descriptions of as nas don't actually appear until the late 19th century, that is, well *after* poker had already arrived in the early 1800s, casting doubt upon the Persian game's status as a possible predecessor.

7. Florence, 2.

8. Chaucer, "The Pardoner's Tale," lines 590-91 (495).

9. Hargrave, 40.

10. For example, from Mrs. John King van Rensselaer's 1890 book *The Devil's Picture-Books: A History of Playing Cards*: "History tells us that Columbus carried cards with him in his ship on the voyage of discovery in 1492, and that his sailors employed every spare moment playing with them, until their superstitious fancies persuaded them that this impious practice was the cause of the long voyage and contrary winds which alarmed them so greatly. During the frenzy caused by this panic, they flung overboard their Jonahs (the cards)" (147). After finally making land, the sailors are said to have regretted tossing the cards overboard and set about fashioning new ones from tree leaves. Like others, Mrs. van Rensselaer evokes the story to explain the introduction of playing cards to North America. "There seems to be more than a probability of truth in this story," suggests Hargrave (281).

11. Cardano, 5.

12. Ibid, 40.

13. Shakespeare, *The Merry Wives of Windsor,* Act IV, scene 5 (360).

14. Johnson, Samuel, 46.

15. Stith, 6-7.

16. Ibid, 26.

17. Fenich, 67.

18. Weyler, 110.

Chapter 3: Poker in Print

1. All quotes come from the first part of Letter XV (*Dragoons*, 128-30). During the early 1830s, occasional passing references to poker can be found in newspapers, the (likely) earliest appearing in the 3 Sep. 1832 edition of *The Globe* (Washington, D.C.) via the *Centre County Democrat* of Pennsylvania. With the 1832 presidential election two months away, the item finds supporters of challenger Henry Clay questioning the character of the incumbent Andrew Jackson by listing the president's many objectionable traits, including his being "notorious for his skill and dexterity at *Lieu* [i.e., the card game loo], *poker* and *Kentucky Brag*." The complaint is somewhat ironic, given Clay's own reputation as a poker player (see Chapter 13).
2. Green, Jonathan Harrington, *An Exposure*, 95.
3. Ibid, 96, 99, 107, 122-27.
4. Ibid, 97.
5. Green, Jonathan Harrington, *Gambling Unmasked*, 199.
6. Green, Jonathan Harrington, *An Exposure*, 98.
7. Ibid, 95.
8. All quotes from Cowell, 93-95.
9. *Hoyle's*, 260-63.
10. R.F. Foster explains how English editions of *Bohn's Handbook* ignored poker entirely until 1884. Meanwhile "The American reprint, which came out in 1850, tacked on a brief description of Poker, and draw Poker was inserted, out of place, in 1887" (*Practical Poker*, 10).
11. All quotes from Bohn, 381-84.
12. Turner, 88.
13. All quotes from Dick, 172-82. (The expanded section on poker appears at least by the third edition.)
14. Hauck, 1.
15. All quotes from "The National Game," 4.
16. "More About Draw-Poker," 2.

Chapter 4: Poker on the Mississippi

1. Asbury, 201.
2. Ibid, 203-04.
3. DeArment, *Knights of the Green Cloth*, 21.
4. Smith, Sol, 111.
5. Edwards, 22-25.
6. Qtd. in Johnson, Merle De Vore. 140.
7. Twain and Warner, 145. While the book was a collaboration between Twain and Warner, the quoted passage comes from a chapter usually attributed to Warner.
8. Twain, *A Connecticut Yankee*, 392.
9. Twain, "Full Report."
10. "Mark Twain Was Particular," 1.
11. Twain, *Life on the Mississippi*, 387.
12. Ibid, 392.
13. Ibid, 394.
14. Devol, 11-12.
15. Ibid, 14.
16. Ibid, 45.
17. Ibid, 136-37.
18. Ibid, 294.
19. Ibid, 296.

20. Ibid, 190.
21. Ibid, 285-86.
22. Ibid, 285.
23. Ibid, 286.
24. Ibid, 286-87.
25. Asbury, 207-09.
26. "Singular Characters," 1.
27. Ibid.
28. Curtis, *Queer Luck*, 131.
29. Ibid, 144.
30. Curtis, *Stand Pat*, 171.
31. Ibid, 213-15.
32. James McManus provides a more particular explanation of the origin of the poker term "river," linking it with the introduction of seven-card stud in which the seventh and last card is dealt face down. That "gave rise to the nickname 'Down-the-River,'" later shortened to just "the river." McManus also connects the term to the phrase "sold down the river," a reference to "troublesome slaves in border states punitively sold to planters in the Deep South, where working conditions were even harsher" (*Cowboys Full*, 168).

Chapter 5: Poker in the Old West
1. Sullivan, 5.
2. "The exact number of gambling houses that blossomed in the first flush of the wild stampede to the California goldfieds is not known, but there were several hundred, at least, and perhaps as many as a thousand" (DeArment, *Knights of the Green Cloth*, 10).
3. Remington, 301.
4. Bogdanovich, 84-85.
5. Ibid, 106.
6. DeArment, *Gunfighter in Gotham*, 3.
7. Ibid, 43.
8. Schwartz, *Roll the Bones*, 162.
9. Ibid.
10. Enss, 147.
11. Nichols, 274.
12. Ibid, 285.
13. Wilstach, 284.
14. Adams, Cecil.
15. Kesey, 77.

Chapter 6: Poker in the Civil War
1. Wiley, *The Life of Billy Yank*, 248.
2. Ibid, 249.
3. Ibid, 250-51.
4. Ibid, 250.
5. Ibid, 251.
6. Ibid.
7. Wiley, *The Life of Johnny Reb*, 36.
8. Ibid, 36-37.
9. Ibid, 37.
10. Ibid, 39.
11. Ibid, 39-40.

12. Flood, 10.

13. Grant, Vol. 17, 429.

14. Grant, Vol. 29, 42.

15. Grant, Vol. 4, 113.

16. Grant, Vol. 29, 108-09n.

17. All quotes from Ward, 2.

18. As described by Ward, Sheridan's call with "nothing" (or at least a hand worth less than a pair of nines) appears odd, perhaps only explained as having been made out of curiosity to see Grant's hand.

19. Qtd. in Thomas, Emory M., 68.

20. Childton, 772.

21. Wiley, *The Life of Johnny Reb*, 36.

22. Foote, 423-24.

23. McManus. 143.

24. Malmuth.

25. Mitchell, 35.

26. Ibid.

27. Ibid, 44.

28. Ibid, 47.

29. Ibid, 766.

30. Butler's line gets reprised in a scene near the beginning of the latter-day western *Dances With Wolves* (1990). During a lull in gunfire amid a Civil War battle in St. David's Field in Tennessee, a Union sergeant notes that "Some of the boys are saying that if we ain't gonna fight we could just settle the whole business with a little high-stakes poker. Wouldn't that be a sight? A bunch of fellas in the middle of this field drawing cards?"

31. All quotes from "Broke Up the Game," 3.

Chapter 7: Poker in Clubs

1. Curtis, *Queer Luck*, 3.

2. Ibid, 13-14.

3. Ibid, 15.

4. Ibid, 224.

5. Carleton, 42-43.

6. The final scene of *A Cure for Pokeritis* somewhat resembles *Sitting Up With a Sick Friend* from Casssius M. Coolidge's "Dogs Playing Poker" series of paintings in which a couple of hat-wearing "female" dogs barge in on a poker game and beat the "male" dogs with umbrellas. As the title indicates, they are upset about having been lied to regarding the true nature of the dogs' gathering (a ruse not unlike the "Sons of the Morning" one pulled in *Pokeritis*). For more on Coolidge's paintings, see chapter 9.

7. Yagoda, 31-32.

8. Harriman, 246.

9. Qtd. in Fadiman, 5.

10. Broun, 66.

11. Broun, 67; Harriman, 234.

12. Broun, 67.

13. Harriman, 234.

14. Marx and Barber, 130. With a few differences (e.g., locating the story in Galesburg, Illinois, not Rockford as Harpo does), Groucho tells the story as well in his 1977 compilation of anecdotes, *The Groucho Phile: An Illustrated Life*.

15. Harriman, 248.

16. Bancroft, 771.

17. Still the state's Attorney General, Ulysses S. Webb would issue an opinion letter on March 1, 1937 reaffirming his position "that commercial draw poker, where it was not operated as a bank or percentage game, was legal and there was nothing in state laws prohibiting it" (Votolato, 18).

18. "Poker Wins Over Prayers," 44.

19. Qtd. in Turner.

20. Hayano, x.

21. Ibid, 20.

22. Ibid, 138-39.

23. Ibid, 18.

24. Ibid, 140.

25. Miles, 111, 115.

26. Spanier, *Total Poker*, 132.

27. Brown, 107.

28. Ibid, 116.

29. Miles, 113.

30. Qtd. in Turner.

31. Walsh, *California Split*, screenplay, 1.

32. All quotes from Walsh, interview.

33. Churm, 1.

34. Truscott, C18.

35. Kerr, C20.

36. Koppleman, "Mayfair Club," 5.

37. Siegel.

38. Koppelman, "Mayfair Club," 5.

Chapter 8: Poker on the Bookshelf

1. Dick, 172.

2. "Letter from Minister Schenck," 4. The letter is dated 16 Jan. 1875. In an 1891 essay titled "Gambling in High Life," Adam Badeau (a former Union officer and member of U.S. Grant's staff) details how Lady Frances Waldegrave was the host responsible for the printing of Schenck's rules. On a printing press "in the house for the use of her cook, who set up his own menus... Lady Waldegrave had a score of little pamphlets, not so large as her hand, struck off and stitched in paper covers." As Badeau explains, a copy "found its way into the hands of an American who had a grudge against Schenck and saw the use that might be made of the paper" (497).

3. Schenck, 1.

4. Ibid, 6.

5. Ibid, 9-10.

6. Ibid, 16.

7. Dizikes, 310.

8. Lillard, 190-91. Badeau disputes stories such as this, maintaining that "General Schenck never played high in English society" (497).

9. Asbury, 34.

10. "Many a man," 208.

11. "The National Game," 4.

12. Elderkin, 21.

13. Winterblossom, 10-11.

14. Ibid, v, 52, 31.

15. Ibid, 56, vi.

16. Ibid, 72.

17. Blackbridge, iii. All quotes from the 2nd edition.

18. Rev. of *A Complete Poker-Player*, 4.

19. Blackbridge, 22.

20. Ibid, 23.

21. Ibid.

22. Ibid, 13-14.

23. Ibid, 49, 55.

24. "Magazines," 175.

25. Rev. of *A Complete Poker-Player*, 4.

26. Maugham, "The Portrait of a Gentleman," 156.

27. Proctor, 497.

28. "Poker Principles," 203. Following pages' worth of especially sober odds and probabilities, Proctor's essay ends with the lighthearted line that "poker-playing generally, as a process for making money more quickly, is much improved and enlivened by a slight degree of intoxication" (515). Perhaps with tongue-in-cheek as well, the *Chicago Tribune* reviewer condemns the recommendation, objecting that "a condition which seems highly problematical if the player is expected to remember the involved mathematical processes which [Proctor] lays down, and certainly implies a moral laxity which makes one sudder at the mere thought." ("Poker Principles," 203).

29. *Talk of Uncle George*, 5.

30. Ibid, 49.

31. Florence, 98.

32. Abbott.

33. Keller, 1.

34. Ibid, 53, 2.

35. Brown, "Preface."

36. Edwards, 9, 12.

37. Foster, *Foster's Complete Hoyle*, 236 (bold in original removed).

38. Foster, *Practical* Poker, xii.

39. Ibid, xi.

40. Ibid, 226.

41. "The Publishers," 31.

42. Kerfoot, 556.

43. Crofton, vii-xii.

44. Ibid, viii.

45. Fisher, 5, 14-15.

46. Ibid, 16-17.

47. Ibid, 29.

48. Pegler, "Fair Enough: Stud Poker Book Fills Old Need," 4.

49. Pegler, "Fair Enough: One Loud Vote for Stud Poker," 8. See Chapter 10 for more on Garner's poker playing.

50. Jacoby, 1.

51. "The publication of 'Oswald Jacoby on Poker'... was a huge success" ("Bridge Master," 66).

52. Yardley, vi, 3.

53. Ibid, 52.

54. Kahn, 233-34.

55. McManus, 240.

56. "A Big Hand for Poker," 33–34.
57. Huggins, 52.
58. Mamet, "A Gambler for Life," 238.
59. Preston, Cox, *Play Poker to Win*, 83.
60. Bradshaw, 178.
61. Sklansky, 9.
62. Alvarez, *The Biggest Game in Town*, 133.
63. Brunson, *The Godfather of Poker*, 177.
64. Brunson, "Poker High Stakes," 17.
65. Brunson, *Super/System*, 503.
66. Ibid, 442.
67. Scarne, *Scarne's Guide to Modern Poker*, vii.
68. Ibid, 2.
69. Ibid, 338.
70. Caro, Mike, *Mike Caro's Book of Tells*, 133, 165.
71. Hellmuth, 243.
72. All quotes from Krieger, interview.
73. The explosion in poker strategy titles accompanying the "poker boom" of the mid-2000s paralleled a larger rise-and-fall pattern of print book sales in the United States. According to Nielsen BookScan, sales of print books in the United States increased every year from 2004 to 2008, then suffered five straight years' worth of declines before rebounding somewhat over recent years though remaining well below the 2008 peak.

Chapter 9: Poker in the Home

1. Blackbridge, 13; *Talk of Uncle George*, 11; Florence, 2–3.
2. Lillard, 126.
3. Crane, 263.
4. Ibid, 264.
5. Ibid, 266–67.
6. Ibid, 267.
7. Barry, 44.
8. "A House Is Not a Home," *Cheers*, season 5, episode 25, NBC, 30 Apr. 1987.
9. "Treehouse of Horror IV." *The Simpsons*, season 5, episode 5, Fox, 28 Oct. 1993.
10. "Sinking Ship." *NewsRadio*, season 4, episode 22, NBC, 12 May 1998.
11. *Roseanne* fans noted how during the short-lived 2018 series reboot the paintings near the door had been removed.
12. Smith and Kiger, 50.
13. Webster, 2.
14. Ibid, 12.
15. Ibid, 14.
16. Ibid, 24.
17. Ibid, 27.
18. Ibid, 24.
19. Thurber, 42.
20. Ibid, 43.
21. Ibid, 44–45.
22. Ibid, 45.
23. Lukacs, 60.
24. Ibid.
25. Simon, 3. Unless noted, subsequent quotes are from the 1968 film directed by Gene

Saks (which in most cases closely follows the original play).

26. Ibid, 7–8.

27. Ibid, 113.

28. "The Laundry Orgy." *The Odd Couple*, season 1, episode 1, ABC, 24 Sep. 1970.

Chapter 10: Poker in the White House

1. Kornitzer, 148.

2. Hayes, 120.

3. George Washington Papers, 48.

4. "Cards for Americans," cover, 71.

5. Lillard, 17–18.

6. Sandburg, 47.

7. Thomas, Benjamin, 116–17.

8. Goodwin, 103.

9. Algeo, 134.

10. Watterson, Henry, 211–12.

11. McCullough, *Mornings on Horseback*, 254.

12. Roosevelt, "At Grand Canyon," 371.

13. Roosevelt, "At the Banquet at Dallas," 321.

14. The story appears in a letter written by Butt to his sister-in-law (Watterson, John Sayle, 87–88).

15. Thompson, Charles Willis, 213.

16. Qtd. in Livingston, *Poker Strategy*, 11.

17. Qtd. in McManus, *Cowboys Full*, 10.

18. Dean, 43–44.

19. Hoover, 48.

20. Trohan, 68.

21. Jackson, Robert, 137, 143.

22. Goodwin, "109th Landon Lecture."

23. Pegler, "One Loud Vote for Stud Poker," 8. Fisher's book is discussed in Chapter 8.

24. Caro, Robert A., *The Years of Lyndon Johnson, Vol. I*, 567.

25. McCullough, *Truman*, 137.

26. Lambert.

27. Vaughn.

28. McKim.

29. Smith, Merriman, 113.

30. Ibid.

31. Ibid, 137, 113.

32. Tidwell, 23; "GOP Candidate," 1.

33. Eisenhower, 88–90.

34. Ibid, 9, 23.

35. Ibid, 142–44.

36. Ibid, 176–78.

37. "Eisenhower Takes Time," 14; "Poker Computation Boosts Popularity," 13.

38. Caro, Robert A., *The Years of Lyndon Johnson: Vol. II*, 126.

39. Johnson, Lyndon Baines, 37.

40. Preston and Dinkin, 8, 111.

41. The memory comes from Lester "Budge" Ruffner, related to Fawn Brodie in an interview on March 26, 1976. See Brodie, 97.

42. Nixon, Interview by J.H. Hanson.

43. Mazo, 37.

44. Kornitzer, 147.

45. Quotes from fellow officers James Udall and Lester Wroble in Jackson, Donald, 66.

46. In a "five-and-ten game" (i.e., $5/$10 limits), Nixon tells of one opponent leading on fifth street and a second raising, then with his royal flush he put in another raise. "Unfortunately, I had established my credibility too well on the small pots. Nobody called me, so I raked the chips – a pretty good pot." (Nixon, Interview by Frank Gannon).

47. Nixon, *RN*, 29.

48. Nixon, *In the Arena*, 185.

49. Nixon, Interview by Frank Gannon.

50. O'Neill, 157-58.

51. Nixon, "Address to the Congress on Stabilization of the Economy." In the speech, Nixon interestingly introduces the analogy as having been suggested to him 15 years prior by a "prominent world statesman" (likely Churchill).

52. Nixon, Conversation No. 275-9.

53. Nixon, Conversation No. 772-8.

54. Nixon, Conversation No. 23-96.

55. Spanier, *Total Poker*, 74.

56. Ford, 46.

57. Brown, Aaron, 178.

58. Scherer and Weisskopf, 30-31. James McManus also shares recollections of poker games from Obama's colleagues at the start of *Cowboys Full* (1-7).

59. Konik.

60. Caselli.

61. Weidman, et al., 26, 28.

Chapter 11: Poker During Wartime

1. Apostolico, xvii-xviii.

2. Unless otherwise noted, information about historical playing cards comes from Gene Hochman's original *Encyclopedia of American Playing Cards*, published by Hochman in six parts from 1976-1981. His work was later consolidated by Tom and Judy Dawson as *The Hochman Encyclopedia of Playing Cards*.

3. Starckx.

4. Purdom, 103.

5. Starckx.

6. Cumings, 850; Nixon, *The Real War*, 254. Acknowledgement to James Matray for highlighting Cumings's argument in "Dean Acheson's Press Club Speech Reexamined."

7. Cronkite, *CBS Evening News*, 27 Feb. 1968.

8. Halberstam, 615.

9. Tiede, 5. For more on the symbolic significance of playing cards and the ace of spades in Vietnam, see McManus, *Cowboys Full* (288-294). Regarding the effectiveness of the Americans' using the ace of spades to spook the Viet Cong, McManus cites "death-card historian Herbert Friedman" suggesting the North Vietnamese fear of the symbol to have been overestimated by the Americans. "The cards motivated and encouraged American troops far more than they terrified the enemy," estimates Friedman (292).

10. Hobert, SR6.

11. Von Neumann and Morgenstern, 186.

12. Not to be confused with the similarly-named hard-boiled writer John D. MacDonald whose series of Travis McGee novels often featured poker.

13. McDonald, John, 21. See Chapter 12 for more on McDonald's explanation of the rele-

vance of game theory and poker strategy to economics and business.

14. Morgenstern, 14.
15. Ibid.
16. Ibid.
17. Ibid, 22.
18. Wiznitzer, 69.
19. See David Spanier's excellent presentation of the Cuban Missile Crisis as a poker game in *Total Poker* (84-92).
20. Burdick and Wheeler, 191.
21. "Sir Ken Adam."
22. Bush, George W.; Klein, 4.
23. "A Dangerous Poker Game With Iraq," 14; Raghavan; Gordon, A7; Cooper; Green, Stephen.

Chapter 12: Poker in the Board Room
1. Buffett.
2. Jefferson, 448-49.
3. Ibid.
4. Blackbridge, v.
5. McDonald, John, 85-87.
6. Ibid, 96. McDonald also explores how this resolution of a complex "industry" into two primary players (or opposing positions) is also a frequent feature of "political economy" (97).
7. Ibid, 108-09.
8. Gates, 18.
9. Ibid, 39.
10. Ibid, 39-40.
11. Ibid, 208-09. Writing in 1995 at during the internet's nascent period, Gates correctly predicts the coming of online poker just a few years away (see Chapter 21). "Gambling is going to be another way to play on the highway," Gates observes, noting how for some (such as himself) the appeal of risking one's money by gambling increases when it requires less time to do so (208).
12. Schwager, *The Market Wizards*, 148.
13. Ibid, 148.
14. Schwager, *The New Market Wizards*, 394.
15. Ibid, 394-95.
16. Ibid, 396.
17. Pulliam, A1.
18. Patterson, 8.
19. Ibid, 7.
20. Ibid, 10.
21. Brown, Aaron, 1.
22. Lewis, 16.
23. Ibid, 16-17.
24. Bjerg, 3.
25. Ibid, 203.
26. Ibid, 208.
27. Ibid, 212.
28. Ibid, 218.
29. Ibid, 222.
30. The quote is of uncertain origin, but can be found in Spanier, *Total Poker* (201).
31. Alvarez, *Risky Business*, 158.

32. Like W.C. Fields saying "The world is getting to be such a dangerous place, a man is lucky to get out of it alive."

Chapter 13: Poker in Folklore
1. Acknowledgement to Barbara Connors, who includes this observation amid her excellent discussion of men and women in poker, "Power Play" (34).
2. Cowell, 94.
3. Qtd. in Boller, 80.
4. Adams, John Quincy, 45.
5. Keller, 50.
6. Florence, 23.
7. Spanier, *Total Poker*, 82.
8. "What is a 'looloo'?," 2.
9. "Senatorial Poker," 2.
10. "Fulls and Flushes," 32. All quotes from this version.
11. The story is usually attributed to *The New York Tribune*; quotes are from the version appearing in *Michigan Farmer*, 17, 36.
12. Syndicated reprints of the story attribute it to *The New York Morning Journal*. All quotes are from the version appearing in Edwards, *Jack Pots* (162-65).
13. Edwards speculates both players must have drawn four aces, guessing further that "some youngster of the family rung in a cold deck on the old gentlemen, and then, when he saw the mischief he had done, was afraid to acknowledge the trick" (165).
14. Alvarez, *The Biggest Game in Town*, 66.
15. Hayano, 139.
16. May, 62.
17. "Gamblers Testify," 1.
18. Pietrusza, 11.
19. "Gamblers Testify," 18, "Raymond to Testify," 22.
20. Bradshaw, 226.
21. Benny Binion would later state that Bernstein, Thompson, and Raymond were "the last three men livin' that was in the room in New York at that famous Rothstein killin'. They was in the room when he was killed" (Binion, Lester Ben "Benny," 43).
22. Hesford, 53.
23. Schwarz.
24. Arrillaga, 10.
25. Li, 30.
26. For example, Frank Deford repeats the story this way in "Three Little Syllables" (30).
27. "The Rambler," 220.
28. Pomeranz and Topik, 123-25.

Chapter 14: Poker in Casinos
1. Schwartz, 353-55.
2. "Gaming, Divorce Bills Signed," 1.
3. Rothman, 7-8.
4. In fact, the nickname "Sin City" predates gambling and the rise of the Strip. According to Nevada historian Michael Green, the moniker first appeared way back in 1906 with reference to Las Vegas's infamous "Block 16" where both liquor and prostitution were permitted without licenses (Kishi).
5. The Golden Nugget issued an identical guide in 1948. Promotional materials discussed here and afterwards are located in the UNLV Special Collections at the Center for Gaming Research.

6. According to *The Golden Nugget Grand Prix of Poker Official 1986 Program*, "The Golden Nugget held its first poker tournament in the early '70s" (3).

7. The 1940 survey was conducted by the Association of American Card Playing Manufacturers, with results included in Oswald Jacoby and Albert Morehead's *The Fireside Book of Cards* (18); the results of a 1947 Gallup poll were reported in Gary M. Pomerantz's *The Devil's Tickets* (230); the 1957 survey was again by the Association of American Card Playing Manufacturers and noted in Albert H. Morehead's article "Bridge: 'Summer Rules' Take Over" (107); and Scarne reports his survey results in *Scarne's New Complete Guide to Gambling* (7).

8. American Gaming Association, 26. Such figures remain constant over several years' worth of surveys conducted by the AGA.

9. In 1963 there were 22,178 slot machines compared to 86 poker tables (about 258 to 1); in 2017 there were 164,996 slots compared to 638 tables (about 259 to 1); the greatest ratio came in 2002 when there were 210,575 slots and 382 tables (about 564 to 1) ("Nevada's Gaming Footprint, 1936-2018").

10. Nevada peaked at 114 poker rooms in 2009 ("Nevada Poker: The Evolution").

11. Binion, Lester Ben "Benny," 39-40.

12. Alvarez, *The Biggest Game in Town*, 27-28.

13. Himes, 56.

14. Binion, Lester Ben "Benny," 22.

15. Jenkins, 1. Subsequent quotes from Jenkins, 1-10.

16. Alvarez, *The Biggest Game in Town*, 30, 32.

17. Holden, *Big Deal*, 19-20.

18. McManus, *Cowboys Full*, 275-76.

19. Quotes from Jack Binion via personal communication, 2 Jun. 2017.

20. Thackrey Jr., "Roulette's a Sucker Game in U.S.," 77.

21. Thackrey Jr., *Gambling Secrets of Nick the Greek*, 3.

22. Boyer, 38. Acknowledgment to *Quote Investigator*, who while investigating the roulette quote also shares a colleague's comment that while Thackrey was well liked and admired as a reporter, "he made up stuff all the time." See <quoteinvestigator.com/2012/09/09/einstein-roulette/>,

23. Preston and Dinkin, 156-57.

24. Brunson, *The Godfather of Poker*, 135.

25. David G. Schwartz notes "there were fewer than 1,800 newspapers in the United States then" ("The Surprisingly Humble, Forgotten Roots Of Poker's Biggest Game").

26. These figures do not include states like California and Florida that host significant numbers of card rooms yet no commercial casinos with poker facilities. The 10 states with neither commercial nor tribal casinos in 2018 were Arkansas, Georgia, Hawaii, Kentucky, New Hampshire, South Carolina, Tennessee, Utah, Vermont, and Virginia (American Gaming Association, *State of the States 2018*, 12-14).

27. American Gaming Association, *State of the States 2018*, 6; National Indian Gaming Commission, "2017 Indian Gaming Revenues Increase 3.9% to $32.4 Billion."

28. Again, revenue generated at the poker tables in Nevada peaked both in general and relative to other games in the late 2000s, reaching highs of almost $168M in 2007 and 1.4 percent of total casino revenue in 2009.

Chapter 15: Poker on the Newsstand

1. Peterson, 51.

2. Ibid, 12-14, 52-56.

3. Holden, *Holden on Hold'em*, 4.

Poker & Pop Culture

4. Alvarez, *Poker: Bets, Bluffs and Bad Beats*, 44.

5. Texas, House of Representatives, H.C.R. 109

6. Jenkins, 50.

7. Bradshaw, 153.

8. Moore, 6.

9. Brunson, 59.

10. Ibid, 69-71.

11. Qtd. in Brunson, *Super System 2*, 76-77.

12. Livingston, "Hold Me," 42.

13. Ibid, 39

14. Gilmore.

15. Hecht, 54.

16. Stoddard, 109.

17. Alvarez's "Reporter at Large (Poker World Series)" appeared in two parts in the 7 Mar. and 14 Mar. 1983 issues of *The New Yorker*.

18. Alvarez, *The Biggest Game in Town*, 9.

19. Ibid, 43.

20. Ibid, 15.

21. Conley, 58.

22. Simpich, 79.

23. "Little Tragedies," 17.

24. Quoted in Gaines, 90.

25. McDonald, Duff, 280.

26. "At the World Series of Poker," 63.

27. Allis, 170.

28. "Cool Hand Duke," 110.

29. "Poker Champ Jennifer Tilly Plays Her Hand," 24.

30. "Business Notes," 62.

31. Skow, 12.

32. Russo, W6.

33. Kadlec, 43. The "mind-set coach," Sam Chauhan, once described in *Bluff* magazine his coaching method as "I meditate empowering energy to my clients and create a powerful frequency through vibration of the powerful mantras" ("Make a Point to Stay Positive," *Bluff*, 7.5, May 2011, 48-49).

34. Axthelm.

35. Goodman, Walter, "Poker as a Way of Life," 76.

36. Ansen, 76.

37. Goodman, Leah McGrath. See also Grove, "11 Serious Problems with Newsweek's Weird Tirade Against Regulated Online Gambling."

38. Shrake, "It Ain't Just Heaven," 65. Interestingly, despite including a lengthy testimonial from Sid Wyman (then part owner of The Dunes) declaring Moss to be "the champion player," no mention is made in Shrake's profile of the inaugural World Series of Poker from the previous spring where Moss was voted the winner – an indication of the WSOP's initially miniscule impact.

39. Shrake, 56.

40. Shrake, "Care to Join Our Little Game?"; Kaplan, "Bet On It."

41. Dionne, "Youth Can Age You," 46.

42. Boyle, 24.

43. Livingston, "A Sawyer Takes the Pot Every Time," 45.

44. Dionne, "If You Play Your Cards Right."

45. Hoffer; Reilly; Habib; Hendrickson.

46. Fariello; Kittredge.

47. Solotaroff.

48. "Vegas Without Shame"; "$5,000 Slot Machines."

49. "Giving Himself Away," 350.

50. Broun, Heywood, 6-7.

51. "Edison Tests Poker Skill in New Quiz," 33.

52. "A MAD peek behind the scenes at Celebrity Poker Showdown," 18-20.

53. Lardner, 45, 110.

54. Hibler, 79, 172.

55. Browne, 179.

56. Ostrow, "According to Whose Hoyle," 105; "When Poker Was Poker," 104.

57. Nelson; Rosenbaum; Berendt; "How to Find and Play a Poker Game"; "The One-Minute Guide to Poker."

58. Schulman, 31.

59. Moss, 87.

60. "I'll Play These."

61. Caro, Mike, "The Art of the Tell," 93, 146.

62. Marquis, 64.

63. Chiappone, 152–56.

64. Mamet, "A Gambler for Life," 239.

65. Stein, 106, 135.

66. "Queen High"; Jordan; Kaplan, "Phil Ivey's New House of Cards."

67. Crain, 258-61.

68. "Sag-Pisces," 20. From 1998 to 2017 there appear no less than 29 articles in *Cosmopolitan* that refer to strip poker.

69. Gifford, 200.

70. Segrest, 46.

71. "Good House," 85; "Made on the Shade," 85.

72. Braniff.

73. Deane.

74. Parlee, 14.

75. Ibid, 15.

76. A report by the Audit Bureau of Circulations (<www.cardplayer.com/packages/media_kit/pdf/ABC_Audit_end_12_08.pdf>) shows *Card Player*'s average circulation per issue to have been 96,402 for July-December 2008, with the highest circulation 105,821 (July 8, 2008). Of that total, just under 79 percent of copies circulated were "non-paid" (i.e., distributed for free). A current "media kit" from *Card Player* (posted in 2018) lists circulation at 45,000 (<www.cardplayer.com/media-kit/magazine>).

77. Bradley.

Chapter 16: Poker in the Movies

1. Hesse, Terris, Zak.

2. Spanier, *Total Poker*, 157.

3. References to the film sometimes also include a parenthetical subtitle "Alaska Gold Rush."

4. Wister, 29.

5. The 1946 version of *The Virginian* directed by Stuart Gilmore and starring Joel McCrea similarly keeps the Virginian away from the poker table early on while repeating the poker metaphor before the final duel ("Never mind the bluff, I'm calling your hand," says Trampas).

6. Taylor, 158.

7. Qtd. in Wertheim, 181.

8. Taylor, 158. According to Taylor, Fields would lie in interviews to say he had been wiped out by the crash. Taylor shares another story illustrating Fields' antipathy toward risk. After having been mugged once as a young man in San Francisco, Fields began opening bank accounts in every city to which he traveled. Some suggest he had as many as 700 accounts all over the world, although at the time of his death his executors only found 30 of them (57, 63-64).

9. Other Fields film titles – many of which bear little significance to the plots – evoke poker maxims such as *You Can't Cheat an Honest Man* (1939) and *Never Give a Sucker an Even Break* (1941).

10. Remade as a talkie in 1934, *The Road to Ruin* again starred Foster (with a different name), in a relatively less tawdry version of the same story, though still plenty controversial by the day's standards. Among the several mostly incidental changes to the story, the party-goers play dice rather than poker as they gamble away their garments.

11. Silberstang, 99.

12. Ibid, 100.

13. Rev. of *The Last Deal*, 216.

14. Shaffer, 23.

15. Poker is played briefly in *The Hustler* (1961), although not by Newman's character, the pool player "Fast Eddie" Felson. In *Hud* (1963), Newman plays a woman-chaser who becomes enamored with a housekeeper, in part because she is a poker player. And in *Nobody's Fool* (1994), Newman plays a construction worker who frequently plays in a home game with the company's owner. Newman himself was not an especially dedicated poker player, at least not according to biographer Shawn Levy. "Despite the evidence of his film work," writes Levy, "he played pool and poker passingly to badly; chess too." When it came to card games, Newman preferred bridge instead, says Levy, spending down time on sets "working out bridge hands silently in his head" (156).

16. Interestingly, the two drones with whom Lowell plays poker appear at one point to collude with one another. In other words, they have not only learned how to play poker but also how to *cheat*, which in turn suggests something about the game (as encouraging cheating) and/or human nature (which the drones' programming mimics).

17. In Medoff's 1979 play, the couple plays bridge, not poker, where the same warnings about cheating perhaps are more readily applicable given that bridge is played with partners.

18. Harris, René.

19. "Gamblers on Titanic Escape by Dressing as Women."

20. The chips and cards can be viewed as part of *Titanic: The Artifact Exhibition* at the Luxor Casino in Las Vegas (acknowledgement to Robert Woolley).

21. Harris, Martin, "Pop Poker."

22. Weddle, 257.

23. Spencer Tracy had originally been signed on to portray Lancey Howard, though "did not agree with the way the script was evolving and bowed out" after a couple of weeks (Bart, 56). "Sam [Peckinpah] agreed that [Edward G.] Robinson was a good substitute, but was disappointed to lose Tracy." Meanwhile Sharon Tate (Ransohoff's then girlfriend) had been picked to portray Christian, but Peckinpah objected and Tuesday Weld was cast; Peckinpah also disagreed with the casting of Ann-Margaret, but lost that battle (Weddle, 259).

24. In addition to Chayefsky, Frank Gilroy and Charles Eastman contributed to early drafts along with Southern and Lardner (Weddle, 258).

25. Michael Wiesenberg once estimated the odds of two such hands occurring as being 45,102,784 to 1 ("The Cincinnati Kid"). "In poker terms, the hand is a joke," judges Anthony Holden, who sees "no evident moral in the way things turn out" (*Big Deal*, 73).

26. An early draft of *The Cincinnati Kid* screenplay, dated 3 Nov. 1964 and attributed only to Ring Lardner Jr. has Eric accusingly say to Lancey after the hand "You were crazy – odds are three hundred to one against" (129). That line's omission from the final version is not only preferable because the odds being cited are imprecise, but to have Eric complain about getting unlucky would confirm his failure to have learned anything from the experience, something Lancey underscores in his response (also omitted from the final version): "I don't play a percentage game. I play stud poker my way. And I got the money and you got the questions. Figure that out" (129).

27. Walsh, *Gambler on the Loose*, 188.

28. Walsh, interview.

29. The fact that Mike makes this argument to Jo directly after having colluded with Worm in the game against the "trust fund babies" actually hurts his position, given that the pair's cheating makes the skill component Mike argues for less meaningful.

30. Proving *Luckytown*'s lack of concern about either poker or realism, at the conclusion of a hand involving Charlie and the younger player, Charlie appears to show two queens as though the game is hold'em, while the other character turns over five cards as though the game is five-card draw.

31. *Rounders* is another obvious source of material for *Shade*, starting with the opening voice-over monologue and including the appearance of a superfluous older card cheat named "The Professor" (played by Hal Holbrook) who conspicuously resembles Professor Petrovsky from *Rounders* when delivering what purports to be sage life advice to Vernon ("Just remember, some things are more important than money").

32. *Casino Royale* (2006) was the 21st film from Eon Productions, considered by Bond fans the sole proprietor of the character and series; other companies produced the earlier *Casino Royale* as well as *Never Say Never Again* (1983).

33. During the tournament considerable effort is made to show Bond discovering Le Chiffre's "tell" – an eye twitch when he bluffs – only to have Le Chiffre later use the tell falsely when he actually has a strong hand to win a big pot off of Bond. However, the fact that Le Chiffre wins the hand with quad jacks versus Bond's aces full of kings renders that effort superfluous, negating the need to have bothered with false tells or bluffs since both players' hands are so strong all the chips were going in, anyway. The 2010 comedy *MacGruber* spoofs the idea of the super intelligent action hero using heightened powers of perception to spot tells at the poker table when the title character assures someone the film's villain is bluffing "by the look in his beady little eyes." With the tip the player shoves all in, and the villain promptly calls with a straight flush.

34. *All In* was barely released, yielding no recorded box office information. By contrast, *Lucky You* opened in 2,525 theaters and endured one of the worst wide openings in box office history, earning slightly more than $2.7 million. With a $55 million budget, the film ultimately grossed just under $8.4 million worldwide (<www.boxofficemojo.com/alltime/weekends/worstopenings.htm?page=WRSTOPN25&p=.htm>). *Lucky You* was based in part on another box office failure, the 1970 film *The Only Game in Town* starring Elizabeth Taylor and Warren Beatty. That film had an estimated $11 million budget and earned only $1.5 million. Meanwhile *Deal*, with an estimated budget of $5 million, earned less than $80,000 at the box office worldwide during its two weeks in the theaters (<www.boxofficemojo.com/movies/?id=deal.htm>).

35. Travers; "The Seagal Report"; Rechtshaffen.

36. With a $6 million budget, *Mississippi Grind* earned just over $130,000 in theaters although was simultaneously released as video-on-demand, the figures for which are not reported (<www.boxofficemojo.com/movies/?id=mississippigrind.htm>). *Molly's Game* writer-director Aaron Sorkin earned an Oscar nomination for his adaptation; the film earned

nearly $60 million in theaters worldwide, almost twice its $30 million budget (<www.box-officemojo.com/movies/?id=mollysgame.htm>).

37. There have been poker documentaries as well, a couple of which are discussed in Chapter 22.

Chapter 17: Poker in Literature

1. Hammett, 87–88.
2. Morgan, 171–77.
3. Maugham, "Straight Flush," 153.
4. Runyon, "Princess O'Hara," 213.
5. Harte, 41.
6. Ibid.
7. Ibid, 45.
8. Ibid, 47.
9. Lydston, 76.
10. Ibid, 49.
11. Ibid, 19.
12. Tarkington, 118.
13. Ibid, 119.
14. Brecht scholars agree his *The Threepenny Opera* collaborator Elisabeth Hauptmann contributed significantly to "Four Men" and other stories, though Brecht alone was listed as author.
15. Jones, 292.
16. Ibid, 296.
17. Updike, 191.
18. Ibid, 193.
19. Auster, 63.
20. Twain, 387.
21. Wister, 25.
22. Ibid, 34.
23. Kelley, 26.
24. Ibid, 34.
25. Oates, 74.
26. Ibid, 77.
27. Bennet, 200.
28. Speaking of connections between the author and his fictional character, May worked as a commentator with the groundbreaking U.K. television show *Late Night Poker* (1999–2002) discussed in Chapter 20, and in fact during the first season he appeared on an episode as a player, too, using the same "Mickey Dane" pseudonym.
29. May, 8.
30. Ibid, 32.
31. Ibid, 140.
32. Kaufman, 13.
33. Hurston.
34. Mamet, "The Things Poker Teaches," SM52.
35. Mamet, *American Buffalo*, 6.
36. Ibid, 40.
37. The original subtitle for Holden's book was "Confessions of a Professional Poker Player," later revised to reflect the scope of Holden's experiment.
38. Holden, *Big Deal*, 62.

39. Amis, 179.

40. Bellin, 241–42.

41. McManus, *Positively Fifth Street*, 21–22.

42. It is also worth noting that British writer and television presenter Victoria Coren's won the £500,000 first prize in a 2006 European Poker Tour event, subsequently recounted in her own poker memoir, *For Richer, For Poorer: A Love Affair With Poker* (2009). Coren won a second EPT Main Event title in 2014 (for €476,100).

43. Curiously, and as if to highlight the literary leanings of Amis's essay, details of his bustout hand as first reported in 2006 have been entirely rewritten for the essay's publication in his 2017 collection *The Rub of Time*. Whereas Amis originally hit the rail following a mundane preflop all-in with pocket sevens vs. ace-king (Amis, "On Poker, Panic and a Pair of Sevens," 24), the revised version has him all in with pocket fives and called by an opponent holding pocket sixes. The 5-J-6 flop gives both players sets, with another 6 on the river knocking Amis from the event. His comment sounds as though the flop is mistaken as he lyrically describes the winning hand as "the mark of the beast: 6-6-6" (Amis, "Losing in Las Vegas," 153).

44. Holden, *Bigger Deal*, 232.

45. Whitehead, 3.

Chapter 18: Poker on the Radio

1. Jewison.

2. "Radio 1929-1941."

3. "Gun Shy Gambler," *The Lone Ranger*, episode 1845, NBC Blue Network, 15 Nov. 1944.

4. "Four Aces for Death," *The Adventures of Wild Bill Hickok*, episode 21, Mutual radio network, 19, Aug. 1951.

5. "The Case of the Poker Murders," *Nick Carter, Master Detective*, episode 236, Mutual radio network, 21 May 1946.

6. "The Case of the Killer Cards," *The New Adventures of Nero Wolfe,* episode 13, NBC radio network, 12 Jan. 13.

7. "Playing Poker with Charles Coburn," *Duffy's Tavern*, episode 322, NBC radio network, 4 May 1949.

8. "Poker Game," *Fibber McGee and Molly*, episode 353, NBC Red Network, 23 Feb. 1943.

9. "The Poker Game," *The Burns and Allen Show*, episode 66, CBS radio network, 7 Mar. 1944.

10. "Be a Pal," *My Favorite Husband*, episode 93, CBS radio network, 18 Jun. 1950.

11. "Poker Game," *Fibber McGee and Molly*.

12. "The Poker Game," *The Burns and Allen Show*.

Chapter 19: Poker in Music

1. MacEvoy, "That Game of Poker!"

2. "Richard A. Saalfield obituary."

3. Saalfield, "Poker; or, That queen."

4. Edwards, 267-68.

5. Sampson, 59.

6. Bundles, 22, 286.

7. Wintz and Glasrud, 179.

8. Bahrampour, A6.

9. Charles also sings the theme song to *The Cincinnati Kid* (1965), with lyrics by Dorcas Cochran and music by Lalo Schifrin.

10. McGuire, "Life in the Fast Lane."

11. Knopper, 43.

12. "National Recording Registry Reaches 500." "The Gambler" earned Schlitz a Grammy for Best Country Song (in 1979) and Rogers a Grammy for Best Male Country Vocal Performance (in 1980). The song and album also helped Larry Butler also win a Producer of the Year Grammy in 1980, the only country music producer ever to win the award.

13. In addition to Schlitz, Cash, and Rogers, three other country artists released versions of "The Gambler" in 1978: Bobby Bare, Hugh Moffatt, and Michael Twitty (Conway's son, recording under the name Charlie Tango).

14. Schlitz.

15. Bernstein.

16. Kilmister and Garza, 137-38.

17. The satirical spelling of America as "Amerikkka" dates back to an article by Preston Wilcox for the July 1970 issue of the journal *Black World* (formerly *Negro Digest*) titled "White Ethics and Black Power: The Emergence of the West Side Organization" (82-84). Gangsta rap artist Ice Cube first popularized the spelling in music with his 1990 album *AmeriKKKa's Most Wanted*.

Chapter 20: Poker on Television

1. Petrie, 70.

2. Ibid.

3. Ibid, 95.

4. In 1950 there were 3.88 million television households in America, representing 9 percent of U.S. homes; by 1965 the total had ballooned to 52.7 million or 92.6 percent. (Steinberg, 142).

5. "Trails's End for a Cowboy," *The Life and Legend of Wyatt Earp*, season 1, episode 14, ABC, 6 Dec. 1955.

6. "Tinhorn," *The Rifleman*, season 4, episode 24, ABC, 12 Mar. 1962.

7. Hargrove, 75.

8. "According to Hoyle" features an interesting reference to the rulebook. Maverick draws a straight and appears to win a big pot from an opponent who has three nines, but she reads him a rule from *Hoyle* suggesting straights don't play in five-card stud "unless it's determined at the commencement of the game that they be admitted" ("According to Hoyle," *Maverick*, season 1, episode 3, ABC, 6 Oct. 1957). Indeed, as discussed in Chapter 3, the 1864 *American Hoyle* does refer to straights not always being allowed, and that "it should always be determined whether they are to be admitted at the commencement of the game."

9. "Rope of Cards," *Maverick*, season 1, episode 17, ABC, 19 Jan. 1958. There have been multiple academic essays written by mathematicians about the scene. See for instance Martin J. Chlond's "Five Pat Hands" in which he provides a mathematical explanation for why when tasked "to arrange 25 randomly dealt playing cards into five pat poker hands [i.e., a straight, a flush, a full house, four of a kind, a straight flush, and a royal flush]... the probabilty of success is about 98%" (164). In Roy Huggins's *Poker According to Maverick*, he (writing as "Bret Maverick") reveals the true odds to be "at least 49 to 1 in my favor" (of making five pat hands).

10. "This TV series spawned a mini-boom in poker much like *Rounders* created a real boom in poker in the 1990s" (Hughes, 79).

11. Two western series in particular, *The Alaskans* (1959-60) and *Alias Smith and Jones* (1971-73) borrowed liberally from *Maverick*, with the latter (for which Roy Huggins wrote, directed, and produced) repeating both the "According to Hoyle" ruse and "Maverick Solitaire" (more than once).

12. The episode adapted Henry Slesar and Jay Folb's story "A Fist Full of Money" that first published in the February 1959 issue of *Playboy*.

13. "The Corbomite Maneuver," *Star Trek*, season 1, episode 10, NBC, 10 Nov. 1966.

14. "A Piece of the Action," *Star Trek*, season 2, episode 17, NBC, 12 Jan. 1968.

15. "The Measure of a Man," *Star Trek: The Next Generation*, season 2, episode 9, syndication, 13 Feb. 1989.

16. "The Outcast," *Star Trek: The Next Generation*, season 5, episode 17, syndication, 16 Mar. 1992.

17. "Descent, Part I," *Star Trek: The Next Generation*, season 6, episode 26, syndication, 21 Jun. 1993.

18. "All Good Things..., Part II," *Star Trek: The Next Generation*, season 7, episode 26, syndication, 23 May 1994.

19. "Crazy Handful of Nothin'," *Breaking Bad*, season 1, episode 6, AMC, 2 Mar. 2008.

20. There are multiple stories of Desi Arnaz's affection for high-stakes poker, including one in which he allegedly won a Palm Springs ranch home near the Thunderbird Country Club in a poker game in 1954. There the couple hosted parties (and more high-stakes games), with poker perhaps having provided at least one source of friction between them prior to their 1960 divorce. TV screenwriter and producer Bob Weiskopf later recalled how Lucy would indirectly insult Desi to others, saying "for example, what had happened in a poker game over the weekend in Palm Springs. In front of him, she'd talk about what stupid plays he had made. I thought, 'Jesus Christ, this guy's a saint.' I would have punched her in the nose" (Schinderette).

21. "A Dog's Life," *The Honeymooners*, season 1, episode 21, CBS, 18 Feb. 1956.

22. "An Evening with Hamlet," *The Adventures of Ozzie and Harriet*, season 2, episode 32, ABC, 23 Apr. 1954.

23. "Rick and Kris Go to the Mountains," *The Adventures of Ozzie and Harriet*, season 13, episode 4, ABC, 7 Oct. 1964.

24. "A Nice, Friendly Game of Cards," *The Dick Van Dyke Show*, season 3, episode 18, CBS, 29 Jan. 1964.

25. "The Card Sharps," *Sanford and Son*, season 2, episode 6, NBC, 27 Oct. 1972.

26. "The Merchant of Korea," *M*A*S*H*, season 6, episode 17, CBS, 20 Dec. 1977.

27. "Your Hit Parade," *M*A*S*H*, season 6, episode 19, CBS, 24 Jan. 1978.

28. "Pick a Con... Any Con," *Cheers*, season 1, episode 19, NBC, 24 Feb. 1983.

29. "Presence." *NewsRadio*, season 2, episode 19, NBC, 14 Apr. 1996.

30. "Blind Date," *30 Rock*, season 1, episode 3, NBC, 25 Oct. 2006.

31. "Casino Night," *The Office*, season 2, episode 22, NBC, 11 May 2006.

32. Preston and Dinkin, 174.

33. "Milton Berle," *I've Got a Secret*, season 1, episode 7, Firestone Syndication Company, 4 Aug. 1972.

34. "Binion's Horseshoe Casino Presents the World Series of Poker," *CBS Sports Spectacular*, CBS, 1973.

35. Scarne, *Scarne's Guide to Modern Poker*, 3-4.

36. Grotenstein and Reback, 120.

37. "2002 World Series of Poker," ESPN, 2002.

38. ESPN employed such inserts for both the 1988 and 1989 WSOP Main Event broadcasts (the first for the network), though abandoned it thereafter. While *The Discovery Channel* shows from 1999-2001 only intermittently focus on actual game play, during the 2000 show something similar was done by identifying players' hole cards briefly via a graphic before their hands are tabled. Meanwhile earlier broadcasts occasionally had trouble even showing hole cards correctly after the showdown, such as during the final hand of the 1994

WSOP Main Event on ESPN when Russ Hamilton goes all in on a 8♣-2♠-6♦ flop holding K♠-8♥ and is called by Hugh Vincent who shows 8♣-5♥ (an impossible hand for him to have, as the 8♣ is on the board).

39. Details of *Late Night Poker*'s origins come via Nic Szeremeta's history of the show, first shared in *Poker Europa* magazine and republished in a series of articles on PokerNews in 2014, starting with <learn.pokernews.com/news/2014/03/the-making-of-late-night-poker-part-1-it-will-never-work-3700.htm>.

40. *Late Night Poker* viewing figures reported by Szeremeta via Gardner.

41. Qtd. in Holden, *Bigger Deal*, 82.

42. Bulwa.

43. In *The Moneymaker Effect*, Eric Raskin's terrific oral history of the 2003 WSOP Main Event, it is revealed that concerns from Nevada gaming regulators almost led to ESPN not employing hole card cameras in their coverage, though ultimately the network managed to obtain the needed approval. "I think we got it resolved just one day before the Main Event started," says Bob Chesterman, then senior coordinating producer for ESPN Original Entertainment. "It was too close for comfort" (59-60).

44. Bulwa.

45. Raskin, 197.

46. "Countdown with Keith Olbermann." season 1, *NBC*, 18 Dec. 2003; "Big Ratings Pot for Bravo Celebrity Poker Finale."

47. Qtd. in Hartley, 115.

Chapter 21: Poker on the Computer

1. Findler, "Computer Model of Gambling and Bluffing," 6.

2. Findler, "Computer Poker," 151.

3. Caro, "Decades later."

4. Rehmeyer, Fox, and Renzi, 186-91.

5. Harris, "Laak-Eslami Team."

6. Bowling et al., 146. The headline's claim is somewhat belied by the study's explanation "that heads-up limit Texas hold'em poker is essentially weakly solved" (a definitional qualification).

7. Moon.

8. Caruso.

9. Spanier, *All Right, Okay, You Win* (190).

10. Redd, 39, 44.

11. Modojo.

12. Some IRC poker players reportedly did assign real-money value to the games by separately settling up wins and losses.

13. Maurer.

14. Weightless.

15. Stoll, 41.

16. Research by Christiansen/Cummings Associates, Inc. qtd. in "National Gambling Impact Study Commission Final Report."

17. Snyder.

18. "We met Randy Blumer."

19. Harroch and Krieger, 221-22. Watterson additionally advises new players unable to detect collusion among their opponents to "*stick to the lowest limits available*," her advice echoing that of John Blackbridge who in 1875 similarly recommended that "gentlemen should play Draw-Poker for the recognized *minimum* of the game" where the chance of encountering card sharps was less likely and the damage caused if one did would be less detrimental (23).

20. The story of Moneymaker winning his 2003 WSOP Main Event seat on PokerStars frequently includes the misreported detail that he won his seat via a $39 satellite (sometimes rounded to $40). In fact, Moneymaker himself added to the confusion with the title of a 2005 memoir he co-authored, *Moneymaker: How an Amateur Poker Player Turned $40 into $2.5 Million at the World Series of Poker*. For the full, accurate story of the satellite, see Brad Willis's account "The Moneymaker Boom that almost wasn't" on the PokerStars blog.

21. Sexton, 105.

22. Laffey, 479; Sexton, 87.

23. Parke, 8.

24. According to the results-tracking site High Stakes Database; see <highstakesdb.com/profiles/Isildur1.aspx?show=2009#graph>.

25. Alvarez, *The Biggest Game in Town*, 43.

26. Kang, "Online Poker's Biggest Winner."

27. Crowson.

28. 888.com's partnership with Caesars would later be extended, with 888's gaming platform subsequently powering WSOP.com's online sites in New Jersey, Delaware, and Nevada starting in 2013. Meanwhile the Fertitta-Full Tilt and Wynn-PokerStars agreements were immediately dissolved in the wake of "Black Friday" (see next chapter).

29. Vardi, 23. The interview with Wynn first appeared online on April 6, 2011 before being published in the April 23, 2011 print issue of *Forbes*.

Chapter 22: Poker Under Siege

1. "The Evils of Stud-Horse Poker."

2. See Chapter 7 for more on how California's erratic legislation in the 20th century helped create conditions for the introduction of poker clubs in the state.

3. Rose, 7.

4. Silver.

5. Contrary to some accounts, the Congressional record does show cursory discussion among House members the night of September 30, 2006 regarding the UIGEA, starting with its inclusion with the SAFE Port Act being commended by Rep. Jim Leach (R-IA) who had proposed the related bill passed by the House in July. Drawing attention to the UIGEA's provisions, Leach alluded to the opinion that "Internet gambling is crack cocaine for gamblers" (echoing somewhat the words of the first person to launch an online poker site – see Chapter 21). Six representatives subsequently questioned the inclusion of the UIGEA with the bill – Linda Sanchez (D-CA), Shelia Jackson-Lee (D-TX), Frank LoBiondo (R-NJ), Ron Paul (R-TX), Jon Porter (R-NV), and Ed Markey (D-MA) – with Markey the only one of that group ultimately to vote against it, as did Jeff Flake (R-AZ). Peter King (R-NY) also noted the UIGEA's inclusion in his comments without voicing objection.

6. U.K.-based FirePay immediately stopped allowing U.S. customers to make transactions starting 13 Oct. 2006, the date the UIGEA was signed into law. Neteller continued to serve the U.S. until Jan. 2007 when its two founders were arrested in the U.S. and charged with money laundering offenses.

7. E.g., "PokerStars has received extensive expert advice from within and outside the U.S. which concluded that these provisions do not alter the U.S. legal situation with respect to online poker. Furthermore it is important to emphasize that the Act does not in any way prohibit you from playing online poker" (Qtd. in Hintze).

8. The infamous heads-up hand began with POTRIPPER limping from the small blind and Marco "CrazyMarco" Johnson checking. After a 4♥-K♦-K♥ flop, Johnson check-called a bet from POTRIPPER, then following the 7♠ turn card Johnson checked and POTRIPPER bet again. This time Johnson, who had been dealt 9♥-2♥, check-raised all in as a semi-bluff,

knowing that if he were called he would still likely have a heart flush draw to win. POTRIP-PER, who had Johnson covered, inexplicably called the shove with just 10♣-9♣, a terrible hand on this board that could only possibly beat a bluff such as the one Johnson had made. The 5♠ river then gave POTRIPPER the pot and the tournament win, his ten-high nipping Johnson's nine-high.

9. Highlighting even further the questionable significance of some offshore sites' "licenses" to operate and the authority of some regulators, both Absolute Poker and UltimateBet were operated by a company called Tokwiro Enterprises ENRG owned by Joe Norton, the former Kahnawake Grand Chief who not coincidentally also was instrumental in establishing the KGC licensing agency.

10. Blackbridge, 23.

11. See, for example, Caldwell, John, "Annie Duke Discusses the Ultimate Bet Scandal," *PokerNews*, 27 Jun. 2008, <pokernews.com/news/2008/06/annie-duke-discusses-ultimate-bet-scandal.htm>.

12. United States, Cong. House Committee on Financial Services.

13. *The Tonight Show with Jay Leno*, episode 3884, NBC, 31 Aug. 2010.

14. *Late Show with David Letterman*, episode 16.82, CBS, 2 Feb. 2009.

15. Garcia; Vasquez; Mudhar.

16. Berzon and Schechner, B2.

17. United States Attorney's Office, Southern District of New York, "Civil Complaint Amended."

18. Berzon, A1.

19. For a more comprehensive rundown of the timeline of events both before and after April 15, 2011, see "Black Friday: Reliving Poker's Darkest Day Five Years Later," *PokerNews.com*, 15 Apr. 2016, <pokernews.com/news/2016/04/black-friday-five-years-later-24506.htm>.

20. United States Attorney's Office, Southern District of New York, "Manhattan U.S. Attorney Announces." Of the 11 site owners and payment processors named in the original "Black Friday" indictment and civil complaint, all but one eventually reached settlements and/or plea agreements resulting in fines and/or prison sentences ranging from a few months to three years. Rafe Furst, Howard Lederer, and Chris Ferguson each separately settled with the DOJ in late 2012 and early 2013, with none admitting any wrongdoing and each forfeiting assets ranging from $150,000 (Furst) to more than $2 million (Lederer, Ferguson).

21. The first state to legalize "riverboat gaming" was Iowa in 1989, and by 1993 Illinois, Missouri, Louisiana, Mississippi, and Indiana had each legalized gambling aboard riverboats with a variety of restrictions regarding the boats' operation and types of games allowed (Fenich 74-75).

Chapter 23: Poker in the Future

1. Wister, 209.

2. Wilde, 4.

3. Ibid, 72.

4. Ibid.

5. Green, Jonathan Harrington, *An Exposure*, 95

6. Harroch and Krieger, 10.

7. Mississippi passed legislation in 2018 to begin offering the lottery in 2019, becoming the 45th state to do so. The District of Columbia also began running a lottery in 1982.

8. *Commonwealth of Pennsylvania v. Walter Watkins.*

9. *United States v. DiCristina.*

10. Lukacs, 58.

11. Not coincidentally, the rise of tournament poker has closely paralleled the increasing prevalence and popularity of lotteries which similarly promise disproportionately large rewards for small investments.

Bibliography

"$5,000 Slot Machines," *Rolling Stone*, 1010, 5 Oct. 2006, 54.

Abbott, "Uncle" Jack. *A Treatise on Jack Pot Poker*. New Orleans: Clark & Hofeline, 1881.

Adams, Cecil. "Was Wild Bill Hickok holding the 'dead man's hand' when he was slain?" *The Straight Dope*, 5 May 1978, <straightdope.com/columns/read/275/was-wild-bill-hickok-holding-the-dead-mans-hand-when-he-was-slain/>.

Adams, John Quincy. *Memoirs of John Quincy Adams*. Philadelphia: J.B. Lippincott & Co., 1887.

Algeo, Matthew. *The President Is a Sick Man*. Chicago: Chicago Review Press, Inc., 2011.

Allis, Tim. "Chatter," *People*, 28.21, 23 Nov. 1987, 170.

Alvarez, Al. *The Biggest Game in Town*. Boston: Houghton Mifflin, 1983.

---. *Poker: Bets, Bluffs, and Bad Beats*. San Francisco: Chronicle Books LLC, 2001.

---. *Risky Business: People, Pastimes, Poker and Books*. London: Bloomsbury, 2007.

American Gaming Association. *2013 State of the States: AGA Survey of Casino Entertainment*, May 2014.

---. *State of the States 2018: The AGA Survey of the Commercial Casino Industry*, August 2018.

Amis, Martin. "Losing in Las Vegas." *The Rub of Time*. New York: Alfred A. Knopf, 2017. 145-55.

---. "On Poker, Panic and a Pair of Sevens," *The Australian*, 21 Oct. 2006, 24-31.

---. "Poker Night." *Visiting Mrs. Nabokov and Other Excursions*. New York: Harmony Books, 1993.

Ansen, David. "The Bottom of the Deck," 132.37, 14 Sep. 1998, 76.

Apostolico, David. *Tournament Poker and the Art of War*. New York: Lyle Stuart Books, 2005.

Arrillaga, Pauline. "To Be a Judge, Be Judged a Winner in This Poker Game," *Los Angeles Times*, 21 Nov. 1999, 10.

Asbury, Herbert. *Sucker's Progress*. New York: Dodd, Mead and Company, Inc., 1938.

"At the World Series of Poker Telly Savalas Left $10,000 on the Table: Baby, Who Loves Ya Now?" *People*, 23.23, 10 Jun. 1985, 63.

Auster, Paul. *The Music of Chance*. New York: Penguin Books, 1990.

Axthelm, Pete. "The Aces of Poker," 93.23, 4 Jun. 1979, 52-53.

Badeau, Adam. "Gambling in High Life," *The Cosmopolitan*, 11, May-Oct. 1891, 493-98.

Bancroft, Hubert Howe. *California Inter Pocula*, Vol. 35. San Francisco: The History Company, 1888.

Barry, Dan. "Artist's Fame Is Fleeting, But Dog Poker Is Forever," *The New York Times*, 14 Jun. 2002, 1, 44.

Bahrampour, Tara. "A club of their own: The story of a secret society started by pioneering African Americans," *The Washington Post*, 8 Sept. 2018, A6.

Bart, Peter, "Director Ousted in Film Dispute," *The New York Times*, 8 Dec. 1964, 56.

Bellin, Andy. *Poker Nation*. New York: Perennial, 2002.

Bennet, Rick. *King of a Small World: A Poker Novel*. New York: Arcade Publishing, 1995.

Berendt, John. "The Poker Game," *Esquire*, 118.3, Sept. 1992, 71, 75

Bernstein, Jonathan. "Kenny Rogers, 'The Gambler' (1978)," *Rolling Stone*, 1 Jun. 2014, <rollingstone.com/music/music-lists/100-greatest-country-songs-of-all-time-11200/20-kenny-rogers-the-gambler-1978-14490/>.

Berzon, Alexandra. "Poker Site Stacked Deck," *The Wall Street Journal*, 21 Sept. 2011, A1.

Berzon, Alexandra and Sam Schechner. "TV Helped Drive Traffic to Online Poker Websites, Irking Justice Department," *The Wall Street Journal*, 26 Jul. 2011, B2.

Bierce, Ambrose. *The Devil's Dictionary*. New York: The World Publishing Company, 1911.

Bjerg, Ole. *The Parody of Capitalism*. Ann Arbor: U of Michigan P, 2011.

"A Big Hand for Poker," *Changing Times* 36.3, Mar. 1986: 33-34.

"Big Ratings Pot for Bravo Celebrity Poker Finale." *Multi Channel News*, 15 Jan. 2004, <www.multichannel.com/news/big-ratings-pot-bravo-celebrity-poker-finale-161322>.

Binion, Jack. Personal communication, 2 Jun. 2017.

Binion, Lester Ben "Benny." "Some Recollections of a Texas and Las Vegas Gaming Operator." Interview by Mary Ellen Glass, 22-23 May 1973, Las Vegas, Nevada.

Blackbridge, John. *The Complete Poker-Player*. 1875. New York: Dick & Fitzgerald, 1880.

Bogdanovich, Peter. *John Ford*, 2nd ed. Oakland: U of California P, 1978.

Bohn, Henry G., ed. *Bohn's New Hand-Book of Games*. Philadelphia: Henry F. Anners, 1850.

Boller, Paul F. *Presidential Campaigns: From George Washington to George W. Bush*. Oxford: Oxford UP, 2004.

Bowling, Michael and Neil Burch, Michael Johanson, Oskari Tammelin. "Heads-up limit hold'em poker is solved," *Science*, 347.6218, 9 Jan. 2015, 145-49.

Boyer, Ed. "Epitaph: Ted Thackrey Jr.: 1918-2001," *Los Angeles Magazine*, 46.10, Oct. 2001, 38.

Boyle, Robert H. "The Poker in the Smoker," *Sports Illustrated*, 18.16, 22 Apr. 1963, 24-30.

Bradley, Lance. Personal communication, 30 Oct. 2018.

Bradshaw, Jon. *Fast Company: How Six Master Gamblers Defy the Odds*. New York: Harper's Magazine Press, 1975.

Braniff, Brenda. "A Husband's Secret Addiction," *Good Housekeeping*, 224.6, Jun. 1997, 92-97.

"Bridge Master Oswald Jacoby, 81," *Philadelphia Daily News*, 28 Jun. 1984: 66.

Brodie, Fawn. *Richard Nixon: The Shaping of His Character*. New York: W.W. Norton, 1981.

Brown, Aaron. *The Poker Face of Wall Street*. Hoboken: John Wiley & Sons, Inc., 2006.

Brown, Garrett. *The Autocrat of the Poker Table: Or How to Play the Game to Win*. 1899. Boston: The Four Seas Company, 1919.

Browne, George F. "Playing Poker to Win," *Esquire*, 17.6, Jun. 1942, 74, 178-79.

Broun, Heywood. "Just One More Round, *Judge*, 83.2144, 2 Dec. 1922, 6-7.

Broun, Heywood Hale. "A Full House," *American Heritage*, 18.1, Dec. 1966, 64-67.

Brunson, Doyle. *The Godfather of Poker*. Las Vegas: Cardoza Pub., 2009.

---. "Poker High Stakes," *The Sunday Telegraph*, 11 Sep. 2005, 17.

---. *Super/System: A Course in Power Poker*. 1978. Las Vegas: Cardoza Publishing, 2002.

---. *Super System 2*. Las Vegas: Cardoza Publishing, 2009.

Buffett, Warren E. Letter To the Shareholders of Berkshire Hathaway Inc., 29 Feb. 1988, Berkshire Hathaway, <www.berkshirehathaway.com/letters/1987.html>.

Bulwa, Demian, "A New Crowd is Saddling Up to the Table," *SFGate*, 27 Oct. 2003, <www.sfgate.com/entertainment/article/A-new-crowd-is-saddling-up-to-the-table-to-play-2580664.php>.

Bundles, A'Lelia. *On Her Own Ground: The Life and Times of Madam C.J. Walker*. New York: Scribner, 2001.

Burdick, Eugene Burdick and Harvey Wheeler. *Fail-Safe*. New York: McGraw-Hill, 1962.

Bush, George W. "The President's News Conference," 6 Mar. 2003.

"Business Notes: Poker Is Hard Work," *Time* 127.12, 24 Mar. 1986, 62.

Cardano, Gerolamo. *Liber de Lude Aleae (Book on Games of Chance)*. 1663. Trans. Sydney Henry Gould. New York: Holt, Rinehart and Winston, 1961.

"Cards for Americans," *Life*, 38.22, 30 May 1955, 71-72.

Carleton, Henry Guy. *The Thompson Street Poker Club*. New York: White and Allen, 1888.

Caro, Mike. "The Art of the Tell," *Playboy*, 49.5, May 2002, 93, 146.

---. "Decades later, poker history repeats itself." 2008. <poker1.com/archives/7948>.

---. *Mike Caro's Book of Tells: The Body Language of Poker*. Secaucus, NJ: Gambling Times Books, 1984.

Caro, Robert A. *The Years of Lyndon Johnson, Volume I: The Path to Power*. New York: Vintage Books, 1982.

---. *The Years of Lyndon Johnson, Volume II: Means of Ascent*. New York: Vintage Books, 1990.

Caruso, Catherine. "Time to Fold, Humans: Poker-Playing AI Beats Pros at Texas Holdem," *Scientific American*, 2 Mar. 2017, <scientificamerican.com/article/time-to-fold-humans-poker-playing-ai-beats-pros-at-texas-hold-rsquo-em/>.

Caselli, Michael. "Donald Trump Fired Up About Poker," *Bluff*, Dec. 2004, <archive.bluff.com/magazine/donald-trump-fired-up-about-poker-11510/>

Chaucer, Geoffrey. *Chaucer's Major Poetry*. Ed. Albert C. Baugh. Englewood Cliffs, NJ: Prentice-Hall, Inc., 1963.

Chiappone, Richard. "Dealer's Choice," *Playboy*, 42.4, Apr. 1995, 152-56.

Childton, R.H., Assistant Adjutant-General, by command of General R.E. Lee. General Orders, No. 127, Hdqrs. Army of Northern Virginia, 14 Nov. 1862. Qtd. in *The War of the Rebellion*, Vol. 19. Washington, D.C.: Government Printing Office, 1887.

Chlond, Martin J. "Five Pat Hands," *Informs: Transactions on Education* 12.3, May 2012, 164-65.

Churm, Steven R. "Legalized Vegas-Style Poker Offers Area Casinos New Deal," *Los Angeles Times*: 12 July 1987: 1.

Commonwealth of Pennsylvania v. Walter Watkins. CP-19-0000746-2008. Superior Court of Pennyslvania. 14 Jan. 2009. Appeal 24 Mar. 2010.

Conley, Kevin. "The Players," *The New Yorker*, 81.20, 11 Jul. 2005, 52-58.

Connors, Barbara. "Power Play." *Women's Poker Night*, ed. Maryann Morrison. New York: Kensington Publishing Corp., 2007, 25-41.

"Cool Hand Duke," *People*, 60.5, 4 Aug. 2003, 110.

Cooper, Tom. *Moscow's Game of Poker: Russian Military Intervention in Syria, 2015-2017*, Warwick, England: Helion and Company, 2018.

Cowell, Joe. *Thirty Years Passed Among the Players in England and America: Part I - England*. New York: Harper & Brothers, 1844.

Crain, Ester. "Playing a Mean Poker Game Is Just the Start... 30 Skills Every Cosmo Girl Must Master," *Cosmopolitan*, 226.3, Mar. 1999, 258-261.

Crane, Stephen. "A Poker Game." *Last Words*. London: Digby, Long & Co., 1902. 263-67.

Crofton, Algernon. *Poker. Its Laws and Principles*. New York: Wycil & Co., 1915.

Crowson, Arthur. "Top Online Poker Winners and Losers," *PokerListings*, 4 Jan. 2011, <pokerlistings.com/top-winners-and-losers-of-2010-76808>.

Culin, Stewart. *Korean Games, with Notes on the Corresponding Games of China and Japan*. Philadelphia: U of Pennsylvania P, 1895.

Cumings, Bruce. *The Origins of the Korean War, Vol. II: The Roaring of the Cataract 1947-1950*. Princeton: Princeton UP, 1990.

Curtis, David A. *Queer Luck*. New York, Brentano's: 1899.

---. *Stand Pat, or, Poker Stories from the Mississippi*. Boston: L.C. Page & Company, 1906.

"A Dangerous Poker Game With Iraq," *The New York Times*, 4 Oct. 1998, 14

Dean, John W. *Warren G. Harding*. New York: Henry Holt and Company, 2004.

Deane, Barbara. "Women and Gambling: Risking It All," *Woman's Day*, 59.4, Feb. 1996, 43.

DeArment, Robert K. *Gunfighter in Gothan: Bat Masterson's New York City Years*. Norman: U of Oklahoma P, 2013.

---. *Knights of the Green Cloth: The Saga of the Frontier Gamblers*. Norman: U of Oklahoma P, 1982.

Deford, Frank. "Three Little Syllables." *Sports Illustrated*, 46.4, 24 Jan. 1977, 30-35.

Devol, George. *Forty Years a Gambler on the Mississippi*. New York: Home Book Company, 1887.

[Dick, William Brisbane.] *The American Hoyle; or, Gentleman's Hand-Book of Games*, 3rd ed. New York: Dick & Fitzgerald Publishers, 1864.

Dionne, Roger. "If You Play Your Cards Right, You Can Make It Big in Tiny Emeryville," *Sports Illustrated*, 62.22, 3 Jun. 1985, 92-95.

---. "Youth Can Age You," *Sports Illustrated*, 30.20, 14 May 1979, 40-46.

Dizikes, John. *Sportsmen and Gamesmen*. Columbia: U of Missouri P, 1981.

Dragoon Campaigns to the Rocky Mountains. New York: Wiley & Long, 1836.

"Edison Tests Poker Skill in New Quiz," *The New York Times*, 11 Jun. 22, 33-34.

Edwards, Eugene. *Jack Pots. Stories of the Great American Game*. Chicago: Jamieson-Higgins Co., 1900.

Eisenhower, Dwight D. *At Ease: Stories I Tell To Friends*. Garden City, NY: Doubleday & Company, Inc., 1967.

"Eisenhower Takes Time to Figure a Poker Hand," *The New York Times,* 10 Nov. 1943, 14

Elderkin, John. *A Brief History of the Lotos Club*. New York: Club House, 1895.

Enss, Chris. *Wicked Women: Notorious, Mischievous, and Wayward Ladies from the Old West*. Helena, MT: Two Dot, 2015.

"The Evils of Stud-Horse Poker," *The New York Times*, 15 Jul. 1884, 3.

Fadiman, Clifton, ed. *The Little, Brown Book of Anecdotes*. Boston: Little, Brown and Company, 1985.

Fariello, Grif. "On Drinking with Professors," *Rolling Stone*, 341, 14 Apr. 1981.

Fenich, George G. "A Chronology of (Legal) Gaming in the U.S." *Gaming Research & Review Journal*, 3.2, 1996, 65-78.

Findler, Nicholas V. "Computer Model of Gambling and Bluffing." *IRE Transactions on Electronic Computers* 10.1, Mar. 1961, 5-6.

---. "Computer Poker." *Scientific American* 239.1 (Jul. 1978): 144-51.

Fisher, George Henry. *Stud Poker Blue Book: The Only Standard Authority*. Los Angeles: The Stud Poker Press, 1934.

Flood, Charles Bracelen. *Grant and Sherman: The Friendship That Won the Civil War*. New York: Farrar, Straus and Giroux, 2005.

Florence, William J. *The Gentleman's Handbook on Poker*. New York: G. Routledge, 1892.

Foote, Shelby. *The Civil War: A Narrative, Volume Three - From Red River to Appomattox*. New York: Vintage Books, 1974.

Ford, Gerald Ford. *A Time to Heal: The Autobiography of Gerald Ford*. New York: Harper & Row, 1979.

Foster, R.F. *Foster's Complete Hoyle: An Encyclopedia of Games*. 1897. New York: Frederick A. Stokes Company, 1909.

---. *Practical Poker*. London: Thomas de la Rue & Co. Ltd., 1904.

"Fulls and Flushes," *The Chicago Tribune*, 21 May 1893, 32.

Gaines, James R. *Wit's End: Days and Nights of the Algonquin Round Table*. New York: Harcourt Brace Jovanovich, 1977.

"Gamblers on Titanic Escape by Dressing as Women," *The Witney Gazette,* 11 May 1912, *Encyclopedia Titanica*, <www.encyclopedia-titanica.org/gamblers-titanic-escape-dressing-as-women.html>.

"Gamblers Testify to Rothstein Loss in Big Poker Game." *The New York Times*, 22 Nov. 1929, 1, 18.

"Gaming, Divorce Bills Signed." *Nevada State Journal*, 20 Mar. 1931, 1.

Garcia, Oskar. "Prosecutions turn online poker into a shaky bet," *Boston.com*, 20 Apr. 2011, <archive.boston.com/business/technology/articles/2011/04/20/prosecutions_turn_online_poker_into_a_shaky_bet/>.

Gates, Bill. *The Road Ahead*. New York: Viking, 1995. 18.

Gaul, Gilbert M. "Players Gamble on Honesty, Security of Internet Betting." *The Washington Post*, 30 Nov. 2008: A1.

Gifford, Susan Korones. "What Keeps a Husband Crazy in Love," *Redbook*, 200.5, May 2003, 200-04.

Gilmore, Nicholas. "Cartoons from the World War II Home Front," *Saturday Evening Post*, 23 Nov. 2016, <www.saturdayeveningpost.com/2016/11/cartoons-world-war-ii-homefront/>.

"Giving Himself Away," *Judge*, 25.633, 2 Dec. 1893, 350.

The Golden Nugget Grand Prix of Poker Official 1986 Program, The Golden Nugget, 1986.

"Good Collateral," *Michigan Farmer*, 31 Aug. 1886, 17, 36.

"Good House," *Good Housekeeping*, 247.5, Nov. 2008, 85.

Goodman, Leah McGrath. "How Washington Opened the Floodgates to Online Poker, Dealing Parents a Bad Hand," *Newsweek*, 163.7, 22 Aug. 2014, <https://www.newsweek.com/2014/08/22/how-washington-opened-floodgates-online-poker-dealing-parents-bad-hand-264459.html>.

Goodman, Walter. "About Men; The Luck of the Draw." *The New York Times*, 7 Aug. 1983: 54.

---. "Poker as a Way of Life," *Newsweek*, 99.21, 24 May 1982, 76.

Goodwin, Doris Kearns. "109th Landon Lecture." 22 Apr. 1997, University of Kansas State, Manhattan, KS.

---. *Team of Rivals: The Political Genius of Abraham Lincoln*. New York: Simon & Schuster, 2005.

"GOP Candidate Says He's 'Too Angry to Speak," *Pacific Stars and Stripes*, 21 Oct. 1952, 1.

Gordon, Michael R. "Inside the War Over Syria: A High Altitude 'Poker Game,'" *The New York Times*, 23 May 2017, A7.

Grant, Ulysses S. *The Papers of Ulysses S. Grant, Vols. 1-32*. Carbonale: U of Illinois P, 1967-2009.

Green, Jonathan Harrington. *An Exposure to the Arts and Miseries of Gambling*. Cincinnati: U.P. James, 1843.

---. *Gambling Unmasked: Or The Personal Experience of a Reformed Gambler*. 1844. Philadelphia: G.B. Zieber & Co. 1847.

Green, Stephen, "The World (War) Series of Poker," *PJ Media*, 9 Mar. 2016, <pjmedia.com/vodkapundit/2016/03/09/the-world-war-series-of-poker/>.

Grotenstein, Jonathan and Storms Reback. *All In: The (Almost) Entirely True Story of the World Series of Poker*. New York: St. Martin's Press, 2005.

Grove, Chris. "11 Serious Problems with Newsweek's Weird Tirade Against Regulated Online Gambling," *Online Poker Report*, 14 Aug. 2014, <www.onlinepokerreport.com/13443/newsweek-got-almost-everything-wrong-regulated-online-gambling/>.

Habib, Daniel G. "Online and Obsessed," *Sports Illustrated*, 102.22, 30 May 2005, 66-78.

Halberstam, David. *The Best and the Brightest*. New York: Random House, 1972.

Hammett, Samuel Adams. *Piney Woods Tavern; or, Sam Slick in Texas*. Philadelphia: T.B. Peterson and Brothers, 1858.

Hardin, John Wesley. *The Life of John Wesley Hardin, As Written By Himself*. Seguin, TX: Smith & Moore, 1896.

Hargrave, Catherine Perry. *A History of Playing Cards*. New York: Houghton Mifflin Company, 1930.

Hargrove, Marion. "This Is a Television Cowboy?" *Life*, 46.3, 19 Jan. 1959, 75-78.

Harriman, Margaret Case. *The Vicious Circle: The Story of the Algonquin Round Table*. New York: Rinehart & Co., Inc., 1951.

Harris, Martin. "Laak-Eslami Team Defeats Polaris in Man-Machine Poker Championship," *PokerNews*, 25 Jul. 2007, <pokernews.com/news/2007/07/laak-eslami-team-de-feats-polaris-man-machine-poker-champions.htm>.

---. "Pop Poker: Holden says 'Too Few Great Poker Movies,'" *PokerListings*, 14 Dec. 2012, <www.pokerlistings.com/pop-poker-holden-says-too-few-great-poker-mov-ies-97264>.

Harris, René. "Her Husband Went Down With the Titanic," *Liberty Magazine*, 23 Apr. 1932.

Harroch, Richard D. and Lou Krieger. *Poker for Dummies*. Hoboken, NJ: Wiley Publishing, Inc., 2000.

Harte, F. Bret. "The Outcasts of Poker Flat." *Overland Monthly* 2.1, Jan. 1869, 41-47.

Hartley, John. *The Little Black Book of Casino Games: The Smart Player's Guide to Gambling*. White Plains, NY: Peter Pauper Press, Inc., 2005.

Hauck, Tommy. "Our Washington Letter." *The Atlanta Constitution*, 4 May 1872: 1.

Hayano, David. *Poker Faces: The Life and Work of Professional Card Players*. Berkley: U of California P, 1982.

Hayes, Kevin J. *George Washington: A Life in Books*. New York: Oxford UP, 2017.

Hecht, Ben. "Swindler's Luck," *The Saturday Evening Post*, 224.28, 12 Jan. 1952, 18-19, 51-58.

Hellmuth, Phil. *Poker Brat*. East Peoria, IL: D&B Publishing, 2017.

Hendrickson, Brian. "Deal With It," *Sports Illustrated*, 114.17, 25 Aprl. 2011, 18.

Hesford, Walter. "*Thousand Pieces of Gold*: Competing Fictions in the Representation of Chinese-American Experience," *Western American Literature* 31.1, Spring 1996, 49-62.

Hesse, Monica and Ben Terris, Dan Zak, "Cal Ripken's favorite baseball movie, and 24 others on the film about their profession," *The Washington Post*, 25 Dec. 2017, <washingtonpost.com/lifestyle/style/cal-ripkens-favorite-baseball-movie-and-21-others-on-the-best-film-about-their-profession/2017/12/25/223c8fb8-e5d0-11e7-833f-155031558ff4_story.html>.

Hibler, Winston. "Dealer's Choice," *Esquire*, 9.4, Apr. 1938, 79, 172.

Himes, Chester. *Cast the First Stone*. 1952. New York: Signet, 1972.

Hintze, Haley. "Poker Stars Affirms Continuing U.S. Market Presence," *PokerNews*, 12 Oct. 2006, <pokernews.com/news/2006/10/poker-stars-continuing-us-market.htm>.

Hobert, Bruce. "Playing Poker With Veterans," *The New York Times*, 25 Feb. 2017, SR6.

Hochman, Gene. *The Hochman Encyclopedia of Playing Cards*. Ed. Tom and Judy Dawson. Stamford, CT: U.S. Games Systems, 2000.

Hoffer, Richard. "The Prime-Timing of Texas Hold'em," *Sports Illustrated*, 99.11, 22 Sept. 2003, 52-56

Holden, Anthony. *Big Deal: Confessions of a Professional Poker Player*. New York: Penguin Books, 1990.

---. *Bigger Deal: A Year Inside the Boom*. New York: Simon & Schuster, 2007.

---. *Holden on Hold'em*. London: Little, Brown, 2008.

Hoover, Herbert. *The Memoirs of Herbert Hoover: The Cabinet and the Presidency*. New York: The Macmillan Co., 1952.

"How to Find and Play a Poker Game," 133.1, Jan. 2000, 25

Hoyle's Games. Philadelphia: Henry F. Anners, 1845.

[Huggins, Roy.] *Poker According to Maverick*. New York: Dell Publishing, 1959

Hughes, Johnny, *Texas Poker Wisdom: A Novel*. Lincoln, NE: iUniverse, 2007.

Hurston, Zora Neale. *Poker!* 1931. Retrieved from the Library of Congress, <loc.gov/item/hurston000007/>.

"I'll Play These," *Playboy*, 21.11 Nov. 1974, 109-116, 158, 184-200, 203-04, 224-27, 231-44.

Jackson, Donald. "The Young Nixon," *Life,* 69.19, 6 Nov. 1970, 54-66.

Jackson, Robert. *That Man: An Insider's Portrait of Franklin D. Roosevelt*. New York: Oxford UP, 2003.

Jacoby, Oswald. *Oswald Jacoby on Poker*. Garden City, NY: Doubleday, Doran & Company, Inc., 1940.

Jacoby, Oswald and Albert Morehead, ed., *The Fireside Book of Cards*. New York: Simon & Schuster, 1957.

Jefferson, Thomas. "Thoughts on Lotteries. February, 1826." Rpt. in *The Works of Thomas Jefferson*, Vol. 18, Ed. Albert Ellery Bergh. Washington, DC: The Thomas Jefferson Memorial Association, 1905.

Jenkins, Don. *Johnny Moss: Champion of Champions*. Odessa, TX: Johnny Moss, 1981.

Jewison, Norman. Audio Commentary. *The Cincinnati Kid*, Warner Bros. Entertainment, 2005.

Johnson, Lyndon Baines. *Vantage Point: Perspectives of the Presidency, 1963-1969*. New York: Holt, Rinehart, and Winston, 1971.

Johnson, Merle De Vore. *A Bibliography of the Works of Mark Twain, Samuel Langhorne Clemens*. New York: Harper & Bros., 1935.

Johnson, Samuel. *The Works of Samuel Johnson, LL.D., Vol. 2*. London: Talboys and Wheeler, 1825.

Jones, James. *From Here to Eternity*. 1951. New York: Dial Press Trade Paperbacks, 2012.

Jordan, Pat. "Is This Man the Future of Poker?" *Playboy*, Jan. 2005, 148-52, 184-89.

Kadlec, Dan. "World Series of Poker: Attack of the Math Brats," *Time* 175.25, 28 Jun. 2010, 40-43.

Kahn, David. *The Reader of Gentlemen's Mail: Herbert O. Yardley and the Birth of American Codebreaking*. New Haven, CT: Yale UP, 2004.

Kang, Jay Caspian. "Online Poker's Biggest Winner," *New York Times Magazine*, 25 Mar. 2011,<nytimes.com/2011/03/27/magazine/mag-27Poker-t.html>.

Kaplan, Michael. "Bet On It at an Annual Golf Outing Exclusively for High Rollers," *Sports Illustrated*, 99.14, 13 Oct. 2003, bonus section.

---. "Phil Ivey's New House of Cards," *Playboy*, 61.6, Jul.-Aug. 2014, 68-71, 190-93.

Kaufman, George S. *If Men Played Cards as Women Do*. New York: Samuel French, 1926.

Kelley, William Melvin. "The Poker Party." 1956. *Dancers on the Shore*. Washington, DC: Howard UP, 1984. 23-35.

Kilmister, Lemmy and Janiss Garza, *White Line Fever*. London: Simon & Schuster, 2002.

Kishi, Stephanie. "Home of Sin City's Original Sin," *Las Vegas Sun*, 15 May 2008, <lasvegassun.com/news/2008/may/15/origination-sin-sin-city/>.

Keller, John W. *The Game of Draw Poker* (New York: White, Stokes & Allen, 1887.

Kerfoot, J.B. "The Latest Books," *Life* 45.1176, 11 May 1905, 556.

Kerr, Peter. "Games People Play, and Where," *The New York Times*, 16 Nov. 1984.

Kesey, Ken. *One Flew Over the Cuckoo's Nest*. New York: New American Library, 1962.

Kittredge, William. "On Drinking with Students," *Rolling Stone*, 341, 14 Apr. 1981.

Krieger, Lou. Interview with the author, 19 Feb. 2010.

Klein, Joe. "The Poker Player in Chief," *Time*, 161.11, 17 Mar. 2003, 4.

Knopper, Steve. "Grand Funk Railroad Drummer Looks Back Down the Tracks," *The Chicago Tribune*, 13 Nov. 1998, 43.

Konik, Michael. "Trump Cards: The U.S. Poker Championship," *Cigar Aficionado*, Mar.-Apr. 1997, <www.cigaraficionado.com/article/trump-cards-the-us-poker-championship-7557>.

Koppelman, Brian. "Mayfair Club: An Elegy for a Carpet Joint," *The New York Observer*, 21 May 2001, 5.

---. "The Beauty of Black Friday." *Grantland*, 20 Jun. 2011, <grantland.com/features/the-beauty-black-friday/>.

Kornitzer, Bela. *The Real Nixon: An Intimate Biography*. New York: Rand McNally & Company, 1960.

Laffey, Des. "The ultimate bluff: a case study of partygaming." *Journal of Information Technology*, 22.4, 479-88.

Lambert, Bruce E., interview by James R. Fuchs, 26 May 1981, Arlington, Virginia, Harry S. Truman Presidential Library & Museum, <trumanlibrary.org/oralhist/lambertbe.htm>.

Lardner, Rex. "Big Poker: The Only Game," *Esquire*, 44.1, Jul. 1955, 45, 110.

Lardner Jr., Ring. *The Cincinnati Kid*, Second Draft Screenplay. Culver City, CA: Metro-Goldwyn-Mayer, Inc., 3 Nov. 1964.

Lake, Stuart N. *Wyatt Earp: Frontier Marshal*. New York: Houghton Mifflin Company, 1931.

"Letter from Minister Schenck," *The New York Times*, 7 Feb. 1875, 4.

Levy, Shawn. *Paul Newman: A Life*. New York: Harmony Books, 2009.

Lewis, Michael. *Liar's Poker: Rising Through the Wreckage on Wall Street*. New York: W.W. Norton & Company, 1989.

Li, David K. "A Game of Poker Could Decide N.M." *The New York Post*, 14 Nov. 2000, 30.

Lillard, John F.B. *Poker Stories*. New York: Francis P. Harper, 1896.

"Little Tragedies of Social New York," *Vanity Fair*, 3.6, Feb. 1915, 17.

Livingston, A.D. "'Hold Me': A wild new poker game... and how to tame it." *Life*, 65.7, 16 Aug. 1968, 38-42.

---. *Poker Strategy and Winning Play*. Philadelphia: J.B. Lippincott Co., 1971.

---. "A Sawyer Takes the Pot Every Time," *Sports Illustrated*, 35.20, 15 Nov. 1971, 41-51.

Lukacs, John. "Poker and American Character." *Horizon* 5.8, Nov. 1963, 56-62.

Lydston, G. Frank. *Poker Jim, Gentleman and Other Tales and Sketches*. Chicago: Monarch Book Co., 1906.

MacEvoy, Charles. "That Game of Poker!" Pond & Co., Wm. A., New York, monographic, 1878. Notated music. Retrieved from the Library of Congress, <www.loc.gov/item/sm1878.02711>.

"A MAD peek behind the scenes at Celebrity Poker Showdown," *MAD*, 452, Apr. 2005, 18-20.

"Made on the Shade," *Good Housekeeping*, 250.6, Jun. 2010, 85.

"Magazines," *Forest and Stream*, 4.11, 22 Apr. 1875: 175.

Maher, Bill. *New Rules: Polite Musings from a Timid Observer*. New York: Rodale Books, 2006.

Malmuth, Mason. "The Most Important Hand Ever Played," UNLV Center for Gaming Research, 19 Dec. 2008. <library.unlv.edu/center-gaming-research/2008/12/mason-malmuth-most-important-hand-ever-played.html>.

Mamet, David. *American Buffalo*. New York: Samuel French, 1975.

---. "A Gambler for Life," *Playboy*, 41.1, Jan. 1994, 178-81, 238-39.

---. "The Things Poker Teaches," *The New York Times*, 20 Apr. 1986, SM52.

"Many a man makes his fame out of the most unexpected materials," *Life*, 15.380, 10 Apr. 1890, 208.

"Mark Twain Was Particular," *The New York Times*, 9 Sep. 1912: 1.

Marquis, Don. "The Crack of Doom," *Playboy*, 3.2, Feb. 1956, 10-16, 64.

Marx, Harpo and Rowland Barber, *Harpo Speaks*. Pompton Plains: Limelight Editions, 1962.

Matray, James. "Dean Acheson's Press Club Speech Reexamined," *The Journal of Conflict Studies* 22.1, Spring 2002, 26-53.

Maugham, W. Somerset. "The Portrait of a Gentleman," *The Complete Short Stories of W. Somerset Maugham, Vol. II*. Garden City, NY: Doubleday & Company, Inc., 1952, 155-160.

---. "Straight Flush," *The Complete Short Stories of W. Somerset Maugham, Vol. II*. Garden City, NY: Doubleday & Company, Inc., 1952. 149-154.

Maurer, Michael. "Michael Maurer's IRC Poker Database." <archive.li/7ztYP#selection-275.1-275.246>.

May, Jesse. *Shut Up and Deal*. New York: Anchor Books, 1998.

Mazo, Earl. *Richard Nixon: A Political and Personal Portrait*. New York: Harper and Brothers, 1959.

McCullough, David. *Mornings on Horseback*. New York: Simon & Schuster, 1981.

---. *Truman*. New York: Simon & Schuster, 1992.

McDonald, Duff. "Poker's Wild," *Vanity Fair*, 535, Mar. 2005, 280-95.

McDonald, John. *Strategy in Poker, Business & War*. New York: W.W. Norton & Co., 1950.

McGuire, Pauly. "Life in the Fast Lane: Poker and the Eagles," *PokerStars blog*, 14 Jul. 2016, <pokerstars.com/en/blog/buzz/2016/life-in-the-fast-lane-poker-and-the-eagl-162403.shtml>.

McKim, Edward D., interview by James R. Fuchs, 19 Feb. 1964, Phoenix, Arizona, Harry S. Truman Presidential Library & Museum, <trumanlibrary.org/oralhist/mckimed2.htm>.

McManus, James. *Cowboys Full: The Story of Poker*. New York: Picador Books, 2009.

---. *Positively Fifth Street*. New York: Farrar, Straus and Giroux, 2003.

Medoff, Mark. *Children of a Lesser God*. New York: Dramatists Play Service, Inc., 1980.

Miles, Dick. "Lowball in a Time Capsule," *Sports Illustrated*, 26.16, 17 Apr. 1967, 110-29.

Milton, John. *Paradise Lost*. 1667. Ed. John Leonard. New York: Penguin Books, 1998.

Mitchell, Margaret. *Gone With the Wind*. New York: The Macmillan Company, 1936.

"Mixed Deal." Rev. of *The Cincinnati Kid*. *Time* 86.19, 5 Nov. 1965, 136.

Modojo, "Zynga Is Way Bigger Than You Thought," *Business Insider*, 22 Mar. 2011, <businessinsider.com/zynga-bigger-than-you-thought-2011-3>.

Moon, Angela. "Machine beats humans for the first time in poker," *Reuters*, 1 Feb. 2007, <in.reuters.com/article/artificialintelligence-poker-idINKBN15G5S3>.

Moore, Evan. "Poker: The National Game of Texas," *Houston Chronicle*, 14 Sep. 1986, 6.

"More About Draw-Poker." *The New York Tribune*, 13 Feb. 1875: 2.

Morehead, Albert H. "Bridge: 'Summer Rules' Take Over, *The New York Times*, 23 Jun. 1957, 107.

Morgan, Benjamin. *Shams; or, Uncle Ben's Experience with Hypocrites*. Chicago: H.J. Smith, Co., 1889.

Morgenstern, Oskar Morgenstern. "The Cold War Is Cold Poker," *The New York Times*, 5 Feb. 1961, 14, 21-22.

Moss, John. "Playboy on Poker," *Playboy*, 4.11, Nov. 1957, 24-28, 83-87.

Mudhar, Raju. "U.S. Prosecutors Not Bluffing with Shutdown of Poker Sites," *Toronto Star*, 24 Apr. 2011, <thestar.com/sports/2011/04/24/mudhar_us_prosecutors_not_bluffing_with_shutdown_of_poker_sites.html>.

"National Gambling Impact Study Commission Final Report." 18 Jun. 1999. <govinfo.library.unt.edu/ngisc/reports/fullrpt.html>.

"The National Game." *The New York Times*, 12 Feb. 1875: 4.

National Indian Gaming Commission, "2017 Indian Gaming Revenues Increase 3.9% to $32.4 Billion," 26 Jun. 2018, <nigc.gov/news/detail/2017-indian-gaming-revenues-increase-3.9-to-32.4-billion>.

"National Recording Registry Reaches 500," *Library of Congress*, 21 Mar. 2018, <loc.gov/item/prn-18-028/national-recording-registry-reaches-500/2018-03-21/>.

Nelson, Peter. "Nine-to-Five Poker," *Esquire*, 105.6, Jun. 1986, 82-88

"Nevada Poker: The Evolution. Statewide annual totals, 1992-2011," UNLV Center for Gaming Research, <gaming.unlv.edu/reports/NV_poker.pdf>.

"Nevada's Gaming Footprint, 1963-2018," UNLV Center for Gaming Research, <gaming.unlv.edu/reports/nv_gaming_footprint.pdf>.

Nichols, George Ward. "Wild Bill," *Harper's New Monthly Magazine*, 34.201, Feb. 1867, 273-286.

Nixon, Richard. "Address to the Congress on Stabilization of the Economy." *United States Capitol*, The United States Government, 9 Sept. 1971.

---. Conversation No. 23-96, White House Telephone, 1 May 1972, White House Tapes, Richard Nixon Presidential Library and Museum, Yorba Linda, CA.

---. Conversation No. 275-9, Executive Office Building, 7 Sept. 1971, White House Tapes, Richard Nixon Presidential Library and Museum, Yorba Linda, CA.

---. Conversation No. 772-8, Oval Office, 7 Sept. 1972, White House Tapes, Richard Nixon Presidential Library and Museum, Yorba Linda, CA.

---. *In the Arena*. New York: Simon & Schuster, 1990.

---. Interview by Frank Gannon, 9 Feb. 1983, Walter J. Brown Media Archives & Peabody

Awards Collection, University of Georgia Libraries.

---. Interview by Special Agent in Charge J.H. Hanson, 17 Jul. 1937, Los Angeles, California, Federal Bureau of Investigation.

---. *The Real War*. New York: Warner Books, 1980.

---. *RN: The Memoirs of Richard Nixon*. New York: Simon & Schuster, 1978.

Oates, Joyce Carol. "Strip Poker." 2007. *Give Me Your Heart: Tales of Mystery and Suspense*. New York: Mariner Books, 2012. 56-82.

O'Neill, Thomas P. and William Novak. *Man of the House: The Life and Political Memoirs of Tip O'Neill*. New York: Random House, 1987.

"The One-Minute Guide to Poker," *Esquire*, 154.3, Oct. 2010, 44.

Ostrow, Albert. "According to Whose Hoyle," *Esquire*, 25.4, Apr. 1946, 104-05.

---. "When Poker Was Poker," *Esquire*, 28.1, Jul. 1947, 104.

Parke, Jonathan et al. *Global Online Gambler Survey*. Nottingham, UK: e-Commerce Online Gaming Regulation and Assurance, Jan. 2007.

Parlee, Mary. "Deal Me In: Why Women Should Play Poker, *Ms.*, 13.7, Jan. 1985, 14-15.

Patterson, Scott. *The Quants: How a New Breed of Math Whizzes Conquered Wall Street and Nearly Destroyed It*. New York: Crown Business, 2010.

Pegler, Westbrook. "Fair Enough: One Loud Vote for Stud Poker," *The Atlanta Constitution*, 17 Aug. 1934, 8.

Peterson, Theodore. *Magazines in the Twentieth Century*. Urbana: U of Illinois P, 1956.

---. "Fair Enough: Stud Poker Book Fills Old Need," *The Atlanta Constitution*, 30 Apr. 1934, 4.

Petrie, Dan, Introduction, "The Night They Made a Bum Out of Helen Hayes." In William I. Kaufman, ed., *The Best Television Plays*. New York: Merlin Press Inc., 1952, 69-97.

Pietrusza, David. *Rothstein: The Life, Times, and Murder of the Criminal Genius Who Fixed the 1919 World Series*, New York: Basic Books, 2003.

"Poker Champ Jennifer Tilly Plays Her Hand," *People*, 64.3, 18 Jul. 2005, 24.

"Poker Computation Boosts Popularity," *Hagerstown Morning Herald*, 10 Dec. 1943, 13.

"Poker Principles," *Knowledge*, 100, 28 Sept. 1883, 203.

"Poker Wins Over Prayers: Gardena Elects Three of a Kind," *Life*, 36.17, 26 Apr. 1954, 44.

Pomerantz, Gary M. *The Devil's Tickets: A Night of Bridge, a Fatal Hand, and a New American Age*. New York: Crown Publishers, 2009.

Pomeranz, Kenneth and Steven Topik. *The World That Trade Created: Society, Culture, and the World Economy, 1400 to the Present*. Armonk, NY: M.E. Sharpe, 2006.

Preston, Amarillo Slim and Bill G. Cox. *Play Poker to Win*. New York: Grosset & Dunlap, 1973.

Preston, Amarillo Slim and Greg Dinkin. *Amarillo Slim in a World Full of Fat People*. New York: Harper Collins Publishers, 2003.

Proctor, Richard A. "Poker Principles and Chance Laws," *Longman's Magazine*, 2.11, 1 Sep. 1883, 497-515.

"The Publishers. Plans of Some of Them -- Forthcoming New Books," *The New York Times*, 14 Jan. 1905, 31.

Pulliam, Susan. "Private Money: The New Financial Order; The Hedge-Fund King Is Getting Nervous," *The Wall Street Journal*, 16 Sep. 2006, A1.

Purdom, Charles Benjamin, ed. *Everyman at War*. London: J.M. Dent, 1930.

"Queen High," *Playboy*, Nov. 1987, 161

"Radio 1929-1941." *Encyclopedia.com*, 2002, <encyclopedia.com/education/news-and-education-magazines/radio-1929-1941>.

Raghavan, Sudarsan. "Years after invasion, the U.S. leaves a cultural imprint on Afghanistan," *The Washington Post*, 28 Jun. 2015.

"The Rambler," *The Book Buyer: A Monthly Review of American and Foreign Literature*, 13.4, May 1896, 215-222.

Raskin, Eric. *The Moneymaker Effect*. Las Vegas: Huntington Press, 2014.

"Raymond to Testify at McManus Trial," *The New York Times*, 29 Nov. 1929, 22.

Rechtshaffen, Michael. "The game is up in 'Cold Deck,'" *Los Angeles Times*, 4 Dec. 2015,

E12.

Redd, William "Si." Interview by Orley B. Caudill, 18-19 Apr. 1983, Hattiesburg, MS, The Mississippi Oral History Program of the University of Southern Mississippi, Vol. 257.

Rehmeyer, Julie and Nathan Fox, Rico Renzi. "Ante Up, Human: The Adventures of Polaris, the Poker-Playing Robot," *Wired*, 16.12, Dec. 2008, 186-91.

Reilly, Rick. "TV Poker's a Joker." *Sports Illustrated* 101.16, 25 Oct. 2004, 156.

Remington, Frederic. "A Quarrel Over Cards -- A Sketch from a New Mexican Ranch," *Harper's Weekly*, 31.1582, Apr. 23, 1887, 301.

Rev. of *A Complete Poker-Player*, *The New York Times*, 10 Apr. 1875, 4.

Rev. of *The Last Deal*, *Moving Picture World*, 6.6, 12 Feb. 1910, 216.

"Richard A. Saalfield obituary," *The New York Times*, 4 Dec. 1912, 13.

Rose, I. Nelson. "Gambling's Fall: You Can Bet on It," *Los Angeles Times*, 17 Aug. 1989, 7.

Roosevelt, Theodore. "At the Banquet at Dallas, Tex., April 5, 1905." Rpt. in *The Works of Theodore Roosevelt, Presidential Addresses and State Papers, Part Three*. New York: P.F. Collier & Son, Publishers, ca. 1906.

---. "At Grand Canyon, Arizona, May 6, 1903." Rpt. in *The Works of Theodore Roosevelt, Presidential Addresses and State Papers, Part One*. New York: P.F. Collier & Son, Publishers, ca. 1906.

Rosenbaum, Jonathan. Rev. of *Rounders*. *Chicago Reader*, <www.chicagoreader.com/chicago/rounders/Film?oid=1063620>. Accessed 3 May 2018.

Rosenbaum, Ron. "Jokers Wild," *Esquire*, 105.6, Jun. 1986, 325.

Rothman, Hal. *Neon Metropolis*. New York: Routledge, 2002.

Runyon, Damon. "The Idyll of Miss Sarah Brown." *A Treasury of Damon Runyon*. New York: The Modern Library, 1958. 3-18.

---. "Princess O'Hara." *A Treasury of Damon Runyon*. New York: The Modern Library, 1958. 209-225.

Russo, Francine. "Ante Up, Ladies," *Time*, 166.18, 31 Oct. 2005, W6, W8, W12.

Saalfield, Richard A. "Poker; or, That queen," New York, monographic, 1883. Notated Music. Retrieved from the Library of Congress, <www.loc.gov/item/sm1883.12768>.

"Sag-Pisces," *Cosmopolitan*, 248.1, Jan. 2010, 20.

Sampson, Henry T. *Blacks in Blackface: A Sourcebook on Early Black Musical Shows, Volume 1*. Toronto: The Scarecrow Press, 2014.

Sandburg, Carl. *Abraham Lincoln: The Prairie Years*. 1926. New York: Dell Publishing Co. 1954.

Scarne, John. *Scarne's Guide to Modern Poker*. New York: Pocket Star Books, 1980.

---. *Scarne's New Complete Guide to Gambling*. New York: Simon & Schuster, 1974.

Schinderette, Susan. "The Real Story of Desi and Lucy," *People* 35.6, 18 Feb. 1991, <people.com/archive/cover-story-the-real-story-of-desi-and-lucy-vol-35-no-6/>.

Schenck, Robert C. *Draw. Rules for Playing Poker*. 1872. Brooklyn: Robert C. Schenck, 1880.

Scherer, Michael and Michael Weisskopf, "High Rollers," *Time* 172.2, 14 Jul. 2008, 30-31.

Schlitz, Don. Interview by the Library of Congress, 10 Apr. 2018, <loc.gov/programs/static/national-recording-preservation-board/documents/DonSchlitzInterview.pdf>.

Schulman, Max. "Five Card Poker and the Hell With It," *Playboy*, 4.8, Aug. 1957, 31.

Schwager, Jack D. *Market Wizards: Interviews with America's Top Traders*. Hoboken: John Wiley & Sons, Inc., 1989.

---. *The New Market Wizards: Conversations with America's Top Traders*. New York: HarperBusiness, 1994.

Schwartz, David G. *Roll the Bones: The History of Gambling*. New York: Gotham Books, 2006.

---. "The Surprisingly Humble, Forgotten Roots Of Poker's Biggest Game," *Forbes*, 5 Jul. 2018, <forbes.com/sites/davidschwartz/2018/07/05/the-surprisingly-humble-forgotten-roots-of-pokers-biggest-game/>.

Schwarz, Hunter. "In most states, tied elections can be decided by a coin toss," *The Washington Post*, 14 Jul. 2014, <www.washingtonpost.com/blogs/govbeat/

wp/2014/07/14/in-most-states-tied-elections-can-be-decided-by-a-coin-toss/>.

"The Seagal Report: Gutshot Straight (2014)," *Wizzley*, <wizzley.com/the-seagal-report-gutshot-straight-2014/>.

Segrest, Susan. "The Hottest Game!" *Seventeen*, 63.5, May 2004, 46.

"Senatorial Poker," *Indianapolis Journal*, 8 August 1894, 2.

Sexton, Mike. *Life's a Gamble*. East Peoria, IL: D&B Publishing, 2016.

Shaffer, George. "Goldwyn Puts Poker Lesson in 'Dead End,'" *The Chicago Tribune*, 18 Jun. 1937, 23.

Shakespeare, William. *The Complete Pelican Shakespeare*. New York: Viking Press, 1969.

Shrake, Edwin. "An Amateur Is Burned at High Stakes," *Sports Illustrated*, 46.23, 29 May 1977, 58-63.

---. "Care To Join Our Little Old Game?" 47.7, *Sports Illustrated*, 15 Aug. 1977, 16-22.

---. "It Ain't Just Heaven, Gambling. There's a Lot You Got to Contend With," *Sports Illustrated*, 34.4, 25 Jan. 1971, 56-66.

Siegel, Alan. "Going All In: An Oral History of 'Rounders,'" *The Ringer*, 20 Sep. 2018, <theringer.com/movies/2018/9/20/17878996/rounders-oral-history-matt-damon-ed-norton-poker-brian-koppelman-david-levien>.

Silberstang, Edwin. *Playboy's Book of Games*. New York: Playboy Press, 1972.

Silver, Nate. "After 'Black Friday,' American Poker Faces Cloudy Future," *The New York Times*, 20 Apr. 2011, <fivethirtyeight.blogs.nytimes.com/2011/04/20/after-black-friday-american-poker-faces-cloudy-future/>.

Simon, Neil. *The Odd Couple: A Comedy*. New York: Random House, 1966.

Simpich Jr., Frederick. "At Ease in the South Seas," *National Geographic*, 85.1, Jan. 1944, 79-104.

"Singular Characters: James Bowie, The Duellist." *The Saturday Evening Post* 29.1510, 6 Jul. 1850, 1.

"Sir Ken Adam -- Filmsets are Forever," Interview by Christopher Frayling, 9-14 Feb. 2003, Berlinale Talent Campus, Berlin, Germany, <archive.li/YWtpD>.

Sklansky, David. *Hold'em Poker*. Las Vegas: Gambler's Book Club, 1976.

Skow, John. "The Big Poker Freeze-Out," *Time*, 135.25, 18 Jun. 1990, 10-13.

Smith, Martin J. and Patrick J. Kiger. *Poplorica: A Popular History of the Fads, Mavericks, Inventions, and Lore that Shaped Modern America*. New York: HarperCollins, 2004.

Smith, Merriman. "How Truman Played Poker," *The Des Moines Register*, 26 Apr. 1953, 113, 137, 139.

Smith, Sol. *Theatrical Management in the West and South for Thirty Years*. New York: Harper & Brothers, Publishers, 1868.

Snyder, Adam. "Wagering on Web is risky business." 23 Jul. 1997. <web.archive.org/web/19980117085341/http://www.msnbc.com/news/130414.asp>.

Solotaroff, Ivan. "Poker's New World Order," *Rolling Stone*, 976, 16 Jun. 2005, 61-68.

Spanier, David. *All Right, Okay, You Win: Inside Las Vegas*. London: Mandarin, 1992.

---. *Total Poker*. New York: Simon & Schuster, 1977.

Starckx, Senne. "Card games as war pastime, and strategic tool," *Flanders Today*, 14 May 2016, <www.flanderstoday.eu/living/card-games-war-pastime-and-strategic-tool>.

Stein, Joel. "A Full Boat," *Playboy*, 52.8, Aug. 2005, 104-06, 132-35.

Steinberg, Cobbett. *TV Facts*. New York: Facts on File, 1980.

Stevenson, Seth. *Newsweek*, 133.20, 17 May 1999, 76.

Stith,William. "The Sinfulness and Pernicious Nature of Gaming." Williamsburg, VA: William Hunter, 1752.

Stoddard, Maynard Good. "It's Called Poker," *The Saturday Evening Post*, 253.6, Sep. 1981, 64-65, 109.

Stoll, Clifford. "The Internet? Bah!" *Newsweek*, 125.9, 27 Feb. 1995, 41.

Sullivan, John L. "Annexation," *United States Magazine and Democratic Review*, 17.1, Jul.-Aug. 1845, 5-10.

Talk of Uncle George to His Nephew About Draw Poker. New York: Dick & Fitzgerald, 1883.

Tarkington, Booth. "The One-Hundred Dollar Bill." *The Fascinating Stranger and Other Stories.* Garden City, NY: Doubleday, Page & Company, 1923. 85-120.

Taylor, Robert Lewis. *W.C. Fields: His Follies and Fortunes.* New York: New American Library, 1949.

Texas, House of Representatives, H.C.R. 109, 15 Jun. 2007, 80th Texas Legislature, <capitol.texas.gov/tlodocs/80R/billtext/pdf/HC00109F.pdf>.

Thackrey Jr., Ted. *Gambling Secrets of Nick the Greek.* Chicago: Rand McNally, 1968.

---. "Roulette's a Sucker Game in U.S.," *Toledo Blade,* 30 Oct. 1968, 77.

Thomas, Benjamin P. *Abraham Lincoln: A Biography.* Carbondale: Southern Illinois of UP, 1952.

Thomas, Emory M. *Robert E. Lee: A Biography.* New York: W.W. Norton & Company, 1995.

Thompson, Charles Willis. *Presidents I've Known.* Indianapolis: Bobbs Merrill, 1929.

Thompson, Howard. Rev. of *The Cincinnati Kid. The New York Times,* 28 Oct. 1965: 48.

Thurber, James. "Everything is Wild." 1932. Rpt. in *The Middle-aged Man on the Flying Trapeze.* New York: Harper and Brothers, 1935, 41-47.

Tidwell, James N. "Political Words and Phrases: Card-Playing Terms," *American Speech* 33.1, Feb. 1958, 21-28.

Tiede, Tom. "GIs Turn Superstitions To Their Own Advantage," *The Corpus-Christi Caller-Times,* 27 Sep. 1966, 5.

Tocqueville, Alexis de. *Democracy in America.* 1835. Trans. Arthur Goldhammer. New York: The Library of America, 2004.

Travers, Peter. Rev. of *Runner Runner, Rolling Stone,* 11 Oct. 2013, <www.rollingstone.com/movies/movie-reviews/runner-runner-111672/>.

Trohan, Walter. *Political Animals.* New York: Doubleday, 1975.

Truscott, Alan. "Bridge: A Celebrated New York Club Has Moved to a New Home," *The New York Times,* 11 Mar. 1988, C18.

Tucker, Betty Jo. "High Stakes." Rev. of *Rounders. Reel Talk,* <www.reeltalkreviews.com/browse/viewitem.asp?type=review&id=3780>. Accessed 3 May 2018.

Turner, Frederick Jackson. "The Significance of the Frontier in American History." 1893. Rpt. in *History, Frontier, and Section: Three Essays.* Albuquerque: U of New Mexico P, 1993.

Turner, Robert. "Gardena: Poker Capital of the World," 24 Apr. 2016, <robertturnerpoker.wordpress.com/2016/04/24/gardena-poker-capital-of-the-world/>.

[Twain, Mark.] Jones, S. Browne. "Full Report of the Proceedings Upon the Examination of Mark Twain on the Charge of Fraud, in the Police Court. The Defendant Found Guilty and Sentenced to Forty-Eight Hours in the City Prison." *The Golden Era,* 16 Jul. 1865, <twainquotes.com/Era/18650716.html>.

Twain, Mark. *A Connecticut Yankee in King Arthur's Court.* 1889. Berkley: U of California P, 1979.

---. "His Speech on the Presentation of His New Play, Ah Sin, in New York." *St. Louis Globe-Democrat,* 4 Aug. 1877.

---. *Life on the Mississippi.* Boston: James R. Osgood and Company, 1883.

Twain, Mark and Charles Dudley Warner. *The Gilded Age: A Tale of To-Day.* 1873. Hartford, CT: American Publishing Co., 1874.

United States Attorney's Office, Southern District of New York. "Civil Complaint Amended to Allege that Full Tilt Poker and Its Board of Directors Operated Company as a Massive Ponzi Scheme Against Its Own Players," 20 Sep. 2011.

---. "Manhattan U.S. Attorney Announces $731 Million Settlement Of Money Laundering and Forfeiture Complaint With Pokerstars and Full Tilt Poker," 31 Jul 2012.

United States, Congressional House Committee on Financial Services. *Hearing on H.R. 2267, Internet Gambling Regulation, Consumer Protection, and Enforcement Act,* 21 Jul. 2010, 111th Cong. Washington: GPO, 2010 (statement of Annie Duke on behalf of the Poker Players Alliance).

United States v. DiCristina. No. 12-3720. United States District Court for the Eastern District of New York. 21 Aug. 2012. Appeal 6 Aug. 2013.

Updike, John. "Poker Night." 1984. *Trust Me*. 1988. New York: Random House, 2014. 186-93.

Vaughan, Harry H., interview by Charles T. Morrissey, 26 May 1981, Alexandria, Virginia, Harry S. Truman Presidential Library & Museum, <trumanlibrary.org/oralhist/vaughan2.htm>.

Van Rensselaer, Mrs. John King. *The Devil's Picture-Books: A History of Playing Cards*. New York: Dodd, Mead, and Company, 1890.

Vardi, Nathan. "He's All In," *Forbes*, 187.7, 23 Apr. 2011, 23.

Vasquez, Michael. "Odds aren't looking good for online poker players," *Miami Herald*, 21 Apr. 2011, <bradenton.com/news/article34510593.html>.

"Vegas Without Shame," *Rolling Stone*, 1010, 5 Oct. 2006, 52-53.

Votolato, Max. *Gardena Poker Clubs: A High-Stakes History*. Charleston: The History Press, 2017.

Von Neumann, John and Oskar Morgenstern. *Theory of Games and Economic Behavior*. Princeton: Princeton UP, 1944.

Walsh, Joseph. *California Split*, First Draft Screenplay. Los Angeles: Won World Productions, 18 Dec. 1973.

---. *Gambler on the Loose*. Los Angeles: Walsh Publications, 2008.

---. Interview with the author, 24 Apr. 2017.

Ward, Ferdinand. "General Grant As I Knew Him," *The New York Herald*, Dec. 19, 1909, 1-2.

Washington, George. George Washington Papers, Series 5, Financial Papers: General Ledger B, 1772-1793, Library of Congress.

Watterson, Henry. *Marse Henry: An Autobiography*, Vol. 2. New York: George H. Doran Company, 1919.

Watterson, John Sayle. *The Games People Play: Sports and the Presidency*. Baltimore: Johns Hopkins UP, 2006.

"We met Randy Blumer, the pioneer of online poker." *Poker Player*. 28 Nov. 2014. < pokerplayer365.com/news/features-news/randy-blumer-is-the-pioneer-of-online-poker-you-could-see-this-was-going-to-be-the-crack-cocaine-of-gambling/>.

Webster, H.T. *Webster's Poker Book*. New York: Simon & Schuster, 1925.

Weddle, David. *If They Move... Kill 'Em! The Life and Times of Sam Peckinpah*. New York: Grove Press, 1994.

Weidman, Jerome and George Abbott, Jerry Bock, Sheldon Harnick. *Fiorello!* New York: Popular Library Inc., 1960.

Weightless. "25 Years of Online Poker: The First Poker Site." *PocketFives*. 28 Oct. 2015. <pocketfives.com/articles/25-years-of-online-poker-the-first-poker-site-591578/>.

Wertheim, Arthur Frank. *W.C. Fields from the Ziegfeld Follies and Broadway Stage to the Screen*. New York: Palgrave, 2016.

Weyler, Karen A. *Intricate Relations: Sexual and Economic Desire in American Fiction, 1789-1814*. Iowa City: University of Iowa Press, 2004.

"What is a 'looloo'?: Its Interpretation Made Plain by a Senator Who Has Traveled." *The New York Times*, 13 Feb. 1893, 2.

Whitehead, Colson. *The Noble Hustle: Poker, Beef Jerky, and Death*. New York: Doubleday, 2014.

Wiesenberg, Michael. "The Cincinnati Kid," 2000, *Poker Pages*, <web.archive.org/web/20071214064346/http://www.pokerpages.com/articles/archives/wiesenberg15.htm>.

Wilde, Percival. *Rogues in Clover*. New York: Appleton & Company, 1929.

Wiley, Bell Irvin. *The Life of Billy Yank: The Common Soldier of the Union*. 1952. Baton Rouge: Louisiana State UP, 1978.

---. *The Life of Johnny Reb: The Common Soldier of the Confederacy*. 1943. Baton Rouge: Louisiana State UP, 1978.

Willis, Brad. "The Moneymaker Boom that almost wasn't," *PokerStars blog*, 16 Feb.

2006, < pokerstars.com/en/blog/2016/the-moneymaker-boom-that-almost-wasnt-160534.shtml>.

Wilkinson, Sir William. "Chinese Origin of Playing Cards." *American Anthropologist*, 8.1, Jan. 1895, 61–78.

Wilson, Des. *Ghosts at the Table*. Edinburgh: Mainstream Publishing Company, 2007.

Wilstach, Frank G. *Wild Bill Hickok: The Prince of Pistoleers*. 1926.

Winterblossom, Henry T. *The Game of Draw-Poker, Mathematically Illustrated*. New York: Wm. H. Murphy, 1975.

Wintz, Cary D. and Bruce A. Glasrud, ed., *The Harlem Renaissance in the American West: The New Negro's Western Experience*. New York: Routledge, 2012.

Wister, Owen. *The Virginian*. New York: Grosset Dunlap, 1902.

Wiznitzer, Louis. "Chess vs. Poker," *The New York Times*, 26 Feb. 1961, 69.

Yagoda, Ben. *About Town: The New Yorker and the World It Made*. New York: Charles Scribner's Sons, 2000.

Yardley, Herbert O. *The Education of a Poker Player*. New York: Simon & Schuster, 1957.

Image Credits

Special thanks to Timothy Peters, Max Votolato, Ann Sludikoff, PokerNews, PokerListings, David G. Schwartz, Su Kim Chung and the Center for Gaming Research at the University of Nevada Las Vegas for their assistance. Photos and illustrations public domain unless otherwise noted.

Chap. 1: "Postcard of three men playing poker in a parlor," University of Nevada Las Vegas University Libraries, Timothy Peters Collection; "Postcard of teen boys smoking, drinking, and gambling," University of Nevada Las Vegas University Libraries, Timothy Peters Collection;

Chap. 2: The Cardsharps (ca. 1594), Caravaggio; Cheat with the Ace of Diamonds (ca. 1635), Georges de la Tour;

Chap. 3: Detail from Dragoon Campaigns to the Rocky Mountains (1836); title page of Hoyle's Games (1845);

Chap. 4: "Celebrated race of the steamers Robt. E Lee and Natchez" (ca. 1883), William M. Donaldson, Library of Congress; drawing of George H. Devol, from Forty Years a Gambler on the Mississippi (1887); William "Canada Bill" Jones, date/source unknown;

Chap. 5: Wild Bill Hickok at Cards (1916), N.C. Wyeth; A Quarrel Over Cards –– A Sketch from a New Mexican Ranch (1887), Frederic Remington, Harper's Weekly, Library of Congress; Wyatt Earp (ca. 1870s), source unknown; Doc Holliday (March 1872), Pennsylvania School of Dentistry; Bat Masterson (ca. 1879), source unknown; Gene Barry as Bat Masterson (1958), NBC Television, Herb Ball; "Poker" Alice Ivers (ca. 1860s), source unknown; "Poker" Alice Ivers (ca. 1920s), source unknown; James Butler "Wild Bill" Hickok, date/source unknown;

Chap. 6: "Petersburg, Va. Officers of the 114th Pennsylvania Infantry playing cards in front of tents" (1864), Library of Congress; "Soldiers playing cards" (ca. 1861-65), Library of Congress; "Two unidentified soldiers in Union uniforms drinking whiskey and playing cards" (ca. 1861-65), Library of Congress; A Pass Time (1863), Winslow Homer, Library of Congress;

Chap. 7: "Photograph of poker players at the Boulder Club, Las Vegas" (ca. 1930s-40s), University of Nevada Las Vegas University Libraries, Davis Collection; title page, The Thompson Street Poker Club (1888), Henry Guy Carleton; stills from A Cure for Pokeritis (1912), dir. Laurence Trimble; still from lost scene from Marx Brothers, Horse Feathers (1932), source unknown; "Inside the Gardena Club" (ca. 1970s), City of Gardena archive via Max Votolato; "The Gardena Club boardman (ca. 1970s), City of Gardena archive via Max Votolato;

Chap. 8: detail from cover of first edition of The Education of a Poker Player (1957), Herbert O. Yardley (author photo); title page, The Intensely Interesting and Classical American Game Draw Poker, Robert C. Schenck (1878); front cover of The Complete

Poker-Player (1875), John Blackbridge; "Photograph of gamblers at the 7th World Series of Poker, Las Vegas (Nev.)" (1976), University of Nevada Las Vegas University Libraries, Binion's Horseshoe Collection;

Chap. 9: "A poker party at George Turner's ranch, Moreno Valley, Colfax County, New Mexico" (1943), Library of Congress; "A Friend in Need" (1903), Cassius M. Coolidge; first edition of Webster's Poker Book (1925), H.T. Webster et al., with accessories (author photo);

Chap. 10: Henry Truman chip set with the presidential seal, National Archives and Records Administration, Harry S. Truman library; "Stand Pat!" pin from Theodore Roosevelt's 1904 campaign; Harry Truman playing poker in a club in Kansas City, Missouri, National Archives and Records Administration, Harry S. Truman library;

Chap. 11: "Soldiers in Washington, D.C. waiting between trains" (Dec. 1943), Library of Congress; "Soldiers in the 42nd Infantry Division ('Rainbow Division') playing cards" (ca. 1915-20), Library of Congress; "Aircraft Spotters" cards created by the U.S. Playing Card Company, U.S. Air Force; "Oflag Ivc Prisonar of War Camp at Colditz Castle, Germany during the Second World War," Imperial War Museums; The War Room with the Big Board from Stanley Kubrick's 1964 film Dr. Strangelove, trailer;

Chap. 12: Wall Street sign, Pixabay; Bill Gates (2013), United States Department of Energy;

Chap. 13: detail from Jack Pots: Stories of the Great American Game (1900), Eugene Edwards, illustration by Ike Morgan; detail from title page of Jack Pots: Stories of the Great American Game (1900), Eugene Edwards, illustration by Ike Morgan;

Chap. 14: "Binion's Horseshoe at night" (ca. 1960s), University of Nevada Las Vegas University Libraries, Binion's Horseshoe Collection; "Print advertisement for the Eldorado Club" (ca. 1950), University of Nevada Las Vegas University Libraries, Binion's Horseshoe Collection;

Chap. 15: "Magazines at newsstand, St. Louis, Missouri" (ca. 1939), Library of Congress; illustrations for "Just One More Round," Heywood Broun, Judge (2 Dec. 1922 issue); front cover, Poker Chips (Oct. 1896 issue);

Chap. 16: still from Dr. Jack (1922), dir. Fred C. Newmeyer, Sam Taylor; still from Hell Bent (1918), dir. John Ford; still from White Oak (1921), dir. Lambert Hillyer; John Wayne and Ward Bond in Tall in the Saddle (1944), dir. Edwin L. Marin, trailer; still from Dr. Jack (1922), dir. Fred C. Newmeyer, Sam Taylor; promotional still from The Lady Eve (1941), National Board of Review Magazine;

Chap. 17: detail of front cover of Poker Stories (1896), John F.B. Lillard; Life on the Mississippi (1883), Mark Twain, illustration by John Harley;

Chap. 18: "Seven people listening to a radio in the Hamilton Hotel, Washington, DC" (ca. 1950), Library of Congress; Ed Gardner as Duffy from the radio program Duffy's Tavern;

Chap. 19: detail of 78 rpm copy of "The Darktown Poker Club" (1914), Bert Williams, Internet Archive, Kahle/Austin Foundation; "That Game of Poker" (1878), Charles MacEvoy, Library of Congress; Kenny Rogers singing "The Gambler" at the 1979 World Series of Poker, Shelley Hill, Gambling Times (Oct. 1979 issue), courtesy Ann Sludikoff;

Chap. 20: Jack Kelly and Richard Long in an episode of the television program Maverick (19 Apr. 1960); James Garner as Bret Maverick and Jack Kelly as Bart Maverick in an episode of the television program Maverick (ca. 1957); "Photograph of Binion and others on the Merv Griffin show, Las Vegas (Nev.)" (Jan. 1976), University of Nevada Las Vegas University Libraries, Binion's Horseshoe Collection; Lon McEachern and Norman Chad at the 2011 World Series of Poker, Jonathan Boncek, courtesy PokerNews;

Chap. 21: poker player Randy Lew multi-tabling online poker, still from "Randy 'nanonoko' Lew's Top 5 Multi-Tabling Secrets - Poker Strategy" (May 2016) by Matthew Showell, courtesy PokerListings, Christopher Hunt; electronic draw poker machines at the Stardust Resorts and Casino, Las Vegas (ca. mid-1970s), University of Nevada Las Vegas University Libraries, Stardust Collection; a video poker machine, Surv1v4l1st, CC0 1.0; lobby for Planet Poker, Burkr, CC BY-SA 3.0;

Chap. 22: judge's gavel, Pixabay; Full Tilt Poker domain seizure notice, U.S. Department of Justice;

Chap. 23: close-up of playing cards, pxhere.

Index

Poker & Pop Culture